Environmental Communication and Community

As society has become increasingly aware of environmental issues, the challenge of structuring public participation opportunities that strengthen democracy, while promoting more sustainable communities has become crucial for many natural resource agencies, industries, interest groups and publics. The processes of negotiating between the often disparate values held by these diverse groups, and formulating and implementing policies that enable people to fulfil goals associated with these values, can strengthen communities as well as tear them apart.

This book provides a critical examination of the role communication plays in social transition, through both construction and destruction of community. The authors examine the processes and practices put in play when people who may or may not have previously seen themselves as interconnected, communicate with each other, often in situations where they are competing for the same resources. Drawing upon a diverse selection of case-studies on the American, Asian and European continents, the chapters chart a range of approaches to environmental communication, including symbolic construction, modes of organizing and agonistic politics of communication.

This volume will be of great interest to researchers, teachers and practitioners of environmental communication, environmental conflict, community development and natural resource management.

Tarla Rai Peterson is a professor in the Department of Communication and Coordinator of RARE Mozambique at the University of Texas, El Paso, USA.

Hanna Ljunggren Bergeå is a researcher at the Division of Environmental Communication, Department of Urban and Rural Development, Swedish University of Agricultural Sciences, Uppsala, Sweden.

Andrea M. Feldpausch-Parker is an assistant professor in the Department of Environmental Studies at the State University of New York College of Environmental Science and Forestry (SUNY ESF), USA.

Kaisa Raitio is an associate professor at the Division of Environmental Communication, Department of Urban and Rural Development, Swedish University of Agricultural Sciences, Uppsala, Sweden.

Routledge studies in environmental communication and media

Culture, Development and Petroleum
An ethnography of the high North
Edited by Jan-Oddvar Sørnes, Larry Browning and Jan Terje Henriksen

Discourses of Global Climate Change
Apocalyptic framing and political antagonisms
Jonas Anshelm and Martin Hultman

The Troubled Rhetoric and Communication of Climate Change
The argumentative situation
Philip Eubanks

Environmental Communication and Travel Journalism
Consumerism, conflict and concern
Lynette McGaurr

Environmental Ethics and Film
Pat Brereton

Environmental Crises in Central Asia
From steppes to seas, from deserts to glaciers
Edited by Eric Freedman and Mark Neuzil

Environmental Advertising in China and the USA
Structures of desire
Xinghua Li

Public Perception of Climate Change
Policy and communication
Bjoern Hagen

Environmental Communication and Community
Constructive and destructive dynamics of social transformation
Edited by Tarla Rai Peterson, Hanna Ljunggren Bergeå,
Andrea M. Feldpausch-Parker and Kaisa Raitio

Environmental Communication and Community

Constructive and destructive
dynamics of social transformation

**Tarla Rai Peterson,
Hanna Ljunggren Bergeå,
Andrea M. Feldpausch-Parker
and Kaisa Raitio**

Routledge
Taylor & Francis Group

LONDON AND NEW YORK

from Routledge

First published 2016 by Routledge

2 Park Square, Milton Park, Abingdon, Oxfordshire OX14 4RN

711 Third Avenue, New York, NY 10017

Routledge is an imprint of the Taylor & Francis Group, an informa business

First issued in paperback 2017

British Library Cataloguing-in-Publication Data
A catalogue record for this book is available from the British Library

Library of Congress Cataloging-in-Publication Data
Names: Peterson, Tarla Rai, editor.
Title: Environmental communication and community : constructive and destructive dynamics of social transformation / edited by Tarla Rai Peterson, Hanna Ljunggren Bergeêa, Andrea M. Feldpausch-Parker and Kaisa Raitio.
Description: New York, NY : Routledge, 2016. | Includes bibliographical references and index.
Identifiers: LCCN 2015044169| ISBN 9781138913868 (hardback) | ISBN 9781315691176 (ebook)
Subjects: LCSH: Communication in the environmental sciences–Case studies. | Environmental management–Social aspects–Case studies. | Environmentalism–Social aspects–Case studies.
Classification: LCC GE25 .E577 2016 | DDC 363.7–dc23
LC record available at http://lccn.loc.gov/2015044169

ISBN: 978-1-138-91386-8 (hbk)
ISBN: 978-0-8153-5921-0 (pbk)

Typeset in Bembo
by Wearset Ltd, Boldon, Tyne and Wear

To Nadarajah Sriskandarajah
Justice crusader
While attentive to power
Maintaining full hope

Contents

Figures

Tables

Contributors

Eduardo Altamirano is the technical assistant of the Sea Turtle Conservation Programme at Fauna and Flora International (FFI) in Managua, Nicaragua.

Elin Ångman is a researcher at the Division of Environmental Communication, Department of Urban and Rural Development, Swedish University of Agricultural Sciences, Uppsala, Sweden.

Irma Arts is an independent researcher in the Netherlands.

Paulami Banerjee is a PhD candidate in the Environmental Science and Engineering Programme at University of Texas, El Paso, USA.

Hanna Ljunggren Bergeå is a researcher at the Division of Environmental Communication, Department of Urban and Rural Development, Swedish University of Agricultural Sciences, Uppsala, Sweden.

Leigh Bernacchi is the programme coordinator of the Water Security and Sustainability Initiative at the Sierra Nevada Research Institute, University of California, Merced, USA.

Arjen E. Buijs is an assistant professor at the Forest and Nature Conservation Policy Group Wageningen University and senior researcher at Alterra Green World Research, Netherlands.

Deborah Cox Callister is a mediation consultant, adjunct assistant professor at University of San Francisco and lecturer in Media Studies at University of California, Berkeley, USA.

Sofia Chavarría is the national coordinator of the Hawksbill Programme at ICAPO in San Salvador, El Salvador.

Brian Cozen is a visiting assistant professor of Communication at University of Nevada, Las Vegas, USA.

Danielle Endres is an associate professor in the Department of Communication and the Environmental Humanities Programme at the University of Utah, USA.

Andrea M. Feldpausch-Parker is an assistant professor in the Department of Environmental Studies at the State University of New York College of Environmental Science and Forestry (SUNY ESF), USA.

Velkiss Gadea is the coordinator of the Sea Turtle Conservation Programme at FFI in Managua, Nicaragua.

Alexander R. Gaos is the co-founder and regional director of ICAPO in San Diego, CA, USA and a PhD candidate in the Joint Doctoral Programme in Ecology at San Diego State University and the University of California, Davis, CA, USA.

Lars Hallgren is a senior lecturer at the Division of Environmental Communication, Department of Urban and Rural Development, Swedish University of Agricultural Sciences, Uppsala, Sweden.

Hans Peter Hansen is an assistant professor at the Division of Environmental Communication, Department of Urban and Rural Development, Swedish University of Agricultural Sciences, Uppsala, Sweden.

Michael J. Liles is the co-founder and national director of the Eastern Pacific Hawksbill Initiative (ICAPO) in San Salvador, El Salvador.

David Melero is the director of the Conservation Tourism and Livelihoods Programme at ICAPO and FFI in León, Nicaragua.

Eric L. Morgan is an associate professor in the Department of Communication Studies at New Mexico State University, Las Cruces, USA.

Megan O'Byrne is a visiting assistant professor, Kutztown University in Pennsylvania, USA.

Israel D. Parker is a research scientist of the Institute of Renewable Natural Resources at Texas A&M University in College Station Texas, USA.

Markus J. Peterson is a professor in the Department of Biological Sciences, University of Texas, El Paso, USA.

M. Nils Peterson is an associate professor in the Department of Forestry at North Carolina State University, Raleigh, USA.

Tarla Rai Peterson is a professor in the Department of Communication and coordinator of RARE Mozambique at the University of Texas, El Paso, USA.

Kaisa Raitio is an associate professor at the Division of Environmental Communication, Department of Urban and Rural Development, Swedish University of Agricultural Sciences, Uppsala, Sweden.

Leah Sprain is an assistant professor in the Department of Communication, University of Colorado, Boulder, USA.

Hilary Swartwood is an MPS student in the Department of Environmental Studies at the State University of New York (SUNY) and an MPA student at Syracuse University, USA.

Anne Marie Todd is a professor in the Department of Communication Studies at San José State University, San José California, USA.

José Urteaga is the co-founder of ICAPO and a PhD student in the Emmett Interdisciplinary Programme in Environment and Resources at Stanford University, Stanford, CA, USA.

Brion van Over is an assistant professor in the Department of Communication, Manchester Community College, Manchester, Connecticut, USA.

Gerard Verschoor is an assistant professor in the Sociology of Development and Change Group, Wageningen University, the Netherlands.

Ingrid Yañez is the co-founder and financial programmes manager at ICAPO in San Diego, CA, USA.

Acknowledgements

The chapters in this book are based on papers and posters presented at the 2013 Conference on Communication and the Environment (COCE). Most of all, we would like to thank the members of the Environmental Communication Programme at the Swedish Agricultural University (SLU) in Uppsala for organizing and hosting the conference. We thank SLU for its strong institutional support, including most of the financial resources needed to host the conference. Additional support was provided by Uppsala University's Centre for Sustainable Development, the Cemus Research Forum, Naturvårdsverket (Swedish Environmental Protection Agency), FORMAS (Swedish Research Council for Environment, Agriculture and Spatial Planning), the International Association for Environmental Communication (IECA), the National Communication Association, and the European Communication Research and Education Association.

All chapters have profited from reviews and conversations associated with their presentation at the 2013 COCE. Reviewers included Ashley A. Anderson, Katelind Batill, Chris Blackmore, Emma Frances Bloomfield, James Cantrill, Serena Cinque, Brian Cozen, Katherine Cruger, Sharon Dunwoody, Peter Edwards, Edna Einsiedel, Joshua Frye, Shiv Ganesh, Jennifer Good, Alberto Gonzalez, Caroline Gottschalk Druschke, Susan Grantham, Damon Hall, Sara Holmgren, Cristi Horton, Ann Jabro, Courtney Johnson-Woods, Pietari Kääpä, Miriah Russo Kelly, Brenden Kendall, Bill Kinsella, Daniela Kleinschmit, Randall Lake, Libby Lester, Magnus Ljung, Callum McGregor, Salma Monani, Eric Morgan, Norbert Mundorf, Helena Nordström Källström, Todd Norton, Ulrika Olausson, Carrie Packwood Freeman, Israel Parker, Jennifer Peeples, Markus Peterson, Nils Peterson, Phaedra Pezzullo, Stina Powell, Jen Schneider, Julie Schutten, Steve Schwarze, Samantha Senda-Cook, James Shanahan, Stacey Sowards, Neil Stenhouse, Bruno Takashaki, Jessica Thompson, David Tschida, Susan Vente, Micheal Vickery, Lotten Westberg, Amy Wolfsen, and Heather Zoller.

As editors, we are grateful to Cristián Alarcón, Anabela Carvalho, Hans Peter Hansen, Nadarajah Sriskandarajah and others for both formal and informal conversations probing possible relationships between environmental communication research, democracy and public policy. We also appreciate our employers providing us with the time to complete this project (State University of New York College of Environmental Science and Forestry, Swedish Agricultural University, and University of Texas at El Paso).

Finally, we thank our capable and supportive editorial and production team at Routledge. We especially want to thank Louisa Earls, whose interest and enthusiasm encouraged us while undertaking this project, and Helen Bell, who was always available to answer our questions, and who exhibited astonishing grace and patience throughout the entire process.

Part I

Introduction and conceptual framing for community constructivity and deconstructivity

1 Introduction

Andrea M. Feldpausch-Parker and
Tarla Rai Peterson

Context: from conference theme to book

In September 2012, we embarked on the process of coordinating conference submissions for the first international Conference on Communication and the Environment (COCE) at the Swedish University of Agricultural Sciences (SLU) in Uppsala, Sweden, in June 2013. The first COCE, organized by James G. Cantrill and Christine Oravec, was held in Alta, Utah, USA in 1991. What started as a small North American conference of communication scholars, who believed that the study of environmental communication (EC) was more than a passing fad, had grown into an international group of individuals interested in how scholars and other citizens of Earth constituted the phenomenon of EC. Stephen Depoe, who was the founding editor of *Environmental Communication*, campaigned tirelessly for the establishment of an organization that would provide institutional support to stabilize these efforts. The 2013 conference in Uppsala followed formalization of the loosely associated group into the International Environmental Communication Association in 2011 and an internationalized roster of participants at the 2011 COCE. Attendees at the 2011 conference, organized and hosted by Stacey Sowards in El Paso, Texas, USA, discussed broadening the geographic scope of the conference, starting with the 2013 conference in Uppsala, Sweden.

The 2013 conference was organized and hosted by the Environmental Communication Programme at SLU, with leadership from Professor N. Sriskandarajah, who personifies the "pracademic" (as coined by Susan Senecah and embraced by many EC scholars) identity more holistically than any other individual. The conference theme of *Participation Revisited: Openings and Closures for Deliberations on the Commons* grew out of Sriskandarajah's commitment to bring EC fully into the theory-to-practice realm, particularly in the service of people who are adrift, alienated, or estranged from their environments, whether because of destitution, genocide, or sea-level rise. The idea for this book emerged from this conference theme and the papers presented there.

This book critically examines a suite of international cases that demonstrate how EC contributes to both the construction and destruction of community.

We recognize that the term community can have multiple geographic, political and cultural definitions, and this book incorporates all of these conceptions as they relate to the environment and environmental issues. Beyond describing and cataloguing, we use these cases as touchstones for understanding and delineating how the communicative dimensions of being in a community contribute to social transformation.

As such, the chapters in this book are grounded in an assumption that communication presents a central political challenge (perhaps *the* central political challenge) to the formation and maintenance of democratic communities throughout the world. The chapters were selected from conference presentations that reflected critically on ways that EC research may contribute to citizen participation in both the development and implementation of more inclusive institutional frameworks for environmental governance. This does not mean we have limited the book to institutional analyses. Rather, as noted in several of the chapters, communication provides its grounding. The chapters collected in this book offer a demonstration of the thought provoking papers that focused specifically on how communicative practices in a variety of communities enable and constrain social transformation.

Theoretical perspective

As society has become increasingly aware of environmental issues, the challenge of structuring appropriate decision-making processes and public participation opportunities has become crucial for many natural resource agencies, industries, interest groups and publics. The processes of negotiating between the often disparate values held by diverse groups, and formulating and implementing policies that enable people to fulfil goals associated with these values, can strengthen communities as well as tear them apart. We use the selected cases to examine the communicative practices put in play when people who would not otherwise meet interact with each other, often in situations where they are competing for the same resources such as land use, energy sources, or wildlife to name a few.

We follow the German sociologist, Nikolas Luhmann's (1989) claim that, as with any system, human society does not directly communicate with its environment, but that people still observe, interpret and incorporate their experiences with the environment into their thought and action. The study of EC examines this space between individual experiences with the *extrahuman* world (Peterson *et al.* 2007) and society-level action or inaction on environmental issues (Latour 2004). We concur with Cox and Pezzullo's (2016) claim that EC includes both constitutive and instrumental dimensions, examining how humanity perceives the extrahuman world and how people can be mobilized through communication to take action toward or on behalf of that world. In addition to these constitutive and instrumental dimensions, we agree with scholars who argue that one characteristic differentiating EC research from more traditional communication studies is that EC includes an explicitly normative dimension (Cox 2007). Although there is considerable debate over what that normativity should encompass, part of it is a commitment to question and analytically explore the various representations whereby humans experience the world beyond themselves. Research coming from this perspective includes critical reflection on how social and biophysical systems interact in the communities where humans live. That reflection opens possibilities for rhetorical (both its material and symbolic dimensions) struggle over the connotations of community. Beyond this generic approach to EC, our theoretical foundation consists of three threads – symbolic construction, modes of organizing and agonistic politics – that, together, are fundamental to community building, its maintenance and potentially or its destruction. Each chapter draws from one or more of these threads, and some integrates all three. We conceptualize these threads as follows.

A theoretical perspective based on symbolic construction enables us to explore how words, images and other symbols constitute meanings and communities, as well as how the tactical use of these symbols functions as a constructive and destructive instrument for existing communities. For example, words and non-linguistic images constitute ways of thinking, acting, and simply *being* in relation to one's environment. They also may be instruments that draw people together or tear them apart.

Chapters in the section on modes of organizing highlight how society's attempts to construct institutional frameworks to enhance political legitimacy enable various types of actions at the same time they disable others. This perspective directs our attention to the variety of spatial and temporal scales where environmental communication operates. They range from individual members of local groups to international organizations, and from immediate livelihood pressures to multi-generational concerns. The chapters in this section also highlight how social networks form, and then build on each other to influence possibilities for community action.

Viewing community construction and/or destruction as agonistic politics enables us to explicitly explore how participatory democracy can facilitate social transformation by disturbing political boundaries, and why people may want to do so. The chapters in this section investigate communicative practices that instantiate Mouffe's (2000) definition of agonism as a productive form of antagonism for engaging in decision-making in pluralistic, heterogeneous societies, or argumentation between "adversaries", adversaries being defined in a paradoxical way as "friendly enemies", that is, persons who are friends because they share a common symbolic space but also enemies because they want to organize this common symbolic space in a different way (13). The chapters in this and the following section explore the ways in which people marshal their communication resources by creatively engaging with traditional political structures and by politicizing activities that had not previously been thought of as political. These practices expand possibilities for citizen involvement in governance through revising the margins of public life.

Preview

This book is divided into three parts: an introduction, a suite of case studies, and a conclusion. In addition to this introductory chapter, the Part I includes a chapter that examines the criticality of conflict communication to the dynamics of social transformation. Part II, which contains the case studies presented here, is subdivided into sections focused on symbolic construction, modes of organizing, and agonistic politics. A fourth section of Part II includes two chapters that integrate symbolic, institutional and agonistic analyses. All of the case studies highlight the creation, maintenance and/or fracturing of community as they interact with other communities, including the extrahuman world. The following provides a brief glimpse of the content found in each chapter.

Conceptual framing for community constructivity and deconstructivity

In Chapter 2, "Reframing Conflict in Natural Resource Management", Hallgren explores constructive and destructive aspects of natural resource management (NRM) conflict and attempts to clarify distinctions between them. The point of departure in this chapter is that NRM conflict is neither solely constructive nor destructive, but involves elements of both. In order to illuminate the distinction between constructive and destructive conflict, the chapter offers a critical analysis of what natural resource managers generally assume is being constructed in a constructive process and destroyed in a destructive process. Hallgren puts Mouffe's (2013) agonistic pluralism into conversation with Habermas's (2001) theory of communicative rationality to form the basis of his argument that what is destroyed/constructed in destructive/constructive conflict processes is the actor's intersubjective ability to understand meaning for the conflict and the differences between agonistic perspectives. To further analyse this process, he introduces the concepts of commonality, mutuality and reciprocity. He concludes by arguing that when social interaction generates intersubjective experiences of equivocal reciprocity, opportunities for pluralistic agonism to emerge are reduced, resulting in destructivity. On the other hand, when social interaction generates increased certainty about reciprocity, those opportunities are expanded, resulting in constructivity. Both scenarios are fundamental to social transformation.

Symbolic construction – instantiating community through language and other symbols

Chapters 3, 4, and 5 address the role of symbols in the construction or deconstruction of community, exploring social attempts to address environmental issues within varying democratic systems. In Chapter 3, "Process literacy", Callister lays out an alternative to traditional forms of stakeholder engagement that could be used in multi-cultural contexts. She notes that, because, democracy suffers multiple encumbrances within these contexts (e.g. Benhabib 1996; Habermas 1984, 1989), making it work requires models of discourse that accommodate and encourage participants to develop their own forms of engagement to create conditions for deliberation within communities and at interfaces with decision-makers (Dryzek 2004). Callister defines process literacy as a "discursive lubricant" that facilitates the construction of community. The chapter explores how it builds an awareness of and the capacity to make choices that encourage productive communication during conflict situations. Process literacy functions to keep communication productive as multi-cultural participants negotiate internal conflict while striving to reach mutual decisions. Most importantly, it pivots conflict communication toward collaboration and deliberative decision-making, while holding open space for dissent. Finally, this chapter frames conflict communication in relationship to these complex processes within a *telos* of consensus.

Chapter 4, "Performances of an international professional community", shifts from considering spatially defined community to interest-based community of energy professionals. The use of carbon capture and storage (CCS) technologies is a significant topic of international deliberation about energy policy, particularly in the face of climate change. In 2005, the Intergovernmental Panel on Climate Change recommended the use of CCS as a strategy for climate change mitigation by reducing CO_2 emissions from the coal-dependent energy sector and other stationary industrial sources (IPCC 2005). This chapter examines the rhetorical dynamics of shifting the name of the community from CCS to CCUS (Carbon Capture, Utilization and Storage). Drawing largely from participant observation, the chapter describes and evaluates the moments of rupture caused by putting the "U" in CCUS. Drawing from social constructivist theories of linguistic meaning-making (Burke 1966), rhetorical boundary-work (Gieryn 1999) and the cultural performance of social drama, the authors argue that the framing shift ruptured the boundaries of the community, calling forth cultural performances of confusion, acquiescence and resistance to the framing shift. They suggest this theoretical perspective has the potential to serve as a powerful heuristic for examining other community ruptures, particularly communities based on shared interests, rather than shared space.

Chapter 5, "How reductive scientific narratives limit possibilities for community participation in biodiversity conservation" focuses on a community of place, exploring discourse surrounding the conservation of whooping cranes (*Grus Americana*) in Texas USA. This chapter identifies and explores the narratives used to describe the endangered whooping crane and its habitat needs along the central coastal bend of Texas (Aransas National Wildlife Refuge 2010). The authors began with a series of semi-structured interviews with people directly involved in crane conservation, most of whom live near or in whooping crane winter habitat. To ensure that the discursive frame that emerged from their study could demonstrate how community members integrated traditional scientific knowledge with local experiential knowledge

(Collins and Evans 2002), they augmented interview transcripts with testimony from a related trial, planning documents developed by government agencies, and scientific studies of whooping cranes and the ecosystem. Both humans and extrahumans played leading roles in the community narrative. Human relations with cranes varied widely, including experiencing the birds as close personal friends, neighbours, objects of study, management responsibility, economic stimulus, local icon and symbol of the natural world. The narrative that emerged from this community indicated that technically oriented discourse both empowered and constrained community participation in crane conservation and, by extension, in biodiversity conservation. Discourse gathered from these sources shows a community locked in conflict over how best to help with crane conservation. The authors argue that their case demonstrates that reductive scientific discourse tends to reproduce an equally reductive public discourse that constrains citizens' awareness of and capacity to make choices, a dimension of citizen engagement that Callister (Chapter 3) identified as crucial for working through the challenges presented by environmental issues. In this case, the community narrative focused almost exclusively on people's inability to provide more blue crab (a primary protein source for cranes), which meant ignoring equally critical issues such as the amount of available habitat.

Modes of organizing – instantiating community through structural means

Chapters 6 through 8 address the construction and maintenance of institutional frameworks for communities involved in environmental management. These communities present opportunities as well as constraints for management in a democratic system. In Chapter 6, "Community conversations on conservation", Banerjee examines the Joint Forest Management (JFM) programme in east Sikkim, India. She notes that, since its inception under the National Forest Policy Act of 1988, JFM has been presented as a powerful tool for sustainable forestry management throughout India (APFD 2001). Despite these claims, JFM in Sikkim has failed to achieve sustained community interest, and conflicts between local communities and the central government over forest use and management continue (Ravindranath *et al.* 2000). Banerjee adopts a critical interpretive framework (Denzin 1989) to evaluate how JFM as a participatory approach to forest conservation and management operates in the state of Sikkim. Through interviews with key actors and analysis of their roles, interests and power within JFM, she explores the highly contextualized socio-cultural, political and economic practices that make up the institution. Her critical exploration of the relationships between local residents and forests demonstrates how identity politics shape interactions between local communities and forest conservation, and provides a basis for understanding how members of these communities ascribe and legitimize the meanings they assign to forests, including both congruence and conflicts among ascribed meanings. She identifies rhetorical strategies used by forest-dependent communities and by professional forest managers to legitimize the various meanings they assign to forests, and examines how the actors use these strategies to leverage their meanings for specific conservation outcomes. The chapter suggests implementing collaborative approaches that encourage Forest Department personnel and local community members to recognize and cultivate their mutual interdependence through an iterative dialogue process similar to that suggested by Callister in Chapter 3.

Chapter 7, "Wildlife conservation as public good", examines the community of wildlife professionals and recreationalists that has emerged around the *North American Model of Wildlife Conservation* (NAMWC), a model for the future of wildlife conservation that supporters claim emerged from the public trust doctrine (PTD). The PTD charges governing authorities with managing natural resources in trust for the long-term benefit of the public. These resources could range from petroleum deposits in the North Sea to fish in the Amazon. Feldpausch-Parker and her co-authors describe the primary tenets of NAMWC, which include protection of special places, restrictions on commercial exploitation of wildlife, laws dedicated to species and habitat conservation, province/state and federal wildlife and landscape management entities, and dedicated funding for wildlife conservation (Geist 2006). The chapter then explores how associations of wildlife professionals and sportspersons throughout North America have institutionalized the NAMWC as a prototype of the PTD. The authors use Mouffe's (2000) democratic paradox as an analytical tool to examine how these organizations' communication characterizes appropriate wildlife management within a democratic political context. They found that consumptive use groups were the dominant voice communicating about the NAMWC, and that their language excluded other groups from participating in the North American conservation community. Feldpausch-Parker and her co-authors argue that recognizing and grappling with the always existing paradox between liberality and democracy could enable a discourse that reverses this exclusionary perspective and encourages the emergence of new ideas about wildlife conservation through practices of agonistic democracy.

In Chapter 8, "Dialogue for Nature Conservation", Hansen and Peterson explore another attempt to frame natural resources as a public good, and nature conservation as an inclusive community of citizens who collaboratively determine how best to manage this commons. The authors characterize this Swedish attempt to envision a new type of nature conservation as an attempt to recover dwindling political legitimacy for Swedish NRM by including a broad range of non-instrumental rationalities in environmental decisions and planning. After summarizing ways that local participation in NRM has been circumscribed by institutionalizing environmental interests within existing political systems, they describe how this institutionalization has also narrowed the spectrum of rationalities used to develop and evaluate NRM policies. The authors turn to Habermas' (1981, 1989) sociological theory of legitimacy to guide a critical discourse analysis of the antecedents and development of the Dialogue for Nature Conservation (DNC). Their analysis identifies the constraints that limited its expansion of the range of rationalities considered acceptable in Swedish NRM. The chapter explores both the program's social context and the political process leading to its implementation, using interviews with key actors, official documents and media prepared for the general public to discover how the goals of transforming nature conservation into a more dialogically based participative process were reinterpreted, culminating in the production and delivery of the DNC program. They argue that following the trajectory of this institutional innovation from an idea proposed by one individual, through the political process, and to the point of programmatic implementation, illuminates both opportunities and challenges encountered when public institutions attempt to incorporate non-instrumental rationalities into the policy arena.

Agonistic politics – instantiating community through dissent and nontraditional practice

Chapters 9 through 11 address the power and place of dissent and nontraditional practices in response to environmental issues. Chapter 9's "Deconstructing public space to construct community", explores a phenomenon known as guerrilla gardening, the cultivation of public space without permission. Todd analyses the communication strategies detailed in guerrilla gardening manuals and on their websites to demonstrate how guerrilla gardening discourse advocates alternative visions of community through sensory appeals to environmental sustainability. As a basis for her analysis, she draws from environmental communication theory regarding the symbolic and embodied transformation of place (Carbaugh and Cerulli 2013; Thompson and Cantrill 2013), on relations between communication and democracy (Peterson et al. 2007, 2010), from environmental education and psychology (Ralston 2012). Using this foundation, she explores how the authors of guerrilla gardening manuals guide guerrilla gardeners through practices that construct social identity and provide political legitimacy their community. As community gardens, these reconstructed places become spaces for discourse about what the commons are and how they should be instantiated. Todd concludes that guerrilla gardening cultivates a sense of place through a radical form of community engagement. Its status as a guerrilla activity foregrounds one of the fundamental challenges of social transformation in liberal democracy, with a relatively peaceful dissent contributing directly to a new consensus.

Chapter 10, "Communicating emotions in conflicts over natural resource management in the Netherlands and Sweden", explores another forbidden dimension of environmental engagement, the inclusion of emotion in environmental decision-making. Ångman and her co-authors provide an empirically grounded analysis of the extent to which emotion is legitimized and delegitimized as part of NRM. The chapter turns to social psychology

(Haidt 2003) for its understanding of communicative openings and closures to discuss how accepted communicative practices open and close space for emotion in the NRM context. The chapter follows Thévenot *et al.* (2000) in claiming that emotional arguments are indicative of and help legitimize valuable community bonds, and that delegitimizing emotions often results in discursive closure of deliberative space for local communities. The case studies show that deliberative spaces for planning relate directly to the struggle over emotions as legitimate within NRM. Emotions and emotional accounts are powerful mobilizers that could enable local communities to organize and construct new identities. The chapter's empirical grounding comes from a Dutch struggle over the management and re-design of an urban forest, and a Swedish conflict over management of a privately owned, but publicly used, forest. In both cases actors were keen to establish their connection to the land, but differed in the sense of place they ascribed to that land. The authors chronicle how communities were simultaneously constructed and deconstructed through protest and collaboration, and how emotional dimensions of the protests, and by extension the protestors themselves, were delegitimized within the NRM context. They suggest that recognizing and understanding emotions as central to NRM is basic to improving the management of environmental conflict.

Chapter 11 explores "Community construction through culturally rooted celebration" in Central America. Liles and his co-authors offer a third nontraditional approach to engaging publics in environmental policy development and deployment. They describe an innovative campaign for sea turtle conservation in El Salvador and Nicaragua. The campaign was motivated by the fact that, in these low-income regions where governing authorities lack the ability and will to enforce conservation laws, primary resource users often self-govern resource use in their local communities (Dietz *et al.* 2003). This reality means that, in Bahía de Jiquilisco (El Salvador) and Estero Padre Ramos (Nicaragua), local residents determine what happens to hawksbill eggs. Since approximately 80 per cent of the endangered hawksbill turtles in the eastern Pacific lay their eggs on these beaches, local residents who own no real estate, have no stock options, and whose livelihoods are based on selling turtle eggs, wield extremely powerful influence in whether or not the turtles will continue to exist (Liles *et al.* 2014). Liles and his co-authors spent years studying how local residents related to the turtles, including (but not limited to) factors that may motivate or discourage their participation in a conservation community that strives to collectively develop and reach shared goals. They frame community with three dimensions (shared ecology, social organization, and shared cultural and symbolic meaning), where a community is considered less robust if one or more dimensions are weak or nonexistent and a community is considered more robust if all three dimensions are strong (Cnaan and Milofsky 2008). Using this multidimensional concept of community, they worked together with local residents to develop the Hawksbill Cup, an annual competition rooted firmly in traditions of local culture. The chapter details how this celebration mobilizes turtles as a symbol of community pride and transforms the role of from invisible workers into protagonists in the hawksbill conservation saga. They argue that this transformation affords local participants a powerful voice in both defining and determining the intertwined fate of human and hawksbill wellbeing in their communities.

Cases that integrate all three perspectives

The theoretical threads (symbolic construction, modes of organization, and agonistic politics) used throughout the book converge in the final two case studies, Chapters 12 and 13. In Chapter 12, "Seized and missed opportunities in responding to conflicts", Raitio critically examines forest conflicts in Inari (Finland) and the Great Bear Rainforest (British Columbia, Canada). Along with Hallgren, she begins from Mouffe's (2013) assertion that, unless conflict and dissent have space within democratic process, they will emerge outside of the recognized political process, delegitimizing the authorities that have excluded them from more formal channels. Like Chapters 9, 10, and 11, Raitio uses her cases to demonstrate the importance and valuable potential of contestation and dissent, noting that, contrary to a common perception, constructivity and destructivity are found in how conflict is addressed, rather than in conflict itself (Glasl 1999). Similarly to Chapters 6, 7, and 8, she uses communication research on the role of conflict in social and institutional change (Ganesh and Zoller 2013), which, together with critical planning theory (Fischler 2000) provides a foundation for her analysis of conflict processes in Finnish and Canadian forests. Like Chapters 3 and 4, she carefully examines how symbols and images are used to craft some meanings rather than others. Raitio uses her cases to provide a ground for examining the dynamics between process design choices, causes of conflict, and social transformation. Her comparative empirical analysis identifies missed opportunities to address underlying cases in the dispute settlement over the Inari forest, as opposed to a settlement that attempted to address a broad spectrum of underlying causes in Great Bear Rainforest. She concludes that differences in how the conflicts were addressed, rather than in the nature of the conflicts, have been decisive for community constructivity and destructivity.

Chapter 13, "Divergent meanings of community", takes its theoretical cue most directly from the ethnography of communication (Philipsen and Coutu 2005), but also includes discussion of how the social construction of meaning through communication interacts with institutions, and how these social constructions eventually potentiate forms of democratic governance that may both compel and constrain social transformation. The authors specify that, although effective public participation may enable solutions that are better adapted to the local context, transform adversarial relationships, lead to joint ownership of decisions, reduce implementation costs and increase the available information (Reed 2008), none of these normative goals are primary to an ethnography of communication. Because communication processes are always prior to and underlying cultural and political action, the speech events (Hymes 1972) wherein publics participate are the focal point of the analysis. Given this focus, Sprain and her co-authors examine these events by querying potential relationships between language and social life, seeking to understand local systems of meaning, values, norms and beliefs exhibited by community members. Only after exhaustive analysis at this level do they turn to an examination of the cultural discourses (Carbaugh 2007) and related discourse practices in play during these events, identifying and exploring the divergent expectations and meanings that citizens and event designers may bring to the situation. Using this approach, they analyse two cases of public participation in water governance in the western United States; the California Marine Life Protection Initiative and a public dialogue on the Poudre River in Northern Colorado. Through comparing and contrasting the two, they demonstrate the significance of understanding locally situated meanings of participation in environmental governance. They explicitly argue for developing theories grounded in local communicative practices, and against broad theorizing that attempts to encompass entire polities. At the same time, they suggest gaining a more complete understanding of the ongoing co-production of meaning that occurs via local communicative practices and how they bring community into existence, may offer valuable insights enabling the design and implementation of participation processes that enrich community life, and at least do not undermine it.

Conclusion

Together, these chapters tell the story of community constructivity and destructivity from multiple levels and perspectives, but all demonstrate the importance of communication, how it contributes to community, and how it influences possibilities for democratic decision-making. Further, they demonstrate and explain multiple possibilities for moving environmental communication research between theory and practice. Finally, they offer grist for discussion about what it takes to build and eventually transform democratic communities in the twenty-first century.

References

APFD (2001) *Joint Forest Management: Forest Conservation with People's Participation, a Saga of Success towards Swarna Andhra Pradesh.* Hyderabad: Andhra Pradesh Forest Department.

Aransas National Wildlife Refuge (2010) Comprehensive conservation plan and environmental assessment. US Fish and Wildlife Service, Aransas National Wildlife Refuge Complex, Austwell, Texas, USA.

Benhabib, S. (ed.) (1996) *Democracy and Difference: Contesting the Boundaries of the Political.* Princeton, NJ: Princeton University Press.

Burke, K. (1966) *Language as Symbolic Action: Essays on Life, Literature, and Method.* Berkeley, CA: University of California Press.

Carbaugh, D. (2007) Cultural discourse analysis: communication practices and inter-cultural encounters. *Journal of Intercultural Communication Research* 36(3): 167–182.

Carbaugh, D. and Cerulli, T. (2013) Cultural discourses of dwelling: investigating environmental communication as a place-based practice. *Environmental Communication: a Journal of Nature and Culture* 7(1): 4–23.

Cnaan, R. A. and Milofsky, C. (eds) (2008) *Handbook of Community Movements and Local Organizations.* New York, NY: Springer.

Collins, H. M. and Evans, R. (2002) The third wave of science studies: studies of expertise and experience. *Social Studies of Science* 32: 235–296.

Cox, R. (2007) Nature "crisis disciplines": does environmental communication have an ethical duty? *Environmental Communication* 1: 5–20.

Cox, R. and Pezzullo, P. C. (2016) *Environmental Communication and the Public Sphere,* (4th edition) Thousand Oaks, CA: Sage.

Denzin, N. K. (1989) *Interpretive Interactionism,* Newbury Park, CA: Sage.

Dietz, T., Ostrom, E. and Stern, P. C. (2003) The struggle to govern the commons. *Science* 302: 1907–1912.

Dryzek, J. (2004) Pragmatism and democracy. *Journal of Speculative Philosophy* 18: 72–79.

Fischler, R. (2000) Communicative planning theory: a Foucauldian assessment. *Journal of Planning Education and Research* 19: 358–368.

Ganesh, S. and Zoller, H. M. (2013) Dialogue, activism and democratic social change. *Communication Theory* 22(1): 66–91.

Geist, V. (2006) The North American model of wildlife conservation: a means of cre-ating wealth and protecting public health while generating biodiversity. In: Lavigne, D. M. (ed.) *Gaining Ground: In Pursuit of Ecological Sustainability.* Guelph, Canada, and Limerick, Ireland: International Fund for Animal Welfare and Univer-sity of Limerick, 285–293.

Gieryn, T. F. (1999) *Cultural Boundaries of Science: Credibility on the Line.* Chicago: University of Chicago Press.

Glasl, F. (1999) *Confronting Conflict: a First Aid Kit for Handling Conflict.* Gloucester-shire, UK: Hawthorne Press.

Habermas, J. (1981) *Theorie des kommunikativen handelns.* Frankfurt am Main: Suhrkamp. 2 vols. McCarthy, T. (trans) as *The Theory of Communicative Action. Reason and the Rationalization of Society* (1984) and *Lifeworld and System: a Critique of Functionalist Reason* (1987). Boston, MA: Beacon Press.

Habermas, J. (1989) *The Structural Transformation of the Public Sphere: Inquiry into a Category of Bourgeois Society.* Boston, MA: MIT Press.

Habermas, J. (1997) *Between Facts and Norms.* Cambridge, MA: Polity Press.

Habermas, J. (2001) Truth and society: The discursive redemption of factual claims to validity. In: *On the Pragmatics of Social Interaction: Preliminary Studies in the Theory of Communicative Action.* Cambridge, MA: MIT Press.

Haidt, J. (2003) The moral emotions. In: R. J. Davidson, K. R. Scherer and H. H. Goldsmith (eds) *Handbook of Affective Sciences.* Oxford: Oxford University Press, 852–870.

Hajer, M. A. (1995) *The Politics of Environmental Discourse: Ecological Modernization and the Policy Process,* Oxford: Oxford University Press.

Hymes, D. (1972) Models of the interaction of language and social life. In: Gumperz, H. H. and Hymes, D. (eds) *Directions in Sociolinguistics: the Ethnography of Communication.* New York: Holt, Rinehart & Winston, 35–71.

Intergovernmental Panel on Climate Change (2005) *IPCC Special Report on Carbon Dioxide Capture and Storage*. New York: Cambridge University Press.

Latour, B. (2004) (Porter, K. trans) *Politics of Nature: How to Bring the Sciences into Democracy*. Cambridge, MA: Harvard University Press.

Liles, M. J., Peterson, M. J., Lincoln, Y. S., Seminoff, J. A., Gaos, A. R. and Peterson, T. R. (2014) Connecting international priorities with human wellbeing in low-income regions: lessons from hawksbill turtle conservation in El Salvador. *Local Environment*. Online, available at: http://dx.doi.org/10.1080/13549839.2014.905516.

Luhmann, N. (1989) *Ecological Communication*. (J. Bednarz, Trans.). Chicago, IL: University of Chicago Press.

Mouffe, C. (2000) *The Democratic Paradox*. New York, NY: Verso.

Mouffe, C. (2013) *Agonistics: Thinking the World Politically*. London: Verso.

Peterson, M. N., Peterson, M. J. and Peterson, T. R. (2007) Environmental communication: why this crisis discipline should facilitate environmental democracy. *Environmental Communication: a Journal of Nature and Culture* 1(1): 74–86.

Peterson, M. N., Peterson, T. R., Lopez, A. and Liu, J. (2010) Views of private-land stewardship among Latinos on the Texas–Tamaulipas border. *Environmental Communication: a Journal of Nature and Culture* 4(4): 406–421.

Philipsen, G. and Coutu, L. (2005) The ethnography of speaking. In: Fitch, K. L. and Sanders, R. E. (eds) *Handbook of Language and Social Interaction*. Mahwah, NJ: Lawrence Erlbaum Associates, 355–380.

Ralston, S. J. (2012) Educating future generations of community gardeners: a Deweyan challenge. *Critical Education* 3(3).

Ravindranath, N. H., Murali, K. S. and Malhotra, K. C. (eds) (2000) *Joint Forest Management and Community Forestry in India: An Ecological and Institutional Assessment*. New Delhi: Oxford and IBH Publishing.

Reed, M. S. (2008) Stakeholder participation for environmental management: a literature review. *Biological Conservation* 141: 2417–2431.

Thévenot, L., Moody, M. and Lafaye, C. (2000) Forms of valuing nature: arguments and modes of justification in French and American environmental disputes. In: Lamont, M. and Thévenot, L. (eds) *Rethinking Comparative Cultural Sociology: Repertoires of Evaluation in France and the United States*. Cambridge, UK: Cambridge University Press, 229–272.

2 Reframing conflict in natural resource management

Mutuality, reciprocity and pluralistic agonism as dynamics of community constructivity and destructivity

Lars Hallgren

This chapter explores constructive and destructive dimensions of natural resource management (NRM) conflict and attempts to distinguish them from each other. The point of departure is that NRM conflict is neither solely constructive nor destructive, but involves elements of both.

In order to identify the distinction between constructive and destructive conflict, the chapter critically examines what is generally assumed to be created in a constructive process and destroyed in a destructive process. Based on Mouffe's concept of agonistic pluralism, as a significant adaptation of Habermas's ideas about communicative rationality, I suggest that what is simultaneously destroyed and created in destructive and constructive conflict processes is the actors' intersubjective ability to understand the meaning of the conflict and the differences between agonistic perspectives. To further analyse this process, I consider the face-to-face level of conversation and elaborate on the concepts of commonality, mutuality and reciprocity. It can be concluded that when social interaction generates intersubjective experiences of equivocal reciprocation, opportunities for pluralistic agonism to emerge are reduced, resulting in destructivity. On the other hand, social interaction that generates increased trust in the likelihood of reciprocation increases opportunities for the emergence of pluralistic agonism, resulting in constructivity.

In ordinary English usage, "conflict", as it pertains to NRM, is often perceived to be the opposite of "community". Conflict is often described as the force that destroys community. Thus developing and sustaining a healthy community is assumed to require protection from conflict through the use of conflict management. However, conflict theorists from multiple disciplines have explored ways that conflict can be constitutive and constructive for community. The sociologist George Simmel (1964), for example, argued that conflict is social interaction that paradoxically constitutes society, as well as dissolving society:

> If every interaction among men [*sic*] is association, conflict ... must certainly be considered as sociation. And in fact, *dis*sociating factors – hate, envy, need, desire – are the causes of conflict.... Conflict is thus designed

to resolve divergent dualisms; it is a way of achieving some kind of unity, even if it be through the annihilation of one of the conflicting parties.

(Simmel 1964, p. 13)

Conflict is a core concept and an important topic in environmental and NRM literature. A literature search on Web of Science in November 2014 revealed that "environmental conflict" appeared in the heading or abstract of 46 journal articles published in that year. There is, of course, some uncertainty built into the concept and the phenomenon. Conflict as a phenomenon can be viewed from multiple perspectives (Peterson and Feldpausch-Parker 2013). In this chapter, I focus on conflict as: 1) a destructive process that causes society to break down and reduces its ability to think and act jointly, and therefore needs to be prevented and resolved; and 2) a constructive process that is constituting society, and that is necessary for pluralism and creativity, and a productive means of informing a society when it has issues that need to be dealt with. "Conflict … cannot and should not be eradicated, since the specificity of pluralist democracy is precisely the recognition and the legitimation of conflict" (Mouffe 2013, p. 7). In the NRM literature, this dual nature of conflict is often not considered, and in fact the concept of conflict is often framed in ways that limit attention to its dissociating processes, at the same time descriptions of its associating processes are often overly simplistic. Although Simmel (1964) explicitly describes conflict as a dialectic between sociating–dissociating factors, the NRM literature mainly concentrates on the dissociating factors. This chapter discusses both types of factors, and relies on Simmel's conceptualization of conflict. Rather than using the sociating and dissociating terms proposed by Simmel, however, I use the terms constructive and destructive, in an attempt to juxtapose my argument more directly with contemporary NRM literature generally, and the arguments laid out in this book particularly.

The point of departure for this analysis is that the process of conflict comprises both constructive and destructive processes. It assumes that disagreement should not be considered as inherently destructive, while recognizing that, at most times, something within society will be generating destructivity. This view is raised by Mouffe in her critique of liberal democratic theory:

Contrary to Habermas … I submit that … emphasis in the ever present possibility of the friend/enemy distinction and the conflictual nature of politics constitutes the necessary starting point for envisaging the aims of democratic politics. Only by acknowledging "the political" in its antagonistic dimension can we pose the central question for democratic politics.

(Mouffe 2005, p. 14)

The problem is that in previous theoretical and empirical discussions, the phenomena associated with conflict have been attributed constructive and destructive qualities, with little clarification of how the distinction between constructivity and destructivity should be derived. Moreover, the concept of conflict is often used in the analysis of environmental communication and NRM with an implicit assumption that it is purely destructive. The aim of the present analysis is thus to develop a theoretical understanding of both the distinction and relationships between constructive and destructive aspects of conflict. Simmel (1964, p. 15) writes about the conditions for of this complicated relationship: "there probably exists no social unit in which convergent and divergent currents among its members are not inseparable interwoven".

Creating a conceptual framework for distinguishing constructivity from destructivity means revisiting the debate between supporters of Mouffe's emphasis on the never-ending agonistic possibilities of any political system, and a Habermasian (2001) perspective focused on building public consensus via engaging all interested parties in genuinely communicative and deliberative discussions that would occur within the public sphere. Based on their extensive work, I continue by scaling down the conflict situation to face-to-face communication and link my discussion of constructivity–destructivity interactionistic, social constructionist communication theory. I go on to discuss asymmetries in conversation dynamics, which helps formulate a tentative suggestion about the distinction between constructivity and destructivity in environmental conflict.

Constructing and destructing what? Revisiting the Mouffe–Habermas debate

The words constructive and destructive have a common etymology in "structure", from the Latin *struera*; to pile or heap up. Constructive is an adjective describing that something is built or put together, in the original meaning something concrete, e.g. a wall. The adjective destructive (destroy) comes from the Latin *destruere*; to tear down. Thus in a constructive conflict, it should be possible to identify the "structure" that has been constructed and in a destructive conflict it should be possible to identify the structure that has been destroyed. It may help in making a distinction between constructive and destructive aspects of NRM conflicts if we can clarify *what* is constructed and destroyed. Often this *what*, the structure built/destroyed in the process of the conflict, is not explained when talking about constructivity and destructivity. Instead, "constructive" is used to describe a conflict that is considered to be developing in a generally "good" direction and "destructive" is used to describe a conflict considered to be developing in a generally "bad" direction.

For making a meaningful distinction between constructivity and destructivity, the same "thing", i.e. a particular structure, which is constructed in a constructive conflict should be destroyed in a destructive conflict. Constructivity and destructivity should be considered not only as a pair of related concepts, but also as social processes that are dialectically related: What is constructed in the constructive phase is the same as that which is destroyed in the destructive phase.

Conflicts are sometimes described as "productive", where productive is used synonymously with constructive. This creates a need for specification; *what* is the conflict producing? In this study, "constructive" is preferred over "productive", since productive can easily be associated with economic goals, e.g. a conflict could be considered "productive" if resulting in "Pareto-optimal distribution", or if alternative costs and transaction costs are lower than the benefit or if the situation contributes to economic growth. This is not the direction to take when searching for a distinction between constructivity and destructivity in conflicts.

Case study descriptions of NRM conflicts commonly describe the conflict as a disagreement or interest divergence on one hand, and implicitly or explicitly as destructive on the other hand (e.g. Silva-Macher and Farrell 2014; Martin *et al.* 2014; Keir and Ali 2014). This would make "consensus" or "agreement" the structure constructed/destroyed in conflict, with the result that conflicts could not be considered constructive at all. One critic of this view is Mouffe (2013), who claims that society "requires a debate about possible alternatives". The present analysis investigates whether her terminology could contribute to identification of what is constructed/destroyed. Mouffe (2013, p. 6) argues that conflict is necessary, e.g. for the constitution of social identities:

> the fundamental question is not how to arrive at a consensus reached without exclusion, because this would require the construction of an us that would not have a corresponding them ... the very condition for the constitution of us is the demarcation of a "them".

Mouffe (2005) emphasizes that society is always facing the possibility of conflict, and that conflict can take the form of antagonism, hostility between groups, but also "agonism". Agonism is when actors challenge others' ideas, not their legitimacy to represent these ideas in a debate. The distinction Mouffe makes between antagonistic relations between actors in a conflict and agonistic relations concerns the extent to which actors involved in conflict see and respond to each other as legitimate.

Mouffe's purpose with this distinction is different than that in the present study; her intention is to emphasize the importance of understanding society as political and to identify opportunities for radical, pluralistic democracy. Her ultimate objective, and that of Habermas (2001), is a normative discussion about how to organize decision-making in society. The political philosophy of Mouffe does not obviously lend itself to the identification of what is constructed/ destroyed in a conflict process. However, we will read Mouffe with the purpose to analytically separate constructivity and destructivity in conflict, and as the first step to identify what it is that is constructed respective to what is destructed.

> Antagonism can take many forms and it is illusory to believe that they could ever be eradicated. This is why it is important to allow them an

agonistic form of expression through the pluralist democratic system.... A democratic society requires a debate about possible alternatives and it must provide political forms of collective identification around clearly differentiated democratic positions.

(Mouffe 2005, pp. 30–31)

[In agonism] ... others are not seen as enemies to be destroyed, but as adversaries whose ideas might be fought, even fiercely, but whose right to defend those ideas is not to be questioned.

(Mouffe 2013, p. 7)

However, Mouffe also stresses the difference between her view on agonism and the proposers of normative dialogue, who typically mean that if disagreeing actors talk with each other in a respectful way, they might together find new solutions to the problem that caused the conflict. This is not what Mouffe seeks. Rather, she claims that, "in an agonistic politics, however, the antagonistic dimension is always present, since what is at stake is the struggle between opposing hegemonic projects which can never be reconciled rationally, one of them needing to be defeated" (Mouffe 2013, p. 9). Her point here is that the always pre-existing hegemonic relations preclude any democratic politics without antagonism.

Mouffe criticizes neo-liberal political philosophy for making universal consensus the goal of politics, and denying the political aspect of politics. However, she confirms that consensus on procedural issues is necessary for pluralistic agonism to arise. Moreover, she stresses that the aim of democracy is not to overcome political distance between groups and sub-communities or to generate integration between segregated groups through unification. Politics, according to Mouffe, should be pluralistic, which includes separation into "us" and "them": "The crucial issue then is to establish this us/them distinction, which is constitutive of politics, in a way that is compatible with the recognition of pluralism" (Mouffe 2013, p. 7).

What is not quite as clear when reading Mouffe from the perspective of distinguishing between constructivity and destructivity is to what extent a community understanding of the difference between contested perspectives is necessary for pluralism. Does "plural" imply that actors involved in conflict are aware of the meaning of the different perspectives? Or would a situation where people who perceive a "we–them" identity, but have no idea about the ideological difference between "them" and "us", equally qualify as "plural"? In the present analysis, I adopted the following standpoint: *to be able to talk about pluralism in a conflict situation, it is necessary for the agonism (argument, debate, dialogue) to result in the actors involved understanding the difference between perspectives.* If confusion and/or misunderstanding about the difference between perspectives increase with agonism, or if what actors know about other actors' propositions is only that they are made by actors different from themselves, but not how they were made, then plurality cannot be claimed to exist. For plurality, it must be possible for actors to understand the range of alternatives. When the relationship between two (or more) opinions is unclear and there is no joint, legitimate method for working that clarifies the difference, then agonism will evolve into antagonism and adversaries will become enemies. This transition should be called destructive.

At this stage of the analysis it is necessary to link Mouffe's approach with Habermas's theory of communicative action, despite these authors having come to quite different conclusions in their work. Mouffe in fact explicitly questions whether there is any opportunity for communicative rationality. However, I believe that communicative rationality is a necessary complement to Mouffe's distinction between agonistic pluralism and antagonism if we are to distinguish between constructive and destructive conflict.

Communicative rationality takes place, according to Habermas (2001, p. 88), in a communicative situation where: i) all claims of validity are allowed to affect discourse until there is consensus about the invalidity of the claim; ii) all claims of validity are evaluated as regards the extent to which the claim is intelligible, true, legitimate and sincere; iii) all actors can raise claims of validity, and iv) all actors can question validity. Mouffe (2013, p. 7) writes that: "Adversaries fight against each other because they want their interpretations ... to become hegemonic, but they do not put into question the legitimacy of their opponent's right to fight for the victory for their position".

What Mouffe describes seems undeniably to be a situation characterized by communicative rationality: actors arguing their respective contrary interpretations, thus making validity claims, and raising questions about validity, but not questioning the right of their opponent to claim validity. This can therefore be interpreted not as a procedure for generating universal consensus, but as a procedure for generating pluralism, thus developing a shared understanding by actors of the difference in ontology and epistemology.

Following this line of thinking, communicative rationality does not result in general consensus about ontology, epistemology, values, ethics, or joint action. Instead, communicative rationality continuously works to establish local, temporary and situated consensus about: i) meta-communicative procedure, i.e. conditions for communicating about the disagreement; ii) the meaning of the concepts used; and iii) the meaning of the difference in perspective and premises of the adversaries. Mouffe (2005, p. 37) confirms that pluralistic agonism is dependent on consensus in meta-communicative questions: "Consensus is no doubt necessary, but it must be accompanied by dissent. Consensus is needed on the institutions constitutive of democracy".

This re-reading of Mouffe and Habermas provides a temporary answer as to *what* is constructed and destroyed in conflict processes, namely the ability to agonize. The ability to agonize should not be considered an individual capacity, but the capacity of a social practice; an intersubjective, temporary and situated capacity that is reconstructed when experienced.

With this view, what is constructed in a constructive conflict is a social practice to investigate the conflict, the foundation and conditions for the antagonism, and the differences in perspectives. What is destroyed in a destructive conflict is the disagreeing actors' joint ability to investigate the conflict, its foundations and conditions, and differences in perspectives. This ability is intersubjective, shared and co-constructed; it is an emergent property of the social interaction in the conflict, not a static property of the individuals involved or a property of the context of the conflict or disagreement as such.

Illustration of the dynamics of constructivity and destructivity in NRM conflict

Before continuing this conceptual and theoretical investigation of constructivity and destructivity in NRM conflicts, the theory can be illustrated with a case study. Note that this does not purport to be a complete, validated analysis of the case, but rather an illustration of the theory discussed here. The case is described in detail in Hallgren (2003).

The small river Emån in south-east Sweden regularly floods the surrounding landscape, occasionally causing damage to societal infrastructure, and often causing crop damage and costs for farmers. During the 1990s, farmers, supported by a parliamentary decision in 1974 on meeting flood protection costs in the area, applied for permission to improve drainage. The proposal encountered resistance from nature conservation authorities and organizations. In the ensuing enquiry and decision-making process, which lasted more than ten years, both sides in the conflict expressed and responded to various arguments in formal texts, debate articles, and public meetings. Farmers argued that the proposed drainage project was necessary for their economic survival and for the development of the area, and would not cause any environmental problems. Nature conservation organizations argued that the proposed drainage would cause serious, multiple environmental degradation and that farm finances and rural development are not dependent on flood protection, as agriculture has been practiced in the area for hundreds of years without these measures. In research interviews, both parties argued that there was no reason for conflict, that no goal interference existed, and that the other party had dark, hidden motives for its action. Each side claimed that the other side was not sincere and/or was deliberately hiding the truth, and that its actions were based on a desire to harm them rather than defending the interests they publicly claimed to represent. One farmer said repeatedly in an interview that "one can hardly believe it's true, how I've been treated" and claimed that civil servants at the county administrative board, as well as the representatives of nature conservation organizations arguing in the case, were "jealous" of farmers. The same farmer stated in a formal letter to the authorities that some of the objections received were written by individuals running a "vendetta" against farmers and with a hatred of farmers as individuals. In interviews, civil servants and representatives of nature conservation organizations claimed that the farmers involved had based their financial plans on unrealistic expectations on farm output, making them recklessly commit to the drainage case, regardless of the consequences. They also claimed that some of the farmers belonged to a certain landlord culture whereby they believed they did not have to care about public interests and decisions by authorities. One member of a nature conservation organization asked the researcher what other people had been interviewed and, when the name of one of the farmers was mentioned, asked "was that possible" (to talk with him).

The disagreement about drainage in Emån had both constructive and destructive aspects, but over time destructivity dominated; the involved actors' shared ability to investigate the conditions and consequences of the disagreement were successively reduced when actors debated the issue with each other. The interviews revealed that when actors had experienced the communication process, they became increasingly convinced that the other party had hidden motives, and speculation about these motives became increasingly advanced. The interviews and scrutiny of the letters exchanged also revealed that actors' faith in, and expectation of, being understood and able to understand was reduced. Communication was increasingly less considered to be a functional means of exercising influence in the issue, and various other forms of exercise of power, such as delegitimizing and excluding the antagonist, were applied. Farmers sometimes reported public officers at the county administrative board to the constitutional court for abuse of power, and to the environmental court for environmental crimes. Farmers also invited politicians to their farms during flooding and told their version of the story. When one Member of Parliament then criticized the authority in the media for bad management procedures, the chief executive of the authority claimed that that criticism was "the lowest low water mark during my 30 years in Swedish politics". In the analysis below, I show that a lot of discursive openings, i.e. opportunities to investigate important issues in society, were made in this case, but they tended not to remain open, but closed due to inability to exploit them. This is what is meant by destructive conflict.

A particular issue in the conflict about drainage in Emån concerned the validity of a research report in which a biologist argued that the population of catfish (*Siluris glansis*) in the river had decreased as a consequence of an earlier drainage project in another part of the same river, and that further drainage should be avoided and regarded as a threat to the survival of the endangered catfish population. That report was based on the statistical analysis of a catch and re-catch sample before and after the drainage project. The report was criticized and discussed in a public exchange of letters (circulated to more than 20 organizations, including the Swedish Environmental Protection Agency (SEPA) and the Ministry for the Environment). The farmers claimed that since the catch and re-catch monitoring had been conducted at different times in the years before and after the drainage project, they were not directly comparable and thus the report was unable to draw valid conclusions about population changes. This exchange involved an argument on differences in views on statistical analysis between farmers and biologists. To some extent this met the criterion defined for constructive conflict in this chapter, as it involved arguments about the statistical theories and procedures on which valid statements about reasons for catfish population changes should be based and how these changes should be evaluated. This procedure could result in farmers and biologists realizing why they disagree; e.g. because of thinking differently about statistical theory, or making these different assumptions about society. However, other arguments also appeared. One farmer claimed that the researchers had written a sloppy, unscientific report, that their research methodology was faulty and that funding bodies should support other researchers instead. One of the biologists replied that: "since you are a technician and not a biologist, I need to point out that biology does not follow mechanistic rules ... in biological issues, it is the freshwater laboratory which has the knowledge and competence". The researcher continued: "with this we consider the personal debate with you closed, and will continue with more constructive work". We will return to this quote later, but note that in this very sentence, the terminology used in this chapter paradoxically back-fires; when the investigative dialogue is classified as destructive (or at least less constructive), then use of the concept "constructive" contributes to destructivity.

What is destructive in this situation is not that the actors disagreed about the size and development of the catfish population or about research methods, but that their joint ability to investigate important differences in ontology, epistemology and ideology, which was the foundation for the disagreement, was successively reduced. For the actors in this conflict, the intentions behind others' actions became increasingly confused and more difficult to interpret, and they increasingly tended to explain the behaviour of the other as being based on illegitimate drivers, rather than legitimate argumentation for a position based in ontological and epistemological assumptions they themselves disagreed about. The conflict about draining the river Emån would have been constructive if the ability to investigate the foundations of conflict could have been reconstructed. As I see it, both constructivity and destructivity are always situated and always changing. In every moment the process can turn around and constructivity can transform into destructivity and vice versa. The ability for joint investigation of conditions and consequences of disagreement is the temporary, dynamic result of the last turns in the interaction between actors in the conflict, and how they choose to respond to each other's previous actions. In the last example above, the researcher responded to the farmer's criticism of the statistical method used for drawing conclusions, in a question that engaged both of them, through writing that the personal debate was finished and that the researcher would now return to more constructive activities. This can be interpreted as: i) a suggestion of a discursive closure; let's end this investigation of our disagreement, and ii) a classification of the exchange so far as non-constructive. However, the exchange only becomes destructive with the response confirming the proposed discursive closure that the investigation of disagreement is ending. From the perspective proposed in this chapter, it is the intersubjective, dynamic consequence of actions that are constructive or destructive, not action in itself. It is the ability to jointly investigate the conditions and consequences that are constructed/destroyed in every communicative action in relation to all other previous actions and all other anticipated future actions.

Constructivity and destructivity as a dynamic response to mutuality and reciprocity

In this section, terminology developed for investigating face-to-face inter-action is used in order to understand the dynamic of constructivity and destructivity in NRM conflicts. Since the theory of communicative action was first introduced, the concrete face-to-face situation has to some extent been the model for understanding the distinction between constructive and destructive aspects of conflict.

Three concepts: commonality, mutuality and reciprocity, frequently are used to describe different levels of sharedness and symmetry/asymmetry in conversations (Grauman 1995; Linell 2010). The basis of the social construc-tionist perspective on conversation is that actions, such as gestures, utterances, etc. are assumed to be both dependent on the context of the conversation *and* creators of the context of the conversation in a dialectical way.

Commonality refers to assumptions about the world, self and other that conversationalists share; knowledge, language, identity. Part of what the con-versationalists share has been generated during the conversation. Mutuality refers to the assumptions the conversationalists make about what they have in common and to what degree; assumptions about what others know/assume, and assumptions about what others assume I know/assume. Reciprocity refers to shared assumptions about the interplay itself and how to reciprocate; assumptions about being involved in an interplay where one is expected to respond to the other, and the other is expected to respond back. Further-more, when involved in an interplay, we expect that the other expects us to respond to their gesture, e.g. if my neighbour says good morning, I expect s/he will expect me to respond. That this is what we expect is evident when we consider the embarrassment we experience if we recognize too late that we did not respond to our neighbour's greetings (Asplund 1987). If this happens, the next time we meet we often become involved in complicated, meta-communicative explanations; "You know, I did not see you, and then when I saw you, you had turned around and that truck was hooting so you did not hear when I shouted".

For example, consider two actors, A and B, who have different perspec-tives on an issue about a resource R, about which both are concerned. A and B have different and contested interests in that if A employs means in order to achieve his/her interest, B's opportunity to realize his/her own interest will be reduced, and vice versa. A and B also disagree about the status of R and about whether A's or B's interest should be prioritized. A and B have a conflict that can develop in a constructive or destructive direction. Thus their joint, co-constructed, intersubjective ability to investigate the meaning of the conflict and its premises can be constructed or destroyed. The point of departure in this chapter is that before A and B initiate their conversation about R, they disagree about R, so only some of their assumptions about R are shared (commonality). Before the conversation, they do not necessarily know what assumptions are common and what assumptions they disagree about. Simultaneously, before the conversation, both parties assume they have enough in common to make conversation possible and meaningful (mutuality), that they can expect some, or even a certain kind of, reciprocation from the other, and that they themselves will be able to reciprocate (in approximately the way they assume the other will expect; reciprocity). These are the basic assumptions to be made if communication is to be initiated at all; a minimum of reciprocal assumptions about mutuality and reciprocity. When communicating, A and B will subsequently investigate their intersubjective commonality. In this case, A and B have much disagreement about R, meaning commonality about R is partly lacking. Simultaneously, A and B are communal in that they more or less share a language for talking about their disagreement of R. This communality gradually grows when they talk about disagreeing about R, thereby creating experiences of understanding and misunderstanding each other. When A and B talk about R, they experience talking and thus they re-evaluate the meaning of the turns they have pursued in relation to the anticipated response and the actual response. Their continued talking will be based on their experiences of talking. Each turn will constitute the interpretive context of the next turn, in a constantly re-constructing process.

When A and B start talking with each other, they do this based on assumptions about what is mutually known, what both of them know. This may be an assumption about sharing concepts that could be used for representing certain perspectives on R, concepts for representing A and B, and concepts representing assumptions about a shared or divergent view on R. When A and B experience talking with each other about R, their assumptions about what is mutually known will change. Since A and B disagree about R, they will gradually discover during their communication that what they both assumed to be mutually known about the issues is something they disagree about. Based on their experience of this communication, they will also develop new assumptions about a mutual view on the disagreement.

When A and B initiate their conversation, they do so on the basis of an assumption that they know when and how they should reciprocate the other's actions, that the other knows when and how s/he should respond to them, and that the other has certain expectations about when and how they should respond. When they have experiences of talking about R and their disagreement about R, their assumptions about how reciprocation takes place in this particular, local conversation gradually change.

There is thus a dynamic and dialectic relation between commonality, mutuality, and reciprocity. If there are great asymmetries in commonality (i.e.

disagreement), this may (but does not have to) generate asymmetries in mutuality, which may then generate asymmetries in reciprocity, and vice versa. Asymmetries in commonality and mutuality can thus generate from asymmetries in reciprocity. This dynamic is connected to constructivity and destructivity, since it decides how the intersubjective ability to investigate the disagreement will be changed in every interactive turn (three or more connected actions; question–answer–response to answer, statement–counterstatement–response to counterstatement, etc.). With this view, the ability to investigate disagreement is (re)constructed or deconstructed in every turn in the interaction, meaning that constructivity and destructivity are situated, local and continuously changing, or reproduced.

I argue in earlier work (Hallgren 2003, Hallgren and Ljung 2005) for a slightly different, but related, definition of destructive aspects of conflict: destructivity is a social interaction during which the interactants' trust in the interaction is decreasing. "Trust in interaction" means that actors assume that they know how they should act in the interaction and what they can expect from the interaction. When actors' trust in interaction reciprocity is decreasing, i.e. when actors doubt they know how to master the interaction situation and subsequently doubt they can influence it through communication, the intersubjective ability to investigate the disagreement declines, resulting in destructivity.

This way of thinking directs attention towards reciprocity in particular. Assumptions about adequate reciprocation are central for a social interaction to be able to handle asymmetries in commonality and mutuality, and are thus the core of constructivity in disagreement. When actors experience equivocal and paradoxical responses, and uncertainty about reciprocation is co-constructed, the communicative tools for investigating the agonism become weaker and destructivity emerges; actors become worse at detecting and repairing misinterpretations, and the co-acting community becomes less tolerant of disagreement. Actors tend to portray their opponents as enemies that should be restricted, rather than as legitimate proponents for their interpretation. The situation then takes the form of antagonism rather than agonism, resulting in reduced plurality.

At the level of face-to-face interaction, we have seen that the ability to investigate conflict can be reduced (destructivity) if there is uncertainty about reciprocation. In this, the micro and macro theories reviewed here intersect. Reciprocation on the micro level is what "institutions constitutive for democracy" is on the macro level. Mouffe (2005, p. 37) writes that "Consensus is needed on the institutions constitutive of democracy". Certainty about reciprocation at the speech act level corresponds to consensus on the institutions constitutive for democracy on the macro level. A precondition for pluralism, and for constructive conflict, is all parties believing that they know how to respond and what (kind of) responses to expect in a communicative encounter, and knowing that they agree with their fellow citizens on the function of democratic institutions, even when they disagree about the ontology and epistemology of the issues being discussed. Consensus on institutions for democracy and symmetry in reciprocation is actually the same, but on different scales; both are about shared assumptions/agreements about the preconditions for reciprocation. The agonistic interplay presupposes that actors acknowledge their adversaries' right to work passionately for their interpretation of the situation to be hegemonic. For actors to give this legitimacy to each other, they must themselves believe they can manage the interaction. If they do, there are opportunities for opposing groups to develop their understanding of the meaning and premises of the conflict, the competing political alternatives then become clear, and agonistic pluralism is realized.

Conclusions

This chapter has identified and developed a number of approaches that may be used for distinguishing constructive and destructive processes in NRM, and suggested how these concepts and the phenomena they represent relate to each other dynamically and dialectically. The perspective advocated here provides immediately practical suggestions for how both environmental communication researchers and natural resource managers could understand and work with both constructivity and destructivity on the basis that *something* is both constructed and destroyed in all conflict processes, and that this *something* is an intersubjective ability to investigate the meaning of the conflict, an ability that is local, situated and temporal, and constantly re-negotiated through the communication processes. Simply recognizing the ordinariness of this process can enable a more productive attitude toward conflict in general. The chapter has also shown that both coherent and paradoxical experiences of reciprocation are important drivers in the emergence of community constructivity and destructivity. These experiences affect constructivity and destructivity in both micro level, face-to-face situations of conflict and macro level conflicts with more complex social and political situations, representation, and communication mediated in public forums.

References

Asplund, J. (1987) *Om hälsningsceremonier, mikromakt och asocial pratsamhet.* Göteborg: Korpen.

Grauman, C. (1995) Commonality, mutuality, reciprocity, a conceptual introduction. In: Markova, I., Grauman, C. and Foppa, K. (eds) *Mutualities in Dialogue.* Cambridge, UK: Cambridge University Press.

Habermas, J. (2001) Truth and society: the discursive redemption of factual claims to validity. In: *On the Pragmatics of Social Interaction: Preliminary Studies in the Theory of Communicative Action.* Cambridge, MA: MIT Press.

Hallgren, L. (2003) *I djupet av ett vattendrag: Om konflikt och samverkan vid naturresurshantering* [*In the Depth of a Water Course: On Conflict and Collaboration in Natural Resource Management*]. Swedish University of Agricultural Sciences.

Hallgren, L. and Ljung, M. (2005) *Miljökommunikation: Aktörssamverkan och processledning* [*Environmental Communication: Collaboration and Process Facilitation*]. Lund: Studentliteratur.

Keir, L. S. and Ali, S. H. (2014) Conflict assessment in energy infrastructure siting: prospects for consensus building in the Northern Pass Transmission Line Project. *Negotiation Journal* 30(2): 169–189.

Linell, P. (2010) Troubles with mutualities: towards a dialogical theory on misunderstanding and miscommunication. In: Markova, I., Grauman, C. and Foppa, K. (eds) *Mutualities in Dialogue*. Cambridge, UK: Cambridge University Press.

Martin, A., Gross-Camp, N., Kebede, B., McGuire, S. and Munyarukaza, J. (2014) Whose environmental justice? Exploring local and global perspectives in a payments for ecosystem services scheme in Rwanda. *Geoforum* 54: 167–177.

Mouffe, C. (2005) *On the Political*. New York: Routledge.

Mouffe, C. (2013) *Agonistics: Thinking the World Politically*. London: Verso.

Peterson, T. R. and Feldpausch-Parker, A. M. (2013) Environmental conflict communication. In: Oetzel, J. G. and Ting-Toomey, S. (eds) *The SAGE Handbook of Conflict Communication: Integrating Theory, Research, and Practice*. Thousand Oaks, CA: Sage, 513–537.

Silva-Macher, J. C. and Farrell, K. N. (2014) The flow/fund model of Conga: exploring the anatomy of environmental conflicts at the Andes–Amazon commodity frontier. *Environment Development and Sustainability* 16(3): 747–768.

Simmel, G. (1964 [1922]) *Conflict and the Web of Group Affiliations*. London: Free Press.

Part II

Constructing and deconstructing community

Symbolic construction – instantiating community through language and other symbols

3 Process literacy

Theory and practice for multi-cultural community-based deliberative democracy

Deborah Cox Callister

Introduction

Democracy suffers numerous encumbrances within multi-cultural contexts (e.g. Benhabib 1996; Cunningham 2002; Habermas 1984, 1991). Making multi-cultural democracy work requires models that open spaces, accommodate and develop new forms of participation to create the conditions for deliberation within communities and at interfaces with sovereign decision-makers (Cox 2010, Dryzek 2004). This chapter focuses on *process literacy* (PL), a type of discursive lubricant during conflict communication that facilitates the construction of community. PL functions to keep communication productive as multi-cultural participants negotiate internal conflict while striving to reach mutual decisions. Moreover, PL pivots conflict communication toward collaboration and deliberative decision-making, while holding open space for dissensus.

PL is informed by democratic theory, conflict theory and contemporary rhetorical theory. More specifically, it draws on deliberative democracy (e.g. Benhabib 1996; Cunningham 2002; Dryzek 2000; Habermas 1984; Mouffe 1993) and especially deliberative communication theory (Dryzek 1990, 2004, 2006; Ellis 2012; Gastil 1993). PL is also informed by dialogue (Arnett 2004; Bakhtin 1981; Bohm 2003; Peters 1999), mediation (Cloke 2001; Folger and Bush 2001; Moore 1986), dispute resolution (Carpenter and Kennedy 1988; Pearce and Littlejohn 1997) and collaborative learning (Daniels and Walker 2001), which includes collaborative forms of argumentation (Makau and Marty 2001; Rieke *et al.* 2012). Finally, contemporary rhetorical theory offers crucial conceptual frameworks (Bitzer 1968; Bone *et al.* 2008; Doxtader 2000; Foss and Griffin 1995; Goodnight 1982; Peterson *et al.* 2005; Welsh 2002) for understanding how PL functions.

Connecting theory constituted by democratic, conflict and contemporary rhetorical tenets enables an explication of PL in the context of multi-cultural group deliberation. Multi-cultural coalitions and groups engage in all three of these complex domains because they use rhetorical tactics and strategies to influence decisions and to negotiate internal conflicts (Callister 2013). This chapter provides a visual representation of group conflict communication in relation to these complex processes with a *telos* of consensus.

An environmental coalition formed to prevent a major inter-basin water transfer project that threatens the socio-economic and environmental health of an arid region in the American West serves as an illustrative case study. This brief case study demonstrates how PL may function as a significant rhetorical strategy for building community, and potentially environmental democracy. For the purposes of this chapter, I draw from Theodori (2005) to define "territory-based" communities, or what Peterson *et al.* (2007) call "land communities" (see also Callister 2013), although I substitute the word "communicative" for the term "social". Thus, land communities are constituted by communicative transaction that "(a) delineates an area as shared territory, (b) contributes to the wholeness of local life [defined broadly, i.e. beyond humans], (c) gives structure, [...], direction, and [meaning] to collective actions, and (d) is [a] source of mutual identity" (Peterson *et al.* 2007, pp. 662–663). Moreover, community constructivity strengthens communicative processes and practices that build these community attributes, while community destructivity weakens them. My purpose in this chapter is to demonstrate how PL contributes to land community constructivity, which fosters a more participatory and deliberative democracy in land-based communities.

To demonstrate the crucial role of PL in constructing and maintaining healthy land communities, this chapter proceeds in seven subsequent sections: (1) why PL matters; (2) a discussion of theoretical underpinnings for the PL model; (3) an overview of field methods used to derive the model; (4) presentation and explication of the PL model; (5) definition of key terms associated with the model; (6) a brief case study to demonstrate best practices in PL; and (7) a discussion of implications, applications and suggestions for future practices and research.

The significance of PL

How can we enact more participatory democracies that support healthy land communities? This is a pressing question in late-modernity. Large-scale applications of democracy suffer encumbrances when seeking inclusivity of diverse and multi-cultural interests (e.g. Benhabib 1996; Cunningham 2002; Habermas 1984, 1991). Making democracy work with multicultural publics and large scale applications requires a model that opens spaces, accommodates and develops new forms of participation, to create the conditions for deliberation within civic spheres and at interfaces with sovereign decision-makers (e.g. Cox 2010; Dryzek 2004). Doxtader (2000) calls for exploration of "how dissent contributes to the formation of consensus" (p. 338). PL responds to this by mapping a space for dissensus within the rhetorical frameworks of multi-cultural group deliberation. Descriptions of new participatory forms such as cultural activism (e.g. Delicath 2004); community dialogues (e.g. Spano 2001); collaborative learning opportunities (Walker 2004), and third-party or alternative dispute resolution (ADR) processes (e.g. Carpenter and Kennedy 1988; Coalition for Utah's Future 1995) have emerged in the literature. These are examples of participatory communication processes that create the conditions for deliberation among diverse publics and institutional decision-makers.

Deliberative democracy calls for mutual decision-making, which entails the dissemination of ideas, dialogue and the negotiation of differences, while attending to the democratic ideals of liberty, equality and justice (Habermas 1984; Dewey 1925). This involves communicative processes at the confluence of contemporary dialogue, conflict and rhetorical theories. PL maps the communicative conditions that are conducive for deliberative decision-making. It draws from rhetoric and dialogue, which stem from different theoretical traditions in the field of communication.

Peters (1999) traces the roots of these different ideas about communication – *dissemination* (the circulation and audience uptake of messages) and *dialogue* (inter-subjective meaning-making interactions) – using Jesus' parables and Plato's *Phaedrus* as metaphors, respectively. Within this work he suggests that the most appropriate concept for communication between self and others is dissemination. Dialogue, he argues, is a more viable project for constructing shared meanings in intra-personal (or self-talk) contexts. For Peters, communication to achieve shared understandings remains mediated, even in the most authentic inter-subjective dialogic contexts. While Peters' argument points to the challenges associated with the project of arriving at shared understandings (at best a failed project from the beginning), deliberative decision-making requires efforts to try to achieve mutual agreements, which involve both the dissemination of charismatic messages (*rhetoric*) and intersubjective meaning making (*dialogic*) processes among participants.[1] In sum, PL adopts a practical perspective with regard to rhetoric and dialogue. It recognizes that communication is a transactional system in which messages (signs, symbols, sounds, gestures and utterances) circulate through time and a variety of channels (e.g. traditional mass media and the Internet), with variable resonance and understanding among diverse interpretive audiences. These messages are inevitably mediated between and among individual subjects through channels that include, but are not limited to face-to-face contexts, including community-based deliberative democracy.

This chapter puts deliberative democratic theory in conversation with conflict theory and contemporary rhetorical theory to explicate the negotiation of internal conflict within the context of large multi-cultural (human) group deliberation (i.e. an environmental coalition). It offers a model of PL, a kind of discursive lubricant that pivots conflict communication toward collaboration. PL, I argue, is an important rhetorical strategy in community constructivity, because it functions to keep communication productive as disparate (multi-cultural) participants negotiate internal conflict while striving to reach mutual decisions.

Theoretical scaffolding

Connecting a theory that is constituted by the tenets of democratic-, conflict- and contemporary rhetorical-theory for this project enables the strengths of each to complement the weaknesses of the others. Simply put, democratic theory informs participation in decision-making; conflict theory informs participation in conflict; and rhetorical theory informs persuasion within decision-making and conflict. Community-based groups engage in all three of these complex theoretical domains because they use rhetorical tactics and strategies to influence decisions and to negotiate conflicts.

Democratic theory provides resources to illuminate the communicative practices and processes that seek to uphold democratic principles such as liberty, equality and justice during conflict communication. For example, Rural Water Defenders (RWD) is a culturally diverse coalition (e.g. environmentalists, ranchers, natives, business owners, government officials, etc.) of participants who are resisting the Urban Water District's (UWD's) proposal to drill for ancient aquifer water in rural desert and mountain states for the purpose of moving the water to metropolitan Urbana.[2] These aqueduct opponents perceive the proposal as a "water grab" (a common epithet used in the western United States for large scale water projects) by powerful elites. They are fighting for freedom to carry on their livelihoods, equality for rural interests, and justice for the inhabitants of a fragile and arid ecosystem (a land community of mutual interest). And while RWD are united by a common threat, they must also find ways to successfully negotiate diverse constituencies and internal conflicts that inevitably arise among coalition participants over strategies to prevent the aqueduct from becoming a material reality.

Deliberative democratic theory emphasizes the importance of communication (e.g. Benhabib 1996; Dryzek 2000; Habermas 1984). This model of democracy opens up a space for and seeks the institutionalization of the *conditions* for deliberative communication in the public sphere and in governmental decision-making processes (Cunningham 2002). Since deliberation entails the interchange of ideas that encourages the identification of collective preferences toward a common good, this approach assumes that specific interests and values get reconstituted through deliberative exchanges among publics and decision-makers over time. Deliberative democracy is a dynamic and communicative approach to democracy, which both contributes to and benefits from PL in community-based conflict communication because community participants must negotiate differences together in order to reach collective and mutual decisions.

Conflict theory describes substantive, relational, and processual dynamics that affect communication climates in the context of (perceived) mutual incompatibilities (e.g. Carpenter and Kennedy 1988; Deetz and Simpson 1999; Kellet and Dalton 2001; Mindel 1995; Pearce and Littlejohn 1997; Zoller 2004). Conflict resolution literature, especially that which treats mediation (e.g. Cloke 2001; Moore 1986), assumes that parties are capable of resolving disputes in a mutually agreeable fashion and that imbalanced power relationships can be sufficiently levelled (Folger and Bush 2001) to allow this to happen. The assumptions in conflict resolution theory are generally compatible with the principles of deliberative democracy outlined above. For example, ADR and collaborative learning literatures contribute to understandings about

creative communicative processes and practices that foster inclusive and democratic participation (Carpenter and Kennedy 1988; Cloke 2001; Daniels and
Walker 2001). Conflict theory also contributes to PL, because it informs communicative processes that facilitate open communication climates for deliberation in the wake of disputes.

Additionally, contemporary rhetorical theory contributes to PL because it
focuses on strategies for influencing audiences. I adopt Dickinson *et al.*'s (2010)
definition of rhetoric as "the study of discourses, events, objects and practices
that attends to their character as meaningful, legible, partisan, and consequen-
tial" (p. 3). This emphasis in rhetorical theory on the framing and resonance of
messages with particular audiences contributes to both conflict theory and PL
by putting rhetorical frameworks into conversation with processual models for
resolving conflicts (e.g. dialogue, facilitation and mediation).

In sum, I draw on democratic-, conflict-, and contemporary rhetorical-
theory to explicate a PL model that functions to shift human communication
toward collaboration and deliberation within multi-cultural large group conflict communication.

Rhetorical field methods

A growing number of scholars have used a combination of rhetorical criticism
and qualitative field methods (e.g. Blair 2001; Conquergood 1992; Middleton
et al. 2011; Pezzullo 2003) to collect primary texts for analysis. For this
research, I have used this approach, or rhetorical field methods (Middleton *et
al.* 2011 p. 387), to gather texts for rhetorical analysis. This included participant observation of eight full day RWD quarterly strategy meetings and ten
1.5–3-hour semi-structured interviews (Lindlof and Taylor 2002) with 11
active RWD participants who represent a diverse range of cultural orientations within RWD. I then analysed roughly 143 pages of field notes and relevant excerpts from interview transcripts. This research spanned three and a
half years. A portion of my findings follows in the subsequent sections.

PL: a model for deliberative democracy

To help conceptualize PL, I offer two diagrams (see Figures 3.1 and 3.2,
below). Figure 3.1 places macro- and meso-terms that I will describe into a
conceptual map. It depicts internal coalition communication within three
overlapping circles that are embedded within a competitive socio-economic
and political milieu of North America. These circles represent three different
approaches to discursive differences and cultural tensions – invitational, deliberative and argumentative – and the complexity of shifting rhetorical
dynamics in internal coalition communication. The perforated boundary
of the bottom circle represents the natural permeation of a competitive
orientation into rhetorical situations for resolving conflicts in Western culture
(capitalized here to distinguish the term from its geographical connotation).

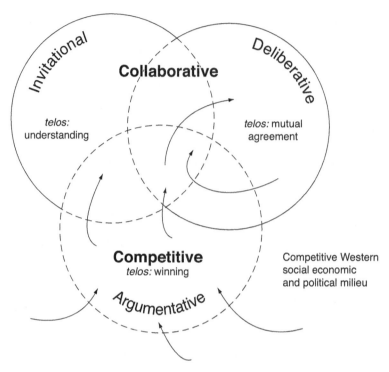

Figure 3.1 Communicative genres and the rhetorical dynamics of internal coalition communication (© Deborah Cox Callister).

Notes: During conflict situations, process literacy (PL) supports movement across rhetorical frameworks toward a collaborative communicative genre and a deliberative rhetorical framework. The perforation on the bottom circle illustrates the natural permeation of competitive approaches to resolving conflicts in Western culture. The curved arrows reflect the tendency for PL to shift the rhetorical dynamics away from competition toward collaboration via an invitational rhetorical framework.

Makau and Marty (2001) note, "much modern argumentation ... has rested on assumptions that ... those who argue must come to the exchange ... favoring an oppositional approach to interaction" (p. 157). These scholars suggest, "ideological commitments to competitiveness, individualism, and winning" undermine the ability to achieve "idealized deliberative communities" (p. 101). In short, Western argumentation practices are predominantly built on competitive models. The solid boundaries around the two upper circles represent a barrier between the predominantly competitive Western culture and collaborative ways of approaching conflict. Changing from a competitive to a collaborative approach when tensions arise is not a natural move for Westerners. It requires knowledge, skill and practice. PL facilitates movement with intentionality in a collaborative direction as indicated by the arrows and perforated lines in locations where

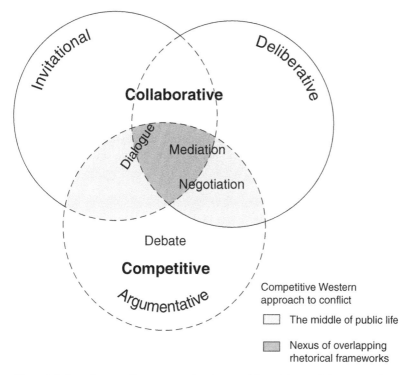

Figure 3.2 Locating conflict communication models – debate, dialogue, mediation, and negotiation – within rhetorical frameworks (© Deborah Cox Callister).

Note: The shaded areas represent the dynamic complexities of conflict communication in the overlapping argumentative, invitational and deliberative rhetorical frameworks. The centre and darkest of this shaded area represents a discursive space for working through differences before moving toward deliberative decision-making. Process literacy (PL) helps to keep this discursive space open and functional. Put another way, PL requires patience. It supports cooperative argumentation, dialogue, mediation, and negotiation, and it discourages the impulse to make collective or so-called "consensus" decisions in the face of dissent.

the three circles overlap. Figure 3.2 depicts the same concepts, but it foregrounds four distinct conflict models – debate, dialogue, mediation and negotiation. The overlapping areas among these three circles represent conflict communication that does not necessarily fall neatly within just one of these circles. For example, the shaded overlapping areas demonstrate that an argumentative approach to conflict can be a collaborative enterprise.

I have organized the PL terms on three levels: macro, meso and micro. The macro level terms refer to communicative genres, the meso level terms refer to rhetorical frameworks, and the micro level terms refer to conflict models. In this chapter, I focus on the macro and meso terms and their connection to PL.

Key PL terms

Communicative genres – macro level terms

The term *communicative genres*, references Bakhtin's (1981) broad conception of them. For Bakhtin, communicative genres are worldviews that influence daily behaviours. Communicative genres carry with them value systems, purposes and a range of action/responses that are learned during primary socialization. As Morson (1991) explains, communicative genres from a Bakhtinian perspective are "models for change and central to how change happens" (p. 1087). Both Figures 3.1 and 3.2 depict competitive and collaborative genres, which I will define next.

Competitive

A *competitive* communicative genre refers to the dominant individualistic and aggressive cultural practices within the Western cultural milieu. As Bohm (2003) explains, "the success of a person's point of view" is often rewarded either socially or financially and "the struggle of each idea to dominate is commonly emphasized in most activities in society" (p. 296). Those who disagree are viewed as "rivals" rather than "resources" (Makau and Marty 2001, p. 88). The model for change within a competitive communicative genre assumes that aggressive and confrontational challenges to the status quo are necessary. This genre subsumes the argumentative rhetorical framework that I have observed in internal coalition communication.

Collaborative

By a *collaborative* communicative genre, I am referring to alternative (non-dominant) Western cooperative cultural practices. The orientation of a collaborative communicative genre adopts a premise of interdependence and mutual respect for others with plural worldviews (Arnett 2004; Makau and Marty 2001). Conflict is viewed as an opportunity to make change in mutually agreeable ways (Daniels and Walker 2001). This communicative genre subsumes two of the three rhetorical frameworks I have observed in multicultural large group communication – invitational and deliberative.

Rhetorical frameworks – meso level terms

In order to understand how PL pivots discourse toward a collaborative communicative genre, it is important to understand what I mean by *rhetorical framework*. The framework (e.g. the overall style, tone and content) of rhetoric is shaped by intention, purpose or *telos*. For example, if the *telos* is to compete, a more aggressive or confrontational approach to the rhetorical situation is likely to ensue. Rhetorical framework references a constellation of rhetorical characteristics that are associated with and influenced by *telos*. Both Figures 3.1 and 3.2 depict three overlapping rhetorical frameworks, each with a unique *telos* that I have observed in internal coalition communication.

Argumentative

Traditionally, an *argumentative* rhetorical framework adopts a win/lose, right/ wrong, or judgmental set of assumptions. The *telos* in an argumentative rhetorical framework is to win audience "adherence" or "informed support" (Rieke *et al.* 2012, p. 4) at the potential expense of someone or something else (losers or losing propositions). I embed this rhetorical framework within the prevailing competitive communicative genre of Western culture.

Invitational

An *invitational* rhetorical framework adopts a type of curiosity or interest in learning, without the intention of persuading audiences toward a particular stance. The *telos* is to understand (Bone *et al.* 2008; Foss and Griffin 1995). Thus, rhetors and audiences are in a dialectic relationship, wherein the subject positions of teacher and student shift between them and are shared. This rhetorical framework is subsumed within a collaborative communicative genre.

Deliberative

A *deliberative* rhetorical framework also falls within the collaborative communicative genre. Within a deliberative rhetorical framework, the *telos* is to reach mutual agreements or decisions that address the primary interests involved. The ideal outcome among deliberators is consensus (Dryzek 1990, 2004, 2006; Ellis 2012; Gastil 1993; Habermas 1984; Makau and Marty 2001).

Conflict models – micro level terms

In Figure 3.2, I locate communicative conflict models within the three rhetorical frameworks described above. Conflict communication models are patterned communicative practices or processes for productively dealing with conflict. These conflict processes can be initiated within any of the three rhetorical frameworks, but each is located in Figure 3.2 within the respective rhetorical framework that is most conducive for operationalizing it. I address these micro-terms elsewhere (Callister 2013), but it is important to understand that conflicts can contribute to the destructivity of community if they are not dealt with productively.

PL and the collaborative genre

The ability to negotiate the complexities of conflict in multi-cultural community-based communication while striving to reach agreement on action steps requires PL. In the case of the RWD, PL entails maintaining productive communication at the nexus of argumentative, invitational and deliberative rhetorical frameworks. PL facilitates movement away from a competitive communicative genre toward a collaborative one. It allows for some shifts from collaborative to competitive communication genres, but it primarily creates openings where these frameworks and genres overlap and finesses interactions toward a deliberative rhetorical framework to arrive at mutual agreements. Next, I will briefly review the meso-terms in Figures 3.1 and 3.2, noting how the macro-terms relate to PL along the way.

Traversing rhetorical frameworks

While PL pivots conflict communication toward a collaborative genre, it also facilitates cooperative forms of argumentation and diminishes the impulse to coerce or force mutual agreements. Thus, PL enables participants to fluently traverse all three rhetorical frameworks – argumentative, invitational and deliberative – in support of community constructivity and deliberative democracy.

An argumentative rhetorical framework

I distinguish an argumentative rhetorical framework from deliberative and invitational rhetorical frameworks by communicative genre (primarily competitive) and by *telos* (winning). Rieke *et al.* (2012) define argumentation as "the communicative process of advancing, supporting, criticizing and modifying claims so that appropriate decisions makers, defined by relevant spheres, may grant or deny adherence" to these claims and conclusions that they support (p. 4). Inherent in this definition of argumentation is a *telos* of persuasion – to *win* the informed backing of audiences (e.g. decision-makers). As discussed earlier, the style, tone and content of messages enacted within an argumentative rhetorical framework typically reflects this competitive (win/lose) purpose.

While deliberation uses argumentation as a means for reaching informed, mutual decisions, and argumentation uses deliberation as a means for honing and advancing key claims, the primary distinction is the communicative genre (i.e. the manner) in which dissent is enacted. This is because the *approach* taken during the act of dissent is vital to the quality of participant relationships, an important aspect of community cohesion and health.

Cooperative argumentation

Makau and Marty (2001) distinguish *cooperative* from *adversarial* forms of argumentation in which "people tend to get locked into their positions" as adversaries instead of focusing on the issues, interests and values that underlie their respective positions (p. 84). This distinction is highly relevant to PL, which pivots dissent toward a collaborative communicative genre in the context of internal coalition communication. If dissent takes place within a competitive (win/lose) argumentative framework, it risks perpetuating a cycle of conflict among participants, which undermines community constructivity because it privileges the advocate's perspective at the expense of others. Alternatively, "cooperative argumentation" as Makau and Marty (2001) suggest, "provides the means for reasoned give-and-take on complex and controversial issues" (p. 115). In sum, argumentation can take place within both competitive and collaborative communicative genres.

Turning back to Figure 3.1, Makau and Marty's (2001) notion of cooperative argumentation falls outside of a competitive communicative genre, and is enacted within a collaborative communicative genre. Figure 3.1 illustrates this in the upper portion of the sphere containing the argumentative rhetorical framework, where it overlaps with both the invitational and deliberative rhetorical frameworks. Similarly, Doxtader (2000) treats these overlapping frameworks in his discussion about the interplay between dissent and consensus. I locate what Doxtader (2000) refers to as "transgressive" (p. 339) forms of rhetoric primarily within the competitive communicative genre or lower portion of the argumentative rhetorical framework. I do this because in describing what he calls "the middle of public life" between "transgressive and consensual modes of communication" Doxtader likens the condition of being in the middle as being "caught between disrespect and mutual support" (p. 345). Thus Doxtader's "middle of public life" is located in the overlapping areas between a competitive and a collaborative communicative genre depicted in Figures 3.1 and 3.2. An invitational rhetorical framework enables movement toward a deliberative rhetorical framework. As such, it is often the route taken to get from a competitive argumentative framework to a collaborative deliberative rhetorical framework (as noted by the flow depicted in Figure 3.1).

An invitational rhetorical framework

Foss and Griffin (1995) introduced the concept of an invitational rhetorical theory that eschews patriarchal impulses to dominate and change others. This rhetorical framework is "an invitation to understanding as a means to create a relationship rooted in equality, immanent value and self-determination. Invitational rhetoric constitutes an invitation to the audience to enter the rhetor's world and to see it as the rhetor does" (p. 5). Bone *et al.* (2008) have responded to criticisms over Foss and Griffin's totalizing linkage of traditional rhetorical strategies with coercive forms of persuasion or more violent forms of rhetoric that trespass on personal integrity. In doing so, these authors suggest that invitational rhetoric is "a move toward civility", which they define as a place where "we cannot pretend that we journey alone, that others are unworthy or without voice, or that our view is the only 'right' view" (pp. 456–457). The ideal result of invitational rhetoric is the understanding of both issues and participants, as they share unique perspectives through listening to one another with a sense of "respect and appreciation" (Foss and Griffin 1995, p. 5).

Thus, invitational rhetoric opens up a communication climate and fosters a shift from a competitive to a collaborative communicative genre. To move beyond genuine inquiry and understanding of diverse perspectives to an evaluative and selective process that involves ranking options and decision-making on a collective course of action, also falls outside of an invitational rhetorical framework. This is because invitational rhetoric eschews rhetorical moves to persuade audiences about what is better or best.

Finally, an invitational rhetorical framework sets the stage for cooperative problem-solving and conflict resolution. As Foss and Griffin (1995) explain, invitational rhetoric *allows* the "*development* of interpretations, perspectives, courses of actions, and solutions to problems different from those allowed in traditional models of rhetoric" (p. 16, emphasis added). In the case of RWD, internal coalition conflict is often met within an invitational rhetorical framework before participants move beyond learning about the diverse perspectives represented in the room toward collaborative decision-making. For example the facilitator might invite participants to offer their diverse perspectives on an exigence or crucial issue such as a recent political development that could affect the outcome of their work to prevent a major water development project from coming to fruition.

A deliberative rhetorical framework

In contrast to invitational rhetoric, a deliberative rhetorical framework engages inventive, suasory, creative, evaluative and collaborative problem-solving toward mutually agreed upon decisions (Doxtader 2000; Ellis 2012; Gastil 1993; Makau and Marty 2001; Welsh 2002). Through participant observation, I have found collaboration to be the predominant communicative genre in RWD strategy meetings. During these meetings, participant communication often shifts back and forth between invitational and deliberative rhetorical frameworks. The progression in this large multi-cultural group begins with invitational rhetoric and ends with deliberative rhetoric as participants move through agenda items and arrive at mutual agreements.

Doxtader (2000), Goodnight (1982), Makau and Marty (2001), Peterson *et al.* (2005) and Welsh (2002) are among the contemporary rhetorical scholars that explicitly theorize deliberative rhetoric outside of legislative contexts. Doxtader (2000) asserts, "the middle of public life appears when individuals, standing between various interests, desires, and discourses, enter into a struggle for recognition" (p. 361). RWD's strategy meetings exemplify this space where deliberative rhetoric happens. As I will demonstrate in the analysis section, PL, within a deliberative rhetorical framework, involves patience and the wisdom to stop short of decision-making if a clear pathway forward is not collectively understood. As such, PL keeps open a space for on-going dissent between deliberative and argumentative frameworks within a collaborative communicative genre.

Turning back to Figure 3.2, we might visualize Doxtader's middle of public life in the overlapping shaded areas, particularly at the nexus (depicted with the darkest shading in the centre), where space is common to all three rhetorical frameworks. Here, in this communicative space, held open by PL, dissent thrives and pathways toward consensus emerge. This is the space between what Doxtader calls transgressive (competitive) and intersubjective (collaborative) dimensions of the public sphere.

In particularly tense conflict situations, when competitive genres emerge and begin to dominate (imagine the overlapping areas in Figures 3.1 and 3.2 shrinking as the bottom circle moves downward, away from the top two circles), PL helps to prevent the attenuation of this space in the middle. In other words, PL acts like a ligament that keeps argumentative rhetoric connected to and pivoting toward collaborative rhetoric.

Analysing how PL helps participants manage to collectively and consistently enter this liminal space and dwell in it, responds to Doxtader's (2000) call for building deliberative rhetorical theory as a space between opposition and agreement. It is a means for determining how dissensus can facilitate consensus. Much has been written about the Habermasian influenced term "deliberation". Within communication, Ellis (2012) defines deliberation as a type of communication based on democratic fairness with five qualities: (1) argument and reason, (2) fair and equal relationships among participants with genuine listening and respect for the ideas and realities of others, (3) consensus as a *telos*, (4) traditional authority and power can be challenged and questioned, and (5) no one group may dominate the interactions. I adopt Ellis' definition of deliberation with help from Gastil (1993) who claims that deliberation entails equal and adequate opportunities to participate in "agenda setting reformulating ... and dissenting" (p. 26). Thus, a deliberative rhetorical framework supports communicative speech acts marked by Ellis' notion of democratic fairness with room for dissent, because pressure to reach agreement can silence inarticulate and marginalized interests (Mouffe 1993; Peterson *et al.* 2005).

We can see in deliberative rhetoric some overlap with Foss and Griffin's (1995) invitational rhetoric in the concepts of: fairness, equality and an openness to questioning the status quo, as well as in honouring equality and inclusive participation. But there is a departure from invitational rhetoric with deliberative rhetoric's underpinnings in argumentation and the motive to reconcile differences or achieve consensus.

In sum, a deliberative rhetorical framework is respectively distinct from argumentative and invitational rhetorical frameworks, because, (1) it steers clear of competitive win/lose orientations, and (2) it seeks mutually acceptable ways to resolve differences. Invitational rhetoric creates an open communication climate in that it invites information sharing and articulation of perspectives. As such, an invitational rhetorical framework is compatible with and sets the stage for a deliberative rhetorical framework – both fall within a collaborative communicative genre. Questions remain, however, "to unravel the puzzle of how public transgression and opposition facilitates dialogue and mutual agreement" (Doxtader 2000, p. 338). PL offers *phronesis* (practical wisdom) to enable these shifts between competitive and collaborative communicative genres. To demonstrate this, I will explicate best practices in PL using the RWD case study.

Case study: troubled waters in Verdant Valley

In 2009, a major conflict among RWD participants occurred over a proposed interstate water compact. Responses to this situation required negotiating serious differences about the compact's value without allowing a competitive communicative genre to dominate.

In late summer of 2009, water bureaucrats from Mountain State and Desert State held a series of promotional meetings for a negotiated two-state compact that allocated specific water rights underlying a basin that straddles the two-state border. Many RWD participants became passionately opposed to this compact, while a few supported it. PL contributed to negotiating a dispute that emerged from a clash between Alonso and Joe.

Alonso is a small business owner in Verdant Valley with a keen sense of humour. His communicative style can be somewhat divisive, and as he claimed when interviewed, he doesn't "take any bullshit". He remarked that the governor of Mountain State would sign the two-state compact "in a New York minute" (or 45 seconds) if it were not for the legal ruling in favour of RWD's arguments and public awareness campaign. Alonso doesn't mince words and he often references his ethnic "radar" when he smells a rat. He makes public his opinions in letters to editors and he does not shy away from personalizing his messages. For example, in response to learning that Joe supported the two-state compact, he called Joe's credibility into question in an open email letter addressed to Joe, which he circulated on the RWD listserv. He wrote:

> When some heard your statement re: the [water rights] split and know you are promoting a compact they said[,] "Is he being bought out?" Your reputation in these parts is being challenged. Stand strong Joe: oppose a compact and continue the long untarnished history you have.

Here, Alonso suggests that Joe's *ethos* is at risk if he continues to support the compact. He cautions him and implies "you're either with us on this issue or you're against us". The overall tone of the entire letter created consternation for many RWD participants, who practice maintaining a collaborative communicative atmosphere within RWD.

Alonso's letter, along with other rumours circulating within the group, precipitated a call within RWD to adopt ethical guidelines. Alonso's strident position and willingness to "call out" Joe in front of his peers was perceived by some members of RWD as a personal attack on Joe that threatened to foreclose the opportunity to continue exploring options for mutual gain in collaboration with Joe, or anyone else that might take a favourable view of the two-state compact. In other words, Joe's competitive tone threatened community constructivity.

Three capacity indicators of PL

Before describing a sustained dialogic session that ensued in response to this controversy, I want to briefly describe three dimensions (or capacity indicators) of PL: (1) facilitation, (2) mediation, and (3) discursive accommodation. The capacity for PL is constituted by the collective skill sets among participants that support these dimensions, which function to maintain a collaborative communicative genre that supports community constructivity.

Facilitation

All of the RWD strategy meetings are facilitated by one of a handful of RWD participants. Facilitators are (disinterested) third-parties that concurrently track communicative group interactions on three levels: processual, substantive and relational (Kaner 2007; Daniels and Walker 2001). I define facilitation as the practice of employing communicative strategies to foster participatory communication toward collectively derived group goals.

Mediation

In RWD, disputants either mediate their own disputes or one particular facilitator (with some background in mediation) mediates them using shuttle diplomacy. Mediation is a democratic, participant-driven, voluntary dispute resolution process that uses the help of a third-party to reach mutually beneficial agreement(s) (e.g. Moore 1986).

Discursive accommodation

RWD participants practice discursive accommodation. Having an awareness of unique cultural symbolic meanings enables a person to build rapport across cultural divides by avoiding certain speech acts that might be perceived by audience members as culturally offensive. This is what I call *discursive accommodation*. It is akin to what Makau and Marty (2001) call "critical self-awareness" (p. 57).

Best practices in PL

I will now demonstrate how best practices in PL enabled community constructivity in a RWD strategy session, and discouraged participants from giving into the impulse to coerce consensus. Best practices in coalition PL include: (1) creating ethical guidelines; (2) containing conflict and attending to the need for confidentiality; and (3) keeping communication participatory across shifting rhetorical frameworks.

After Alonso's letter stirred turmoil among participants, the group drafted and adopted ethical principles that emphasized the need to refrain from "personal attacks", to "respect similarities and differences", and to remember that "confidentiality" of internal conflicts and sensitive information is "crucial". The participants agreed that "breaches" to "what happens here stays here" would result in sanctions including a "3 strikes you're out!!" rule. Containing conflict and threatening sanctions can have a dampening effect on participation, but in the case of RWD, it fostered engagement across all three rhetorical frameworks (argumentative, invitational and deliberative) and communicative genres (competitive and collaborative).

The two-state compact issue was still a controversial topic several months after the ethical guidelines had been adopted by RWD. At the next strategy meeting, Rita invited participants in the circle (25–30 individuals) to share their opinions about the two-state compact (an invitational framework). Before opening up participation, she told the group that a consensus was not a viable goal since there were strong disagreements over the issue. This framing of the discussion tacitly conveyed that the group would fall short of mutual agreement (a deliberative *telos*).

In the dialogic session that followed, there were no fewer than 66 turns taken over a period of about 1.5–2 hours averaging between 1.5–2 minutes per speaker (1 September 2010). During this time, individuals weighed in with their opinions about the controversial two-state compact. Aside from calling the names of the next speakers, Rita took five of the 66 turns. Not only did she facilitate a highly participatory communication process during conflict, she helped the group to move between invitational and deliberative rhetorical frameworks as the rhetorical situation shifted in the room. For example, at one point, Rita stated, "This is your valley, not mine. Folks from the valley, what would work for you?" This is an example of facilitating to identify options for mutual gain within a deliberative rhetorical framework. It also privileges voices from inhabitants of the local land community. Some 17 turns later, Ian facilitated a shift to an invitational rhetorical framework by explaining why those who would be directly impacted by the two-state compact might value the compact more than others. This is an example of paraphrasing disparate perspectives to signal that diverse concerns have been heard and understood. Another 17 turns later, a participant from the valley in question asked, "So what if we all agree against the compact? What do we do?" This question raised a red flag for Rita, as the facilitator, because it implied that the majority opinion in the room constituted a consensus.

At this juncture, Rita chose to straddle an invitational and deliberative rhetorical framework by reminding the group that a viable mutual agreement was not feasible. While cooperative argumentation and sharing of perspectives in a deliberative fashion were germane to the situation, mutual agreement was not. Rita, replied, "We can't agree. There is too much diversity in the group". Some 22 turns later, Rita signalled that it was time to wrap up the dialogue, "We need to recap and move on the agenda". A proponent of the two-state compact spoke next within a cooperative argumentative framework. And Rita reiterated, "We need to recap this discussion. Can we discuss points to improve [our situation]?" Sarah, spoke next, "This has been a good discussion with important points made". Appu spoke with optimism, "We still have a chance to move forward without the compact". At this point, Rita cautioned, "We haven't imploded. There have been a variety of ideas". Then, she changed the discussion topic by asking David to complete the report on plans for the Mountain State's legislative session.

This scenario requires unpacking to better understand the importance of PL, which kept communication participatory while engaging conflict. As is typical in the RWD meetings, Rita called on participants as they raised their hands. She often stated three or four names in sequence as a way to regulate turn taking and manage participant expectations. During this rhetorical situation, at least 21 out of 26 participants chose to speak. The primary proponent for the two-state compact, Joe, took about ten turns, Ian (who argued pros and cons from supportive, opposing, and legal perspectives) took approximately eight, Alonso took three (but walked in and out of the room towards the end of the discussion), and everyone else took anywhere from one to five turns. Participation from almost everyone in the room, during a controversial discussion, is exemplary of a participatory communicative process (Kaner 2007).

Throughout this two-state open discussion participants traversed argumentative, deliberative and invitational rhetorical frameworks within a collaborative communicative genre. Rita kept the turns rolling and maintained a diversity of voices. In spite of strong oppositional opinions, there was never an attempt on her part to flatten or reframe the differences in the room. Put another way, the distinctions among all of the different perspectives, as articulated by each participant, remained in relief. While the topic was highly controversial, participants offered up a wide range of diverse ideas and opinions, sometimes expressing positions within a cooperative argumentative rhetorical framework using logic to persuade others. The process of turn-taking involved making sure that differences in opinions and concerns regarding issues were articulated with time for re-articulation, especially from Joe, who held the minority opinion in the room. This appeared effortless, but as Rita revealed to me later that day, "There were moments when I wasn't sure we were going to make it through the meeting".

Toward the end, when Appu spoke with optimism implying that the group was close to a consensus on the two-state compact, Rita cautioned everyone, "We haven't imploded", and quickly moved the discussion to a different topic. This is an example of backing away from the impulse to reach an agreement. Knowing when to back off of this *telos* is a best practice of PL within a collaborative communicative genre.

In summary, PL enabled a highly participatory strategy session and the practical wisdom (*phronesis*) to hold open a discursive space for dissensus across shifting rhetorical frameworks in the context of internal coalition conflict.

Implications for applying PL

This chapter has illuminated the significant role that PL holds in navigating community conflicts. As a type of discursive lubricant during conflict communication, PL facilitates the construction of community by keeping communication productive as multi-cultural participants negotiate their differences while striving to reach mutual decisions. Importantly, PL works to pivot conflict communication toward collaboration and deliberative decision-making, while holding open space for dissensus. This loci of dissent is an opening for dialogue that can lead to more informed decision-making.

Additionally, PL responds to Doxtader's call for exploration of the ways in which dissent and opposition can lead to consensus. It is PL that enabled RWD participants to negotiate a major internal conflict and remain a cohesive community working to prevent a serious threat to the land community. PL helped RWD to create ethical guidelines in support of healthy coalition participant relationships, to contain the conflict by maintaining confidentiality about the controversy within the group, and to encourage inclusive participation across shifting rhetorical frameworks. These best practices in PL served group cohesion and resilience for weathering internal disputes that otherwise threatened division among participants. As such, PL is a significant rhetorical strategy in environmental coalition maintenance, and by extension it is an important communicative component in the construction and maintenance of healthy land communities.

By maintaining communication in a collaborative genre across shifting rhetorical frameworks such as cooperative argumentation, invitational rhetoric, and deliberative discussions, the opportunity for collaborative learning occurs. This process can improve outcomes that range from clearer understandings of (in)commensurate views, to the fomentation of ideas that illuminate plausible pathways forward. Taking time for dissensus in deliberative democracy requires expertise in PL and patience. This is not a process that leads to simple- or super-majority decisions; rather it is a process in which dissensus is viewed as an opportunity to dwell in and learn through difference until such time as it makes sense to leave and return to this space, as needed.

PL also includes three important dimensions or capacity indicators: (third-party) mediation, facilitation and discursive accommodation. The stronger the skillsets of these dimensions among community members, the greater the capacity for PL. But the question remains, how can this theory of PL be applied to other contexts to support more informed and sustainable land community decisions?

One obvious long-term implication is the importance of teaching young children how to mediate their own disputes in order to build capacity within land communities. There are culturally appropriate problem-solving and peer mediation programmes that can begin as early as age three in preschool. Adults can learn these skills, too. In the case of RWD, facilitation is shared among a handful of participants that have some natural capabilities for holding open a space in the middle for dialogue. Other environmental organizations and coalitions may do well to do the same. For governmental agencies that deal with environmental decision-making, it is important to budget money to hire professional third-parties to facilitate processes for communities to work through thorny issues. Moreover, the money used to pay for these services is best pooled among participants to make the contract for services a collective one. Each can pay according to their ability. The main concern, here, is to prevent government agencies (or anyone else) from "buying" the process. The more the selection process of a third-party can be shared among stakeholders in the land community, the better the decision outcomes will be. Facilitators and mediators hold tremendous power, and the selection of a third-party is no small matter.[3]

In sum, RWD provides a case study that shows how PL can enable deliberative democracy to work within other multi-cultural organizational and community contexts. However, the maturity levels and previous experiences of the participants in this particular coalition must be taken into account. The RWD is comprised of seasoned activists with long-standing relationships that date back to anti-nuclear campaigns in the 1980s. The maturity-levels, relational histories, and the collective wisdom among the silver-haired participants in RWD are factors that lend themselves to best practices for negotiating difference, especially discursive differences and cultural tensions that constitute land communities. Best practices may be more difficult to achieve in land communities lacking these attributes. I propose that PL, offers a key strategy in deliberative democracy, for identifying functional pathways forward toward sustainable futures at watershed levels, such as the level of the RWD.

Future research might explore PL within other land community contexts where participants have less relational histories or less activism experience and/or a younger or more diverse participant demographic. In sum, the findings in this case study point to several loci for future research. Given that water is the lifeblood of ecosystems on Earth, I suggest that studies in land community communication in the context of water conflicts is critical and fertile ground for gaining insights into practical ways to foster participatory and deliberative participation in an environmental democracy – one in which more than human inhabitants of land communities can also participate.

Notes

1 This, of course, assumes that participants *want* to achieve mutual agreements. PL cannot generate the will to achieve mutual decisions, but it can explicate the communicative conditions that are conducive for doing so without resorting to coercive practices.

2 Pseudonyms are used throughout this chapter to protect the anonymity and confidentiality interests of associated individuals and organizations.
3 I use the term disinterested to mean that the third-party facilitator or mediator must not have a stake in the outcome of the dispute. A disinterested party is extremely interested in the quality of the communicative processes that lead to a decision and far less interested in the substantive outcomes. Of course, the outcome must be appropriate to the consensus achieved through participant dialogue.

References

Arnett, R. (2004) A dialogic ethic "between" Buber and Levinas: a responsive ethical "I". In: Anderson, R., Leslie, A. and Cissna, K. (eds) *Dialogue: theorizing difference in communication studies*. Thousand Oaks, CA: Sage Publications, 75–91.

Bakhtin, M. (1981) *The dialogic imagination: four essays by M. M. Bakhtin*. (M. Holquist, ed.; C. Emerson and M. Holquist, trans.). Austin: University of Texas Press.

Benhabib, S. (ed.) (1996) *Democracy and difference: contesting the boundaries of the political*. Princeton, NJ: Princeton University Press.

Blair, C. (2001) Reflections on criticism and bodies: parables from public places. *Western Journal of Communication* 65: 271–294. Online, available at: http://dx.doi.org/10.1080/10570310109374706.

Bohm, D. (2003) *The essential David Bohm*. London: Routledge.

Bone, J. E., Griffin, C. L. and Schol, T. M. L. (2008) Beyond traditional conceptualizations of rhetoric: invitational rhetoric and a move toward civility. *Western Journal of Communication* 72: 434–462. Online, available at: http://dx.doi.org/10.1080/10570310802446098.

Callister, D. C. (2013) *Immersed in water conflict: humor and process literacy as rhetorical strategies in internal coalition maintenance*. (Doctoral Dissertation). Retrieved from ProQuest. (UMI Number: 3561528).

Carpenter, S. and Kennedy, W. (1988) *Managing public disputes : a practical guide to handling conflict and reaching agreements* (1st edition). San Francisco, CA: Jossey-Bass.

Cloke, K. (2001) *Mediating dangerously: the frontiers of conflict resolution*. San Francisco, CA: Jossey-Bass.

Coalition for Utah's Future (September, 1995) *Community and wild lands futures: a pilot project in Emery County, Utah*. Callister, D. C. (ed.). Online, available at: www.worldcat.org/title/community-wild-lands-futures-disputing-parties-heading-onto-cooperative-public-lands-trail-a-pilot-project-in-emery-county-utah/oclc/84277140.

Conquergood, D. (1992) Ethnography, rhetoric, and performance. *Quarterly Journal of Speech* 78: 80–123. Online, available at: http://dx.doi.org/10.1080/00335639209383982.

Cox, R. (2010) *Environmental communication and the public sphere*. (2nd edition) Thousand Oaks, CA: Sage.

Cunningham, F. (2002) *Theories of democracy: a critical introduction*. New York: Routledge.

Daniels, S. and Walker, G. (2001) *Working through environmental conflict: the collaborative learning approach*. Westport: Praeger.

Deetz, S. and Simpson, J. (1999) Critical organizational dialogue: open formation and the demand of "otherness". In: Anderson, R., Baxter, L. and Cissna, K. (eds) *Dialogue: theorizing difference in communication studies*. Thousand Oaks, CA. Sage Publications, 141–158.

Delicath, J. (2004) Art and advocacy: citizen participation through cultural activism. In Depoe, S., Delicath, J. and Elsenbeer, M. (eds) *Communication and public participation in environmental decision making*. Albany, NY: SUNY Press, 255–266.

Dickinson, G., Blair, C. and Ott, B. (eds) (2010). *Places of public memory*. Tuscaloosa, AL: University of Alabama Press.

Doxtader, E. (2000) Characters in the middle of public life: consensus, dissent, and ethos. *Philosophy and Rhetoric* 33: 336–369. Online, available at: http://doi.dx.org/10.1353/par.2000.0026.

Dryzek, J. (1990) *Discursive democracy: politics, policy, and political science*. Cambridge: Cambridge University Press.

Dryzek, J. (2000) *Deliberative democracy and beyond: liberals, critics, contestations*. Oxford: Oxford University Press.

Dryzek, J. (2004) Pragmatism and democracy. *Journal of Speculative Philosophy* 18: 72–79.

Dryzek, J., Downes, D., Hunold, C., Schlosberg, D. and Hernes, H. (2003) *Green states and social movements: environmentalism in the United States, United Kingdom, Germany, and Norway*. Oxford: Oxford University Press.

Ellis, D. G. (2012) *Deliberative communication and ethnopolitical conflict* (First printing). New York: Peter Lang Publishing.

Folger, J. and Bush, R. (2001) *Designing mediation: approaches to training and practice within a transformative framework*. New York: Institute for the Study of Conflict Transformation, Inc.

Foss, S. and Griffin, Cindy (1995) Beyond persuasion: a proposal for an invitational rhetoric. *Communication Monographs*: 62: 2–18. Online, available at: http://dx.doi.org/10.1080/03637759509376345.

Gastil, J. (1993) Identifying obstacles to small group democracy. *Small Group Research* 24: 5–27. Online, available at: http://dx.doi.org/10.1177/1046496493241002.

Goodnight, G. T. (1982) The personal, technical, and public spheres of argument: a speculative inquiry into the art of public deliberation. *Journal of the American Forensics Association* 18 (4): 214–227.

Habermas, J. (1984) *The theory of communicative action*. Boston: Beacon Press.

Habermas, J. (1991) *Structural transformation of the public sphere* (T. Burger, trans.) Cambridge, MA: MIT Press.

Kaner, S. (2007) *Facilitator's guide to participatory decision-making* (2nd edition). San Francisco, CA: Jossey-Bass.

Kellett, P. and Dalton, D. (2001) *Managing conflict in a negotiated world*. Thousand Oaks: Sage Publications.

Lindlof, T. and Taylor, B. (2002) *Qualitative communication research methods*. (2nd edition). Thousand Oaks, CA: Sage Publications.

Makau, J. M. and Marty, D. L. (2001) *Cooperative argumentation: a model for deliberative community*. Prospect Heights, IL: Waveland Press.

Middleton, M., Senda-Cook, S. and Endres, D. (2011) Articulating rhetorical field methods: challenges and tensions. *Western Journal of Communication* 75: 386–406. Online, available at: http://dx.doi.org/10.1080/10570314.2011.586969.

Mindell, A. (1995) *Sitting in the fire: large group transformation using conflict and diversity*. Portland, OR: Lao Tse Press.

Moore, C. (1986) *The mediation process: practical strategies for resolving conflict*. San Francisco, CA: Jossey-Bass.

Morson, G. S. (1991) Bakhtin, genres and temporality. *New Literary History* (22): 1071–1092. Online, available at: www.jstor.org/stable469079.

Mouffe, C. (1993) *The return of the political*. London, Verso.

Pearce, B. and Littlejohn, S. W. (1997) *Moral conflict: when worlds collide*. Thousand Oaks: Sage Publications.

Peters, J. D. (1999) *Speaking into the air*. Chicago: University of Chicago Press.

Peterson, M. N., Peterson, M. J. and Peterson, T. R. (2005). Conservation and the myth of consensus. *Conservation Biology* 19, 762–767. Online, available at: http://dx.doi.org/10.1111/j.1523-1739.2005.00518.x.

Peterson, M. N., Peterson, M.J. and Peterson, T. R. (2007) Response to Cox; environmental communication: why this crisis discipline should facilitate environmental democracy. *Environmental Communication* 1: 74–86. Online, available at: http://dx.doi.org/10.1080/17524030701334292.

Pezzullo, P. (2003) Resisting "national breast cancer awareness month": the rhetoric of counterpublics and their cultural performance. *Quarterly Journal of Speech* 89: 345–365. Online, available at: http://dx.doi.org/10.1080/0033563032000160981.

Rieke, R., Sillars, M. and Peterson, T. R. (2012) *Argumentation and critical decision making* (8th edition). Boston, MA: Pearson.

Spano, S. (2001) *Public dialogue and participatory democracy*. Cresskill, NJ: Hampton Press, Inc.

Theodori, G. (2005) Community and community development in resource-based areas: operational definitions rooted in an interactional perspective. *Society and Natural Resources: An International Journal* 18: 661–669 Online, available at: http://dx.doi.org/10.1080/08941920590959640.

Walker, G. (2004) The roadless areas initiative as national policy: is public participation an oxymoron? In: Depoe, S., Delicath, J. and Elsenbeer, M. (eds) *Communication and public participation in environmental decision-making*. Albany, NY: SUNY Press, 113–136.

Welsh, S. (2002) Deliberative democracy and the rhetorical production of political culture. *Rhetoric and Public Affairs*: 679–707. Online, available at: http://dx.doi.org/10.1353/rap. 2003.0020.

Zoller, H. (2004) Dialogue as global issue management: legitimizing corporate influence in the transatlantic business dialogue. *Management Communication Quarterly* 18: 204–240. Online, available at: http://dx.doi.org/10.1177/0893318904265126.

4 Performances of an international professional community

CCS/CCUS and its national contexts

Danielle Endres, Brian Cozen, Megan O'Byrne and Andrea M. Feldpausch-Parker

Introduction

The climate crisis is the most pressing sustainability challenge we face today (Intergovernmental Panel on Climate Change 2007, 2015). Despite the scientific consensus that confirms the materiality of anthropogenic climate change, it "presents perhaps the most profound and complex challenge to have confronted human social, political, and economic systems" (Dryzek *et al.* 2011: 17). The complexity largely stems from the international and intergenerational nature of climate change as well as the uneven distribution of both the sources of greenhouse gas emissions and the negative impacts across nations. Given the role of fossil fuels and their greenhouse gas emissions in worsening climate change, rethinking energy policy is a crucial aspect of any response to the climate crisis. This response must be international, because the catastrophic implications of climate change will not respect national political boundaries. An international response, therefore, requires the construction and maintenance of an international community that can not only monitor and regulate greenhouse gas emissions but can also address the unique circumstances of particular national communities and their varying roles in contributing to the climate crisis.

While community can be defined in a variety of conflicting ways (Shepherd and Rothenbuhler 2000), we define community simply as a group of people with shared interests. This definition is not limited to a geographical or political conception of community (e.g. the United States), but also allows for communities that cross a variety of geographical or political boundaries. The range of communities involves "relationships, families, neighborhoods, voluntary associations, municipalities, regions, or nation states" (Depew and Peters 2000: 3). Across this range, Benedict Anderson (2006) differentiates between actual and imagined communities. Actual communities are premised on everyday face-to-face interaction between members (and are therefore practically limited in size). Imagined communities are social constructions that are imagined by the people who identify as members, such as a nation, within which it would be impossible to have face-to-face interaction with everyone in the community. While there is overlap between the actual and imagined communities, these concepts are useful towards thinking through the role of rhetoric and communication in community construction. Anderson (2006: 9) argues that a nation, and we would add an international body, is "an imagined political community". In this case, both an international community to address climate change and a national community fall within Anderson's notion of an imagined community.

Yet, as we know, while there is an international community of concern about climate change, creating lasting and binding agreements has been an ongoing challenge (Giddens 2009) including the long-standing reluctance of the largest emitters – namely, the United States and China – to sign international CO_2 reduction agreements, and the failure of the UN Framework Convention on Climate Change to achieve binding agreements (most recently held in Geneva, Switzerland in February 2015) (Klein 2014).[1] Unfortunately, effective international action on climate change is not easily achieved, as evidenced by the fact that it has been over 20 years since the first definitive findings of the greenhouse effect and climate change debuted. Therefore, a guiding assumption of this chapter is that the lack of an international community that can effectively address climate change is the most pressing sustainability issue faced by humanity today.

We do not intend to solve this problem of a lack of an effective international community to address climate change in this chapter (although we wish it could be that easy). Instead, the purpose of this chapter is to examine, from a rhetorical perspective, some of the constraints on building this sort of international community to address climate change through energy policy. In particular, we examine how national policies and contexts constrain an international community's ability to take action. As much as we talk about globalization and the collapsing of national boundaries, the reality is that national communities are still relevant towards creating the regulatory environments needed to address climate change as an international issue. This tension between national and international is not new. Indeed, the argument of this chapter may be intuitive and unsurprising. Yet, there is power in unpacking this tension in a particular case study and revealing the complex ways in which national communities constrain international action.

We narrow our focus to one representative anecdote (Burke 1969) of this tension between international community action and national community action. A representative anecdote is a single anecdote that represents a larger phenomenon. In this case, we use the international community of carbon capture and sequestration (CCS)[2] and carbon capture, utilization, and sequestration (CCUS)[3] professionals working on the research, development, and implementation of CCS/CCUS as a suite of low-carbon energy technologies. This collection of professionals functions as an example to highlight the larger phenomenon of the tension between international community and national community with regard to climate change.

The distinction between CCS and CCUS, mainly the insertion of *utilization* in 2012, partially stemmed from political barriers to the passage of climate legislation (most notably in the United States) and industry desire to commodify anthropogenic CO_2 for processes such as enhanced oil recovery (EOR) (Endres *et al.* 2013). Although research into CCS began in the late 1980s, it did not become an important facet of international deliberation about energy policy and the climate crisis until the early 2000s (Herzog 2001), particularly after the Intergovernmental Panel on Climate Change (IPCC) recommended CCS as a primary strategy for climate change mitigation (Intergovernmental Panel on Climate Change 2005). CCS/CCUS are overarching terms for a variety of technologies that reduce CO_2 emissions from coal-based energy production and other stationary industrial sources (e.g. cement plants, ethanol plants, refineries, and iron and steel mills) (Intergovernmental Panel on Climate Change 2005; US Department of Energy 2008). CCS is a suite of transitional energy technologies that seek to lower the CO_2 emissions from a fossil fuel energy source (or in the case of CCUS, benefit secondarily from the CO_2 capture process for use in other industrial operations), and are therefore different from alternative energy technologies that reduce dependence on fossil fuels, such as wind and solar. CCS/CCUS technologies, however, have enough similarities with other low-carbon energy technologies to merit serving as a case study for our larger question about the constraints on building an international community to address climate change through energy policy.

We turn our attention to the communicative rhetorical practices of the CCS/CCUS professional community as a way to understand how national communities constrain international community action on energy and climate change. *We define communication, from a rhetorical perspective, as a form of symbolic action in which symbols (language, visuals, etc.) are mobilized to influence how we make sense of the world.* Symbols act as terministic screens that reflect, frame and constitute an understanding of the world (Burke 1966). Kenneth Burke states, "even if any given terminology is a *reflection* of reality, by its very nature as a terminology it must be a *selection* of reality; and to this extent it must also function as a *deflection* of reality" (1966: 45). In other words, rhetoric is, consciously or not, constructed to make sense of the world through emphasizing certain things and deemphasizing others, or emphasizing one way of viewing the world over others. One of the ways we make sense of our world is through the creation of and identification with communities. Communication is crucial to the development of community because of its representative and constitutive functions (Shepherd and Rothenbuhler 2000).[4] For the international CCS/CCUS professional community, evidence of their existence can be seen in the way people talk about them and in how the mobilization of symbols has consequences on the construction, maintenance and deconstruction of community.

The international community of CCS/CCUS professionals acts as a bridge between two other relevant forms of imagined community: international climate change community and national community. The CCS/CCUS professional community is both an actual and an imagined community, made up of people with a shared interest in developing and promoting CCS/CCUS technologies as a part of the solution to reducing greenhouse gas emissions and curbing climate change. This community is actual in the sense that it is premised on a variety of networks between its members, who often meet up in face-to-face or virtual meetings. It is imagined in the sense that it articulates a vision of an international solution to climate change through CCS/CCUS technologies that is not dependent on actual face-to-face contact. This community is made up of basic and applied scientists and engineers from academic, industry and governmental sectors; representatives of energy corporations; non-governmental organizations (NGOs) related to CCS/CCUS, energy policy, or climate change; and government agencies. The CCS/CCUS professional community is a transdisciplinary network across these sectors in pursuit of a shared solution to a real world problem that transcends one discipline or perspective (Sprain *et al.* 2010). The CCS/CCUS professional community is not a geographically or politically bounded community, but is made up of people from a variety of locations and political affiliations with a common interest in CCS/CCUS technologies. In this way, it is an international community in that its members extend across the globe, but it also has intersections with more geographically and politically bounded national communities through its members. As such, the CCS/CCUS community situates itself as part of a broader imagined community to address climate change. Yet, it is made up of people who are also members of imagined national political communities. This professional community, then, intersects with other international and national community responses to climate change and energy policy. That is, the actions of the CCS/CCUS professional community with regard to climate change and energy do not happen in a vacuum, but are always related back to the actions of other international communities (e.g. the UN) and national communities (e.g. the United States, China, etc.). As we will show, the laws and policies of national political communities form a constraint on the ability of the international CCS/CCUS community to address climate change, either through collaboration with another international body like the UN or on its own.

One of the major nodes of community development and maintenance for CCS/CCUS professionals is the conference, where community members meet face-to-face to discuss the technological and societal implications of CCS/CCUS technologies. As such, to access the rhetorical practices that relate to the role of CCS/CCUS professionals in the construction or deconstruction of an international CCS/CCUS community aimed at reducing CO_2 emissions, we conducted participant observation within the CCS/CCUS community. We have been involved with research on the social and cultural dimensions of CCS/CCUS covering eight years. Our backgrounds not only arguably make us peripheral members of the CCS/CCUS professional community but also allow us to participate in a variety of venues where

CCS/CCUS professionals gather, including the attendance of the annual spring CCS/CCUS conference in Pittsburgh, Pennsylvania. Although this conference is held annually in the United States, it is an international conference that draws speakers and participants from countries such as Canada, Norway, Japan, China, the United Kingdom, the United States, and others. In this chapter, we focus on the eleventh Annual CCUS Conference (2012)[5] to analyse the communication strategies used in relation to the topic of the role of CCS/CCUS in international efforts to address climate change. This conference is significant because it signi-fied a transition of CCS/CCUS community thinking from mainly climate change mitigation to CO_2 commodification and climate change mitigation.

In the case of CCS/CCUS, efforts to build international community are fundamentally limited by the laws, regulations, and cultural practices of the national political communities in which CCS/CCUS technologies must be situated. The rhetorical practices of the CCS/CCUS professional community offer a window into how these constraints materialize in everyday conversa-tions among these professionals. The CCS/CCUS professional community has to negotiate the boundaries within and outside their community to address the tension between national and international communities. This type of rhetorical boundary-work – breaking down, reinforcing and creating anew the boundaries that demarcate national and international community – highlights the significant role of communication in the (de)construction of community especially in this context, wherein international politics and pol-icies complicate the communication at hand. Even though our case study primarily focuses on a failure in international community construction, there are practical lessons that can contribute to alternate strategies.

We begin by further clarifying a theoretical framework that draws from boundary-work. Then, we discuss our methodological approach, which uses rhetorical field methods to better understand the ongoing practices of boundary negotiation within the CCS/CCUS professional community. The subsequent section presents a discussion of our findings. Finally, we conclude with implications for future study and practical lessons.

Theoretical framework: negotiating boundaries within communities

In professional conversations that situate CCS/CCUS as a part of a suite of energy technologies that can address climate change, the professional CCS/CCUS community contends with negotiating boundaries between the national and international community, particularly as related to the tension between national laws and regulations that can constrain or enable an inter-national community response to climate change. Examining CCS/CCUS technologies and how professionals talk about those technologies also con-tends with boundaries between science and society; in other words, bound-aries are constructed between what the technology produced by the community can do and the enabling and constraining factors of implementing these technologies in messy societies with conflicting laws, policies, attitudes, ideologies and politics. In this case, the boundaries between national and international community and science and society play an important role in energy and climate change. As stated above, we argue that national communities serve as constraints on the development of an effective international community, which is an important part of any solution to anthropogenic climate change. This is seen in the discourse of CCS/CCUS professionals seeking to envision how their technologies can be put into the service of new climate-conscious energy policies. Yet, these boundaries are neither essential nor fixed. Rather, they are socially constructed by communities and communication, and are "ambiguous, flexible, historically changing, contextually variable, internally inconsistent, and sometimes disrupted" (Gieryn 1983: 792), a point that we will return to in the conclusion.

In order to better understand the national and international boundaries at play in the CCS/CCUS professional community, we turn to academic studies of boundary-work and demarcation (e.g. Gieryn 1983, 1999; Kinsella *et al.* 2013; Taylor 1996) that examine the discursive construction of boundaries within technoscience, such as energy technology's role in addressing the climate crisis. Boundary-work comes out of both science, technology and society (STS) and rhetoric of science (RoS) traditions to focus on how science functions as a cultural, social and rhetorical practice that enables scientists and engineers to construct (evolving) boundaries. These boundaries can be used as a way to, for example, name and define their activities, garner credibility and speak to the social implications of their work. Although much boundary-work scholarship focuses on scientific laboratory practices, the concept is not limited to those practices (Taylor 1996). Boundary-work comes into play in a broad range of scientific and technical practices, including grant work, public outreach and professional scientific and technical conferences.

While an examination of CCS/CCUS professionals could be used to explore boundary-work across scientists and the public, as has been done in much boundary-work, our vantage point and purpose highlight the negotiation of boundaries between national communities within the international CCS/CCUS professional community. The majority of rhetorical work on demarcation and boundary-work has examined the boundaries between science and non-science (i.e. fraud or bad science) or between science and the public (e.g. Condit 1996; Derkatch 2012; Holmquest 1990; Keränen 2005; Kinsella 2001). Through our analysis of the interdisciplinary CCS/CCUS professional community, we highlight the boundary work that happens in professional conversations about the application of CCS/CCUS, and its relationship to national and international political communities. Gieryn suggests that "boundary-work is strategic practical action. As such, the borders and territories of science will be drawn to pursue immediate goals and interests of cultural cartographers, and to appeal to the goals and interests of audiences and stakeholders" (1999: 23). Cultural cartographers include individuals within the community seeking to frame its goals and interests, whereas audiences and stakeholders are members of the community that have an interest in the outcome of the framing. Community members can shift between cartographers, audience members and stakeholders, depending on the situation. As we demonstrate in our analysis, however, it is more complicated than this. The drawing of boundaries within a professional scientific community is constrained by its interaction with other communities. In this case, while the CCS/CCUS community has the power to name and frame its own goals and interests through boundaries, it does not have the power to make its goals mesh with external community standards, laws, and policies.

Rhetorical field methods

Using rhetorical field methods (Middleton *et al.* 2011), we gained access to the everyday rhetorical practices of CCS/CCUS professionals in action. Rhetorical practices are "mundane, embodied, repetitive actions; they are the daily arguments and compromises that compellingly convince us of who we are and how we ought to act" (Senda-Cook 2012: 131). We focus our analysis on one moment in our ongoing research of the CCS/CCUS professional community: the 2012 Annual CCUS Conference. Our participant observation at this conference – data including field notes (e.g. Emerson *et al.* 2011), ethnographic interviews (e.g. Lindlof and Taylor 2010), transcribed plenary speeches, and conference materials (e.g. the conference program, fliers from exhibition tables, copies of presentation slides, etc.) – illuminates the negotiation of boundaries in action. In line with rhetorical field methods, we used rhetorical criticism as our mode of analysis of the data we collected through fieldwork. This allows us access to an untraditional rhetorical text for analysis, giving an important window into *in situ* rhetorical practices (as opposed to already documented texts, which are the mainstay of traditional rhetorical criticism).

The National Energy Technology Labs (NETL) and Exchange Monitor Publications – a private technical publishing house devoted to nuclear and CCS technologies – convened the eleventh Annual CCUS conference in 2012. This conference included a wide variety of participants, ranging from industry (e.g. Shell, Electronic Research Power Institute (EPRI), and Schlumberger Carbon Services) to basic and applied scientists and engineers from academic, governmental and non-governmental organizations. The conference boasted roughly 600 participants from 22 countries and a total of 300 technical posters and papers presented on CCS/CCUS research and development (R&D) efforts. This clustering of professionals presented a diverse audience of attendees representing competing and/or complementary interests in relation to the climate mitigation strategy of CCS/CCUS technological implementation. The conference theme was unique in relation to these participants. The theme for the conference was "Building a Business Case for Carbon Capture, Utilization, and Sequestration: Good for the

Economy and the Environment". Building a business case for CCUS refers to developing strategies to make the technologies economically viable for businesses to implement successfully (i.e. with a profit margin). This theme is important because it reflects how the community was focused not purely on the scientific and technical feasibility of CCS, but rather on a more normative goal of promoting the value of CCS as a response to climate change that can also be good for the economy. The theme spanned the boundary between science and society in its focus on a business case for CCUS that converged economic and environmental motivations. To the extent that this theme served as a starting point for conference discourse, the intersections between technical feasibility and societal achievability of CCS/CCUS were predominant themes throughout the conference.

Bruno Latour (1988) argues that technoscientific communities are best understood through their everyday, on the ground practices, and in this case professional conferences serve as an important node of the practices of the CCS/CCUS professional community (see also Latour and Woolgar 1986). Indeed, while the laboratory or field research sites are most commonly associated with the everyday practice of technoscientists, these communities also practice across a variety of different sites (Hine 2007; Lorenz-Meyer 2011). Professional conferences are a relatively understudied but crucial site of technoscientific communities in action (Heath 1998; Krauss 2011, 2009). CCS/CCUS conferences are a particularly important site of localized practices for the CCS/CCUS professional community because, besides journal articles, it is one of the major sites in which CCS/CCUS professionals engage in conversation about their research. Unlike journal articles that sustain a distanced and timeless conversation, CCS/CCUS professional conferences involve emplaced and time-bound interpersonal conversations about research and its societal implications. This allows for co-presence and chance encounters (Henke and Gieryn 2008) where cross-disciplinary CCS/CCUS professionals converge to present, discuss and develop new scientific ideas. For a topic as transdisciplinary and politically charged as CCS/CCUS, conferences serve as a crucial localized site of knowledge production and interaction. As we will show, much of the conversation in the plenary sessions particularly was focused on normative claims about CCS/CCUS and its role in society.[6] It was within this context that we observed the tension between national and international community.

Setting the scene – CCS/CCUS as energy solution

The conference actively engaged with the societal implications of CCS/CCUS technologies, thus breaking down a supposed boundary between science and society from the start. This was not a conference solely devoted to scientific and technical details about the feasibility of CCS/CCUS (although some sessions did address this component). Rather the theme and the spirit of the panels, particularly the plenary sessions, emphasized and debated the role that CCS/CCUS could play in relation to societal needs for environmental protection (climate change) and promoting the economy. One of the most important themes that emerged was the idea that CCS/CCUS is good for the environment because it reduces CO_2 emissions and addresses climate change but it is not yet good for the economy – it is very expensive and not currently economically viable. The goal of making the "business case" for CCS/CCUS highlighted the economic viability and benefits of CCUS (taking the environmental benefits as a given).[7] The conference chair, in his introduction of the first speaker of the conference, set the conference theme by foregrounding the economic and policy work of CCUS. He noted that making a business case for CCUS and developing a clear image for its role in the future of energy and climate mitigation was "maybe some of the most important work going on in the energy sector". This highlights the important linkage between policy and R&D of new technologies, especially low-carbon energy-related technologies (Feldpausch-Parker *et al.* 2013). This situates CCS/CCUS within an international community of professionals committed to this technology as a part of the solution to climate change and the related necessity of re-envisioning energy policy. This sort of an international community contends with the particular legal and policy contexts of national communities, creating a tension in the boundary between national and international community.

Participants at the conference talked about CCS/CCUS as a mechanism to reduce greenhouse gas emissions and address the climate crisis. The CEO of an international centre to promote CCS (with substantial funding from the Australian government) stated: "Decreasing CO_2 emissions at the end of it all is really the key reason for pursuing CCS". This sentiment was echoed throughout the conference by presenters representing a variety of countries, international bodies and sectors (academic, governmental and industry). Yet, concomitant to the feasibility of CCS/CCUS to reduce greenhouse gas emissions was the recognized need for aligned national and international agreements on reducing greenhouse gas emissions that also put a price on CO_2 through a carbon tax or cap and trade. The same CEO noted that global agreements are one of the five central challenges that need to be met to move faster on CCS/CCUS. In the absence of stronger international greenhouse gas emission reduction targets and a carbon tax or cap and trade system, CCS/CCUS is expensive. The conference's focus on the "business case" for these technologies is an attempt to think about the viability of CO_2 mitigation in the absence of these sorts of international agreements. As an official in the US Department of Energy (DOE) noted in his headliner plenary address, "That was appropriate at a time when we were looking at things like carbon tax or cap and trade, but I'm here to tell you today it's about a business case". These examples reveal that the societal application of CCS/CCUS technology was a central component of this conference. The conference started with an assumption of the failure of international agreements and attempted to make an international business case for CCS/CCUS. Yet, as we will demonstrate, this goal was also constrained by national communities and their specific contexts and policies.

Findings and discussion – national community policy as constraint

We found that the discussion of the viability of CCS/CCUS as an inter-national solution to climate change always tied back to the constraints within national political community laws, regulations and policies. This highlights a tension between the community's desire to promote CCS/CCUS as an inter-national solution to an international problem and the reality that the success of such a solution depends on national conversations and policies that could undermine international goals. The boundaries and inconsistencies between national political community approaches to climate change and energy create a constraint on international action. In this section we highlight speakers from the United States, Canada, Norway, China and the European Union (EU), whose rhetoric reveals the boundary-work between national and international community. We selected these countries because they were more strongly represented at the plenary sessions and other conference activities than other countries. While many participants understood the need for an international agreement to reduce emissions and price CO_2, discussions of topics including implementation of CCS/CCUS technology, international technology transfer to promote CCS/CCUS, and the need for economic incentives for CCS/CCUS consistently came back to discussions about national contexts as lim-itations to developing CCS/CCUS as an international solution. These discus-sions involved participants both reflecting on their own national community as well as on other national communities. The US national context was pre-dominantly featured in the conference due to its location, co-sponsorship by the Department of Energy, and the demographics of the majority of confer-ence attendees. Yet, the US context did not dominate as there were explicit efforts to bring international NGOs, and representatives from other countries into the plenary sessions of the conference. We will begin with a discussion of the US national community context, and then address some of the other national communities represented.

In the US context, there was a strong argument for moving to a primary focus on CCUS with EOR as the business case, or the economically viable way to implement CCS technologies. The plenary headliner, a ranking offi-cial at the US DOE, explained the need for shifting from an emphasis on CCS alone to an emphasis on CCUS with EOR, noting the constraints of US policy. He argued that US policy has been slow to create a regulatory climate conducive to CCS such as a carbon tax, some other mechanism to make CO_2 a commodity, or stricter limitations on greenhouse gas emissions. Within this regulatory climate, the US community is more amenable to something like EOR that utilizes carbon as a commodity and puts it in the hands of industry, wherein industry needs a business case or an economically rational reason to deploy this technology. He noted, "in the absence of carbon policy" enhanced oil recovery is a win–win type of situation to get "oil out of the ground that otherwise wouldn't be available to you ... get a benefit for our security in this country and create jobs, generate tax dollars, etc., etc. and get the tangible benefit of sequestering CO_2". In this regulatory context, the US DOE has a strong interest in and incentive to deploy and commercialize technologies that work with the policies and regulations set forth by the US government and that make sense from a business perspective.

This brings the conversation to the high cost of CCS/CCUS. An explicit assessment of the costs with R&D and eventual commercial deployment of CCS/CCUS is required to determine its potential for deployment and commercialization (Feldpausch-Parker *et al.* 2013; Johnsson 2011). On the capture side, it costs money to build and maintain the additional infrastructure needed to retrofit current coal-fired power plants and to build new ones. CCS also costs energy because a coal-fired power plant fitted with capture technology needs to burn more coal to produce the same amount of electricity. From one vantage point, these costs can be evaluated in relation to the benefit of mitigation of anthropogenic greenhouse gas emissions and responding to the climate crisis. Yet, if anthropogenic climate change is not recognized as a significant problem, if there is no price on CO_2, and if there are not strict limits on emissions, the added costs of CCS do not justify its addition to an energy portfolio. However, CCUS with EOR, as presented in the conference, provides a business-friendly alternative that appears to be both economically viable and environmentally beneficial (Tomski *et al.* 2012). This example shows the tension in developing an international community to address climate change through energy policy when the regulations of a particular national community serve as limitations to the use of a particular technology.

Within this context, the conference theme of a business case for CCUS represents an attempt to overcome the economic limitation by making CCS more economically viable through adding EOR to the CCS process. This theme strongly represents the US and North American context. The regulatory context of the national US community constrains the industry's ability to move forward with a technology that could help provide a transition away from fossil fuels. Ironically, the solution is to combine these technologies with industry practices that would actually increase reliance on fossil fuels and tap into previously inaccessible oil reserves. US-centred governmental and industry presenters used the framing shift to sell CCUS as something that could revive CCS, perceived to be dying because of a lack of good legislation and regulation and a deficient business case without utilization (i.e. the U in CCUS). The case of the United States points to how the rhetorical appeal of the CCUS narrative is always dependent upon its political context. An implication of this is that it entrenches a perspective that given a failure in policy to address climate change mitigation, the immediate response is to shift to the market as a potential solution.

Yet, the conference's focus on the US regulatory context also created boundaries between the US community and other national communities, both highlighting the differences between national contexts and revealing the constraints to international community building around CCS/CCUS technologies. What makes sense for the US national community does not necessarily make sense for other national communities with their own set of contexts and regulations, thus further breaking down the ability to create an international community response to climate change. Indeed, the CEO of an international institute to promote CCS noted that while CCUS–EOR works well given the context of the US community, it does not work well in other national community contexts. He noted,

> One of the challenges with EOR is that while it is a highly viable, incredibly affordable approach in North America, it is not the same experience in much of the rest of the world. The opportunity for EOR from all that we can understand is actually vastly more limited with few exceptions. So in many nations, CCS has to be on the back of climate change policy.

And even in those countries where EOR is possible, it may still be limited by differing governmental regulations. For example, an executive from a Canadian energy company focused his plenary presentation on the success of CCUS demonstration projects in Canada, noting that while the regulatory environment in Canada makes it difficult to build new CCUS-capable (with EOR) power plants, retrofitting has allowed Canadian projects to move forward.

We turn now to a discussion of Norway as an example of how national communities that promote international community are also limited. In other words, Norway's position, as represented by participants at the conference, was to do what it could to support international efforts to deploy CCS/CCUS in order to address climate change.[8] At a plenary presentation, the CEO of Statoil deemphasized the conference's primary focus on making a business case for capturing CO_2 for EOR and re-presented CCS as more importantly about climate mitigation, claiming that "climate change is the true elephant in the room", and should not be lost in discussions about the economic viability of CCS/CCUS. Statoil represents the Norwegian government in holding oil reserves in the North Sea in trust for Norwegian citizens, as described in more detail in Chapter 7's discussion of the PTD. This structure may have enabled the CEO to describe the costs of CCS as necessary toward achieving and outweighing the benefits of reducing greenhouse gas emissions to use "CCS for a better climate". As one researcher noted, this unabashed acknowledgement from an industry executive might signal a different perception of climate change by the Norwegian government and energy industry. This executive's plenary presentation reveals how, within a different national community context, it is appropriate and possible for a publically owned corporation to prioritize climate change over economics and regulations. All of this is not to say that economics and regulations are unimportant, rather Norwegian (and more broadly EU) regulations and their economic implications support the further development of CCS. Norway has a strong CO_2 tax, which provides a crucial tax incentive for sequestration. In other words, Norway's regulatory structure does what the international community cannot in terms of making CCS viable through climate regulation. It also has strong government investment in the commercialization of CCS through this corporation in particular. This national context may enable a broader approach to incentivizing CCS than the more short-term promotion of the business case that was emphasized throughout the international community gathered for this conference.

In addition to revealing a tension between differing national community responses to CCS/CCUS, the case of Norway also raises an additional constraint to CCS/CCUS's role in international action to prevent climate change. The Norwegian executive noted that CCS makes little sense unless it is deployed internationally. As such, it is in the interest of Norway to promote international community partnerships. Indeed, the corporation's website states:

> The programme focuses on new approaches and innovation, as well as on professional and international cooperation. The objective is to contribute to achieving lower costs for CCS, and to ensure that this essential technology is implemented internationally sooner that would otherwise have been possible.

Yet, those partnerships are limited by national and industry community interests in retaining control over CCS/CCUS R&D. The Norwegian CEO called for more partnerships across countries (as opposed to industries who are more interested in protecting intellectual property) "to share the knowledge" toward wide scale deployment. He noted that Norway has an open invitation for others to come and bring their technology for research collaboration and demonstration projects. Sharing intellectual property, especially across national borders, often comes with strings attached. National governments have, in many cases, been a driving economic force (whether through tax incentives or grants) behind the research that has thus far promoted CCS/CCUS R&D. Transferring intellectual property, gained literally at national expense, is tricky in most cases and specifically prevented in others. Further, when the focus is shifted to a business case that puts more responsibility on business to pursue CCUS, intellectual property sharing from industry is even less likely to occur. In the case of Norway though, where nearly all CCS research is state-funded, this presenter argued that the role of the state was to share knowledge and promote international cooperation rather than to protect intellectual property. Even in a case where a national community actively promotes international community cooperation, we see that this advocacy still comes back to national community both in that it is in the interest of Norway to promote CCS and that international cooperation is not in the interest of all national contexts. Norway's rhetorical efforts to mobilize an effective international community to address climate change through sharing knowledge and technology about CCS as a key part of the solution are still constrained by boundaries between different national community contexts.

China provides another perspective on the tension between national and international communities. China came up frequently in the discussions of CCS/CCUS, both in terms of a fear of China's future emissions and in terms of the solid progress being made in China to address greenhouse gas emissions with CCS/CCUS.[9] We focus on the latter because it was a more prominent theme across the conference. Similar to Norway, the Chinese context sees climate change as a crucial problem. A corporate executive from a government-run mining and energy company in China discussed the "social obligation" to reduce emissions. Further, given China's reliance on coal, "clean coal" types of technologies such as CCS/CCUS are very important to its ability to address climate change, reduce greenhouse emissions and use its coal reserves. The 2012 conference coincided with a new Chinese strategic plan that "clearly, and unambiguously identifies CCS and CCUS as a priority in their climate change" plan, according to the CEO for an international CCS institute. Additionally, the president of a Chinese institute on low-carbon energy stated that "we have a strategic imperative in terms of reducing carbon intensity" in China. Indeed, the CEO of the international CCS institute identified the emergence of China in the CCS/CCUS community as an important game changer. He argued, "Don't underestimate China", and continued:

> From my perspective, Chinese commitment and achievement can't be doubted. Now, this is not a threat. This is a big policy duplication for the cost of the technology, and undoubtedly China can, and I'm sure, will play a very large role in lowering that cost of capture, as well as demonstrating a lot of scale, CCS and CCUS, in a range of different industries.

This speaker continued:

> So what about CCS and China? What has the government's response actually been? I would say that it's smart. I would say it's largely been very highly committed. We're very impressed with the reduction of carbon intensity. There are a number of projects underway. You might call them demonstrations. Another colleague from China will present a number of those projects … and many of those activities are joint activities with other partners around the world, including the US.

As represented by these speakers, the national community of China is positioning itself to be a leader of CCS/CCUS technology nationally and internationally. This leadership is not only related to an obligation within China to reduce GHG emissions, but also related to innovations, scaling, and economizing CCS. Yet, although there is some mention of collaboration with other countries, China's leadership is still framed within a national community context.

Although China's efforts as described by these presenters are laudable and impressive, China's technological development in CCS is primarily geared toward its national GHG emission goals and national interest. Even though China made an aggressive emission reduction pledge at the Copenhagen climate convention in 2009, China was also one of the countries that fought against a legally binding international agreement. More recently, in early 2014, the UN's chief climate official, Christiana Figueres, praised China's national standards and regulations related to reducing greenhouse gas emissions and promoting alternate energy and efficiency (Yoon 2014). Yet, she also noted that climate goals need to "feed the national interest", and that "They're [China] not doing this because they want to save the planet. They're doing it because it's in their national interest" (as cited in Yoon 2014). China, despite all of its efforts to promote, innovate, and deploy CCS, is not motivated by international community, but is rather motivated by a social obligation and a desire to promote its own national community interest. An international legally binding agreement was not something in which China was willing to participate, signalling a constraint to the development of international community. Yet, similar to Norway, international cooperation can play into China's national interest as related to CCS/CCUS, but that is unlikely to come in the form of a formal legally-binding agreement. China's national community context further demonstrates how the national constrains the international, even if there is some interest in the international community.

The conference was not just made up of representatives from national communities, but also included a fair number of international NGOs. In the rhetoric of NGOs, we see attempts to centre the international CCS/CCUS community on economics over the environment, thus tying into the business case theme, but on an international instead of national level. A European NGO seeking to radically lower CO_2 emissions illustrated the discussion of cost as the key stasis point for the deployment of CCS/CCUS. The communication director of this NGO – whose stated goal is to make CCS commercially viable by 2020 – named cost as the key challenge to widespread deployment. Yet, he attempted to turn the economic argument against CCS on its head by arguing "without CCS, it will cost us 70 per cent more to reach our global climate change targets. That is 1.3 trillion dollars extra every single year we're considering. We need to move this [CCS] in the space of being deployable". This presenter subsumes climate change within cost, highlighting the economic costs of climate change as outweighing the costs of deploying CCS. Playing off the Norwegian representative's metaphor, the elephant has been re-located in the room to make way for the 800-pound gorilla. While previous presentations made it clear that CCS/CCUS is a potentially viable, if costly, technology, this European NGO representative reminded the audience that there is a larger goal than simply selling a technology or promoting R&D. The goal remains to reduce greenhouse gas emissions and begin to remediate climate change, and CCS can help meet that goal while also saving money in the long term. In the face of a variety of international policy barriers keeping this technology at bay, this presenter embraced the economic frame and highlighted the global economic consequences of not adopting CCS/CCUS.

Conclusion

In summary, our findings suggest that despite the desirability of creating an international CCS/CCUS professional community to contribute to the reduction of greenhouse gas emissions, the construction of this community always has to contend with and is limited by national community contexts. Our discussion of the differing national contexts between the United States, Canada, Norway and China reveals that national policies and regulations related to climate change and CCS/CCUS have an inescapable grip on the ways that nations can contribute to international solutions. Even non-governmental industries or groups are still bound to the national communities in that they are the entities that make regulations. Yet, as we have shown, it is not as simple as just arguing that the national constrains the international. Rather, our findings reveal the complex boundaries and boundary negotiations and tensions between national and international that happen in the professional CCS/CCUS community.

There are several significant implications from our findings. First, using boundary-work as a theoretical framework offers a powerful heuristic that may be useful in examining similar professional communities involved with low-carbon energy technology and climate change mitigation. As we noted, we see the CCS/CCUS professional community as a representative anecdote for a tension that spans across communities committed to addressing climate change with changes in energy. That tension between the national and international communities may never be resolved, but it is an important tension that must be accounted for and contended with in any consideration of how to address the climate crisis. Further, this heuristic could potentially extend beyond the context of climate change and energy to other issues that involve the negotiation of tension across international and national communities.

Second, studying technoscientific professional communities through our method – rhetorical field methods – offers a unique vantage point from which to examine the everyday, on the ground rhetorical practices of a professional community. In the case of CCS/CCUS professionals, this approach allows for examination of how this group negotiates boundaries in their rhetorical practices among themselves. Evidence of these practices may not be accessible in other forms of communication such as journal articles, websites and other documented texts. The rhetorical field methods approach allows for a unique approach to science communication.

Third, we draw two practical lessons from this case in the spirit of promoting an international community to address climate change through changes in energy practices. As much as globalization and the collapsing of national boundaries are important aspects of the climate crisis, we cannot escape the notion that national communities matter. In the absence of a strong international agency that can create and enforce binding agreements, we are left with influencing the policies of particular national communities. As noted above, this is a conclusion that Figueres of the UN may have come to wherein she advocates that mitigating climate change has to be conceived within national interest. This is challenging, given the variety of national interests involved in such a case, but it does provide some guidance towards possibly more effective solutions. The lesson, in our mind, is not that we give up on an international community to address climate change, but that the challenge lies in doing the difficult work of putting national community interests and contexts more into alignment with a larger international goal. Although we mainly focused on the national community as constraint, we might start to think of how national community can also enable. Norway may serve as a positive example of a national community interest and a set of national policies that are aligned with and promote international community as well. Further, it might be argued that, even in the absence of a binding international agreement, strong national actions from the United States, China and the other largest emitters could set an example for additional nations to follow.

Second, society should be sceptical of turning to industry and the economy to solve the climate crisis. The "business case" conference theme represents an attempt to get around national constraints and the lack of climate change regulations that would enable CCS by turning it to industry to find a way to make it profitable. In addition to showing through our analysis that an international business case is equally constrained by national communities, there are significant risks to a market-based solution, namely that, as Naomi Klein (2014) argues, the global capitalist system is at the root of the climate crisis.

The CCUS/CCS professional community is just one example of a group that is grappling with how to address climate change and energy. This is admittedly only one small sliver of a complex array of issues that constrain an international response to climate change. Yet, in some important ways it can serve as a representative anecdote for thinking through local and global community responses to climate change.

Notes

1 Although the United States and China recently committed to new limits on greenhouse gas emissions, no legally binding international agreement has codified their commitments.
2 A broad spectrum of low-carbon energy technologies have the potential to reduce greenhouse gas emissions, ranging from renewable energy sources, such as wind or solar, to what have been called "clean coal" technologies, such as CCS, that reduce the impact of fossil fuels on global warming. At its best, we see CCS as a suite of transitional technologies that can reduce the impact of coal while society develops a better infrastructure for renewable energy sources and energy conservation.
3 CCUS refocuses the process of CCS to emphasize commercial utilization of the captured emissions prior to, or as part of, sequestering it. Utilization includes a variety of uses, such as carbonation for the beverage industry, enhanced hydrocarbon recovery and others. The utilization most often discussed is injecting captured CO_2 into oil wells for enhanced oil recovery (EOR), which allows

harvesting oil from otherwise inaccessible deposits through a displacement process where the CO_2 pushes out the oil and remains in the ground. For a more detailed discussion of the relationship between CCS and CCUS see Endres *et al.* (2013).

4 For an interesting discussion of the historical development of the conceptual relationship between communication and community, which is beyond the scope of this chapter, see (Depew and Peters 2000).

5 Prior to 2012, the conference was called the CCS conference, but the name was changed to CCUS conference in 2012. See Endres *et al.* (2013) for more on this name change.

6 Of note, many of the technical sessions were more focused on the technical details of these technologies. Research scientists and engineers presented the findings of their research and only briefly, if at all, focused on the societal implications of their findings.

7 The environmental benefits are not necessarily automatic. Although CCS reduces CO_2 emissions from coal-fired electricity plants, its implementation reduces the plants' efficiency, thus requiring emission of additional greenhouse gas emissions to produce the same amount of electricity. CCUS for EOR *reduces* greenhouse gas emissions, but then *creates* greenhouse gas emissions not only through the carbon capture process but also through enabling the further use of oil, another greenhouse gas emitting fossil fuel.

8 While CCS is more viable in the Norwegian context, Norway is open to supporting CCUS as a solution that would work better in other national contexts.

9 In the Chinese context, CCUS is not limited to, or even primarily discussed as a means of EOR. Rather, representatives from a state-run Chinese energy company highlighted the utilization of captured CO_2 for the beverage industry.

References

Anderson, B. R. O. (2006) *Imagined Communities: Reflections on the Origin and Spread of Nationalism*. London: Verso.

Burke, K. (1966) *Language as Symbolic Action: Essays on Life, Literature, and Method*. Berkeley, CA: University of California Press.

Burke, K. (1969) *A Grammar of Motives*. Berkeley, CA: University of California Press.

Depew, D. and Peters, J. D. (2000) Community and communication: the conceptual background. In: Shepherd, G. J. and Rothenbuhler, E. W. (eds) *Communication and Community*. New York: Routledge, 3–21.

Dryzek, J. S., Norgaard, R. B. and Schlosberg, D. (2011) Climate change and society: approaches and responses. In: Dryzek, J. S., Norgaard, R. B. and Schlosberg, D. (eds) *The Oxford Handbook of Climate Change and Society*. Oxford: Oxford University Press, 3–17.

Emerson, R. M., Fretz, R. I. and Shaw, L. L. (2011) *Writing Ethnographic Fieldnotes* (Chicago guides to writing, editing, and publishing), 2nd edition. Chicago: University of Chicago Press.

Endres, D., Cozen, B., O'Byrne, M. and Feldpausch-Parker, A. M. (2013) Putting the U in carbon capture and storage: Performances of rupture within the CCS scientific community, paper presented at the *Conference on Communication and the Environment*, 8 June, Uppsala, Sweden.

Feldpausch-Parker, A. M., Ragland, C. J., Melnick, L. L., Chaudhry, R., Hall, D. M., Peterson, T. R., Stephens, J. C. and Wilson, E. J. (2013) Spreading the news on carbon capture and storage: a state-level comparison of US media. *Environmental Communication: A Journal of Nature and Culture* 7 (3): 336–354.

Giddens, A. (2009) *Politics of Climate Change*. Malden, MA: Polity.

Gieryn, T. F. (1983) Boundary-work and the demarcation of science from non-science: strains and interests in professional ideologies of scientists. *American Sociological Review* 48 (6): 781–795.

Gieryn, T. F. (1999) *Cultural Boundaries of Science: Credibility on the Line*. Chicago: University of Chicago Press.

Heath, D. (1998) Locating genetic knowledge: picturing Marfan Syndrome and its traveling constituencies. *Science, Technology and Human Values* 23 (1): 71–97.

Henke, C. R. and Gieryn, T. F. (2008) Sites of scientific practice: the enduring importance of place. In: Hackett, E. J., Amsterdamska, O., Lynch, M. and Wajcman, J. (eds) *The Handbook of Science and Technology Studies*. Cambridge, MA: The MIT Press, 353–376.

Herzog, H. J. (2001) What future for carbon capture and sequestration? *Environmental Science and Technology* 35 (7): 148A–153A.

Hine, C. (2007) Multi-sited ethnography as a middle range methodology for contemporary STS. *Science, Technology, and Human Values* 32 (6): 652–671.

Intergovernmental Panel on Climate Change (2005) *IPCC Special Report on Carbon Dioxide Capture and Storage*. New York: Cambridge University Press.

Intergovernmental Panel on Climate Change (2007) *Climate Change 2007: Impacts, Adaptation and Vulnerability*. Cambridge, UK: Cambridge University Press.

Intergovernmental Panel on Climate Change (2015) *Climate Change 2014 Synthesis Report*. Geneva, Switzerland: IPCC.

Johnsson, F. (2011) Perspectives on CO_2 capture and storage. *Greenhouse Gases: Science and Technology* 1 (2): 119–133.

Kinsella, W. J., Kelly, A. R. and Kittle Autry, M. (2013) Risk, regulation, and rhetorical boundaries: claims and challenges surrounding a purported nuclear renaissance. *Communication Monographs* 80 (3): 278–301.

Klein, N. (2014) *This Changes Everything: Capitalism vs. The Climate*. New York: Simon & Schuster.

Krauss, W. (2009) Localizing climate change: a multi-sited approach. In: Falzon, M. A. (ed.) *Multi-Sited Ethnography: Theory, Praxis and Locality in Contemporary Research*. Abingdon, UK: Ashgate, 149–164.

Krauss, W. (2011) Migratory birds, migratory scientists, and shifting fields: the political ecology of a northern coastline. In: Coleman, S. and von Hellerman, P. (eds) *Multi-Sited Ethnography: Problems and Possibilities in the Translocation of Research Methods*. New York: Routledge, 146–160.

Latour, B. (1988) *Science in Action: How to Follow Scientists and Engineers through Society*. Cambridge, MA: Harvard University Press.

Latour, B. and Woolgar, S. (1986) *Laboratory Life*. Princeton: Princeton University Press.

Lindlof, T. R. and Taylor, B. C. (2010) *Qualitative Communication Research Methods*, 3rd edition. Thousand Oaks, CA: Sage Publications, Inc.

Lorenz-Meyer, D. (2011) Locating excellence and enacting locality. *Science, Technology and Human Values* 37 (2): 241–263.

Middleton, M. K., Senda-Cook, S. and Endres, D. (2011) Articulating rhetorical field methods: challenges and tensions. *Western Journal of Communication* 75 (4): 386–406.

Senda-Cook, S. (2012) Rugged practices: embodying authenticity in outdoor recreation. *Quarterly Journal of Speech* 98 (2): 129–152.

Shepherd, G. J. and Rothenbuhler, E. W. (2000) *Communication and Community*. Mahwah, NJ: Lawrence Erlbaum.

Taylor, C. A. (1996) *Defining Science: A Rhetoric of Demarcation*. Madison: University of Wisconsin Press.

Tomski, P., Kuuskraa, V. and Moore, M. (2012) *US Policy Shift to Carbon Capture, Utilization, and Storage Driven by Carbon Dioxide Enhanced Oil Recovery*. Washington, DC: The Atlantic Council.

US Department of Energy (2008) *2008 Carbon Sequestration Atlas of the United States*, 2nd edition. Washington, DC: US Department of Energy.

Yoon, S. (2014) Biggest emitter China best on climate, Figueres says. *Bloomberg*, 14 January. Online, available at: www.bloomberg.com/news/2014-01-13/top-global-emitter-china-best-on-climate-change-figures-says.html.

5 How reductive scientific narratives constrain possibilities for citizen engagement in community-based conservation

Leigh Bernacchi and Tarla Rai Peterson

Understanding relationships between scientific and lay discourses

This chapter stems from a desire to understand the relationship between conservation narratives circulating among formally recognized scientific experts and those circulating among the lay public. We were especially interested in clarifying how lay publics interpret and apply scientific narratives within their communities, and how this constricts or expands possibilities for community participation in biodiversity conservation. Public participation in conservation management arguably lends to improved democratic acceptance, contribution and creative and cooperative solutions (Peterson *et al.* 2007; Senecah 2004). To better understand this process, we studied the public interpretation and adaptation of scientific narratives around the whooping crane (*Grus Americana*) in its winter range along the central coastal bend of Texas (USA) (see Figure 5.1). We define environmental communication as the socio-symbolic representation of environment, with the caveat that symbolicity does not render communication immaterial. Second, we follow Peterson *et al.*'s (2007) and Callister's (2013) interpretation of Leopold's land community, which explicitly includes both human and *extrahuman* residents. Although this study focuses on communication between humans, it is important to recognize the possibility of communicative interaction with extrahuman members of the community. Members of this community are social actors (Latour 2004) who sometimes require spokespersons (Peters 1999) to communicate their needs and desires to other members of the community. All have the potential to modify each other's experiences and consequences.

The study builds from the tradition of Wynne (1992) and others who have followed his approach to public understandings of science (Blok 2007; Locke 1999) in that we are primarily interested in improved understanding of the lay public's knowledge, but we do not privilege it as somehow better than formalized scientific knowledge (Durant 2008). As Eden (1996) observed, "the role of science can still be critical, if not determinant, in the more 'participatory' model ... because of the political and cultural demand for scientific rationality" (p. 190). Rather than comparing or contrasting traditional

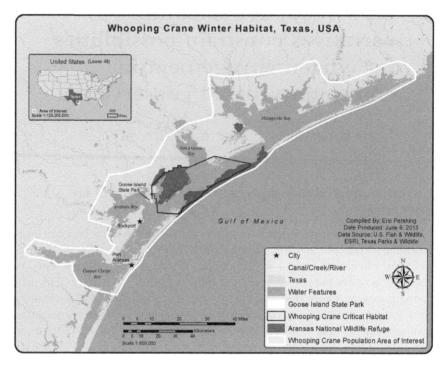

Figure 5.1 Whooping crane habitat in wintering grounds, Texas, USA (source: map by Eric Pershing, 2015; adapted from Aransas National Wildlife Refuge, 2010).

Note: Whooping crane winter habitat includes bays, bayous, freshwater ponds, affected by development, freshwater inflows, precipitation, barrier islands and sea level. The boundaries of designated critical habitat and Aransas National Wildlife Refuge are protected public lands

scientific and lay approaches to knowledge about conservation, for this chapter we explored communicative interactions between community residents and scientists who are responsible for conservation in the region. By paying attention to how members of the lay public talk about scientific knowledge, we sought to discover unrealized opportunities to construct positive community involvement in biodiversity conservation.

We have drawn our descriptions of expertise from an abundant literature on personal experience, local ecological knowledge (Abram 1996), and expert knowledge (Collins and Evans 2007). We adapted Collins and Evans's (2007) *periodic table of expertise* to inform three forms of expertise: personal experience, social expertise and subject expertise. No single type of expertise is garnered without interacting with the others, and that interplay depends upon participating individuals, audiences and available discursive formations. Though expertise and knowledge are not necessarily learned for rhetorical ends, we observed how expertise was exercised as a rhetorical device and affected interpretations of what could and should be done on behalf of extra-human nature. Considering the situation from a classical rhetorical perspective, we found that personal experience often functioned as an appeal to ethos, lending credibility to those with direct observations; social expertise functioned as pathos, appealing to the sympathetic and emotional aspects of trust; and subject expertise typically functioned as an appeal to Logos, or claims of logic and objectivity (Killingsworth 2005).

In this chapter, we first summarize the chapter's conceptual framework which is centred on relationships between scientific expertise and opportunities for community participation in policy development and implementation. Second, we explain our research methods. We rely on a qualitative case study of the land community (Callister 2013) surrounding the whooping crane's winter habitat to explore how multiple types of scientific expertise are woven into a scientific narrative that interacts with public participation. We identify the scientific narratives used to describe the endangered whooping crane and its habitat needs. We report our findings of how these narratives influenced public narratives about viable options for managing the species and associated habitat. Finally, we discuss potential interpretations of those findings and their implications for deeper community participation in biodiversity conservation.

We chose to focus on a community that juxtaposes humans with whooping cranes, because the challenges faced by the denizens of this community exemplify many of the concerns that emerge in biodiversity conservation efforts across Earth. Endangerment in the United States is legally defined by the Endangered Species Act (ESA) as "any species which is in danger of extinction throughout all or a significant portion of its range" (Stanford Environmental Law Society 2001, p. 46). The whooping crane was designated as endangered in 1967 under the predecessor of the current ESA, the Endangered Species Preservation Act of 1966, and remains listed because it is in danger of extinction in its only wild population due primarily to the likelihood that "human population growth will continue to reduce and degrade its suitable migration and winter habitat" (USFWS 2009). Although many endangered species remain relatively unknown to the public, the whooping crane illustrates charismatic endangered species that garner significant public interest and support (Leader-Williams and Dublin 2000), if only by virtue of its large size, distinctive call, and life history characteristics such as life-long monogamous partnering and 5,000-mile migration (Audubon Nature Institute, Gulf Coast Bird Observatory). The threat of species endangerment and extinction is directly tied to concerns about loss of biodiversity.

Approaches to scientific knowledge

In science and technology studies (STS) literature, scientific knowledge generally is assumed to be communicated and verified through three mutually informing and inextricable, yet different, processes: personal experience; social expertise; and knowledge about a subject, or subject expertise (Collins and Evans 2007, Petts 1997). Although personal experience can be organic, individualized and visceral, to be valued as a form of scientific expertise it also must include an explicitly noted rigor that comes via participation in appropriate reference groups and in-depth study of a subject. Social expertise refers to the trust that emerges when someone is seen as authoritative because of established patterns of interacting with others – both fellow experts and lay persons. Subject expertise refers to formalized knowledge about something. All three interact to establish what is considered valuable knowledge.

Although Bruno Latour (1999, 2004) and subsequent STS scholars have done much to destabilize a simplistic view of science as all-knowing, simply adding the term "scientific" to one's statement or claiming to have followed the scientific method continues to confer "some kind of merit or special kind of reliability" (Chalmers 1999, p. xix), within management, legal and lay public discourses. Chalmers (1999) argues that, although claims of being based on facts, or sensory calculations, have generated a belief that science simply represents reality, reflexive scientists admit that reality is immediately translated into "statements", and therefore pinned to the Procrustean bed of theory and prior experience. Contributory knowledge is then constructed by the formulation of these statements. And, Chalmers notes, "it [is] the statements that constitute the facts" (p. 10). Scientific expertise, in all three forms, therefore, hinges more directly on conceptual frameworks than evidence. Returning to Collins and Evans' discussion of science, they suggest scientists take a reflexive perspective on knowing something as real, while not being completely separated from that thing; arguing that scientists' "raw material is expertise mixed with experience" (p. 9). We now explain our interpretation of the three types of scientific knowledge identified by Collins and Evans.

Personal experience

In this study, we conceptualize personal experience as inclusive of senses, perceptions and observations. Phenomenologically, the individual body organizes information collected by the senses (Abram 1996). Yet personal experience is more than bodily experience: materiality and constructivism interact in the formation and validation of scientific expertise.

Understanding the nature of personal expertise requires awareness of external materiality, personal experience and interactions between both. People of all socioeconomic and geographic situations engage with their environments, acting as naturalists, consumers and tourists. Research about local ecological knowledge (LEK) and traditional ecological knowledge (TEK) shifts attention from externally imposed scientific methods to how people encounter extrahuman nature or the more-than-human world (Abram 1996; Durant 2008; Young and Matthews 2007), and how extrahuman nature encounters humans (Callister 2013). Invocation of phenomenological knowledge of conservation may be seen as an attempt to wrest power from formalized scientific control over democratic decisions, expanding the truncated decision space available to lay persons (Peterson 1997). We see explicitly valuing personal experience as one means for deconstructing an exclusionary conservation community, to make way for a more inclusive community that welcomes multiple and diverse members. Via John Dewey, Brown (2009) suggests that the experience of individuals living in a place, motivated by knowledge of what is true in their reality, is critical to any democratic decision-making process.

Individual experience gains relevance through its communication (Collins and Evans 2007), and when that communication is overwhelmingly skewed by failure to legitimize some participants, it can lead to malformed community. As Fischer (2000) explains:

> Because of the fundamental differences in the legitimacy and power of their respective languages – technical versus everyday language – the interaction between the technocratic planners and the members of the local community tends to give shape to an unequal communicative relationship, or what Habermas has described as "distorted communication".
>
> (p. 18)

This distortion is exacerbated as bureaucratic regimes impose regulations on speech, truncating communication by sanctioning who gets to speak and, more importantly, how they may speak and legitimately exercise influence (Senecah 2004). Upon moving from the visceral and individual worlds to the political sphere, personal experience necessarily translates into language and in each step, loses more connection to its direct referent (Latour 2004). The changing of personal experience to fit public participation structures established through national legislation is particularly truncated: language and experience are codified immediately for acknowledgement and response. Reinforced by the legislated structures of public participation, personal experience is simplified and coded as a collective set of preferences for a management plan. In this way, personal experience is often rendered disjunctive from where it was formed through body–place interactions (Jamal and Hollinshead 2001).

Social expertise

Collins and Evans further discuss how personal expertise merges into social expertise, explaining that "popular understanding of science is also transmissible from one person to another to a certain extent – transmissible as a set of ideas rather than a set of formulae" (2007, p. 20). Arguably, audience is the most central aspect of this communication process. Social expertise understands the social norms, appeals to the audience's preferences, respect, trust and other emotions, and in turn provides some level of validity to an otherwise abstracted and impersonal subject expertise. In this way social expertise enables subject expertise to be relevant and persuasive. For example, popular media scientists like Bill Nye the Science Guy and Crocodile Hunter Steve

Irwin have mastered social expertise, and enjoy a platform through which to share their subject expertise (Brown 2010).

Social expertise is engendered through social interactions, primarily supported by belief in the ethos of the expert, and sometimes, regardless of technical knowledge. Although in-group pressure to perform expertise socially varies across cultures (Yuan *et al.* 2013), charismatic scientists are able to lead responses to environmental problems because they have gained acceptance, trust and respect in their communities. Social expertise can be won through developing a positive ethos: belonging to the affected community (Rogers 2003); maintaining racial and gendered status quo (McCright and Dunlap 2011); and providing celebrity support for issues contributes positive valence to both personal and subject expertise (Brown 2010).

Most of what people know is through relationships with others. Arguing that "truth is based on trust", Devereux (2013) argues that, since the environment "goes beyond any one of us, and thus beyond the experience of any one of us, we must rely on social relations and their environmental knowledges to transcend these gaps and gulfs of space and time" (p. 227). The democratic and phenomenological nature of experiencing the extrahuman world is inherently too large to construct individually, and thus environmental knowledge is entrusted to experiences that occur relationally (Carolan and Bell 2003).

Collins and Evans (2007) separate social expertise into interactional and contributory expertise. Interactional expertise is the capacity to communicate as if one is an expert on a subject, while contributory expertise is the capacity to add knowledge to the subject through research. The two function together, with interactional experts honing their expertise through spending time and learning to value what has been established as worthwhile via the discourse of contributory experts.

Scientists can enhance their social expertise by performing functions that community residents who have demonstrated interest and active involvement in conservation practices and decisions request (Lach *et al.* 2003; Peterson *et al.* 2004). For example, active stakeholders frequently ask scientists working for NRM agencies to define and explain the available decision space (Daniels and Walker 2001). In our case, the active stakeholders clearly stated their desire for formally trained ecologists to explain how they integrated science into decisions about management of whooping cranes.

Subject expertise

Subject expertise refers to the third type of expertise that is important to constructing inclusive conservation communities, and addresses having in-depth knowledge about a subject. Similarly to social expertise, subject expertise emerges both through interaction with other members of the community and through contributing new knowledge to the topic of conservation. Interactional subject experts can participate fully in the language of the specialist domain, and contributory subject experts communicate their expertise by publication in peer-reviewed journals, obtaining research funding from scientific foundations and other demonstrations of their acceptance by existing hierarchies in the scientific establishment.

Much of scientific communication consists of validating other scientists' subject expertise, along with their own. The process of validating and verifying one's subject expertise happens through training experience; speaking and writing about the topic among peers of similar calibre and focus; and adhering to the rigorous and established rules of data collection, analysis and interpretation.

Scientific communication of those practices, both internally and externally directed, is truncated for a variety of media that cannot fully express the process of knowledge building (Latour 2003). For example, internal communication is run through the sieve of specificity for professional journals, and external communication is minimized to dualities of truth/falsehood when moderated by legal proceedings and simplified to soundbites for public consumption. Although subject experts are careful to clarify that they seek to alleviate, rather than eliminate, uncertainty, this simplification contributes to unrealistic expectations that certainty should emerge from science. While satisfying such expectations is problematic for any environmental concerns, in cases where scientists are charged with managing the recovery of endangered species, neither biological processes nor policy decisions wait for certainty to emerge. Social studies of science have largely employed an intersubjective and constructivist framework for critiquing the notion of scientific objectivity, focusing on the symbolicity and interactions of scientists, rather than science. In doing so, much of their research concentrates on the social components and interactions.

Collins and Evans' (2007) contribution is unusual in that they attempt "to treat expertise as real and substantive" (p. 2). From their perspective, subject expertise describes real knowledge of a topic, established through a variety of trainings, experiences and interactions. Eventually subject expertise becomes second nature, and is exercised unreflexively by the expert. For example, one need not consciously consider the physics involved with tires contacting the road in order to be a good driver. Similarly, when doing science, subject experts do not necessarily consider every step of the scientific method when seeking new knowledge. They assimilate experience, social norms and their deep knowledge of the subject to contribute to that new knowledge.

Heuristic processing of scientific expertise

In a classic psychology study, Chaiken (1980) described heuristic processing, or the cognitive process whereby people judge the validity of information. She found that people "rely on typically more accessible information such as the source's identity or other non-content cues" (p. 1387). When Manfredo *et al.* (2008) applied Chaiken's work to a wildlife-related issue, they found that respondents could identify only one reason for voting a certain way on a controversial amendment regarding wildlife trapping. They concluded that, "in heuristic processing, a thorough assessment of consequences is abandoned in favour of a more simple approach to forming an attitude and behaviour" (Manfredo *et al.* 2008, p. 35). Similarly, Li (2008) found that persuasive information was only persuasive to those who are "sufficiently motivated or have sufficient cognitive resources" to engage in argumentation. Numerous media analyses have found that not only do audiences find messages that corroborate existing beliefs to be more credible, but people also choose to watch and listen to media they expect to echo pre-existing beliefs, and avoid media they expect to do otherwise (Feldpausch-Parker *et al.* 2013).

Conservation biologists must demonstrate both subject and social expertise because they are making claims, based on science, about both what *is* happening and about what *should* be done about it. As practitioners of a self-designated crisis discipline (Soulé 1985), they must synthesize scientific knowledge into practicable projects for species, habitats and permits. Rather than existing separately, their personal experience, their subject expertise and their social expertise transform each other. Personal observations and the structure of scientific narratives fit into and around each other. People who disagree with a dominant scientific narrative often are excluded from discourse about a politically or communally salient topic because they do not operate within the recognized communicative structure (Haraway 1988).

As Latour (1999) has shown in tracking the isolations of measurements in ecology, and as Collins and Evans (2007) contend, "Any redescription of events in the core of science, even when it is designed for a professional audience, is bound to simplify; when the description is for a popular audience, it will simplify more brutally" (p. 21). In this way, scientific communication is most expansive when it is for an audience of peers, but even then it will exclude aspects of the research being discussed. Further interaction between internal science communication and communication intended for the lay public leads to additional simplification and reduction, which means that both the quantity and quality of opportunities to participate in the conservation community are reduced.

In Chapter 8, Hansen and Peterson discuss the importance of developing a genuinely deliberative public debate that is accessible to all members of the polity. As they note, one of the most fundamental contributions Habermas (i.e. 1984, 1987) offers for constructing expanded environmental communication communities is an analysis of how crucial communicative competence (Hymes, 1966) among community members is, especially those who desire to act as agents of change.

Especially when coupled with the various forms of expertise described in this chapter, heuristic processing helps explain how a simplistic scientific narrative may take root within a group and limit the possibilities for policy development by mitigating against the development of new perspectives that could challenge existing beliefs. When a simplistic, parsimonious explanation is available, audiences are more likely to select it as correct and to employ it to guard against the instability that comes with change.

Methods

Our primary resource for this case study was a set of semi-structured interviews with people who were directly involved in crane conservation. We augmented the transcripts with court testimony and decision (from *The Aransas Project* [TAP] v. *Bryan Shaw* 2010), planning documents developed by international and national organizations responsible for crane recovery, and reports of scientific studies on the land community of interest. In accordance with Texas A&M University's Institutional Review Board for Human Subjects (IRB 10–0355), all names have been changed to preserve the confidentiality of our informants.

We developed an interview approach within the paradigm of privileging individual truths rather than attempting to determine a single truth (Lincoln and Guba 1985). We conducted informant-directed interviews (ranging from 45 minutes to three hours in length) with 35 people involved in whooping crane conservation. Their relationships with whooping cranes varied widely, including experiencing them as objects of scientific study, management responsibility, economic stimulus, local icon and symbol of the natural world. Interviews were digitally recorded, transcribed and then analysed with NVivo10.0 qualitative software (QSR International, Doncaster, Victoria, Australia).

To obtain informants, we employed snowball sampling, and also garnered informants through web searches and articles found in local media. Most informants ($n = 22$) lived in communities surrounding the area where whooping cranes spend the winter. Others worked with government agencies or environmental organizations that are responsible for the management of natural resources that affect the cranes. Agencies, educators, business owners and non-profit organizations represent some of the most important sectors to crane conservation.

We analysed these texts to discover how scientific narratives appear to empower and constrain options for community participation in whooping crane conservation. We used emergent coding of the interview transcripts to guide a qualitative thematic analysis. After an initial coding, we further categorized all claims of scientific knowledge. We ran analyses with respect to their sources of information, and relationships to different community members. The results section presents the narratives of scientific knowledge that emerged. Quoted extracts are identified by a unique number.

Results

Dominant scientific narrative

The predominant response to our queries about whooping cranes was the statement that cranes are dependent upon the blue crab (*Callinectes sapidus*) as a food source. At the time of this analysis, many residents were concerned about a season with unusually high rates of crane mortality. They associated this and previous die-off events of the crane population with drought years, especially the winter of 2008–2009, and with concurrent blue crab population declines under low freshwater inflow conditions. The narrative that cranes rely on blue crab as the most crucial protein source, combined with concerns about salinity levels determined by freshwater inflows as a critical constraint on the crab population, is well established (Canadian Wildlife Service and USFWS 2006). As we learned, the formal scientific claims have carried into the public realm; having been publicized in posters from the International Crane Foundation, featured in news stories and Whooping Crane Festival presentations, and having provided the basic premise for two lawsuits. The results we report here illustrate ways community members expressed this narrative and how personal experience, social expertise and subject expertise contributed to their understanding of the narrative.

The precise origin of the dominant scientific narrative is difficult to pinpoint because scientists, research institutions, industry and government agencies have examined the bay system over time – to differing ends. For example, a 1990 lawsuit sought to purchase instream water rights for whooping cranes (17). And another manager said, "I think it was the mid-90s when I said to Tom Stehn, 'we need to be thinking about freshwater inflows and crabs'" (29). For this analysis, however, we were more interested in identifying and exploring contemporary producers, supporters and dissenters of this narrative.

The causal relationship of low freshwater inflows negatively affecting whooping cranes was clearly explicated by all informants. Some stated it scientifically:

> The whooping cranes are endangered and without crab they can't make it, and with these two dry years, then the whooping cranes have to have crab. They have to have the river flowing to have the right pH factor for the crabs to survive and reproduce.
>
> (20)

Informants referred to the diets of cranes and their dependence on blue crab with absolute confidence: "the crab is an important food source for cranes", "the major food source", and "a staple for their food" (3, 5), and "it's an enormous amount of blue crab. It's not a little – it's not a few blue crab" (9). Informants shared information about crab habitat requirements less assuredly, but many described the importance of freshwater and cycling to the bay ecosystem as a whole. Through media coverage, listserv emails, and the unofficial Aransas National Wildlife Refuge (NWR) crane report, that 23 cranes had died had become common knowledge (7, 27 and 30).

We found that scientists and managers described complementary variations of the dominant narrative. The wildlife managers charged with the state, federal and international responsibilities presented this narrative in planning documents:

A simple inverse relationship exists between blue crab catch rates and mean salinity within an estuary. Inflows are already at times insufficient and reduced over historic levels, leading to increases in mean salinity and decreases in blue crabs, the primary food of the whooping cranes.

(Canadian Wildlife Service and USFWS 2006, p. 21)

Citing whooping crane specialist and Aransas NWR biologist, Tom Stehn, the comprehensive planning document for Aransas NWR states, "The whooping crane's primary food source (blue crabs), are directly affected by lack of freshwater inflows, which in turn may affect whooping crane survival" (Aransas NWR 2010, pp. 4–15). As per National Environmental Policy Act (NEPA) requirements, the United States Fish and Wildlife Service (USFWS) responded to public comment on the plan. The nutritional value of blue crabs emerged as a central issue of concern among the public comments to the Aransas NWR comprehensive conservation plan. "With respect to whooping cranes, there is concern that reductions in freshwater inflows into San Antonio Bay and outflow through Cedar Bayou may severely affect the blue crab population, which is a critical food source for whooping cranes" (Aransas NWR 2010, pp. 2–16).

Personal experiences in support of the dominant scientific narrative

Many respondents had personal experiences connected to the heuristic of the dominant scientific narrative. Local informants observed strange behaviours and changes in distributions of the tall, white, conspicuous bird during drought years, and correlated it to the health of the bay and estuary system. During drought, established human residential areas became homes for cranes, because "there was nowhere for them to go eat, and they didn't have any more territory" (27). Respondents also observed declines in the blue crab populations during the drought years. While guiding daily fishing trips through the bays, fisher people observed lower numbers of blue crabs than expected:

Well, see, I make my living fishing in water about that deep [holds up hand to show about 6 inches].... And the last three years, because of the drought, I mean, you can fish all day and not see one [blue crab].

(24)

When the drought broke and rain flooded the watershed, the relationship between water and crabs was reconfirmed for informants. As one exclaimed, "there are thousands and thousands of blue crabs, little ones, quarter sized" (13).

The focus on blue crabs was not universal among our informants. Many identified with the USFWS stated goal of increasing the total population of cranes as part of the effort to recover this species. They discussed the need for more crane habitat (both terrestrial and marine) and risks posed by increased interaction with humans. In response to the question, "What do you think are the most important things that need to happen for crane survival?" one informant immediately declared, "Habitat, habitat, habitat" (26). Though development had coincidentally declined at the same time as the crane population, property was difficult to acquire for conservation. A developer had recently outbid a local conservation organization for a key piece of property that would have provided excellent crane habitat. Some informants followed the report of the recent transactions with an explanation that losing coastal habitat is particularly risky, since natural processes chew at existing land. Others acknowledged the threats of climate change to the narrow peninsulas. "You have to have habitat for the population to grow into. So protection, preservation of good habitat for them to expand their range is critical" (14).

Social expertise in support of the dominant scientific narrative

Unless drought drives whooping cranes into close proximity with human residences, personal experience with whooping cranes is limited due to the birds' secretive nature, limited number and difficult terrain of their preferred habitat. Community members rely on tourism, fishing and management boats and planes for information about cranes. Informants attributed their understanding of the ecosystem to interactions with trusted community members who have lived in the area or invested in its conservation for many years, often generations. Many of the boat tour guides had been trained by other boat guides in the area. Some of them spoke of connections with the late Connie Hagar, a trusted lay public ornithologist and regional conservationist (4, 20). In addition to person–person reports, the community also relied on trusted networks of newsletters and listserv emails (25). Although this information did not pass through rigorous peer review in the scientific sense, due to the connectedness of the community, it served as a social expertise form of peer review.

Social expertise includes knowledge by proxy: in addition to lay public validated observations, community members gained information about the cranes through social interaction with local, often charismatic, fisheries and wildlife managers. Instead of scientific reports, individual scientists, often identified by name, were a direct source for information about cranes and crane–crab–water causative narratives. Familiarity with practising scientists was common, given that Texas A&M University, Texas State University, and University of Texas have centres that conduct research in the region. Two individuals noted "good coastal estuary program professors" and the Mission-Aransas National Estuary Research Reserve (9, 17). These experts gained credibility through their social status and years spent interacting with other community members. Many named wildlife and fisheries refuge managers and scientists who had worked on landmark management of natural resources in the area for decades, and others named scientists who visited as experts on cranes, usually at the annual crane festival, "where anybody who knows anything at all about whooping cranes and their habitat; they show up there" (4).

Tom Stehn, a local biologist for the USFWS (now retired), was named by 16 informants as their primary resource for tourist interpretation (2), management of habitat and supplemental feeding (26), distributions (11), counting methods (13), and connecting with larger scale crane conservation efforts (6). Stehn, who was often referred to as "Mr. Crane", had worked at Aransas NWR for more than 30 years. He conducted a census of the population annually and shared the results, along with supporting material in a report available via email so the community would know when the report came out and be aware of the practice of collecting data (2, 25 and 15). In a region where residents have long expressed active hostility to the USFWS and other federal agencies, our informants placed unique faith in Stehn: "I think the cranes function very well. Except for Tom Stehn, I believe if the federal government will leave them alone they would function a lot better" (7). In contrast to Stehn's willingness to share information with the entire community, one informant noted, "the regional USFWS leaders were very quiet about this. I mean, 23 cranes died" (28). Many respondents regularly reported their crane and habitat observations to Stehn (2, 13), reinforcing the social nature of science.

An information source such as Stehn has the potential to serve as an outspoken proponent of the dominant scientific narrative from his privileged status as a formally trained biologist. He explained why the crane status was so markedly poor during the drought years, mostly focusing on low levels of crabs:

> On today's flight, an unusually high 52 cranes were on unburned uplands, 4 were on the C14 refuge burn, 13 were in open bays, two were at a game feeder south of the Big Tree on Lamar, and 182 (72 per cent) were in salt marsh. Blue crabs are at extremely low levels and the cranes are having to look for other sources of food. This is a very stressful time of winter for the whooping cranes.
>
> (TAP 2010)

In these publicly available reports, Stehn rarely included direct references to controversial water issues, those citing him often juxtaposed the lack of crabs with low freshwater inflows (Aransas Project 2010).

Eventually his perspective was collected during his testimony in one of the court cases related to whooping crane conservation, with payment for his expert witness fee split equally between both the plaintiff and the defence to avoid appearance of bias (Berryhill 2012). Here he made use of his social expertise, with an emotional appeal that connected with sympathetic community members: "I know these cranes ... I've been watching some of the same ones since 1982. I hate to be – what's the word? – anthropomorphic, but it's almost like they're my kids out there" (Stehn quoted in Berryhill 2012; *TAP* v. *Bryan Shaw* 2010). Further quotations in newspaper and press releases presented appeals to logic and reason. For example, "still, Mr. Stehn worries that insufficient water flows in the future could shrink the size of the flock, by far the largest in the world and the only one left that migrates without human help" (TAP 2010) and, "one likely cause for the population decline could be changes in habitat, Stehn said. A drought in Texas severely affected the whooping crane's foods of blue crabs and berries" (Fisher 2009).

Subject expertise in support of the dominant scientific narrative

Social expertise provides a bridge between personal experience and subject expertise by motivating people to listen to the subject expert and link what they hear to their personal experience. For example, one local landowner who wanted to make his property into appealing habitat for whooping cranes expressed his appreciation for the deep knowledge and reflexive expertise shared by subject experts:

> We spent a good part of the day, them educating me about ... what kind of habitat cranes require during their wintering time here. Tom [Stehn], in his infinite wisdom, having worked with cranes probably most of his adult career, began to hold court and tell us here is an area I know cranes are using on the refuge or on pre-existing or existing conserved and pro-tected land. And here's some areas where there are cranes setting up ter-ritories every year.
>
> (11)

Among the wisdom shared was a warning about the need to trim back the brush in order to minimize predation. Our informant said he had been dubious about this suggestion until

> a bobcat ran out of the brush and flew in the air and caught a whistling duck in its mouth,... and I show up right after that happens and I'm thinking, "Boy, Tom Stehn is so much on his game. He's so smart. I'm gonna be right out there and trim that brush tomorrow".
>
> (26)

We heard several similar stories, where informants' personal experience had validated Stehn's subject expertise.

As is always the case in science, some subject experts disagreed with the dominant scientific narrative. We offer the *San Antonio Guadalupe Estuarine System* (SAGES) report as a representative anecdote for alternative narrat-ives. SAGES found that, although whooping cranes eat blue crab, they have a much more diverse diet than had previously been claimed. Further, they found an inverse relationship between freshwater inflows and crab abun-dance, which directly contradicted the dominant narrative. Only four of our informants directly discussed the report by name, and they lived outside of the study area. Their understanding was that it reported "when blue crab population is not as robust, the cranes will go eat snails or clams or other things" (22). Partly because of its potential to influence Texas state politics, the study became a central point of argument in the state's ongoing legal battle over water.

Bolstering the dominant scientific narrative through the legal system

Together, the Guadalupe-Blanco River Authority, San Antonio River Authority, San Antonio Water System and Texas Water Development Board manage watersheds that provide water for two of Texas' largest cities, where the majority of their constituents and water consumers live. Because increased water consumption in these cities and their surroundings directly decreases freshwater inflows into San Antonio Bay, they have an interest in reducing support for the narrative that whooping cranes rely primarily on blue crab for protein, and that increased salinity leads to decreases in the blue crab population. These water management organizations funded the SAGES study, which found that "blue crab abundance tends to increase with bay salinity", and "that the diet of whooping crane is varied and included blue crabs, wolfberry fruit, clams, snails, and insects" (Slack *et al.* 2009, p. vi). SAGES was presented as evidence that the Texas Commission on Environmental Quality (TCEQ) did not need to mandate increased freshwater inflow into San Antonio Bay, thereby allowing upstream water users to continue existing practices.

In 2010, The Aransas Project (TAP) brought suit against the TCEQ for mismanagement of water allocations and illegal take of the endangered whooping cranes that had died during the most recent drought year (*TAP* v. *Bryan Shaw* 2010). The lawsuit provided a public platform for debate of the validity of the dominant scientific narrative, presenting a duality between those who accepted the dominant narrative (plaintiff) and those who supported the SAGES findings (defendant).

Both the social and subject expertise of those who contributed to SAGES was systematically dismantled through the trial. For example, the trial led to the discovery that field technicians who collected the data for SAGES had received no training and that the poor quality of images used to support findings about the cranes' diet precluded their value for identifying whether the cranes were eating (much less *what* they were eating) or engaging in other behaviours (Days 2 and 6, *TAP* v. *Bryan Shaw* 2010). The SAGES lead scientist's social expertise suffered further when he responded to questions about a claim he had made in the report with, "I just made it up" (*TAP* v. *Bryan Shaw*, p. 213).

Stehn's census methods had been criticized as outdated and, while his unusually long tenure as lead biologist at Aransas NWR had endeared him to the local community, it ran counter to established USFWS practice (Berryhill 2012). Despite his strong social expertise, the prosecution chose not to use Stehn as their chief expert witness, and instead brought in Dr Felipe Chavez-Ramirez, an internationally respected scientist working with the International

Crane Foundation, to provide evidence that supported the dominant scientific narrative (*TAP* v. *Bryan Shaw*, 2010). The main story to emerge from the lawsuit was the strong connection between whooping cranes and blue crabs, with equally relevant issues such as habitat destruction and water policy taking a back seat.

Throughout the time of the lawsuit, local residents demonstrated their personal concern by seeking relief for the cranes. They talked about inventing ways to deliver blue crab to the cranes, move the cranes to where the crab were), and grow more blue crab. One informant suggested the health of the crane population would improve "if we can find a food that will replenish them like a blue crab, the protein in blue crab, and put it where they're feeding now", or "get the blue crab to go where they're [cranes] feeding now more" (7). Another informant was looking into aquaculture as a way to farm-raise blue crab for cranes (6).

Some claimed personal experience with observing enforced changes in the whooping crane diet personally: "They eat anywhere from 80–90 blue crab a day, and there's not any there today. They're eating out of deer feeders now" (7). Deer feeders, used to attract deer to hunting areas, supply corn, which is a food commonly eaten by whooping crane during migration. But a diet of too much corn can lead to malnutrition: "it would be like you and I eating steak and potatoes every day, and then all of a sudden you're just getting food supplements and artificial food" (5). The USFWS and Texas Parks and Wildlife Department (TPWD) reinforced the narrow focus on blue crab as the limiting factor for whooping crane populations by cooperating to extend the no-crabbing zone, with "no objection by the crab-fishing community" (3).

Discussion

In many ways, the dominant scientific narrative was unifying, providing a focal point where the community came together to meet the perceived needs of the crane and acted in solidarity regarding perspectives that seemed to attack their local perspective. Within this knowledgeable, responsive community, the crane–crab heuristic is useful as a starting point. At the same time, it stifles creative interpretations that might focus on other relevant dimensions of the situation, such as water policy and habitat encroachment.

Our findings also support Chaiken's (1980) claims about how heuristic processing may oversimplify perceptions of reality. This may seem counterintuitive, given that heuristics are intended to encourage investigation (Harper 2013). On the other hand, Chaiken (1980) explains that under a "heuristic view of persuasion, recipients exert comparatively little effort in judging message validity: rather than processing argumentation, recipients may rely on more accessible information such as the source's identity or other non-content cues in deciding to accept a message's conclusion" (p. 752). This approach to processing communication simplifies complex, dynamic interactions, and in this case it simplified crane conservation and being about animals that rely on blue crabs. This simplified heuristic of a food chain limits options for management, and the general understanding of this complex ecosystem.

In this case, challenges to the dominant scientific narrative were communicated overtly through the SAGES report and TCEQ's claims that freshwater inflow was not critical for crane recovery. This could have opened up the discussion to include habitat concerns, including but not limited to water quantity. The ESA includes requirements to designate critical habitat for animals listed as endangered, but this aspect of whooping crane conservation did not receive emphasis within the existing heuristic, which was largely limited to discussion of dietary limitations on the crane population. The narrowness in the dominant scientific narrative meant that many possibilities for community constructivity were ignored. This seems particularly problematic, given that habitat is generally agreed to be the most severe limitation to conservation, and the community where we conducted our interviews is vigorously supportive of conservation. Our informants introduced no ideas for obtaining additional habitat or increasing the quality of existing habitat for whooping cranes. When we introduced the topic, few followed up on it. Instead, they talked about sites they had lost or their wish that cranes would make more use of the habitat they had provided.

By limiting whooping conservation to the availability of blue crab, something that, at least for the present, local conservationists have little ability to change, the dominant narrative excludes this potentially responsive community from participation in recovery efforts for whooping cranes, beings they regard as neighbours (despite their awareness that anthropomorphizing the birds is frowned upon). Our informants included influential community leaders who have power and expertise to influence local development through means such as zoning, habitat preservation efforts, and alternative economic growth models. This community of educated, politically savvy, conservationists has been caught in heuristic processing that unnecessarily limits its potential. Any way of seeing also is a way of not seeing, and dominant narratives or heuristics are difficult to change. Still, we remain hopeful that, through vibrant efforts to reconstitute what it means to be a conservation-oriented community, some of the currently buried options for action may be excavated.

Conclusion

In this chapter we sought to demonstrate how public participation in biodiversity conservation interacts with scientific narratives to constrain possibilities for community-based conservation, and also to identify ways that different forms of expertise come together around an environmental issue. We maintain that all individuals bring their personal experience to their interpretation of science, and this experience is the most basic building block for community-based expertise. Further, these individual experiences interact to form social expertise, which, in turn, shapes how community members will interpret and value subject expertise. Our case illustrates the urgent need to recognize the complexity of any scientific narrative, and the importance of recognizing that narratives have multiple uses that may be (but are not necessarily) complementary. Recognizing this complexity could be a first step toward encouraging experimentation with public participation structures that support multiple forms of knowing.

As for heuristics, we do not intend to claim that they necessarily lead to reductive responses that limit community involvement in biodiversity conservation; merely that over-reliance on established heuristics is likely to mask many of the nuances that matter to community members who share an environment with non-domestic beings. There are many ways to represent cranes and the habitats and communities in which they live. Perhaps future opportunities for management toward species recovery could be expanded by strategic integration of multiple ways of knowing these extrahuman residents of Earth.

Acknowledgements

We are grateful for financial support from the US Fish and Wildlife Service, the Tom Slick Senior Graduate Fellowship at Texas A&M University; Nancy Payne for editing; and to informants who shared their perspectives and experiences with us.

References

Abram, D. (1996) *Spell of the sensuous.* New York: First Vintage Books.

Aransas National Wildlife Refuge (2010) Comprehensive conservation plan and environmental assessment. US Fish and Wildlife Service, Aransas National Wildlife Refuge Complex, Austwell, Texas.

Audubon Nature Institute (2014) Audubon animals: whooping crane. Online, available at: www.auduboninstitute.org/animals/whooping-cranes/whooping-crane-1949.

Bernacchi, L. A., Ragland, C. J. and Peterson, T. R. (2015) Engaging active stakeholders in implementing community-based conservation: whooping crane management in Texas, USA. *Wildlife Society Bulletin* 39: 564–573.

Berryhill, M. (2012) Crane man. *Texas Monthly.* Online, available at: www.texasmonthly.com/story/crane-man.

Blok, A. (2007) Experts on public trial: on democratizing expertise through a Danish consensus conference. *Public Understanding of Science* 16: 163–182.

Brown, M. B. (2009) *Science in democracy: expertise, institutions, and representation.* Cambridge, MA: MIT Press.

Brown, W. J. (2010) Steve Irwin's influence on wildlife conservation. *Journal of Communication* 60: 73–93.

Burchell, K. (2007) Empiricist selves and contingent "others": the performative function of the discourse of scientists working in conditions of controversy. *Public Understanding of Science* 16: 145–162.

Callister, D. C. (2013) Land community participation: a new "public participation" model. *Environmental Communication* 7: 435–455.

Canadian Wildlife Service and US Fish and Wildlife Service (2007) Whooping Crane Eastern Partnership: International recovery plan whooping crane (*Grus americana*). Online, available at: www.bringbackthecranes.org/technicaldatabase/recovery/recoveryplan2007.htm (accessed 4 April 2014).

Carolan, M. S. and Bell, M. M. (2003) In truth we trust: discourse, phenomenology, and the social relations of knowledge in an environmental dispute. *Environmental Values* 12: 225–245.

Chaiken, S. (1980) Heuristic versus systematic information processing and the use of source versus message cues in persuasion. *Journal of Personality and Social Psychology* 37: 1387–1397.

Chalmers, A. F. (1999) *What is this thing called science?* (3rd edition). Indianapolis, IA: Hackett Publishing Company.

Collins, H. M. and Evans, R. (2007) *Rethinking expertise.* Chicago, IL: University of Chicago Press.

Collins, H. M. and Evans, R. (2002) The third wave of science studies: studies of expertise and experience. *Social Studies of Science* 32: 235–296.

Corbett, J. B. (1995) When wildlife make the news: an analysis of rural and urban north-central US newspapers. *Public Understanding of Science* 4: 397–410.

Daniels, S. E. and Walker, G. B. (2001) *Working through environmental conflict: the collaborative learning approach.* Westport, CT: Praeger.

Davies, C. S. (1986) Life at the edge: urban and industrial evolution of Texas, frontier wilderness: frontier space 1836–1896. *Southwestern Historical Quarterly* 89: 443–554.

Devereux, E. (2013) Traditional ecological knowledge: learning from the landscape. *Archaeology Online.* Online, available at: http://archaeologyonlinejournal.wordpress.com/vol-1-no-1-september-2013/traditional-ecological-knowledge-learning-from-the-landscape-emma-devereux/.

Durant, D. (2008) Accounting for expertise: Wynne and the autonomy of the lay public actor. *Public Understanding of Science* 17: 5–20.

Eden, S. (1996) Public participation in environmental policy: considering scientific, counter-scientific and non-scientific contributions. *Public Understanding of Science* 5: 183–204.

Feldpausch-Parker, A., Ragland, C. J., Melnick, L. L., Chaudhry, R., Hall, D. M., Peterson, T. R., Stephens, J. C. and Wilson, E. J. (2013) Spreading the news on carbon capture and storage: a state-level comparison of US media. *Environmental Communication* 7: 336–354.

Fischer, F. (2000) *Citizens, experts, and the environment: the politics of local knowledge.* Durham, NC: Duke University Press.

Gulf Coast Bird Observatory (2014) 5,000 miles, round trip. Online, available at: www.gcbo.org/default.aspx/MenuItemID/326/MenuGroup/1000+Whoopers.htm.

Habermas, J. (1984 [1981]). *Theory of communicative action volume one: reason and the rationalization of society.* McCarthy, T. A. (trans.). Boston, MA: Beacon Press.

Habermas, J. (1987 [1981]). *Theory of communicative action volume two: lifeworld and system: a critique of functionalist reason.* McCarthy, T. A. (trans.). Boston, MA: Beacon Press.

Hansen, Anders (2010) *Environment, media and communication.* New York, NY: Routledge.

Haraway, D. (1988) Situated knowledges: the science question in feminism and the privilege of partial perspective. *Feminist Studies* 14: 575–599.

Harper, D. (2013). *Online etymology dictionary.* Online, available at: www.etymonline.com.

Hymes, D. H. (1966) Two types of linguistic relativity. In: Bright, W. (ed.) *Sociolinguistics*. The Hague: Mouton. 114–158.

Jamal, T. and Hollinshead, K. (2001) Tourism and the forbidden zone: the underserved power of qualitative inquiry. *Tourism Management* 22: 63–82.

Killingsworth, M. J. (2005) *Appeals in modern rhetoric: an ordinary-language approach*. Carbondale, IL: Southern Illinois University Press.

Kim, J. N. and Grunig, J. E. (2011) Problem solving and communicative action: a situational theory of problem solving. *Journal of Communication* 61: 120–149.

Lach, D., List, P., Steel, B. and Shindler, B. (2003). Advocacy and credibility of ecological scientists in resources decisionmaking: a regional study. *BioScience* 53: 170–178.

Latour, B. (1999) *Pandora's hope*. Cambridge, MA: Harvard College.

Latour, B. (2004) *Politics of nature: how to bring the sciences into democracy*. Cambridge, MA: Harvard University Press.

Layzer, J. A. (2008) *Natural experiments: ecosystem-based management and the environment*. Cambridge, MA: MIT Press.

Leader-Williams, N. and Dublin, H. T. (2000) Charismatic megafauna as "flagship species". In: Entwistle, A. and Dunstone, N. (eds) *Priorities for the conservation of mammalian diversity: has the panda had its day?* Cambridge, MA: Cambridge University Press, 53–81.

Leopold, A. (1949) *A Sand County almanac and sketches from here and there*. London: Oxford University Press.

Li, X. (2008) Third-person effect, optimistic bias, and sufficiency resource in Internet use. *Journal of Communication* 58: 568–587.

Lincoln, Y. S. and Guba, E. (1985) *Naturalistic inquiry*. Newbury Park, CA: Sage Publications.

Locke, S. (1999) Golem science and the public understanding of science: from deficit to dilemma. *Public Understanding of Science* 8: 75–92.

Manfredo, M. J., Fulton, D. C. and Pierce, C. L. (2008) Understanding voter behavior on wildlife ballot initiatives: Colorado's trapping amendment. *Human Dimensions of Wildlife* 2: 22–39.

McCright, A. M. and Dunlap, R. E. (2011) Cool dudes: the denial of climate change among conservative white males in the United States. *Global Environmental Change* 21: 1163–1172.

Pernecky, T. and Jamal, T. B. (2010) (Hermeneutic) Phenomenology in tourism studies. *Annals of Tourism Research* 37: 1055–1075.

Peters, J. D. (1999) *Speaking into the air: a history of the idea of communication*. Chicago, IL: University of Chicago Press.

Peterson, M. N., Allison, S. A., Peterson, M. J., Peterson, T. R. and Lopez, R. (2004) A tale of two species: habitat conservation plans as bounded conflict. *Journal of Wildlife Management* 68: 743–761.

Peterson, M. N., Peterson, M. J. and Peterson, T. R. (2007) Environmental communication: why this crisis discipline should facilitate environmental democracy. *Environmental Communication* 1: 74–86.

Peterson, T. R. (1997) *Sharing the Earth*. Raleigh, NC: University of South Carolina Press.

Petts, J. (1997) The public–expert interface in local waste management decisions: expertise, credibility and process. *Public Understanding of Science* 6: 359–381.

Polly, K. (2012) Whooping crane lawsuit threatens continued water delivery in Texas. Guadalupe-Blanco River Authority. Online, available at: www.gbra.org/documents/litigation/April_2012.pdf.

Rahn, M. E., Doremus, H. and Diffendorfer, J. (2006) Species coverage in multi-species habitat conservation plans: where's the science? *BioScience* 56: 613–619.

Rogers, E. M. (2003) *Diffusion of innovations* (5th edition). New York, NY: Free Press.

Senecah, S. (2004) The trinity of voice: the role of practical theory in planning and evaluating the effectiveness of environmental participatory processes. In: Depoe, S. P., Delicath, J. W. and Elsenbeer, M. A. (eds) *Communication and public participation in environmental decision-making*. Syracuse, NY: State University of New York Press, 13–33.

Slack, R. D., Grant, W. E., Davis, S. E., Swannack, T. M., Wozniak, J., Greer, D. and Snelgrove, A. (2009) *San Antonio Guadalupe estuarine system: linking freshwater inflows and marsh community dynamics in San Antonio Bay to whooping cranes*. Online, available at: www.twdb.state.tx.us/publications/reports/contracted_reports/doc/0704830697_SAGES.pdf (accessed 20 November 2014).

Slack, R. D., Grant, W. E., Davis, S. E., Swannack, T. M., Wozniak, J., Greer, D. and Snelgrove, A. (2010) Comments, responses, executive summary. Online, available at: www.gbra.org/studies/default.aspx.

Soulé, M. E. (1985) What is conservation biology? *BioScience* 35: 727–734.

Stanford Environmental Law Society (2001) *The endangered species act*. Stanford, CA: Stanford University Press.

The Aransas Project (TAP) (2010) Online, available at: http://thearansasproject.org/whooping-cranes/tom-stehns-jan-21-whooping-crane-census-reports-one-chick-dead-and-a-lack-of-food/.

The Aransas Project v. *Bryan Shaw*. Case No. 2:10-cv-075 (2010) Memorandum and opinion. Expert testimony transcriptions. Online, available at: www.blackburncarter.com/BC/TAP_v_Shaw.html.

Ungar, S. (2000) Knowledge, ignorance and the popular culture: climate change versus the ozone hole. *Public Understanding of Science* 9: 297–312.

United States Fish and Wildlife Service (USFWS) (2009) Spotlight species action plan: whooping crane. Online, available at: http://ecos.fws.gov/docs/action_plans/doc3055.pdf.

United States Fish and Wildlife Service Southwest Region (2014) Ecological services: habitat conservation plans and incidental take permits. Online, available at: www.fws.gov/southwest/es/austintexas/ESA_HCP_FAQs.html.

Wiens, J. A., Stralberg, D., Johnsomjit, D., Howell, C. A. and Snyder, M. A. (2009) Niches, models and climate change: assessing the assumptions and uncertainties. *Proceedings of the National Academy of Sciences, USA, 106*, 19729–19736.

Wynne, B. (1992) Misunderstood misunderstanding: social identities and public uptake of science. *Public Understanding of Science* 1: 281–304.

Yearley, S. (2000) Making systematic sense of public discontents with expert knowledge: two analytical approaches and a case study *Public Understanding of Science 9:* 105–122.

Yoon, C. K. (2009) *Naming nature: the clash between instinct and science*. New York: W.W. Norton & Company, Inc.

Young, N. and Matthews, R. (2007) Experts' understanding of the public: knowledge control in a risk controversy. *Public Understanding of Science* 16: 123–144.

Yuan, Y. C., Bazarova, N. N., Fulk, J. and Zhang, Z.-X. (2013) Recognition of expertise and perceived influence in intercultural collaborations: a study of mixed American and Chinese groups. *Journal of Communication* 63: 476–497.

Modes of organizing – instantiating community through structural means

6 Community conversations on conservation

A case study of Joint Forest Management in East Sikkim, India

Paulami Banerjee

Introduction

The Joint Forest Management (JFM) programme in India is defined as a "concept of developing partnerships between fringe forest user groups and the Forest Department (FD) on the basis of mutual trust and jointly defined roles and responsibilities with regard to forest protection and development" (TERI, undated: 1). Since its inception under the National Forest Policy 1988, JFM has increasingly been recognized as a powerful tool for sustainable forestry management in India. Based on the principles of "care and share" (WBFDCL, undated), the primary objective of JFM is to provide local communities with active roles and meaningful opportunities in the management and protection of forests, and to share the benefits derived from these forests. As of 2005, the total forest area under JFM was estimated to be around 214,300 km², with 99,000 Joint Forest Management Committees (JFMCs), involving over 13.8 million families across 28 states throughout India (Sudha and Ravindranath, 2004; Vemuri, 2008). Despite claims of successful implementation of the programme since its inception in the early 1990s, JFM in India continues to face challenges. In response to various administrative, ecological, institutional, political and technological barriers, JFM has been driven by external donors, rather than by local communities, and has been oriented toward ecological targets to the near exclusion of social concerns (Murali *et al.*, 2000). By marginalizing the needs and desires of the human communities, JFM may be ensuring short-term success, but endangering programme sustainability.

In this chapter, I critically analyse how livelihoods and identity politics shape interactions between local communities and forests, focusing on implications for JFM in Sikkim, India. By "communities", I mean spatially connected groups of people sharing common interests. I further demonstrate how JFM in Sikkim has often functioned as an agent of community destruction, and suggest that an iterative dialogue process may enable JFM proponents to alter this trajectory to modify JFM as a contributor to more sustainable communities.

To provide a context for understanding and evaluating participatory forest management in India and its implications on the socio-cultural context and

nature of JFM in the state of Sikkim, I first summarize the evolution and performance of JFM in India, including the history of organized forestry management, and the adoption and functioning of the JFM programme in
Sikkim. I then describe the ethnographic research methods used in the study.
Following which, I provide a detailed analysis of interviews and focus group
discussions with forest fringe communities and forest department personnel to
characterize the multiple symbolic meanings that nature and environment
take on, and their implications on the functioning of JFM in the state. The
results of the study demonstrate that participatory forest management outcomes are often undermined by (1) differences of opinion between forest
users and resource managers about the benefits derived from forest conservation and management; (2) failure of the state to understand how relations and
structures of power influence and shape the politics of everyday life within
the context of participatory forest management in Sikkim; and (3) lack of
opportunities for residents of forest fringe communities to meaningfully participate in deliberations on JFM.

The context: JFM in India

The origins of community-based natural resource management (NRM) in
India can be traced back to the Arabari Experiment, 1971, and the Sukhomajri integrated watershed management project, 1975. The Arabari experiment
was undertaken by forest fringe communities of the Arabari Forest Range,
Midnapore, West Bengal, to re-establish, manage and protect degraded *Sal*
(Shorea robusta) forests (Sudha and Ravindranath, 2004). This experiment
was one of the earliest attempts by a state forest department to directly engage
locals in the co-management and protection of forests. In exchange for their
participation, the villagers were allowed to collect fuel wood and fodder from
the forests at an ecologically sustainable rate, and had rights to 25 per cent of
the profits arising from timber sales. The Arabari experiment was successful in
promoting greater transparency, accountability and equitability in the forest
management process, leading to mutual trust and better understanding
between the state forest department and the local communities. The success
of the Arabari experiment led to the implementation of the West Bengal
Social Forestry Project in 1981 and, consequently, efforts were taken to
organize forest-based communities into village forest protection committees
(FPCs) in five districts of South West Bengal, India (Balooni, 2002; Harrison
and Ghose, 2000; Roy, 1992; Sudha and Ravindranath, 2004; WBG, 2007).

Another successful attempt at community-based NRM in India during the
1970s was the Sukhomajri Project initiated in Sukhomajri, Haryana (Sudha
and Ravindranath, 2004). The project was a collaborative endeavour between
the villagers, the Chandigarh Forest Department, the Central Soil and Water
Conservation Research and Training Institute (CSWCRTI), Chandigarh and
the Ford Foundation to promote rainwater harvesting and soil conservation
techniques alongside forest regeneration in catchment areas. With the active

involvement of the villagers in every stage of the integrated watershed management programme, the Sukhomajri project, over the course of the next two decades, became one of the most successful community-based NRM initiatives in India (Sudha and Ravindranath, 2004).

The success of the Arabari and the Sukhomajri projects as decentralized, bottom-up approaches to NRM ushered in a new era in India's forest management regime. The National Forest Policy, 1988, launched the JFM programme in India, whereby, the state governments were directed by The Ministry of Environment and Forests (MoEF), Government of India, to create a "massive people's movement" through the active participation of village communities for the re-establishment, management and protection of degraded forests (Sudha and Ravindranath, 2004: 3). It was hoped that JFM as a people's project would empower local communities by making them an integral part of environmental decision-making processes, minimize conflicts between the locals and the forest department, and allow for the sharing of benefits derived from the co-management and protection of forests.

Since its adoption in the early 1990s, JFM in India has undergone progressive changes to make the programme more inclusive of the sustenance and livelihood needs of local forest users, along with greater involvement of local communities, state forest departments, and environmental NGOs in the planning, implementation and monitoring of the programme (Sudha and Ravindranath, 2004). The JFM Guidelines 2000 and 2002 were regarded as positive steps towards institutionalizing and strengthening the JFM programme in India. With the aim of strengthening community participation, the key focus of the JFM Guidelines 2000 were on the participation of women, the preparation of micro plans, giving legal status to JMFCs, setting up village forest committees (VFCs), conflict resolution committees, and the monitoring and evaluation of the JFM programme. The JFM Guidelines 2002 emphasized on further strengthening the role of local communities in JFM, building strong relationships with the Panchayats, signing a memorandum of understanding (MOU) between JFMCs and the state forest department, and the inclusion of provisions for the collection of non-timber forest products (NTFPs) in the JFM working plans (Sudha and Ravindranath, 2004).

Brief evaluation of JFM in India

The JFM programme in India has mostly been evaluated on its ecological, economic, and institutional impacts, with less emphasis given on supporting and encouraging interconnectedness between humans and other inhabitants of the forests. Evaluations on ecological impacts mostly dealt with JFM's impacts on biodiversity (Ravindranath and Hall, 1995), forest cover (Ostwald, 2000), production of NTFPs (Hill and Shields, 1998), biomass and density of trees (APFD, 2001; TERI, undated), harvesting of plantations, forest fires (Gupta, 2003), forest regeneration and survival (PRIA and Samarthan, undated; TERI, undated; WBG, 2007). Research on economic impacts focused primarily on economic incentives for timber sales (KFD, undated), biomass productivity (Hill and Shields, 1998; TERI, undated), production and marketing of NTFPs (TERI, undated) and livelihoods (Gupta, 2003). Institutional assessments of JFM included the spread of JFM throughout the nation, the legal status of JFM, institutional structure and networks (APFD, 2001; Blunt *et al.*, 1999; Gupta, 2003; Rao *et al.*, 2004; TERI, undated), functions of JFMCs (TERI, undated), implementation of JFM policies in the states (TERI, undated) and capacity building (PRIA and Samarthan, undated). Despite claims of its widespread success, critics have expressed doubts about the effectiveness of JFM as a community-based, forest management programme, and question the ecological, economic and institutional parameters used by government and donor agencies to measure the success of JFM in the country. According to Rao *et al.* (2004), most of the JFM evaluations were undertaken by state forest departments, the MoEF, and donor agencies, and often neglected the perspectives of community members, thereby, presenting only a partial view of its overall performance.

Assessments of the ecological impacts of JFM revealed that most of the regenerated forests comprised exotic firewood species with a relatively low percentage of timber as well as non-timber species, resulting in the decline of biodiversity over the years (Murali *et al.*, 2002a; Ravindranath and Hall, 1995). Higher species diversity was often reported in those forests managed outside the purview of JFMCs, particularly in community forestry systems managed by local residents using traditional forest management and silvicultural practices (Rai *et al.*, 2000; Ravindranath *et al.*, 2000). According to Murali *et al.* (2002a), for JFM to have any significant impact, there is a need to adopt an "integrated village ecosystem", where not just forests, but all land-use categories (including village common lands and private lands) are included and managed according to site-specific plans. According to Murali *et al.*, site-specific plans would lead to "adaptive forest management", whereby decisions on forest regeneration, biomass productivity, species varieties and extraction strategies of forest products are made based on the subsistence and commercial needs of the local communities (ibid., p. 527).

Assessments of the economic impacts of JFM on local livelihoods showed less than favourable outcomes. According to Sarin (1999), the failure of JFM to incorporate the subsistence needs of the rural poor increased the economic differences between the poor and their wealthier counterparts. Profits from the collection and sales of NTFPs were mostly appropriated by middlemen, traders and the rural elite groups, at the cost of the marginalized groups (Sarin, 1999; Vemuri, 2008).

JFM in India also has been widely criticized on institutional grounds. Kumar (2002) argued that JFM failed to adequately involve marginalized people, as membership to JFMCs was often restricted to elected members of the *gram panchayat* or village council, who mostly represented the views of the dominant class. The limited success of JFM has also been attributed to the failure of the government to devolve power and control at the desired levels. Ravindranath *et al.* (2000) point out that JFMCs failed to emerge as autonomous institutions, with decision-making authority remaining in the hands of the state forest departments. Most of the JFMCs registered under the forest departments had no legal identity. While villagers were entrusted with the duties of protecting the forests, forest departments retained control over the planning and implementation of working plans, revenue collection, allocation of funds and other important management decisions. According to Kapoor (2001), organizational hierarchy within JFMCs hindered bottom-up participation, resulting in political and administrative barriers. Despite the modifications to the JFM policy in 2000 and 2002 mandating the inclusion of women and poor landless villagers in VFCs, very little was changed in terms of overall implementation. Lack of opportunities to meaningfully participate in the management and protection of forests often compelled marginalized villagers to engage in unlawful activities against the forest department (Vemuri, 2008).

For JFM to be successful as a bottom-up participatory forest management programme, Rao *et al.* (2004) call for the adoption of a "multi-institutional approach" that considers the perspectives of all concerned stakeholders in the JFM process (p. 30). According to Khare *et al.* (2000), as orientations of forest policies change over time, one needs to take into account the competing claims and relative influences of the key stakeholder groups. They further argue that policy debates tend to stereotype people into apparently homogenous groups, failing to account for the heterogeneity within these groups. The ultimate aim, therefore, should not only be to capture the authenticity of diverse viewpoints, but also to formulate and implement policies that recognize all viewpoints.

Conservation context: Sikkim, India

Nestled in the Eastern Himalayas, the state of Sikkim is surrounded by the Tibetan Plateau in the north, Bhutan in the east, West Bengal in the south, and Nepal in the west (see Figure 6.1).

The total forested area in Sikkim of 3,359 km², accounts for 47.3 per cent of its total geographical area (FEWMD, 2007). One of the most densely forested areas in the country, Sikkim is also the least populated state in India, with only 0.02 per cent of the country's total population (Government of India, 2011; JICA, 2009). The state's population is almost entirely rural (91 per cent), and many depend heavily on forests for their livelihoods. The Forest, Environment and Wildlife Management Department (FEWMD) of Sikkim, has administrative control over 81 per cent of the total geographical area of the state (FEWMD, undateda; JICA, 2009) (See Figure 6.2).

As the greenest state in India (SikkimFirst.in, 2013), Sikkim boasts a historically sustainable natural resource conservation paradigm in conjunction with steady economic development. The state's success in the fields of NRM, wildlife protection, environmental sustainability and economic development earned Sikkim the first and second positions (among low population density states in India) in the *States Sustainability Competitiveness Report 2011* (IFC,

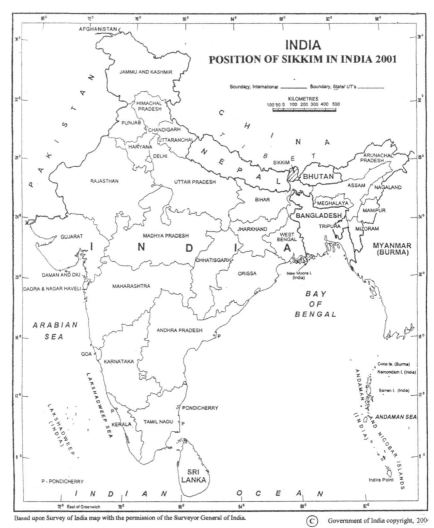

Figure 6.1 Location of Sikkim in India (source: Census of India 2001; District Census
Handbook, Part XII-A & B; Series 12-Sikkim).

2011) and *Environmental Sustainability Index 2009* (IFMR, 2009), respectively. Sikkim ranked highest in India's *Green Protection Index* (0.903) in 2004 (Sethi, 2004). The state was also recognized as the top performer in the country in *Performance in Land Use 2008*, and *Conservation of Natural Resources 2009* (FEWMD, undated b), and is home to the "Greenest Chief Minister of India", whose conservation paradigm "not growth *versus* green but growth *with* green" calls for a greener Sikkim through people's participation (FEWMD, 2009; FEWMD, undated a; Government of India, 2013).

Modern forest management in Sikkim

The origins of modern forestry management in Sikkim date back as far as 1909 under the ruler Sidkeong Tulku, the tenth Chogyal of Sikkim. Considered the "father of forestry" in Sikkim, Sidkeong Tulku was instrumental in bringing the forests of Sikkim under an organized body, and in undertaking the surveying and demarcation of forests on a scientific basis. As the kingdom of Sikkim was not directly under the British Colonial Administration, the administrative and managerial control of forests rested with the landlords directly under the Chogyal until 1947. The year 1905 saw the demarcation of "Reserve Forests", classified as forests not under human occupation, and where "no rights and concessions exist". In 1911, isolated patches of forests within the villages, and forests along the fringes of reserved forests and villages were delineated as "*Khasmal*" and "*Goucharan*" forests. *Khasmal* forests were those where people had rights to a free supply of timber and firewood after obtaining formal permission from the forest department, while *Goucharan* forests were demarcated as those where local people had rights to graze their cattle and collect firewood and fodder (FEWMD, 2009). A forest manual was adopted in 1914 that categorically stated the functions of the forest department regarding forest administration and management. In 1952, the first cadastral survey in Sikkim was undertaken to officially demarcate revenue and forest lands, in which cultivated lands were recorded in the name of their owners, while lands not under the ownership of any individual were recorded as Reserved, *Khasmal* and *Goucharan* forests. These pioneering steps towards organized forestry management under the Chogyals laid the foundations for modern day forest management in Sikkim (FEWMD, 2009).

Sikkim became a part of the Indian Union in 1975, and subsequently the Indian Wildlife Protection Act 1972 and Indian Forest Act 1927 were extended to Sikkim for the protection of its wildlife and forests respectively. Later, the Indian Forest Act 1927 was replaced by the Sikkim Forests, Water Courses and Roads Reserve (Preservation and Protection) Act in 1988. The Forest (Conservation) Act, 1980, was adopted in order to strike a balance between development and conservation, emphasizing on managing the diversion of forested lands for non-forest use (FEWMD, 2009). The year 1995 saw the adoption of "*Harit Kranti Dashak*" (Revolution for a Green Decade) for a "greener Sikkim through people's participation" (FEWMD, 2009).

JFM in Sikkim

The call for community participation in forest management and protection in Sikkim was further strengthened through the adoption of JFM in 1998. It was hoped that the JFMCs, and subsequently the Eco-Development Committees (EDCs), and *Pokhri Sanrakshan Samitis* (Lakes and Wetlands Protection Committees or PSS), which were established as community-based NRM organizations, would promote greater transparency, accountability and equity in forest governance through the decentralization of financial and administrative powers, and would provide meaningful opportunities for rural residents to "enhance their livelihoods through forestry, ecotourism, and other income generation activities" (FEWMD, undated a: 23).

In 2006, the FEWMD, Sikkim, issued notification that each of the 907 village wards in the state were required to establish either a JFMC or EDC, which would be the "nodal agency for all programmes related to forests, land use and environment, medicinal plants, watersheds and wildlife and biodiversity" (JICA, 2009: 19). Each JFMC consists of a General Body (comprising one member from each household in the ward), and an elected Executive Committee (EC). The main duties of the JFMCs include the protection and maintenance of forests and plantations (with an emphasis on monitoring trespassing and grazing activities in JFMC areas), preventing forest theft and helping forest officials prevent and control forest fires. JFMC activities are carried out under the provisions outlined in the National Afforestation Programme (NAP). The NAP mandates the adoption of micro plans prepared with the involvement of local communities. The activities included in the micro plans are: (1) forest plantation and regeneration; (2) entry point activities (EPA) to help create community assets through small-scale assistance; (3) awareness programmes; (4) soil conservation; (5) fencing; and (6) monitoring and evaluation of JFM. Funds are provided to JFMCs by the MoEF, Government of India, through the appointed Forest Development Agency (FDA) in the state (JICA, 2009).

In the years since its adoption, JFM in Sikkim has been proclaimed successful at integrating the livelihood needs of its forest-dependent communities along with the forest conservation and management goals of the state. As of 2009, there were 158 JFMCs established in the state, with provisions for including additional ones in 90 newly created intervention villages, bringing another 3,600 ha of afforested land under the purview of JFMCs by 2015 (FEWMD, 2009, undateda). Despite these claims of success, critical evaluations call for a close scrutiny of JFM in the state of Sikkim (Bhat *et al.*, 2000; Kapoor, 2001; Murali *et al.*, 2002b, 2000; Sarin, 1999).

Methods

Selection of study sites

I conducted the study in the east district of Sikkim; one of the four administrative districts of the state (See Figure 6.2). The east district has a

TIBET

North Sikkim

BHUTAN

NEPAL

West Sikkim

South Sikkim

East Sikkim

Very Dense Forest
Mod. Dense Forest
Open Forest
Scrub

WEST BENGAL

Figure 6.2 Forest cover map of Sikkim (source: India State of Forest Report 2009; Forest Survey of India; online, available at: http://sikenvis.nic.in/write readdata/sd8.pdf).

population of more than 245,040 persons, with the rural population estimated at 78.4 per cent. The total geographical area of the district was estimated to be 954 km², of which the area under forest cover was recorded to be 699 km² (73.27 per cent) in 2011 (FEWMD, 2007; Government of India, 2013). The east district is also home to three wildlife sanctuaries: (1) Fambong Lho Wildlife Sanctuary; (2) Kyongnosla Alpine Sanctuary; and (3) Pangolakha Wildlife Sanctuary – a trans boundary protected area bordering Bhutan, China and Neora Valley National Park (a UNESCO World Heritage site) in West Bengal, India. I focused on 13 JFMCs within the Rongli sub-division of east district, Sikkim. Of the 13 selected JFMCs, nine fall under the territorial jurisdiction of Rongli Range, and four under the jurisdiction of Phadamchen Range (see Table 6.1).

I selected the locales for study on the basis of (1) how dependent the human populations were on forests, and (2) their inclusion under JFM in the east district of Sikkim. Approximately 80 per cent of the population in the selected JFMC intervention villages depend either directly or indirectly on forest resources for their daily livelihoods. As of 2005, the population of the selected villages stood at 21,494 persons, with a total of 4,155 households (DESME, 2005).

Table 6.1 Joint Forest Management Committees (JFMCs) within Rongli and Phadamchen Mountain Ranges, Rongli sub-division, East District, Sikkim, India

JFMCs–Rongli Range	JFMCs–Rongli Range(contd.)	JFMCs–Phadamchen Range
Aritar	North Regu	Gnathang
Chujachen	South Regu	Lingtam
Dalepchand	Rolep	Phadamchen
Kopchey	Rongli	Subaneydara
Lamaten		

Ethnographic fieldwork

I adopted a qualitative, naturalistic inquiry, based on ethnographic fieldwork. The project is grounded in qualitative research principles (Denzin and Lincoln, 2011) and governed by a desire to study material practices in their natural settings, given that my goal was to understand how people construct meanings for their social experiences and to delve deeper into the complexities of their "multiple constructed realities" (Marshall and Rossman, 2006: 53). In an attempt to understand the social context, I spent nine months in East Sikkim during 2010–2012 to identify key informants for interviews and focus groups and to engage in casual conversations with potential informants.

In 2014, I returned to East Sikkim to conduct multi-sited ethnographic research. I lived in East Sikkim that year, and recruited local field assistants to assist with data collection and analysis. Together, we conducted more than 200 interviews (including focus groups) with local residents and other key informants in the 13 selected JFMC intervention villages. I conducted more than 50 additional interviews with *gram panchayat* members and officials from the FEWMD, Sikkim. Furthermore, I undertook participant observation during forest plantation activities and forest evaluation and monitoring activities organized by FEWMD, Rongli Sub-Division, East Sikkim, documenting my experience with thick description field notes (Denzin, 1989).

Data collection

My data collection was driven by the material conditions in these communities. Mostly, I walked the roads and paths of the selected areas, inviting residents I met to participate. Because forest professionals usually had offices equipped with telephones, I made advance appointments to talk with most of them. I adopted Patton's (1990) interview categories: (1) informal conversational interview; (2) general interview guide approach; and (3) open-ended interview for the study. Informal conversational interviews helped me to establish rapport with the selected participants, while open-ended questions enabled me to obtain detailed, uninhibited opinions and viewpoints of the respondents. Participants for the interviews and focus groups were purposively selected to provide variety in role, gender, caste, ethnicity, power and position within the JFM process in Sikkim. When recruiting, I affirmatively sought participation by women and members from racial or ethnic minority groups within the study area. Interviews were conducted in Nepali, Hindi, or English, depending on each participant's choice. Locations for interviews and focus groups were determined according to the convenience and preference of participants. The interviews and focus groups were audiotaped, with the permission of the respondents, and transcribed and translated to English. I used triangulation and informant validation and verification to help identify and manage possible methodological biases and data inaccuracies. The research was conducted in accordance with the requirements of the Institutional Review Board at Texas A&M University (IRB Protocol No. 2012–0327). I obtained oral consent from all parties, and removed names from interview transcripts, replacing them with Arabic numbers. When cited in the text, interview numbers are separated from utterance number by a full stop. For example, the third utterance in the twentieth interview would be designated as 20. 3. In addition to primary data collection, I obtained secondary data from both governmental and non-governmental sources.

Data analysis

Data analysis and interpretation was based on grounded theory (Glaser and Strauss, 1967). Following this approach, I derived analytic categories from the data itself that reflected the interaction between my informants and myself, leading to a deeper understanding of the participants' experiences, both while participating in the study and in the broader context of their lives (Charmaz, 2001). I first read through all interview and discussion transcripts, and compared them with field notes taken during participant observation. After noting incongruities and congruities between the two types of data, I coded the interviews, searching for emergent themes. Categories established through line-by-line and focused coding helped me identify and probe participants' individual perspectives and categorize them into themes.

Findings

The three most common themes to emerge from the analysis of interview and discussion transcripts were:

1   Differences of opinion between local forest users and professional forest managers about the benefits derived from forest conservation and management.
2   Failure of the state to understand how relations and structures of power in everyday life influence and shape the context of JFM in Sikkim.
3   Lack of opportunities for residents of forest fringe communities to meaningfully participate in deliberations on JFM.

Forest conservation and management benefits

Owing to Sikkim's location, varied topography and high annual precipitation, the state is home to more than 4,500 species of flowering plants, over 550 species of orchids, 36 species of rhododendrons, and over 400 species of medicinal plants, making it one of the "richest botanical treasures" of India (FEWMD, undateda). The physical remoteness of this tiny landlocked Himalayan state has created inseparable linkages between forests and people. For these rural, forest-dependent communities of Sikkim, not only are the forests their primary source of livelihood, but are also inextricably linked to their social, cultural, spiritual and emotional wellbeing (JICA, 2009). While the rich floral and faunal biodiversity has historically sustained the rural communities of Sikkim, who have in turn helped preserve and protect forests through accumulated location-specific ecological knowledge (Arora, 2004, 2006), environmental policies in the early 1990s led to the enclosure of forest areas for biodiversity conservation and the protection of natural resources. Elaborating on the impacts of enclosure on his daily livelihood, a villager despairingly commented:

> We have no access to forests,... I have no land of my own, and now I cannot enter the forests. Where will I go now? Whatever little I used to earn by selling milk and curd is now gone. I have no means to buy grass to feed my cow, the only one that's left now. Most of us in this village owned cows as many as 10, 11, but now we have 1 or 2 at the most.
>
> (55. 9)

Prior to forest enclosure, this villager pastured his cows in the forest and, from his perspective, an increase in forest cover offers no immediate benefit. Further, by banning his entry into the forest, JFM has severed his existing connection with the forest. Another informant explained:

> We have derived no benefits from forests since the ban. On one hand we are not allowed to enter the forest to collect grass or firewood, while on the other, we do not get enough work. Yes, the forests are growing, and Sikkim is greener, but we the poor are becoming poorer.
>
> (74. 15)

Poverty, coupled with the lack of access to forest resources, often compelled the villagers to enter the forests illegally to collect firewood, fodder and other minor forest produce. Some villagers admitted taking their cattle inside the reserved forests for grazing, while others admitted to entering the forests to collect highly-valued medicinal plants and selling them illegally. Aware of the logistical impossibility of the strict monitoring of forests by the state forest department, one villager stated:

> I know it is illegal to enter the forests, but what can I do? I need firewood, especially during winter. I sneak in, and so do others who live

close to the forest boundary. It is risky, and if caught, we have to pay a hefty fine, but it is impossible for the department to catch offenders. This is a huge area, miles and miles of forests, and only a few forest guards. No one has yet been caught.

(76. 7)

Admitting the lack of financial and human resources to effectively monitor illegal entries into forests, forest department personnel have shifted their focus from forest boundary policing to "social fencing", whereby locals are encouraged to collectively protect forests and grazing lands through optimal use and self-policing (Chaudhuri, 2013; Mishra and Sarin, 1988). Emphasizing the need to involve local communities in the forest monitoring activities, a JFMC EC member stated:

Physical fencing works no more. What we need is social fencing. People need to be more consciously involved if they want to save the forests. We can stop illegal activities in the forests only if we collectively come forward to help. You cannot just sit at home and expect the government to do everything for you.

(80. 11)

In 2013, Sikkim became the only state in India to have recorded an increase in forest cover over the last two decades. The state forest cover grew from 43.95 per cent in 1993 to 47.34 per cent in 2013 (SikkimFirst.in, 2013). However, while secondary forest cover showed a steady increase, primary forests continued to be depleted due to numerous developmental activities in the state (FEWMD, 2009; Government of India, 2008; Lama, 2001). Studies show that JFM plantation schemes in East Sikkim have so far mostly been unsuccessful in the regeneration of primary oak forests due to a thick undergrowth of quick growing exotic species (JICA, 2009). While the impacts of replacing primary forests with secondary forests of exotic species on Sikkim's biodiversity has not yet been widely researched, global studies show that secondary forests often fail to maintain species biodiversity and other crucial environmental services (Farley, 2007; Farley and Kelly, 2004; Jagannatha Rao *et al.*, 2002; Murali *et al.*, 2002a; Ravindranath and Hall, 1995; Robbins, 1998). One villager verified this when describing the forest plantations undertaken by JFMCs:

Forests are not what they used to be 20–30 years ago. The species are not native to our area. The forest department brings saplings from just about anywhere. The survival rates of saplings are very low. You need to nurture them and undertake regular weeding, but the forest department cares less about these things. Most saplings die within weeks of planting, and those that survive will be of no value to us in the future.

(104. 4)

Although secondary forests of exotic species held little value for this villager, a JFMC Elected Body (EB) member stated secondary forests were important for their quick, regenerative capacities:

> This forest area was considered as degraded land eight years ago, and you would not find a single tree here; but look at this place now, trees all around. We have undertaken massive plantation projects over the years through our JFMC, and have been successful in afforesting Sikkim.
>
> (100. 7)

Planting of non-indigenous species has also resulted in increased threats from wild animals in the forest fringe areas. Forced to leave their natural habitats, animals have taken to foraging the villages, inconveniencing and endangering villagers: According to an irate informant:

> Animals like bears, deer and porcupines do not feed on the non-native species that are being planted in the forests. Lack of food in the forests force the animals to enter our villages and destroy our crops. Porcupines are the worst menace. Twice in three years I have had my crops destroyed by porcupines, and I have not been compensated by the forest department. They ask me to bring a photograph of the animal as a proof. You tell me – is that possible?
>
> (103. 11)

While the state has invested more than ₹10 crore ($100 million) over the past eight years in planting indigenous species of trees, shrubs, fruits, medicinal plants, etc. under the State Green Mission (PTI, 2013), benefits are yet to be realized by the poor, forest fringe communities. As one villager stated categorically:

> I do not know about state policies. There are so many, that I have stopped taking interest in them. The state can have as many missions as they want. We, the poor, have only one mission, to be able to feed our children. Do you know of any state policy that guarantees to benefit our children and protect our forests too? No, there are none. It is an option, and we the poor are more often on the receiving end of such forest conservation policies of the state. Our state is getting greener, but our stomachs are getting thinner.
>
> (83. 16)

To sum up, my informants indicate that JFM does not always have positive outcomes and its benefits are unequally apportioned. While conservation goals focus on protecting nature from people who have been traditionally dependent on forests, local residents are unlikely to perceive significant benefits derived from forest conservation and management. They have seen neither benefits from increased revenue nor from conservation outcomes. From their perspective, JFM has done little to empower poor and marginalized residents of rural, forest-dependent communities of Sikkim.

Community relations and power structures

The importance of understanding social dynamics in participatory NRM initiatives has gained increasing recognition worldwide. Reed *et al.* (2009) claim that the failure of policy makers to pay adequate attention to the interests and relationships among stakeholders often results in biased management decisions and the marginalization of crucial groups, thereby endangering the viability of environmental policies in the long-term. According to Blaikie and Springate-Baginski (2007), forest policy processes cannot be understood without acknowledging the inherent political nature of all forest related issues.

Vemuri (2008) found that hierarchical bureaucracy, which was the quintessence of the exclusion-based forest regime in pre-independent India, prevails in its post-colonial forest management practices, with decision-making authority remaining in the hands of the central and state governments. Sarin (1998), documented how the dominant groups (mostly rural non-poor) that benefitted from the lack of formalized tenure laws and by appropriating control over forest management decisions, further marginalized the poor. Kapoor (2001) notes that attempts to decentralize the management of forests have been severely compromised by administrative complexity and corruption. One informant expressed his displeasure at how JFMCs are constituted and function in Sikkim:

> JFMC EC members should be elected every five years. This is not taking place. The villagers are never involved in the process of selecting committee members. It is an undemocratic process. The current members have been in position since the existence of the JFMC – some for eight to ten years, or even longer. If they are unable to serve the committee, their family members automatically get selected. I say this is wrong. I want to know what happens behind those closed door JFMC meetings.
>
> (88. 22)

On the other hand, one JFMC member justified his stint as a JFMC president for over 11 years as a matter of expediency:

> This is a high altitude border area, a restricted area, and we have to obtain authorizations from the central government to undertake any activities in the forests. By God's grace, I have good rapport with the central government defence and military officers here. We have to work with them in order to preserve and protect the forests. We ask the villagers every five years to elect an Executive Committee for the JFMC.

People decide who gets elected, and we have to abide by their decisions. They say that we will elect those who can help us get benefits through the JFMC. Now, because of my rapport with the military officers, people have re-elected me. This is my second term as the JFMC president. I tell my people I am getting old, elect someone else, but they want me as the president.

(84. 19)

Limited accountability and a lack of transparency in the forest management process have further limited the effectiveness of JFM in Sikkim. A villager described the lack of transparency in the allocation and use of JFM funds:

I have heard from a reliable source that this year the JFMC has received funds to undertake plantations in our village. The year is almost coming to an end now, but where are the plantations? I ask where did the money go? Vanished into thin air? Will I be allowed to check their bank accounts? No. Never! It is none of my business, they would say. The EC members of the JFMC complain that they are not paid for their jobs. I say, who needs a salary from the government when you can make more money this way? I do not trust the committee. I will neither get involved in their activities, nor will allow any of my family members to do so. Who wants to get into this mess after knowing everything?

(41. 16)

A JFMC EC member mentioned his awareness that accusations of financial misappropriations were circulating throughout the area, along with an alleged lack of transparency in JFMC activities, but argued they were not correct:

These allegations are baseless. No money has been sanctioned for plantation activities this year. Check our JFMC account. You will find no discrepancies. Who am I to decide what to do with the funds when they are released from the department? I just follow orders from above. People think we make a lot of money as elected members of the JFMC. In reality we do not. I want to make one thing clear. We are not paid by the department to do this job. No remuneration. This is a thankless job.

(35. 14)

Lack of accountability within the JFM process has also compromised its popularity among forest-dependent communities. As one villager disappointedly stated:

What we say hardly matters because we cannot hold anyone accountable in the forest management committee. I do not think the EC is either answerable or can be held accountable by those right above them, for example, the Range Officer or the Assistant Conservator of Forests.

This individual qualified her remarks by stating that, "the problem is in the system itself". She suggested that, "good examples should be set by those higher up in the ladder, and only then can the followers walk in the right direction". She connected JFM problems with engrained power relationships, noting that, "I sometimes feel bad for the committee people. They may want to do the right thing, but can they ever go against the wishes of the department? Their hands are tied" (65. 22).

Expressing his frustration at the State Forest Department's underlying organizational bureaucracy, a JFM EC member commented:

> It is disheartening to see that JFM has not been very successful in our area. Through our JFMC we try our best to bring in necessary funds for plantations and other related activities into our village so that people can get some employment. But a lot is still needed to make JFM a grand success. Our knowledge is limited, and with this limited knowledge we cannot do a lot. People need to understand this. We need the forest department to train us on how to better manage our JFMCs. We do not have the necessary skills or knowledge to maintain accurate records. Also, we do not have the basic resources like calculators, record books, receipt books, etc. to facilitate these tasks. Time and again our requests for much needed training programmes and funds have fallen on deaf ears. If we go to the RO, he says he cannot do anything, for the powers rest with the officers posted in Gangtok. There have been several occasions where I have procured stationeries for our JFMC out of my own pocket. I have not asked for reimbursement. But I am a poor man and I cannot continue to incur such expenses out of pocket on a regular basis.
>
> (90. 26)

Although some studies have attributed the limited success of JFM to the failure of the government to adequately devolve power and control (Behera, 2003), the devolution of decision-making authority does not necessarily mean that decision-makers will seek to empower local resource users, especially those who are already marginalized by characteristics such as gender, caste, or ethnicity. My informants believed that the government, including JFM personnel, does not understand the importance of ordinary interactions and existing community patterns and power relationships, and that this lack of understanding limits the potential success of JFM in Sikkim.

Participation in deliberations on JFM

Through decentralized community-based management, JFM seeks increased popular participation as a means to resolve disputes emanating from conflicting forest management priorities (Kant and Cooke, 1999). It was hoped that the implementation of JFM through various training programmes, seminars, workshops and meetings would open avenues for better communication between villagers and foresters, reducing the mutual mistrust that has plagued forest departments and forest-dependent communities in the past. While official sources (FEWMD, 2009, undateda) claim that JFM in Sikkim has been successful in integrating the livelihood needs of its rural forest-dependent communities with the conservation and management goals of the state, little has been achieved in terms of providing meaningful opportunities for the local residents to participate in JFM decision-making processes. According to an informant, a lack of access to relevant information about upcoming JFMC meetings has prevented him from participating:

> We never know when or where the meetings are held. If I know in advance I will definitely attend the meetings. I am interested in knowing what is going on in the village, about the funds that have been allocated for plantations, and the projects and schemes sanctioned by the government. But often I hear about the meetings after they have taken place. What is the use of holding such meetings then? I think the committee does this on purpose; if no one is present they can do whatever they want. No one will ever come to know where the funds have gone.
>
> (98. 19)

A JFMC president vehemently protested that,

> Such claims are utterly baseless. How can anyone say that we do not provide them with accurate information about the JFM meetings on a regular basis? Every year we hold at least two General Body (GB) meetings where all villagers, being members of the GB, are invited and requested to actively participate. We have an information officer who is responsible for informing the *gram panchayat* and the villagers about the meetings. The *panchayat* too informs people. Meetings are almost always held in places that are easily accessible by most.
>
> (91. 23)

Another JFMC president commented on the importance of engaging the villagers in JFMC decision-making processes:

> It is necessary to engage the locals in all our activities. All decisions concerning our forests should be made jointly with the people. I cannot decide on my own what needs to be done in order to protect our forests. The villagers have a lot of experience and local knowledge too. Together we can protect our forests.
>
> (91. 19)

While several JFMCs claim to have instituted awareness programmes to encourage active local participation, awareness is only a first step in gaining the trust and confidence of the residents of forest fringe communities.

Although many villagers mentioned their inability to attend JFMC meetings because they lacked information, a lack of trust in JFM officials is another contributor to low levels of participation. As one villager stated:

> What is the use of attending these meetings if what we say never matters? The officials note down our concerns in a copy, and then forget about it altogether. They say they will take necessary actions but they never do. Perhaps, if I were someone influential and important, my problems would have been solved by now. But I am not. Initially, I used to take an active interest in the meetings as I thought it was a platform to express my concerns and problems to the authorities, but now I know better. I have stopped attending these meetings altogether.
>
> (87. 15)

As this informant explained, participation opportunities must be seen as a meaningful part of decision-making regarding how forests will be managed, rather than an empty signifier.

Limitations on participation in decision-making processes on forest management among residents of these forest fringe communities include a lack of awareness, high costs of participation (relative to residents' resources), and a lack of incentives. When coupled with generations of mutual mistrust between forest fringe dwellers and forestry professionals employed by the state, it should not be surprising that JFM has remained far removed from its policy goals of garnering sustained community support for and involvement in the co-management of forests in Sikkim. In this social and political milieu, collaborative NRM is unlikely to be achieved.

Working towards more collaborative management of forests in Sikkim and beyond

The responses from my informants suggest that, in the case of JFM in Sikkim, the most immediate needs are to integrate the plurality of perspectives into policy dialogue and to recognize the ongoing challenges imposed by the differential power dynamics among the residents of these communities. Residents of these communities described a failure of JFM in Sikkim to fully incorporate meaningful participation of local forest resource users. To construct a community that includes both forest fringe dwellers and forest professionals, the JFM programme must take into account a holistic mechanism that recognizes and responds to both the long- and short-term resource needs of the forest dependent communities, as well as the individuals who make up these communities. The likelihood of success for a collaborative resource management programme may be enhanced by recognizing and building upon the differing viewpoints as well as including dynamic collaborative management as a process of understanding the needs, goals and interests of all community members. Through joint and collaborative learning initiatives that encourage and respect interdependence and mutual appreciation among different stakeholders, the JFM programme can work toward its desired conservation outcomes, while also contributing to the livelihoods of those communities dependent on such natural resources.

Achieving JFM's goals as a community-based forest management programme in Sikkim necessitates the recognition of forest-based communities as co-owners and equal partners in forest conservation and management. No collaborative NRM effort can be successful unless trust is established and sustained. Through an ongoing dialogue between different individuals and groups within these communities, there is a greater possibility for the voices of the previously unheard to be heard and respected by others. This would lead to better understanding and respect for each other's perspectives, and recognition of the interdependency among the diverse groups that care about forests. Recognizing and cultivating this interdependency may contribute to an environment conducive to joint learning and working together towards the realization of common goals.

Lessons learned

In a growing effort to address the conflicts and challenges arising out of traditional mechanisms for citizen participation in environmental decision-making, several strategies have been designed and implemented in order to promote collaborative planning and decision-making (Buck *et al.*, 2001; Gray, 1989; Purnomo *et al.*, 2004; Western, 1994; Yaffee and Wondolleck, 2000). Walker (2004) suggested collaborative decision-making, which involves constructive, open dialogue, with an emphasis on learning and the sharing of power between stakeholder groups. Consistent with collaborative management as a dynamic, ongoing process of understanding the needs, goals and interests of each actor group, Buck *et al.* (2001) emphasized social learning, or the encouragement of diverse stakeholder groups to recognize and understand the importance of interdependency and joint working towards common goals and ends. This mutual learning encourages participants to arrive at decisions through interactive, iterative and reflective processes. Highlighting the importance of stakeholder interdependence in collaborations, Gray (1989) pointed out that an increased awareness of interdependence often sparks those who are participating in conflict to seek opportunities that benefit all parties.

All of this research suggests that, for collaboration to succeed, there is a need to build trust among key stakeholder groups and to provide them with the opportunities and resources necessary to come together on a common platform and engage in active interaction and constructive dialogue related to their concerns. Trust, which forms the core of any collaboration, plays a critical role through promoting information sharing, open communication and building relationships through reciprocation (MacKenzie, 2008). By adopting a problem-solving approach that works toward establishing trust and favours discussions, conversations, information sharing and learning, groups can arrive at consensually agreed upon recommendations or workable solutions for their concerns (Daniels and Walker, 2001). The importance of public engagement in the production of substantively and procedurally legitimate natural resource policies is further emphasized by Peterson (2003), who notes that policies that lack social acceptability and broad legitimacy are more difficult to implement and are rarely sustainable.

One key to understanding the complex nature of participatory governance is to assess the level of participation vis-à-vis the inclusivity and the intensiveness of participation. Inclusive participation, according to Malena (2009), is not exemplified by making every individual participate in every policy-making decision, but rather, by ensuring that there is equitable representation of the interests of disadvantaged and marginalized groups. Over time, higher representations from marginalized groups and improved sharing of relevant information between government officials and citizens may evolve into mutual trust and understanding, which leads to more meaningful, intensive and effective forms of public participation.

The degree to which participation may be inclusive and intensive is a complex interplay of varied institutional, organizational, relational and societal-level factors contingent upon context and circumstance. For an in depth analysis of how participatory governance works under specific context and circumstance, it is important to understand that governance practices involve many actors (both state and non-state), each with their own interests, rights and responsibilities. While the literature on participatory governance tends to focus on two primary sets of actors: (1) the state or government; and (2) civil society actors, Malena (2009) points out that these spheres are not homogenous, monolithic entities, but, rather, represent a motley collection of actors and their interests. Further, amidst the state and civil society actors, there is a third set of actors that bridges across government and civil society.

There is an increasing consensus among scholars and practitioners that participatory governance is most effective when state and civil society actors jointly participate in mutually negotiated and agreed upon initiatives, rather than when such linkages and ties are weak or absent. Greater participation by both civil society actors and state actors leads to more accountable, transparent and effective governance processes. Citizen participation may generate quality information based on the needs of marginalized sections of society, which leads to a more informed and appropriate decision-making and policy implementation process. Broadly based participatory governance leads to the empowerment of citizens and "legitimacy, effectiveness, popularity, resources, and political stability for government actors" (Malena 2009: 14).

Recognizing that ongoing natural resource conservation and management processes include both professional resource managers and residents of local communities, collaborative approaches that encourage forest department personnel and local community members to recognize and cultivate their mutual interdependence through an iterative dialogue process can help open up spaces previously controlled exclusively by resource managers to local communities. At the same time, when local community members become regular and respected occupants, political spaces that previously lacked public legitimacy may become legitimate venues for engaging in difficult discussions and reaching policy decisions. Collaborative decision-making opportunities, while not a panacea, can help not only validate public participation, but also transform it from a pro-forma exercise for defending predetermined policy decisions, to one where citizens' inputs and questions influence forest management decisions (Martin, 2007; Peterson, 1997; Senecah, 2004; Walker, 2004). This shift can help construct sustainable communities among the JFM areas of Sikkim, as well as other regions throughout the world that struggle to develop inclusive conservation communities.

References

APFD. (2001) *Joint forest management: forest conservation with people's participation, a saga of success towards Swarna Andhra Pradesh*. Hyderabad: Andhra Pradesh Forest Department.

Arora, V. (2004) *Just a pile of stones! The politicization of identity, indigenous knowledge, and sacred landscapes among the Lepcha and the Bhutia tribes of contemporary Sikkim, India*. Unpublished PhD thesis: University of Oxford.

Arora, V. (2006) The forest of symbols embodied in the Tholung sacred landscape of North Sikkim, India. *Conservation and Society* 4(1): 55–83.

Balooni, K. (2002) Participatory forest management in India: an analysis of policy trends amid management change. *Policy Trend Report*: 88–113.

Behera, B. (2003) *Determinants of sustainable management of natural resources: the case of Joint Forest Management (JFM) in India*. ZEF: University of Bonn.

Bhat, P. R., Rao, R. J., Murthy, I. K., Murali, K. S. and Ravindranath, N. H. (2000) Joint forest planning and management in Uttara Kannada: a micro and macro level assessment. In: Ravindranath, N. H., Murali, K. S. and Malhotra, K. C. (eds) *Joint Forest Management and community forestry in India: an ecological and institutional assessment*. New Delhi: Oxford and IBH Publishing, pp. 48–98.

Blaikie, P. M. and Springate-Baginski, O. (2007) Introduction: setting up key policy issues in participatory forest management. In: Springate-Baginski, O. and Blaikie, P. M. (eds) *Forests, people and power: the political ecology of reform in South Asia*. London, UK: Earthscan, pp. 1–24.

Blunt, M., Fisher, M. J., Mitra, K. and Sarin, M. (1999) *Forestry project: impact assessment report*. Government of Himachal Pradesh Forest Department and British Department for International Development, India: 1–99.

Buck, L., Wollenberg, E. and Edmunds, D. (2001) Social learning in the collaborative management of community forests: lessons from the field. In: Wollenberg, E., Edmunds, D., Buck, L., Fox, J. and Brodt, S. (eds) *Social learning in community forests*. Jakarta: Center for International Forestry Research, pp. 1–21.

Charmaz, K. (2001) Grounded theory. In: Emerson, R. (ed.) *Contemporary field research: perspectives and formulations*. Long Grove, IL: Waveland.

Chaudhuri, T. (2013) From policing to "social fencing": shifting moral economies of biodiversity conservation in a South Indian tiger reserve. *Journal of Political Ecology* 20: 376–394.

Daniels, S. E. and Walker, G. B. (2001) *Working through environmental conflict: the collaborative learning approach*. Westport, CT: Praeger.

Denzin, N. K. (1989) *Interpretive interactionism.* Newbury Park, CA: Sage.

Denzin, N. K. and Lincoln, Y. S. (eds) (2011) *Introduction: the discipline and practice of qualitative research.* Thousand Oaks, CA: Sage.

DESME. (2005) *Socio-economic survey of Sikkim.* Gangtok, Sikkim: DESME.

Farley, K. A. (2007) Grasslands to tree plantations: forest transition in the Andes of Ecuador. *Annals of the Association of American Geographers* 97(4): 755–771.

Farley, K. A. and Kelly, E. F. (2004) Effects of afforestation of a páramo grassland on soil nutrient status. *Forest Ecology and Management* 195: 281–290.

FEWMD. (2007) *Annual administrative report*: Government of Sikkim: Forests, Environment and Wildlife Management Department.

FEWMD. (2009) *Centenary report: 100 years of service, Sikkim forestry.* Government of Sikkim: Forests, Environment and Wildlife Management Department.

FEWMD. (Undateda) *Forestry and environment mission Sikkim 2015.* Government of Sikkim: Forests, Environment and Wildlife Management Department.

FEWMD. (Undatedb) *Tangible results accrued and overall growth.* Online, available at: www.sikkimforest.gov.in/Reports%20and%20Publications/15years/27_Chapter%20 VI%20Results%20pg%20115-1119.pdf.

Glaser, B. G. and Strauss, A. L. (1967) *The discovery of grounded theory: strategies for qualitative research.* Chicago: Aldine.

Government of India. (2008) *Sikkim development report.* New Delhi: Planning Commission, Government of India.

Government of India (2011) *Population census 2011.* New Delhi, Census Organization of India.

Government of India (2013) *Forest and tree resources in states and union territories: Sikkim.* New Delhi: Forest Survey of India.

Gray, B. (1989) Collaboration: the constructive management of differences. *Collaborating: finding common ground for multiparty problems.* San Francisco, CA: Jossey-Bass, pp. 1–26.

Gupta, A. K. (2003) Emergence of second generation issues in operationalizing joint forest management. National workshop on technological innovation and research advancements for application in joint forest management. ICFRE and FAO.

Harrison, S. and Ghose, A. (2000) Small-scale forestry systems in India. In: Harrison, S. R., Herbohn, J. L. and Herbohn, K. F. (eds) *Sustainable small scale forestry: socio-economic analysis and policy.* Cheltenham, UK: Edward Elgar, pp. 165–189.

Hill, I. and Shields, D. (1998) *Incentives for Joint Forest Management in India. Analytical methods and case studies.* Technical Paper 394. Washington, DC, World Bank.

IFC. (2011) *States sustainability competitiveness report.* Online, available at: http://comp etitiveness.in/2011/08/11/press-release-sustainable-competitiveness-report-2011/.

IFMR. (2009) *Environmental sustainability index for Indian states 2009.* Online, available at: www.sikkimforest.gov.in/docs/News%20Clips/ESI2009.pdf.

Jagannatha Rao, R., Murali, K. S. and Ravindranath, N. H. (2002) Joint forest planning and management (JFPM) in Karnataka: current status and future potential. *Wasteland News* 17(3): 14–27.

JICA. (2009) *Preparatory study on integrated project for sustainable development of forest resources in Sikkim.* DWEFM.

Kant, S. and Cooke, R. (1999) Jabalpur District, Madhya Pradesh, India: minimizing conflict. In: Buckles, D. (ed.) *Cultivating peace: conflict and collaboration in natural resource management.* Washington, DC: IDRC, World Bank

Kapoor, I. (2001) Towards participatory environmental management? *Journal of Environmental Management* 63: 269–279.

KFD. (Undated) Economic impact assessment of JFM: Western Ghats Forestry Project. Bangalore: Karnataka Forest Department.

Khare, A., Sarin, M., Saxena, N. C., Palit, S., Bathla, S., Vania, F., Satyanarayana, M. (2000) *Joint forest management: policy, practice and prospects*. London: IIED World Wide Fund for Nature.

Kumar, S. (2002) Does "participation" in common pool resource management help the poor? A social cost-benefit analysis of Joint Forest Management in Jharkhand, India. *World Development* 30(5): 763–782.

Lama, M. P. (2001) *Sikkim human development report 2001*. New Delhi, Government of Sikkim, Social Science Press.

Malena, C. (ed.) (2009) *Building political will for participatory governance: an introduction*. Sterling, VA: Kumarian.

Marshall, C. and Rossman, G. B. (2006) *Designing qualitative research*. Thousand Oaks, CA: Sage.

Mishra, P. R. and Sarin, M. (1988) Social security through social fencing, Sukhomajri and Nada, North India. In Conroy, C. and Litvinoff, M. (eds) *Greening of aid: sustainable livelihood practices*. London: Earthscan, pp. 22–28.

Murali, K. S., Sharma, M., Rao, R. J., Murthy, I. K. and Ravindranath, N. H. (2000) Status of participatory forest management in India: an analysis. In: Ravindranath, N. H., Murali, K. S. and Malhotra, K. C. (eds) *Joint Forest Management and community forestry in India: an ecological and institutional assessment*. New Delhi: Oxford and IBH, pp. 25–58.

Murali, K. S., Murthy, I. K. and Ravindranath, N. H. (2002a) Joint Forest Management in India and its ecological impacts. *Environmental Management and Health* 13(5): 512–528.

Murali, K. S., Rao, J. R. and Ravindranath, N. H. (2002b) Evaluation studies of Joint Forest Management in India: a review of analytical processes. *International Journal of Environment and Sustainable Development* 1(2): 184–199.

Ostwald, M. (2000) *Local protection of tropical dry natural forest, Orissa, India*. Göteborg: Göteborg University, Department of Physical Geography.

Patton, M. Q. (1990) *Qualitative evaluation and research methods*. Newbury Park, CA: Sage.

Peterson, T. R. (2003) Social control frames: opportunities or constraints? *Environmental Practice* 5(3): 232–238.

PRIA and Samarthan. (Undated) *Village resource development programme and eco-development project in Madhya Pradesh: mid-term evaluation of VRDP and EDP in Madhya Pradesh*. Unpublished mid-term evaluation report, New Delhi and Bhopal.

PTI. (2013) Sikkim becomes only state to increase forest cover. *Times of India*. Online, available at: http://articles.economictimes.indiatimes.com/2013-08-18/news/41422618_1_forest-area-forest-cover-sikkim.

Purnomo, H., Mendoza, G. A. and Prabhu, R. (2004) Model for collaborative planning of community-managed resources based on qualitative soft systems approach. *Journal of Tropical Forest Science* 16(1): 106–131.

Rai, A., Nayak, A., Misra, M. R., Singh, N. M., Nayak, P. K., Mohanty, S., Rao, Y. G. (2000) Gadabanikilo – an example of community forest management with a difference. In: Ravindranath, N. H., Murali, K. S. and Malhotra, K. C. (eds) *Joint Forest Management and community forestry in India: an ecological and institutional assessment*. New Delhi: IBH.

Rao, J. R., Murali, K. S. and Murthy, I. K. (2004) Joint Forest Management studies in India: a review of the monitoring and evaluation methods. In: Ravindranath,

N. H. and Sudha, P. (eds) *Joint Forest Management in India: spread, performance and impact*. Hyderabad: Universities Press, pp. 26–40.

Ravindranath, N. H. and Hall, D. O. (1995) *Biomass, energy and environment: a developing country perspective from India*. London: Oxford University Press.

Ravindranath, N. H., Murali, K. S., Murthy, I. K., Sudha, P., Palit, S. and Malhotra, K. C. (2000) Summary and conclusions. In: Ravindranath, N. H., Murali, K. S. and Malhotra, K. C. (eds) *Joint Forest Management and community forestry in India: an ecological and institutional assessment*. New Delhi: IBH, pp. 279–318.

Reed, M. S., Graves, A., Dandy, N., Posthumus, H., Hubacek, K., Morris, J., Prell, C., Quinn, C. H. and Stringer, L. C. (2009) Who's in and why? A typology of stakeholder analysis methods for natural resource management. *Journal of Environmental Management* 90: 1933–1949.

Robbins, P. (1998) Paper forests: imagining and deploying exogenous ecologies in arid India. *Geoforum* 29(1): 69–86.

Roy, S. B. (1992) Forest protection committees in West Bengal. *Economic and Political Weekly* 27(29): 1528–1530.

Sarin, M. (1998) From conflict to collaboration: institutional issues in community management. In: Poffenberger, M. and McGean, B. (eds) *Village voices, forest choices: Joint Forest Management in India*. New Delhi: Oxford University Press, pp. 165–209.

Sarin, M. (1999) *Policy goals and JFM practice: an analysis of institutional arrangements and outcomes*. India: World Wide Fund for Nature.

Sethi, N. (2004) *Forest facts: delving deeper*. Online, available at: www.downtoearth.org.in/node/11291.

SikkimFirst.in. (2013) *Sikkim India's greenest state, 47.3 percent land forested*. Online, available at: http://sikkimfirst.in/2013/08/18/sikkim-indias-greenest-state-47-3-percent-land-forested/.

Sudha, P. and Ravindranath, N. H. (2004) Evolution of forest policies and the spread of Joint Forest Management in India. In: Ravindranath, N. H. and Sudha, P. (eds) *Joint Forest Management in India: spread, performance and impact*. Hyderabad: Universities Press, pp. 1–25.

TERI. (Undated) *Study on joint forest management*. India: MoEF.

Vemuri, A. (2008) Joint Forest Management in India: an unavoidable and conflicting common property regime in natural resource management. *Journal of Development and Social Transformation* 5: 80–90.

Walker, G. B. (2004) The roadless areas initiative as national policy: is public participation an oxymoron? In: Depoe, S. W., Delicath, J. W. and Elsenbeer, M. F. A. (eds) *Communication and public participation in environmental decision making*. Albany, NY: State University of New York Press, pp. 113–136.

WBFDCL. (Undated) *JFM: people's participation*. Online, available at: www.wbfdc.com/jfm.html.

WBG. (2007) *State monitoring report*. West Bengal: Government of West Bengal.

Western, D. (1994) *Natural connections: perspectives in community-based conservation*. Washington, DC: Island.

Yaffee, S. L. and Wondolleck, J. M. (2000) Making collaboration work: lessons from a comprehensive assessment of over 200 wide ranging cases of collaboration. *Environmental Management* 1: 1–8.

7 Wildlife conservation as public good

The public trust doctrine and the North American model of wildlife conservation

Andrea M. Feldpausch-Parker, Israel D. Parker, Hilary Swartwood, M. Nils Peterson, and Markus J. Peterson

Introduction

Governments around the Earth have claimed authority over such entities as air, water, landscapes, wildlife, and the ocean and its shores for the public benefit under various permutations of what is now typically termed the "public trust doctrine" (PTD) since at least the Roman Institutes of Justinian (~533 CE; Caspersen, 1996; Horner, 2000; Sax, 1970). Modern articulations of the PTD include four key elements: (1) the object of the trust (e.g. air, oceans, wildlife) that cannot be owned by individuals or other entities; (2) the trustee (e.g. the state) responsible for acting in the best interest of trust beneficiaries; (3) the beneficiary (the public) who holds title to the trust; and (4) the settlor (e.g. natural law, God, Mother Nature) who creates the trust. Scholars and advocates of the PTD typically leave the identity of the settlor open, suggesting entities such as God, Mother Nature, or Natural Law as creator of the trust (Caspersen, 1996; Horner, 2000).

This legal tradition, as embodied in English common law, was imported into Great Britain's North American colonies. It was reiterated in the fledgling United States by the Northwest Ordinance of 1787, which declared that navigable waters of the Mississippi River "shall be common highways and forever free ... to the citizens of the United States" (1 Stat. 50, Art. 4). Although the primary emphasis of the PTD has been aquatic resources, it has become important to terrestrial as well as aquatic wildlife conservation efforts in North America. In *Martin v. Waddell* [41 US 367 (1842)], the US Supreme Court held that the state of New Jersey not only held rivers and bays in trust for the public good, but also the lands under these waters and the fisheries therein. The Supreme Court then upheld the importance of state governments controlling lands under public waters in *Illinois Central Railroad Company v. Illinois* [146 US 387 (1892)] in what became the lodestar in US public trust law (Sax, 1970). Also during this period, the US Supreme Court held in a chain of cases[1] culminating in

Geer v. *Connecticut* [161 US 519 (1896):529] that the states held wildlife "as a trust for the benefit of the people" (Goble and Freyfogle, 2002). By 1900, the PTD was firmly established in US case law, and has been explicitly extended to many natural resources including both aquatic and terrestrial wildlife.

In Canada, public lands, wildlife and other publically held entities are considered assets of the Crown, which in modern times could be construed as being held in trust for the people (Batcheller *et al.*, 2010). However, as Henquinet and Dobson assert:

> A rudimentary public trust doctrine exists in Canada, but it is an austere announcement of the public right to navigate and fish in navigable waters. It is a dormant doctrine to say the least. There are very few cases that deal with public trust issues and almost none of which actually articulate a public trust doctrine.
>
> (Henquinet and Dobson, 2006: 368)

In their legal reviews, Hunt (1981) and Elwell and Dyck (2002) reached similar conclusions. Perhaps because of the dormant nature of the PTD in Canadian jurisprudence, over half of the provinces and territories have incorporated language identifying wildlife as publically held entities in their environmental statutes (Batcheller *et al.*, 2010). The fact that provincial law and policies have explicitly specified this relationship indicates intent to treat wildlife as public trust resources regardless of the rudimentary nature of the PTD at the national level.

The North American Model of Wildlife Conservation (NAMWC) emerged in part from the legal basis offered by the PTD (Geist, 1995, 2001, 2006; Geist and Organ, 2004). The NAMWC, as articulated by Geist *et al.* (2001), is comprised of seven tenets they advocate as guiding principles for wildlife management and policy. This model makes specific reference to elements of the PTD by giving Canadian and US governments the role of trustee, including the moral and legal authority to (1) eliminate wildlife markets and (2) allocate wildlife by law (rather than markets). The original authors and advocates of the NAMWC suggest several other ideals of wildlife management that supposedly emerge from the PTD, such as (1) requiring that wildlife only be killed for legitimate purposes; (2) defining wild animals as international resources; (3) requiring that science be used as the tool for discharging wildlife policy; and (4) legally enforcing hunting and trapping as democratic activities (Geist, 1995, 2006; Geist *et al.*, 2001; Geist and Organ, 2004; Organ and Batcheller, 2009). Some wildlife management professionals consider the NAMWC, grounded in the PTD, to have been a resounding success (Geist, 1995, 2000, 2006; Geist *et al.*, 2001; Organ *et al.*, 2012; Prukop and Regan, 2005), while others see it as plagued with complications or in need of fine tuning (Jacobson and Decker, 2006; Jacobson *et al.*, 2010; Organ and Batcheller, 2009; Organ *et al.*, 2012).

The PTD, and later the NAMWC, created "communities of practice" or "collection[s] of people who engage on an ongoing basis in some common endeavor" (Eckert, 2006: 683). The construction of these communities comes about from shared values and, in many cases, knowledge of and experience with natural resources. For example, the PTD arguably underlies decisions to allow standing for groups unhappy with how the US Fish and Wildlife Service administers the Endangered Species Act (ESA), and certainly underlies community-level support for endangered species conservation (Peterson *et al.*, 2002). It also gives many stakeholders legal rights to comment publically on wildlife and water related decisions at the local level. Such assemblages include wildlife professionals, academic institutions and wildlife interest groups (both consumptive and non-consumptive users). These communities of practice not only influence what decisions are made, but also how these decisions are carried out. In essence, these communities influence how the commons (i.e. publicly shared resources; Hardin, 1968) are managed for public benefit. These communities of practice are perhaps most obvious among hunters and anglers who explicitly tie their group identity to the PTD and the NAMWC (e.g. the Wildlife Society; Organ *et al.*, 2012), and arguably are behind communities of practice such as the "Riverkeepers" organizations that have emerged throughout the United States (Cronin and Kennedy, 1997).

In this chapter, we use Mouffe's (2000) democratic paradox to provide a theoretical framework for examining online texts compiled by wildlife communities of practice to determine how interpretations of the NAMWC influence wildlife management in liberal democracies such as those in Canada and the United States. According to Mouffe, liberal democracy engenders tension between two opposing but desirable ideals emanating from the liberal and democratic traditions:

> On one side we have the liberal tradition constituted by the rule of law, the defense of human rights and the respect of individual liberty; on the other the democratic tradition whose main ideas are those of equality, identity between governing and governed and popular sovereignty.
>
> (Mouffe, 2000: 3)

These tensions play out in the political arena through the articulation and re-articulation of approaches to public policy such as the NAMWC, which for many in the wildlife management field has taken on an almost sacred quality. The PTD itself brings this internal tension to the fore with the idea that some things should be held in common for all citizens. The directive that some political entity should be formally designated (often by rule of law) as responsible for ensuring the protection of such common goods, and that each individual has a right to access the commons in her/his own way, is consistent with the liberal tradition. At the same time, the PTD draws assumptions that the legitimacy of that political entity relies on consent of the governed (popular sovereignty) and a belief that all citizens must have equal access to the commons from the democratic tradition. Despite claims that the NAMWC is grounded in the PTD, we question whether the NAMWC incorporates the democratic paradox as completely as does the PTD, and suggest that there are limitations that may result from a failure to do so. The privileging of some communities of practice to the near exclusion of others potentially tilts the dynamics of power beyond the limits of public acceptability.

The PTD places wildlife into a limited commons ostensibly protected from misuse by a vigilant trustee. However, when applied through the discourse of the NAMWC, some communities of practice may be underrepresented, or may not be represented at all (Jacobson *et al.*, 2010). This undermines the broad plurality that is supposed to underpin trust protection and to legitimize decisions. Because the NAMWC has become central to the management ideals promulgated by professional wildlife communities of practice (such as the Wildlife Society), it is important to understand how communication of the NAMWC by communities of practice either opens or constrains opportunities for pluralistic dialogue and broad-based public participation in wildlife conservation.

Our investigation is based on a principle underlying the PTD: that management of the commons is improved through participation by a diversity of stakeholders representing the greater public for which the resource is held in trust (Dietz *et al.*, 2003). Our specific objective in this study is to determine how wildlife communities of practice throughout North America implicate the democratic paradox in their interpretations of the NAMWC, and how these interpretations may promulgate and trouble existing hegemonic relations between different communities of practice.

Methods

We analysed the online content related to the NAMWC by accessing relevant organizations' webpages to discover (1) how broadly (or narrowly) articulations of the NAMWC and the PTD reflect the diverse communities of practice involved in wildlife conservation; and (2) whether articulations of the NAMWC and the PTD exhibit ideals of both liberality and democracy, as theorized by Mouffe, or whether they rely on one tradition over the other when discussing wildlife conservation.

Because the Internet serves as an increasingly important space for environmental discourse and debate (Feldpausch-Parker and Peterson, 2015; Parker and Feldpausch-Parker, 2013), we used online texts to address these questions. The Internet as a public space has a multitude of effects on democratic processes, ranging from radicalization (Downey and Fenton, 2003) to serving as electronic forums for stakeholders (Heng and De Moor, 2003). Because of these varying effects, it is a useful space for research analysing stakeholder influence on democratic practice. We used the Google search engine (accessed in September 2014) to collect English language material from wildlife organizations with web content that mentioned the NAMWC. We used a list of search terms to facilitate the search. We started data collection with the following search terms: "North American Model of Wildlife Conservation", "Public Trust Doctrine", "NAMWC", "seven sisters", and "tenets of wildlife management". We used a grounded theory approach (Charmaz, 2001), allowing for the inclusion of emergent terms that were relevant to our analysis such as "North American game model", "North American model of wildlife management", and "7 principles of NAMWC" (see Table 7.1 for a complete list of search terms).

Once texts from these organizations were collected we categorized the organizations as state/province/territory agencies, consumptive-use interest groups, non–consumptive/multi–use interest groups, professional organizations, extension services and partnerships (between federal, state/province/territory and other organizations) (see Table 7.2). In addition, each organization's mission statement (if there was no mission statement then we used the *about us* page to provide mission orientation) and position statement on NAMWC was collected for analysis. After reading material on all sites, we eliminated sources not meeting our full search criteria from further consideration.

A codebook was developed to ensure coding consistency across a priori categories developed to address the democratic paradox (see Table 7.3 for the complete codebook). Coding categories included individual rights and freedoms, freedom and equality, and equality and popular sovereignty. In the NAMWC text, we coded for direct or indirect mentions of the PTD and inclusive or exclusive population references (e.g. hunters, the public). We also coded for protection of interests and purpose of organization to provide context for the organizations' interpretations of the NAMWC. We conducted a qualitative content analysis of the online organizational text using the qualitative software NVIVO 10.0 (QSR International, Doncaster, Victoria, Australia). Coding was completed by two of the researchers using a consensus-based coding process (Krippendorff, 2013; Parker and Feldpausch-Parker, 2013). Once coding was complete, we compared coded content by the six organizational categories listed in the previous paragraph.

Table 7.1 Terms used in web-based search

Search terms	
North American Model of Wildlife Conservation	Public Trust Doctrine
NAMWC	Seven Sisters
Tenets of wildlife management	North American model of wildlife management
North American game model	7 Principles of NAMWC

Table 7.2 Organizations whose web pages included the NAMWC data analysed in this chapter

Consumptive use interest groups	Non-consumptive and multi-use interest groups	Professional organizations	State/province/territory agencies	State extension agencies	Federal/state/consumptive use interest group partnership
American ProCatters Association	Bear Trust International	The Association of Fish and Wildlife Agencies	Arizona Game and Fish Department	Michigan State University Extension	Wildlife and Sport Fish Restoration Program
American Wildlife Conservation Partners	Conservation Hub	The Wildlife Society	Florida Fish and Wildlife Conservation Commission	Oregon State Extension	
Boone and Crockett Club	Mountain Lion Foundation		Georgia Department of Natural Resources		
Ducks Unlimited	Tread Lightly		Mississippi Wildlife, Fish and Parks		
Montana Trappers Association	Public Land–Water Access Association		Montana Fish, Wildlife and Parks		
National Bobwhite Conservation Initiative	West Virginia Sierra Club				
National Wild Turkey Federation					
New Mexico Wildlife Federation					
Orion The Hunter's Institute					
Rocky Mountain Elk Foundation					
The Council to Advance Hunting and the Shooting Sports					
Theodore Roosevelt Conservation Partnership					
Utah Wildlife Network					
Mississippi Wildlife Federation					

Table 7.3 Codebook outline

Coding theme	Codes
Democratic paradox	• Mentions individual rights and freedoms (e.g. ability to hunt) • Mentions both freedom and equality • Mentions equality and popular sovereignty (e.g. managing for "public interest", equal access)
Mentions of the PTD directly or indirectly in the NAMWC text	• Presence • Absence (not coded)
Inclusive/exclusive populations	• Inclusive population reference—mentions the "public" or similar sentiment • Exclusive population reference—mentions specific populations (e.g. hunters and/or scientists)

Goals/agenda/purpose of organization	• Mentions of:
	  • Wildlife conservation
	  • Wildlife preservation (of the resource, not of the right to hunt)
	  • Protection of interests
	• Purpose of organization

Results

Types of organization

We found 30 wildlife organizations that referenced the NAMWC in their text. Of these 30 organizations, 14 were consumptive use groups, six were non-consumptive or multi-use groups, two were professional organizations, five were state/province/territory wildlife agencies, two were extension agencies, and one was a US partnership between federal and state agencies, and consumptive use partners (Table 7.2). It should be noted that federal agencies, specifically the US Fish and Wildlife Service, were only represented in this study because of their inclusion in a partnership that referenced the NAMWC. They did not have any independent web content addressing their position on the model. Most of the interest groups included in our search were consumptive use organizations, such as the Boone and Crockett Club, Rocky Mountain Elk Foundation and National Wild Turkey Federation (Table 7.2). State/province/territory agencies referencing the NAMWC were predominantly from the western and southern regions of the United States. We found few professional organizations that mentioned the model. Although a small number of extension agencies directly referenced the NAMWC, some, such as Texas Agrilife Extension, made passing reference to the model in their educational materials, but did not include a position or description of the model.

Public trust doctrine in NAMWC texts

As outlined in the introduction to this chapter, the PTD is treated as a central pillar to the NAMWC. As such, interpretations of the PTD within the context of the NAMWC inform how these wildlife communities of practice perceive resource access and ownership. As a first step in our investigation, we examined the NAMWC position statements for each organization regarding mentions of the PTD, searching for presence or absence, as well as how the PTD was used. We found that the majority of coded material from interest groups and state/province/territory agencies included a direct or indirect reference to the PTD (i.e. specifically mentioning the "public trust" or mentioning wildlife as a shared resource). Only about half of the content from professional organizations and extension agencies, however, mentioned the PTD in relation to the NAMWC. These included the Wildlife Society, which has written extensively on the NAMWC and the PTD, and Michigan State University Extension, which addressed how "Wildlife populations reside in the public trust" (Cook, 2014). Organizations typically referenced the PTD when they were discussing the seven tenets of the NAMWC or, more often, the history of model development. For example, according to the Wildlife Society, "The Public Trust Doctrine ... is considered the keystone of the North American Model of Wildlife Conservation. It represents the common law foundation for trust status of wildlife resources in the United States" (TWS, 2013). Conservation Hub expanded upon this idea by stating:

> North America's model of wildlife conservation holds wildlife in the public trust, with state and/or federal government providing oversight to manage fish and wildlife. Alternatively, if an individual owns a piece of land in which wildlife lives, he/she cannot own this wildlife. Instead, it is preserved by all citizens.
>
> (Conservation Hub, 2013)

Almost all of the statements involving the PTD focused on wildlife as a resource held in the public trust and managed accordingly by the state. The organizations, however, diverged on what this meant. For example, the PTD supports the idea of ownerless wildlife (Sax, 1970), but these sources tended to assign ownership to various entities. Additionally, the sources credited a narrow set of groups for financially supporting wildlife management. This narrow financial basis of the NAMWC accounts for considerable discussion regarding inclusivity versus exclusivity of wildlife management communities of practice.

Inclusion/exclusion of wildlife communities of practice

We now demonstrate some of the differences in how these communities frame the NAMWC, noting that their framing has direct implications for wildlife management. These implications include, but are not limited to, the potential exclusion of many citizens who may have a strong interest in wildlife conservation, given that more than twice as many consumptive use groups as non-consumptive use groups (14 to 6) engage directly with the NAMWC.

Relationship between wildlife and humans

As noted above, a variety of interpretations of ownership were displayed in the text in reference to the PTD and the NAMWC. Legally, the public is seen as the beneficiary of the trust, not the owner of the resources (Sax, 1970). However, many of the coded statements described wildlife as natural resources "owned" by the public. The nature of this ownership varied amongst wildlife communities of practice. For instance, the Florida Fish and Wildlife Conservation Commission stated, "The North American Model of Wildlife Conservation directs that throughout the United States, fish and wildlife are held in common ownership by the *states* for the benefit of all people" (FWC, 2014; emphasis added). In the Georgia Department of Natural Resources website, they refer to wildlife held in the public trust as "Through shared *ownership* and responsibility, opportunity to enjoy wildlife is provided to all" (GDNR, 2014; emphasis added). Additionally, the Boone and Crockett Club argued that, "wildlife conservation in the US and Canada is based on the notion that *wildlife belongs to the people–not the government, private landowners, or individuals*" (BCC, 2014; emphasis added). They later expand on this line of thinking, stating that:

> Wildlife belongs to the people and managed in trust for the people by government agencies. Who *owns* wildlife was determined by a Supreme Court decision at the time the New World was flexing its new independence from European rule. The Public Trust Doctrine is the pillar of North American conservation, but it took time for citizens to fully understand the responsibilities that came with this *ownership*.
>
> (BBC, 2014; emphasis added)

This reduction of wildlife to owned entities was the most common practice amongst a handful of the surveyed organizations. However, some organizations provided explanations more in line with legal definitions such as the National Bobwhite Conservation Initiative, which stated:

> The state fish and wildlife agencies have the legal authority and stewardship responsibility for wild quail in their respective states. This authority is grounded in the Public Trust Doctrine of wildlife management in North America, which holds that wildlife resources are owned by no one, but are held in trust by government for the benefit of present and future generations of the people.
>
> (McKenzie, 2014)

This wide array of interpretations demonstrates a surprisingly limited understanding of what the PTD entails, and serves to only perpetuate a continued diversity of understandings in relation to owner versus beneficiary.

Wildlife conservation funding

The direct links between financial support, wildlife conservation, and recreational hunting and angling are a common refrain in many wildlife communities of practice. For instance, the American ProCatters Association stated, "Hunters and anglers were among the first to crusade for wildlife protection and remain some of today's most important conservation leaders" (APC, 2012). This role comes packaged with a burden of responsibility as described again by the American ProCatters Association, "In the mid-1800s, hunters and anglers realized they needed to set limits in order to protect rapidly disappearing wildlife, and assume responsibility for managing wild habitats" (APC, 2012). The Boone and Crockett Club built upon the same sentiment when they stated, "Sportsmen and women subsequently stepped forward and gladly accepted their role in funding conservation" (BCC, 2014). The Ducks Unlimited website proclaimed that,

> The strength of the NA Model is found in the willingness of resource users – hunters and anglers – to levy fees on themselves to directly pay for the management of fish and wildlife, as well as finance the protection and management of habitat.
>
> (Ducks Unlimited, 2014)

Demonstrated ability and willingness to pay for conservation makes these recreational hunters and anglers indispensable to wildlife conservation. The presumed permanence of this relationship is reflected in state agency texts in the United States, such as this statement by the Arizona Game and Fish Department:

> Hunting and angling are the cornerstones of the North American Model of Wildlife Conservation…. There is no alternative funding system in place to replace the potential lost funds for conservation. If hunting ends, funding for wildlife conservation is in peril.
>
> (AGFD, 2013)

We found that organizations representing recreational hunters and anglers often mentioned their financial support of wildlife management as justification for their access to wildlife resources. This access was then tied to the foundations of citizenship.

> Over time the Club has seen many challenges to the North American Model of Wildlife Conservation, which it helped to create, as well as to

the traditions of hunting. When and where necessary, the Club has taken action to protect this Model, our wildlife resources, the habitats that support them, and hunting and other forms of outdoor recreation.... Every citizen has the freedom to hunt and fish.... Public access to wildlife, regardless of social or economic status, including hunting, fishing, and trapping is a right of citizenship.

(BCC, 2014)

Text provided by a multi-use group, the Public Land/Water Access Association, was in line with the consumptive use groups when stating, "Hunters and anglers, standing virtually alone, created this 'conservation movement', gave it political force and social leadership and provided for financial support" (PLWA, 2014). Text from the New Mexico Wildlife Federation illustrated that the agent designated as trustee for the public prioritized the community of recreational consumptive users:

Because sportsmen fund virtually every penny of the Department of Game and Fish budget, we keep sportsmen informed about upcoming State Game Commission meetings and what's on the agenda. Then we attend the meetings, and afterward send out a report so hunters and anglers know how their dollars are being spent.

(NMWF, 2014)

There were no similar statements about reporting to other interested communities.

Statements such as these made by consumptive and multi-use groups indicate a high level of entitlement to the resource, at least for certain purposes, as in the Boone and Crockett claim that "Public access to wildlife, ... including hunting, fishing, and trapping is a right of citizenship" (BCC, 2014). Statements by state organizations in the United States that express similar sentiments indicate support for this entitlement, often with an implicit distinction being drawn between communities that are entitled to wildlife access and others that are not so entitled, as in the Arizona Game and Fish Department's statement that, "hunting and angling are the cornerstones of the North American Model of Wildlife Conservation". For instance, the Boone and Crockett Club (2014) invoked basic rights when they said, "Public access to wildlife, regardless of social or economic status, including hunting, fishing, and trapping is a right of citizenship". This rhetoric was not found on the websites of organizations representing non-consumptive wildlife communities of practice.

Science as foundation for policy

The websites we studied tended to frame science as integral to sound policy decisions. This was the only link non-consumptive communities of practice drew between themselves and the NAMWC. For example, according to Conservation Hub (2013), "effective scientific management practices are essential to managing and sustaining wildlife and habitats in North America". Bear Trust International claimed that it

> believes in the North American Model of Wildlife Conservation, and all of our STEM [Science, Technology, Engineering and Math] conservation education lesson plans are rooted in this Model. Specifically, we believe that wildlife conservation should be based on sound science.
>
> (BTI, 2014)

State agencies in the United States, consumptive use groups and extension agencies all carried this common refrain of the importance of science in wildlife management. As the Arizona Game and Fish Department stated, "the North American Model of Wildlife Conservation … strives to sustain wildlife species and habitats through sound science and active management" (AGFD, 2013). The Boone and Crockett Club, an example of a consumptive use organization, stated, "the best science available will be used as a base for informed decision-making in wildlife management" (BCC, 2014). And, according to the Michigan State University Extension website, "science-based management should underpin policy" (Cook, 2014).

All wildlife communities of practice included in this study were unified in their message about the importance of using science as a foundation for wildlife management and decision-making. This relative agreement on the importance of science was an exception to the diverse interpretations of most aspects of the NAMWC.

Discussion

We found that a select portion of wildlife communities of practice referenced the NAMWC as a foundation for wildlife management and policy. The most vocal groups in relation to the model were recreational hunters and anglers, followed closely by state wildlife regulatory agencies in the United States. These groups dominated conversation about the NAMWC and closely aligned recreational hunting and angling with wildlife conservation. Framing of the NAMWC varied greatly in focus amongst the different types of organizations. Many of these organizations were interest groups or agencies that traditionally work closely with these interest groups, and they framed the NAMWC and the PTD to fit their viewpoints. They framed this close relationship as existential: wildlife conservation was unthinkable without recreational hunting and angling and vice versa. Beyond framing recreational hunting and angling as essential to wildlife conservation, this discourse excludes non-consumptive users from membership in the community of people who contribute to wildlife conservation. These implications were shaped by interpretations of the NAMWC and the PTD in a variety of ways related to ownership, financial contribution to wildlife conservation, and the interplay between science and policy. Framings of these focus areas often lent themselves to the exclusion of a broader-based public.

Wildlife: owned resources versus objects of the public trust

As detailed in the introduction to this chapter, the PTD consists of four key elements: (1) the object of the trust that cannot be owned by individuals or other entities; (2) the trustee responsible for acting in the trust's best interest; (3) the beneficiary who holds title to the trust; and (4) the settlor who creates the trust. Despite the fact that legal ownership is not a component of the PTD, much of the text we evaluated nonetheless assigned wildlife ownership to various entities, including publics, natural resource agencies, or state governments. Given the PTD's status as a central pillar of the NAMWC, it is logically erroneous and potentially harmful for proponents of the NAMWC to frame wildlife as natural resources that are owned by anyone. Given the ascendency of neoliberal economic and political systems that have dominated industrial and post-industrial nations at least since the 1970s (Aune, 2001; Duménil and Lévy, 2004; Harvey, 2005), this assumption of wildlife ownership should not be surprising. Because neoliberal economic thought assumes everything of value is either owned (or the owner), this error is predictable; there is no a priori reason to assume natural resource policy should be different from other political issues. There are, however, reasons for those seeking a fully democratic orientation to environmental conservation to problematize this trend.

The dominance of economic liberalization policies since the late 1970s – such as privatization, deregulation and unqualified support of "free" markets – has resulted in a situation where few people even questioned whether Adam Smith's invisible hand would invariably result in the best outcome for the economy and policy generally until the financial crisis of 2008 (Aune, 2001; Duménil and Lévy, 2004, 2011; Harvey, 2005; Peterson *et al.*, 2013). Similarly, many conservation biologists argued that neoliberal policies would positively revolutionize biodiversity conservation (e.g. Mandel *et al.*, 2010; Miles and Kapos, 2008; Wunder, 2007). In addition, multiple academic journals commonly address this topic). After all, a neoliberal perspective specifies that resources such as wildlife populations will be destroyed in tragedies of the commons scenarios unless (1) resources are privatized and turned over to the supposedly efficient and inexpensive invisible hand running the market, or (2) cumbersome and expensive command and control governance is implemented (Mansfield, 2004; Peterson *et al.*, 2010a; Robertson, 2004). For these reasons, one would expect that authors of most of the texts we evaluated would indeed assume that someone or some legal entity must own wild animals. Regardless, there are a number of potential problems with considering wildlife to be owned natural resources and uncritically accepting neoliberal rationales as the basis for wildlife conservation.

For example, if wildlife are owned by the public, then it is reasonable for communities of practice that have traditionally footed the bill for wildlife conservation (i.e. hunters and anglers) to control wildlife management objectives and practices even if other communities in practice are marginalized in the process. Conversely, public ownership of wildlife also could imply that the vast majority should dictate what happens with publically owned wildlife regardless of who pays the bill, which could in turn marginalize hunters and anglers because they make up only a small proportion of the public in Canada and the United States. Regardless of struggles among communities of practice to control wildlife conservation, ownership of wildlife inevitably places wildlife on the slippery slope to commodification. After all, if wild animals are owned, then they can be sold and privatized. Native wild animals indeed have been privatized in many states, and provinces (Anonymous, 1988; Benson, 1992; Freese and Trauger, 2000; Peterson *et al.*, 2010b) despite the objections of consumptive communities of practice that rather ironically argued that wildlife were owned entities.

Although the threats that wildlife ownership poses for the NAMWC are quite real, the neoliberal baggage associated with such ownership probably poses a greater problem for wildlife conservation than for the model itself. Conservationists have increasingly recognized these potential threats during the last decade. For example, Peterson *et al.* (2005) explored the unfavourable consequences of the rush to so called consensus-based approaches to environmental conflict resolution that currently undergird neoliberal conservation. Chan *et al.* (2007: 64) warned that conservationists "must guard against the assumption that economics can single-handedly rescue conservation. To assume this would be to believe (in the face of contrary evidence) that market forces would always favor conservation". Walker *et al.* (2009: 149) reviewed regulatory biodiversity trading and concluded that "delivery of no net loss or net gain [of biodiversity] through biodiversity trading is … administratively improbable and technically unrealistic". Similarly, Vira and Adams (2009: 161) concluded that "there is … a strategic risk in justifying biodiversity conservation primarily in terms of ecosystem services" to humanity. Peterson *et al.* (2010a: 117) maintained that under neoliberal logics,

> the concept of ecosystem services has decoupled [ecosystem] function from [ecosystem] service sufficiently that many people may be aware of the economic value of a given ecosystem service without recognizing human dependence on local and global ecosystems. Not surprisingly, then, there are numerous instances in which commodification of nature has not resulted in conservation of biodiversity.

Finally, Büscher *et al.* (2012: 23) "delineated neoliberal conservation both as inherent to broader capitalist processes, and as a particular set of governmentalities that seeks to extend and police profitable commodification processes based on artificial and arbitrary separations of human society from biodiverse-rich (non-human) natures". If Büscher *et al.* are correct, neoliberal conservation is not only oxymoronical, but also unlikely to produce meaningful conservation objectives.

On the one hand, if all communities of practice interested in wildlife conservation are willing to rely on the invisible hand of the market despite problems associated with wildlife ownership, commodification and neoliberal conservation, then there is little need for public engagement regarding wildlife conservation – the market will take care of it in the best possible manner. On the other hand, those who doubt that neoliberal economics will invariably benefit wildlife conservation should seriously consider the importance of grounding the NAMWC in the classically defined PTD. This would include defining wildlife as objects of the public trust rather than owned entities, where multiple publics hold title to the trust, and states (or provinces) act as trusties (rather than either the public or the states acting as owners). Although this distinction may seem esoteric, it has immediately practical ramifications. Most basically, it would mean that all communities of practice interested in wildlife conservation have real opportunities to become actively involved in the democratic processes that ensure states (trustees) act in the best interest of those holding title to the trust. This need would justify all the hard work required to negotiate the democratic paradox embodied in the examples discussed next.

"Pay to play" applied to wildlife access

Wildlife conservation is currently structured in a way that makes it highly dependent upon consumptive use funds. This limited funding mechanism has led many wildlife communities of practice to argue that wildlife conservation in the twenty-first century requires new legal and financial commitments from a broad-based public. Current funding structures (e.g. hunting license fees, Pittman-Robertson funds) inevitably favour consumptive user voices in wildlife decision-making because of their support. As noted above, consumptive use groups championed their leadership role in wildlife conservation due to funding and engagement in management decisions. From this privileged stature, perceptions of ownership and access to the resource arose. This has dire implications for an inclusive, deliberative process. As Mouffe (2000) argues, "the unchallenged hegemony of neo-liberalism represents a threat for democratic institutions" (p. 6).

This place of privilege has already limited the conversation of the NAMWC and PTD to issues largely important to consumptive users. This close relationship between consumptive use and financial support for wildlife conservation has lent a strong argument to the importance of recreational hunting and angling. In its current form, the NAMWC is largely about maintaining and expanding this relationship. The relative silence of non-consumptive use groups on the model suggested that these groups rely upon different concepts of conservation and conservation history. The consumptive use groups and even the multi-use groups often rallied around the concept of access in the so-called democracy of hunting (one of the seven tenets outlined in the NAMWC). This democracy only allowed for access to those wishing to participate in recreational hunting or angling. Access as detailed by our data included physical access to hunting areas, access to huntable populations through appropriate management, and access to the process of determining appropriate management actions. Although, never directly excluding other activities, consumptive use was the primary driver and democracy, in its limited sense, extended only to these user groups.

Consumptive use groups did occasionally acknowledge non-consumptive uses of wildlife as important or valuable, and in some cases they even expressed a desire for expanded conservation funding that could come from non-consumptive users in the form of a new excise tax on additional categories of outdoor gear. However, with such a dominant voice on behalf of consumptive use groups, the question is whether communities of practice can maintain access to the process of wildlife management decision-making.

The dominant voice of consumptive groups, and to a degree state agencies in the United States, appears to exhibit fear of their own potential exclusion from wildlife access. Consumptive use proponents of the NAMWC often discuss outside threats to the PTD (e.g. limitations on traditional resource uses such as hunting and trapping) (Mahoney *et al.*, 2009). This is especially ironic, given that their focus on the small subset of wildlife communities of practice that engage in hunting and other consumptive activities excludes other wildlife conservationists. This exclusion deconstructs wildlife communities of practice into factions of use instead of seeking benefits from a broadly based coalition with a unified goal of conservation. This bias toward one community of practice undercuts the PTD, creating an insider–outsider paradigm between consumptive and non-consumptive members of the wildlife community. Consumptive use rhetoric is explicitly stated in the NAMWC tenets (e.g. promoting hunting and trapping participation), thus leading to the further perpetuation of the hegemony demonstrated by our data. This is compounded by the fact that the majority of communities of practice advocating the model are also consumptive users or dependent upon consumptive use for conservation funds. Decker *et al.*'s (2009) critique of the model for its focus on user-pay, at the same time it claims to ensure equal access for all, addresses the issue:

> A philosophical question with practical implications is: should a model to fulfill the public trust doctrine rely on funding originating so heavily from a few "user" groups?... No matter how broadly the mandate for management of wildlife as a public trust resource may be interpreted philosophically or legally, funding source – who pays – for wildlife conservation and management invariably affects focus.
>
> (p. 33)

Although attention to the conservation of non-hunted wildlife has increased in the latter part of the twentieth century (Wagner, 1989), managing wildlife for recreational hunting and angling remained a core strategy. Wildlife management agencies expend considerable resources to maintain access and opportunities for recreational hunters and anglers. Wildlife managers have attempted to provide some standing for other communities of practice, the fact that much of wildlife conservation funding in North America comes from consumptive users limits these efforts.

Support for science in wildlife conservation policy

All organizations whose texts we studied seemed to support science-based wildlife management strategies. The underlying implication by the organizations was that science is the best provider of basic knowledge necessary for making informed management decisions. Such statements are, however, nebulous. None of the coded statements provided details about the nature of "science". Certainly, research has indicated that all sides of wildlife debates can claim that science supports their viewpoint (Parker and Feldpausch-Parker, 2013) so the details of what constitutes acceptable science needs to be specified and will most likely continue to be a space for contention. The fact that both consumptive use and non-consumptive use groups supported science in wildlife management revealed very little about potential cooperation or how they would like science incorporated into the democratic process.

Conclusions

Efforts to increase the sense of community and social identification with wildlife conservation require the communication of messages that are relevant to a broad swathe of society. This could start with a de-emphasis on the ownership of wildlife that is more in line with an accurate representation of the PTD. Especially when considered within the context of contemporary liberal democracies that are emerging throughout Earth, the citizenry that frequently live in close proximity with wildlife require meaningful input and access to wildlife management decision-making. We recognize that including diverse viewpoints in policy decisions increases complexity and introduces new tensions. Wildlife management will undoubtedly struggle with the task of representing such divergent viewpoints, but this contestation of wills is at the least necessary, and perhaps desirable in functioning democracies. Mouffe (2000) argued that, "instead of trying to erase the traces of power and exclusion, democratic politics requires us to bring them to the fore, to make them visible so that they can enter the terrain of contestation" (pp. 33–34). She goes on to state that conflict should not be viewed as problematic, but instead as confirmation that democracy "is alive and inhabited by pluralism" (p. 34). Without opposition, dominant discourses prevent the incorporation of new ideas, despite widespread calls for change. For a more complete treatment of this dynamic, see Hallgren's discussion of pluralistic agonism in Chapter 2.

It is through this contestation of ideas that society is able to enact changes in democratic practice in response to contemporary needs, in this case as they relate to wildlife management. Proponents of the NAMWC use it as a demonstration of their dedication to pluralistic and democratic protection of the commons. However the dominance of a single community limits the model's value as a means of building alliances between conservation communities that enable collaboration when their values coincide, as in the case of wildlife conservation. Instead of multiple communities sharing an interest in protecting a commonly held resource and valuing it in their diverse ways, dominant interpretations of the NAMWC as an embodiment of the PTD focus on a community of practice devoted to the recreational and consumptive use of wildlife. Rather than a unifying influence in wildlife conservation, these interpretations actively exclude large swathes of the people necessary for future conservation success.

Peterson *et al.* (2005) argued that, public policy and practice are "not producing anything remotely sustainable, from an ecological perspective, and will not unless the current power structure can be challenged to incorporate new information on the consequences of human action" (p. 765). We would add that current sanctification of the NAMWC unnecessarily limits the open thinking that may enable the emergence of new ideas about wildlife conservation through practices of agonistic democracy. Current discursive framing of the NAMWC and the PTD presents wildlife conservation as the exclusive domain of a single community of practice, which threatens to alienate other communities that also care deeply about wildlife conservation.

Note

1 The chain of US Supreme Court cases culminating in *Geer* v. *Connecticut* [161 US 519 (1896)] and the states holding wildlife in trust for the people include *Martin* v. *Waddell* [41 US 367 (1842)], *Smith* v. *Maryland* [59 US 71 (1855)], *McCready* v. *Virginia* [94 US 391 (1876)], and *Manchester* v. *Massachusetts* [139 US 240 (1890)] (Goble and Freyfogle, 2002).

References

AGFD. (2013) *North American model of wildlife conservation: managing today for wildlife tomorrow.* Online, available at: www.azgfd.gov/h_f/northamericanmodel.shtml (accessed 9 December 2014).

Anonymous. (1988) Privatising America's west: profits from the wild. *Economist* 309(7573): 27–28, 30.

APC. (2012) *The seven pillars: a North American wildlife conservation model.* Online, available at: http://americanprocatters.com/2012/08/north-american-wildlife-conservation-model/ (accessed 9 December 2014).

Aune, J. A. (2001) *Selling the free market: the rhetoric of economic correctness.* New York, New York, USA: Guilford Press.

Batcheller, G. R., Bambery, M. C., Bies, L., Decker, T., Dyke, S., Guynn, D., McEnroe, M., O'Brien, M., Organ, J. F., Riley, S. J. and Roehm, G. (2010) *The public trust doctrine: implications for wildlife management and conservation in the United States and Canada.* Technical Review 10–01, Bethesda, MD: The Wildlife Society.

BCC. (2014) *Boone and Crockett Club position statement: the North American model of wildlife conservation.* Online, available at: www.boone-crockett.org/conservation/conservation_NAM.asp?area=conservation (accessed 9 December 2014).

Benson, D. E. (1992) Commercialization of wildlife: a value-added incentive for conservation. In: Brown, R. D. (ed.) *The biology of deer.* New York: Springer-Verlag, pp. 539–553.

BTI. (2014) *NA model of wildlife conservation.* Online, available at: http://beartrust.org/na-model-of-wildlife-conservation (accessed 9 December 2014).

Büscher, B., Sullivan, S., Neves, K., Igoe, J. and Brockington, D. (2012) Towards a synthesized critique of neoliberal biodiversity conservation. *Capitalism Nature Socialism* 23(2): 4–30.

Caspersen, A. R. C. (1996) The public trust doctrine and the impossibility of "takings" by wildlife. *Boston College Environmental Affairs Law Review* 23(2): 357–391.

Conservation Hub. (2013) *North American conservation model.* Online, available at: www.conservationhub.org/research/north-american-conservation-model/ (accessed 9 December 2014).

Chan, K. M. A., Pringle, R. M., Ranganathan, J., Boggs, C. L., Chan, Y. L., Ehrlich, P. R., Haff, P. K., Heller, N. E., Al-Khafaji, K. and Macmynowski, D. P. (2007) When agendas collide: human welfare and biological conservation. *Conservation Biology* 21(1): 59–68.

Charmaz, K. (2001) Grounded theory. In: Emerson, R. M. (ed.) *Contemporary field research.* Los Angeles: Waveland Press, pp. 335–352.

Chase, L. C., Schusler, T. M. and Decker, D. J. (2000) Innovations in stakeholder involvement: what's the next step? *Wildlife Society Bulletin* 28(1): 208–217.

Cook, B. (2014) *North American wildlife model.* Online, available at: http://msue.anr.msu.edu/news/north_american_wildlife_model (accessed 9 December 2014).

Cronin, J. and Kennedy, R. F., Jr. (1997) *The river keepers: two activists fight to reclaim our environment as a basic human right.* New York: Scribner.

Decker, D. J., Organ, J. F. and Jacobson, C. A. (2009) Why should all Americans care about the North American model of wildlife conservation. *Transactions of the North American Wildlife and Natural Resources Conference* 74: 32–36.

Dietz, T., Ostrom, E. and Stern, P. C. (2003) The struggle to govern the commons. *Science* 302: 1907–1912.

Downey, J. and Fenton, N. (2003) New media, counter publicity and the public sphere. *New Media and Society* 5(2): 185–202.

Ducks Unlimited. (2014) *Presidential transition: wildlife conservation.* Online, available at: www.ducks.org/conservation/public-policy/presidential-transition-wildlife-conservation (accessed 9 December 2014).

Duménil, G. and Lévy, D. (2004) *Capital resurgent: roots of the neoliberal revolution.* Cambridge, MA: Harvard University Press.

Duménil, G. and Lévy, D. (2011) *The crisis of neoliberalism.* Cambridge, MA: Harvard University Press.

Eckert, P. (2006) Communities of practice. *Encyclopedia of Language and Linguistics* 2: 683–685.

Elwell, C. and Dyck, T. (2002) *Water grab #2: province of Ontario's plans to transfer local water systems and services to the private sector: a breach of the public trust?* Ontario: Canadian Institute for Environmental Law and Policy.

Feldpausch-Parker, A. M. and Peterson, T. R. (2015) Communicating the science behind carbon sequestration: a case study of US Department of Energy and regional partnership websites. *Environmental Communication*: Ahead of Print.

Freese, C. H. and Trauger, D. L. (2000) Wildlife markets and biodiversity conservation in North America. *Wildlife Society Bulletin* 28(1): 42–51.

FWC. (2014) *The North American model of wildlife conservation.* Online, available at: www.myfwc.com/fishing/freshwater/black-bass/executive-summary/north-american-model/ (accessed 9 December 2014).

GDNR. (2014) *North American Model of Wildlife Conservation.* Online, available at: www.georgiawildlife.com/Hunting/NorthAmericanModel (accessed 9 December 2014).

Geist, V. (1995) North American policies of wildlife conservation. In: Geist, V. and McTaggart Cowan, I. (eds) *Wildlife conservation policy*. Calgary, Canada: Detselig, pp. 77–129.

Geist, V. (2000) A century of wildlife conservation successes and how to repeat it. In: Mansell, W. D. (ed.) *Proceedings of the 2000 Premier's Symposium on North America's Hunting Heritage*. Eden Prairie, MN: Wildlife Forever, pp. 17–22.

Geist, V. (2006) The North American model of wildlife conservation: a means of creating wealth and protecting public health while generating biodiversity. In: Lavigne, D. M. (ed.) *Gaining ground: in pursuit of ecological sustainability*. Guelph, Canada and Limerick, Ireland: International Fund for Animal Welfare and University of Limerick, pp. 285–293.

Geist, V., Mahoney, S. P. and Organ, J. F. (2001) Why hunting has defined the North American model of wildlife conservation. *Transactions of the North American Wildlife and Natural Resources Conference* 66: 175–185.

Geist, V. and Organ, J. F. (2004) The public trust foundation of the North American model of wildlife conservation. *Northeast Wildlife* 58: 49–56.

Goble, D. D. and Freyfogle, E. T. (2002) *Federal wildlife statutes: texts and contexts.* New York: Foundation Press.

Hardin, G. (1968) The tragedy of the commons. *Science* 162(3859): 1243–1248.

Harvey, D. (2005) *A brief history of neoliberalism*. New York: Oxford University Press.

Heng, M. S. H. and De Moor, A. (2003) From Habermas's communicative theory to practice on the internet. *Information Systems Journal* 13(4): 331–352.

Henquinet, J. W. and Dobson, T. (2006) The public trust doctrine and sustainable ecosystems: a Great Lakes fisheries case study. *NYU Environmental Law Journal* 14(2): 322–373.

Horner, S. M. (2000) Embryo, not fossil: breathing life into the public trust in wildlife. *Land and Water Law Review* 35: 23–75.

Hunt, C. D. (1981) The public trust doctrine in Canada. In: Swaigen, J. (ed.) *Environmental rights in Canada*. Toronto: Butterworths, pp. 151–194.

Jacobson, C. A. and Decker, D. J. (2006) Ensuring the future of state wildlife management: understanding challenges for institutional change. *Wildlife Society Bulletin* 34(2): 531–536.

Jacobson, C. A., Organ, J. F., Decker, D. D., Batcheller, G. R. and Carpenter, L. (2010) A conservation institution for the 21st century: implications for state wildlife agencies. *Journal of Wildlife Management* 74(2): 203–209.

Krippendorff, K. (2013) *Content analysis: an introduction to its methodology*. Thousand Oaks, CA: Sage Publications.

McKenzie, D. (2014) *Strengths and limitations*. Online, available at: http://bringback bobwhites.org/blogs/nbci/56-strengths-a-limitations (accessed 9 December 2014).

Mahoney, S. P., Geist, V., Organ, J., Regan, R., Batcheller, G. R., Sparrowe, R. D., McDonald, J. E., Bambery, C., Dart, J., Kennamer, J. E., Keck, R., Hobbs, D., Fielder, D., DeGayner, G. and Frampton, J. (2009) The North American model of wildlife conservation: enduring achievement and legacy. In: Nobile, J. and Duda, M. D. (eds) *Strengthening America's hunting heritage and wildlife conservation in the 21st century: challenges and opportunities*. Washington, DC: Sporting Conservation Council, pp. 7–24.

Mandel, J. T., Donlan, C. J. and Armstrong, J. (2010) A derivative approach to endangered species conservation. *Frontiers in Ecology and the Environment* 8(1): 44–49.

Mansfield, B. (2004) Neoliberalism in the oceans: "rationalization", property rights, and the commons question. *Geoforum* 35(3): 313–326.

Miles, L. and Kapos, V. (2008) Reducing greenhouse gas emissions from deforestation and forest degradation: global land-use implications. *Science* 320(5882): 1454–1455.

Mouffe, C. (2000) *The democratic paradox*. London: Verso.

NMWF. (2014) *NMWF guided by North American model of wildlife conservation*. Online, available at: www.nmwildlife.org/about/model (accessed 9 December 2014).

Organ, J. F. and Batcheller, G. R. (2009) Reviving the public trust doctrine as a foundation for wildlife management in North America. In: Manfredo, M. J., Vaske, J. J., Brown, P. J., Decker, D. J. and Duke, E. A. (eds) *Wildlife and society: the science of human dimensions*. Washington, DC: Island Press, pp. 161–171.

Organ, J. F., Geist, V., Mahoney, S. P., Williams, S., Krausman, P. R., Batcheller, G. R., Decker, T. A., Carmichael, R., Nanjappa, P., Regan, R. Medellin, R. A., Cantu, R., McCabe, R. E., Craven, S., Vecellio, G. M. and Decker, D. J. (2012) *The North American model of wildlife conservation*. The Wildlife Society Technical Review 12–04, Bethesda, MD: The Wildlife Society.

Parker, I. D. and Feldpausch-Parker, A. M. (2013) Yellowstone grizzly delisting rhetoric: an analysis of the online debate. *Wildlife Society Bulletin* 37(2): 248–255.

Peterson, M. J., Hall, D. M., Feldpausch-Parker, A. M. and Peterson, T. R. (2010a) Obscuring ecosystem function with application of the ecosystem services concept. *Conservation Biology* 24(1): 113–119.

Peterson, M. N., Hansen, H. P., Peterson, M. J. and Peterson, T. R. (2010b) How hunting strengthens social awareness of coupled human-natural systems. *Wildlife Biology in Practice* 6(2): 127–143.

Peterson, M. N., Peterson, M. J. and Peterson, T. R. (2005) Conservation and the myth of consensus. *Conservation Biology* 19(3): 762–767.

Peterson, M. N., Peterson, T. R. and Liu, J. (2013) *The housing bomb: why our addiction to houses is destroying the environment and threatening our society*. Baltimore, MD: Johns Hopkins University Press.

Peterson, M. N., Peterson, T. R., Peterson, M. J., Lopez, R. R. and Silvy, N. J. (2002) Cultural conflict and the endangered Florida Key deer. *Journal of Wildlife Management* 66(4): 947–968.

PLWA. (2014) *The North American model of wildlife conservation*. Online, available at: www.plwa.org/viewarticle.php?id=36 (accessed 9 December 2014).

Prukop, J. and Regan, R. J. (2005) In my opinion: the value of the North American model of wildlife conservation – an International association of fish and wildlife agencies position. *Wildlife Society Bulletin* 33(1): 374–377.

Robertson, M. M. (2004) The neoliberalization of ecosystem services: wetland mitigation banking and problems in environmental governance. *Geoforum* 35(3): 361–373.

Sax, J. L. (1970) The public trust doctrine in natural resource law: effective judicial intervention. *Michigan Law Review* 68(3): 471–566.

TWS. (ed.) 2013. *Final TWS position statement: the North American model of wildlife conservation*. Bethesda, MD: The Wildlife Society.

Vira, B. and Adams, W. M. (2009) Ecosystem services and conservation strategy: beware the silver bullet. *Conservation Letters* 2(4): 158–162.

Wagner, F. H. (1989) American wildlife management at the crossroads. *Wildlife Society Bulletin* 17(3): 354–360.

Walker, S., Brower, A. L., Stephens, R. T. T. and Lee, W. G. (2009) Why bartering biodiversity fails. *Conservation Letters* 2(4): 149–157.

Wunder, S. (2007) The efficiency of payments for environmental services in tropical conservation. *Conservation Biology* 21(1): 48–58.

8 Dialogue for Nature Conservation

Attempting to construct an inclusive environmental policy community in Sweden

Hans Peter Hansen and Tarla Rai Peterson

Introduction

Public policy relating to environmental conservation has undergone dramatic changes over the past century. The first half of the twentieth century saw widespread environmental devastation, ranging from air and water pollution that directly impacted human health to rising rates of species extinctions that most humans were not even aware of. In response to the agitation that emerged from increased public awareness of the anthropocentric causes of these problems, environmental concerns moved from the fringes to the centre of politics. Public interest in, and chemical companies' hostility toward Rachel Carson's *Silent Spring* (1962) prompted executive action by US president John F. Kennedy and secretary of the interior Stewart Udall, who remained in his post through the subsequent presidency of Lyndon B. Johnson (Lear, 2009). The unusually enthusiastic public response to the book, followed by scientific studies that validated Carson's claims that environmental degradation directly impacted human health, contributed to expanded pesticide regulation, as well as other environmental policy, in Europe, the United Kingdom and the United States (Jameson, 2012; Waddell, 1998). The Stockholm Declaration (UNEP) of the 1972 United Nations Conference on the Human Environment stated that people have a "fundamental right to freedom, equality, and adequate conditions of life, in an environment of a quality that permits a life of dignity and wellbeing". It proclaimed a "solemn responsibility to protect and improve the environment for present and future generations". During the 1970s, green parties became part of the official political scene in several European nations, and in 1984 the first Greens were elected to the European parliament (Bomberg, 1998; Global Greens; Jordan and Adelle, 2012). And in the United States, candidate after candidate proclaimed himself to be the future "environmental president" (Peterson, 2004).

Public support for efforts to preserve and restore environmental quality has eroded during the latter decades of the twentieth and the first decade of the twenty-first centuries, however (Rowell, 1996). According to regular studies such as Eurobarometer, Europeans continue to list protecting the environment as "very important" and to position its importance similarly to economic factors, but were not likely to change their behaviours for environmental reasons (see Eurobarometer 2008). Polls have found US residents to be less concerned with environmental issues at the beginning of the twenty-first century than they were during the 1970s and 1980s (Swanson, 2013).

Some of the erosion of public support can be explained by "corporate ventriloquism", where industry works with image consultants to brand themselves as supportive of local culture, and then uses "trade associations and advocacy organizations that produce websites, advertisements, videos, and other messages ... to create the impression of broadly based support" (Bsumek, *et al.*, 2014: 22). For example, when coal companies in the United States claim to speak for the residents of Appalachian communities that historically have provided the company's labour force, they may or may not be fully representing those communities. Another reason for increased public apathy, and even hostility, to environmental law and policy may be the ways that community involvement in environmental policy has been circumscribed within institutionalised political and economic systems (Jordan and Liefferink, 2004; Petersen *et al.*, 2008). The same political process that has institutionalized conservation has also narrowed opportunities for citizen engagement in environmental issues. Although we do not dispute the strategic importance of institutionalization, it has brought unexpected problems in the form of citizen disengagement from policy development and implementation related to environmental issues. For example, Laessoe (2007) argues that, in Denmark, citizen participation in environmental debates has changed "from a grassroots movement to professionally – indeed even commercially – mediated involvement; from contestation of values and political ideology to dealing with household technologies; from confrontation to consensual actions" (p. 232). The shift to a professionally managed process that replaces contestation with consensus may discourage citizens from participation because their participation has become irrelevant to results. Von Essen *et al.* (2015) suggest yet another potential cause, rooted in a split between rural and urban populations, where rural residents claim that environmental policy is made without attending to their input.

Governments and agencies responsible for administering environmental management tasks have recognized the risks attendant to a disinterested, or even hostile, public and have attempted to reinvigorate participation opportunities. These attempts are formally embodied in laws such as the National Environmental Policy Act (NEPA), in the United States (1970) and the Convention on Access to Information, Public Participation in Decision-making and Access to Justice in Environmental Matters (Aarhus Convention) in Europe (2001). While both NEPA and the Aarhus Convention mandate some form of public participation in the assessment of activities that are likely to impact the environment, they do not respond directly to concerns about bureaucratic barriers to citizen involvement in environmental issues.

While recognizing that the structure of neoliberal democracies across much of Europe and the United States enables corporate ventriloquism by privileging markets over all else, we work from the optimistic perspective that, having been constructed, social structures may be de- and reconstructed. Or, as Burke (1950) put it, "the crumbling of hierarchies is as true a fact about them as their formation" (141). Dramatic events may create sufficient disturbance to crack open the hegemonic configuration formed by neoliberal ideology, and individual subjects can slither through these temporary spaces to transgress existing expectations.

Attempts to respond to the growing alienation toward environmental policy provide opportunities to examine alternatives to traditional bureaucratic responses. For example, Whiteside *et al.* (2010) explored how France's "*Grenelle de l'environnement*" opens new possibilities for democratic participation within the French administrative system. Klassen and Feldpausch-Parker (2011) explored how local and regional institutions can provide voice to communities by expanding their roles beyond traditional bureaucratic functions. Westberg, *et al.* (2010) described the Swedish Dialogue for Nature Conservation (DNC) as a response that attempted to provide NRM professionals with the communicative competence to act as change agents who would facilitate greater public participation in the environmental policy arena. In this chapter we examine the genesis of the DNC to identify some of the opportunities and challenges faced by those who attempt to create and maintain a space for meaningful community participation in both planning and implementing environmental policy.

The most basic terms for our analysis are rhetorical communication, community and democracy. Although communication can be defined much more broadly, we are focused on its rhetorical dimension, or "the use of language as a symbolic means of inducing cooperation in beings that by nature respond to symbols" (Burke, 1950, 43). Like all communication, rhetoric includes both constitutive and instrumental dimensions that simultaneously construct and deconstruct the realities that humans experience. For example, a coal company may find the possibility of regulations requiring coal mining to internalize more of the damages done to air, water and human health in mining communities to be unsatisfactory. So, the company broadcasts a photograph of happy, healthy-looking children under the banner, "Coal is Life" to help viewers experience that warm fuzzy feeling prompted by smiling children, and to believe they are contributing to these children's happiness by cooperating with the coal industry. On the other hand, an environmental organization may seek public cooperation in establishing regulations requiring the coal industry to internalize these damages. It may broadcast a photo of children standing outside a school that is downwind and downstream of a coal mining operation, along with numbers indicating the significantly higher rates of respiratory diseases among children living in such environments, in an attempt to persuade people to revise their positive attributions of coal as conducive to life. While there is no guarantee that either experience will lead to changes in personal or political behaviours, the reality experienced by people in that situation has changed. In both cases, an individual or an organization is attempting to construct a community of like-minded citizens.

Similarly to Callister (Chapter 3), we define community as constituted by communicative transactions, such as those described above, that delineate a shared space, contribute to the quality of life experienced by those who inhabit that space, and guide collective action among members of the group. We draw from Peterson *et al.* (2007) the idea that community extends beyond humans to include extrahuman citizens of Earth, although our focus here is on human-to-human communication. Our understanding of the democratic practices people use to promote such a community is guided by Huspek and Kendall's definition of democracy as, "a field of discursive struggle defined by political participants competing to get their words and meanings accepted by others in an effort to secure limited material and symbolic resources" (1991: 1). And, rhetorical communications are attempts to construct a democratic community by establishing, maintaining and increasing common ground among community members. Communication, community and democracy come together in the tension-filled practices of building, destroying and rebuilding a temporary political consensus about any environmental policy. As quickly as people join together to constitute a community that supports, for example, development of a nature reserve, divisions within the community begin to emerge; between leaders and followers, supporters and opponents, insiders and outsiders. And these divisions provide community members with rhetorical material for imagining and then substantiating various rankings among themselves. In this chapter, we examine the process of imagining and implementing a framework that could enable institutions charged with environmental management to align themselves with the individual subjects who make up these communities.

The DNC programme was envisioned as a means to construct a sense of democratic community for natural resource management (NRM) in Sweden by including a broad range of people and their concerns in management discussions (Regleringsbrev för budgetåret, 2003; Westman, 2011), and has been praised for its success in EU publications (i.e. DNC, 2009). In this chapter, we critically examine the antecedents and development of the programme to identify constraints that may have limited this effort to expand democratic participation opportunities, and therefore minimized its potential for community constructivity, and even supported the continuation of community destructivity for Swedish NRM. To understand to what extent the programme reflects the awareness of a loss in political legitimacy and of a need to reverse this trend, we explored both the social context and the political process leading to its implementation. We used interviews with key actors, supplemented by official documents and media directed to the general public, to discover how the goals of transforming nature conservation policy into a more deeply participative process shifted and were reinterpreted at various governmental levels, culminating in producing content and delivering the

DNC program. The analysis illuminates both the opportunities and challenges encountered when public institutions attempt to fully incorporate residents of local communities, including their value-based rationalities, into the decision space of environmental policy.

We first summarize the theoretical perspective that led us to explore the DNC program, concluding with a summary of our central research questions. Second, we explain the methods we used for our analysis. Third, we describe the development of the DNC program, from its ideational inception, through political negotiations, and finally, to planning for its implementation. In our discussion, we explore what the genesis and development of the DNC programme can teach us about relationships between individual citizens, democratic community participation, and environmental conservation.

Theoretical context

From a sociological perspective public apathy and cynicism toward politics has been linked with one of the most profound challenges of modernity; or how to incorporate multiple rationalities into the public sphere. No one has been more influential to the study of political legitimacy problems in modern society than Jürgen Habermas (see, for example, 1981, 1989, 1997), whose theories on the rationalities and communicative dynamics of modern society have provided a touchstone for understanding politics and democracy in Western societies.

Within the environmental sector, political pressure on the legitimacy of political institutions in Europe and the United States has increased dramatically (Jameson, 2012; Rowell, 1996). In some countries the pressure has been linked with political radicalization and a shift toward more conservative governments (Hansen, 2008; Jensen and Hansen, 2008). As a response to political pressure on their legitimacy, environmental authorities continually try to maintain and strengthen their ability to fulfil their missions. These efforts have increasingly incorporated communicative strategies conceptualised as democratic and participative measures (see, for example Beierle, 2002; Naturvårdsverket, 2003; Swedish Government, 2001; Naturvårdsverket and Skogsstyrelsen, 2005). In the literature, however, there is common acknowledgement that the success of these communicative strategies, including efforts to legitimate the sponsoring institutions, has been limited from a democratic point of view, (Boonstra and Frouws, 2005; Elling, 2008; Innes, 2004). One reason may be that these institutionally initiated measures to enhance participation reflect a relatively instrumental understanding of the underlying drivers of the problem.

Over the past decade, various experiments related to environmental conservation and community development have been implemented as efforts to repair people's detachment from policy-making and increase the potential for community driven participatory processes (i.e. Nielsen and Nielsen, 2006, 2007; Packham and Sriskandarajah, 2004; SLIM, 2004; Hansen, 2008). Several have focused on emancipating citizens through collective processes of social learning and interactions between citizens, technical experts, political authorities, etc. Some of these experiments in social learning and citizen interaction offer a significant break with mainstream political culture, but that very break is also their weakness. Because they are not formally connected with the political power structures of society, they are free to explore directions that may be closed to more official endeavours, but that freedom leaves them disconnected from actual policy. Even well-organized processes of social learning and deliberative processes at community levels are seldom capable of influencing the dominating institutional rationalities.

The public hostility toward institutions responsible for environmental conservation combines with structural barriers to certain rationalities to constitute an apparent paradox. On the one hand, public institutions require political legitimacy to carry out their tasks. They attempt to strengthen their legitimacy by demonstrating transparency, detailing the instrumental rationale used in decision-making. When successful, the ironic result of such activities is that making instrumental rationality transparent ignores or marginalizes many public values and hopes, which then delegitimizes the institutions that attempted to make themselves and their practices more legitimate.

Habermas (1981, 1989 and 1997) argued that a lack of legitimacy emerges from the failures of contemporary political institutions to exceed the boundaries of the (dominating) instrumental rationality of modernity. From this perspective, instrumental rationality entails a science of technical interests seeking to explain the natural and social worlds by logic and empirical observation. Also inherent to this category is strategic action with the intent of achieving an ability to exert control. Communicative rationality, on the other hand, has to do with reasonable decision-making that occurs in communities of rationally-minded decision-makers. Although there are numerous differences between these two types of rationality, the relative centrality of community and conversation is most important for this chapter. While instrumental rationality does not oppose the concept of community nor the practice of conversation, neither does it value or need them; communicative rationality, on the other hand, requires the practice of conversation within a community to emerge.

In this volume, Feldpausch-Parker *et al.* (Chapter 7) explored one example of the instrumental rationality that permeates modernity. In the case they examined, the dominance of neo-liberal economic logic has limited public understanding of the relations between humans and extrahumans such as wildlife to owner and owned, closing off the multiple varieties of self and other relations that could enable innovative wildlife conservation efforts. These boundaries prevent the institutional inclusion of the full spectrum of values, knowledge and future visions for how humans might inhabit Earth. Values, knowledge and visions from beyond the boundaries set up by neo-liberal rationality are often excluded from the decision-making process and are rarely integrated into policy. One way to open up these possibilities is to engage in genuinely communicative and deliberative interaction within the public sphere. We follow Habermas, in considering political legitimacy as fundamentally a sociological condition that cannot be attained through purely constitutional and legalistic means. It requires meaningful and open communication among the polity.

This communicative constraint of public institutions raises the crucial question of whether they are capable of exceeding the instrumental rationality of modernity to create a genuinely democratic and participative democracy where citizens and their desires make a difference. An additional and equally relevant question is whether it is possible and/or desirable from a democratic point of view for public institutions to institutionalise the public sphere through various modernization processes. The problem of legitimacy questions the whole process of ecological modernization (Hajer, 1995). As with any potentially controversial policy arena, it can be argued that the institutionalization of environmental politics has contributed to a lack of legitimacy that has enabled the political backlash that those agencies responsible for environmental policy have experienced.

Public legitimacy, thus becomes a question of collaborative identification of common social values, rather than optimizing the immediate and personal interests of individual actors. Rather than presuming that, within liberal democracies, institutions (both governmental and nongovernmental) serve as the primary receptacles of social values, this approach would emphasize the importance of the individual subjects to whom social values adhere, and who have varying degrees of freedom. These subjects jointly construct social values through their interaction with other subjects. Institutions of course remain significant, but no longer are the only important players. From this perspective environmental policy-making would be more effective if it could focus on enhancing both horizontal communicative processes between citizens of society, and vertical democracy (e.g. legal rights and regulations). With this sort of approach, questions of communicative ethics at the level of interpersonal encounters become equally important, with questions of procedural fairness and accountability, and measures of formal representation at the organizational level. In other words, this strategy of public administration has the potential to completely transform the role of environmental professionals from instruments of legal process and components of institutional structures to individual subjects who have both the ability and responsibility to engage in political action along with their fellow citizens.

In this analysis, we scrutinized the significance of the legitimacy problem, especially as it applies to environmental policy, by probing the inception of the DNC program, which was initiated by the Swedish government and developed by the SEPA.[1] In the following section, we describe the sociopolitical processes that led to the programme and begin to identify some of the challenges faced by the public institutions that attempt to expand the community of environmental decision-makers by instantiating diverse societal values and hopes into the decision calculus. We explore how the programme attempted to exceed traditional limitations by enabling environmental NRM professionals to incorporate multiple types of rationalities into their decision processes. Specifically we ask, to what extent the socio-political processes leading to the launch of the DNC maintained and reflected the broader political awareness and focus on legitimacy; and in what ways those who were involved in developing the programme were able to contribute to the goal of transforming environmental policy into a more dialogically based and participative policy process. We also question whether the planning process for the programme seriously included the objective of a more dialogically based and participative process for developing and implementing environmental policy, and if so, how ideas for expanding the community of those involved in environmental policy were operationalized. Finally, we explore how the initial concerns with democratic legitimacy shifted during the course of planning for the program, and how this may limit the DNC's utility for enabling a more inclusive political process.

Data and methods

We utilized both qualitative and critical methods to develop an appreciation for the intents of the individual subjects who envisioned and began planning for the DNC, and to refine our understanding of the programme itself. We collected data primarily through informant-directed interviews (Peterson *et al.*, 1994), with archival analysis providing supplementary texts. We selected a purposive sample of interviewees from those who contributed to development of the DNC program, including individuals drawn from multiple levels of governance. These interviews provided information on individual subjects' understanding of environmental policy, as well as their reflexivity regarding acceptable modes of rationality and what constituted democratic legitimacy. All interviews were audio recorded and completely transcribed. In keeping with qualitative research conventions, we have protected informant confidentiality by referring to most of our informants as team members. Because they played important leadership roles that meant they could be easily identified by any reader wishing to do so, however, we requested and received permission to use the names of Peter Westman and Björn Reisinger. We refer to interviews by date. For example, Westman, 26.09.12 refers to an interview conducted with Westman on 26 September 2012 and Team, 26.09.12 refers to an interview conducted on the same date with a team member whose identity remains confidential. We used archival analysis of government documents (both formalized and supporting materials) to clarify the political context, or the policy environment, within which the DNC was developed. This enabled us to more fully understand the rationalities motivating the institutional practices associated with development of the program.

A presumption that discourses constitute historically and culturally specific ways of being in the world through constructing different subject positions for all individuals guided our analysis. For more on the significance of communication as a construct of community, see Sprain *et al.*'s analysis of water conflicts (Chapter 13). We built on our interpretive approach to interviewing by subjecting the interview transcripts to critical discourse analysis, looking especially for the ways that participants differentiated between instrumental and communicative rationality. We considered statements that focused on how the programme contributed to the generic competence of individual employees of the institution to emanate from a more instrumental rationality, and statements that focused on how the program, the identities of individual employees, and the community where interactions occurred mutually constructed the meaning of competence to emanate from a more communicative rationality. In line with van Dijk (2001), we see discourse as more than language, and are interested in both the symbolic and material practices of discourse. Thus, it was crucial to contextualize the talk generated during interviews within ideas and beliefs about the social world where our informants' discourse existed, and continues to be produced. The government documents we found through archival research provided a glimpse at the institutional practices and power relationships that framed both informal social practices and ways of organizing that channelled the DNC from an ephemeral idea to a concrete program.

The DNC

The appropriation directive from the government to the Ministry of the Environment (hereafter the Ministry) for budget year 2007 included the spending authority and specification of the allocation of the appropriated funds, directing the SEPA to launch a programme to develop "competence in dialogue, local participation and local governance and conflict resolution mechanisms addressing practitioners working with nature conservation and natural resource management" by 30 September 2007 (our translation) (*Regleringsbrev för budgetåret 2007*, 2006, Mål 3). The formal statement of this goal (mål) in the section titled "Operational Measures to Protect Biodiversity" was the culmination of a multi-year process of recognizing and then responding to a growing legitimacy problem within Swedish NRM policy. The directive was the eventual result of a concerted attempt to transform Swedish nature conservation into a programmatically deliberative governance process that included local community participation. As part of this effort, the directive also marked the beginning of the development and implementation of the DNC program, a competence development programme that has become one of the most popular training programmes for Swedish civil servants workings with nature and nature conservation on regional as well as national levels. At the time of writing, more than 700 participants had been through the program.

Negotiating the political landscape

The impetus for the programme was a political transformation in the nature conservation policy of the Swedish Social Democratic Party in the 1990s.

After the Swedish parliament election in 1998 the political mandate of the Social Democratic government under prime minister Göran Persson was extended for an additional four years. Prime Minister Persson appointed Kjell Ingemar Larsson as minister of the environment. Although the Social Democrats have not historically identified the environment as a central issue (Swedish Social Democratic Party; Tipton and Aldrich, 1987), Larsson was especially interested in nature conservation and outdoor recreation. Larsson responded positively when Peter Westman and other members of his staff suggested the need for a stronger nature conservation policy (Westman, 22.06.11). The main argument offered for establishing a stronger policy was the fact that the Swedish state budget on biodiversity (which included nature conservation) had increased rapidly from approximately 200 million Swedish kroner, to two billion Swedish kroner. Policy and guidelines had not changed to reflect the larger budget, and the staff around Minister Larsson therefore produced an internal memorandum listing 13 reasons why the government should develop a new nature conservation policy. Consistent with values traditionally espoused by the Swedish Social Democratic Party, these reasons included (1) Nature conservation should become an engine for local development; (2) The protection of nature and cultural heritage are two aspects of the same landscape; (3) Local participation and dialogue are a precondition for successful nature conservation (Westman, 26.09.12).

Westman, who served as the director of natural resources for the Ministry, played a crucial role in systematizing the general idea into formal policy (Team, 11.07.11; Risinger, 28.09.12; Westman, 22.06.11). He emphasized that the new policy was intended to change the definition of Swedish nature conservation from a set of practices that excluded people from nature, into a set of practices that included people as part of the natural world and provided opportunities for local development. Based on previous experience as a development worker in Africa and Asia, Westman recognized the importance of involving local people when implementing conservation policies, and noted that the international development projects supported by Sweden demonstrated strong "participatory methods of involving local stakeholders, local communities, indigenous people" (Westman, 22.06.11). He found it ironic that awareness of the importance of local participation and control did not transfer from international development to domestic nature conservation, where he saw a striking lack of institutions or procedures for consultation with the general public, including local residents who were likely to be directly impacted. On the contrary, he experienced what he referred to as "a conservatism", especially at a regional level, that opposed spending resources intended for nature conservation on public involvement of any kind.

Westman (22.06.11) further emphasized that the Ministry intended both local participation and open dialogue to be crucial dimensions of the new policy. They assumed this would mean more direct participation from local governments, including (but not limited to) municipalities. He also noted an awareness that, although local control was the best way to ensure that those living most closely to the nature being conserved would be part of the polit-ical process, it was not necessarily synonymous with open and inclusive dia-logue, given that practices to exclude certain individuals are not the sole province of national-level governments.

The programme that eventually became the DNC grew out of this com-mitment to reform Swedish nature conservation policy into a political pro-gramme based on enhanced local participation, open dialogue and a stronger linkage between conservation policy and community development. The process of designing, planning and implementing the new Swedish nature conservation policy continued through the decade following 1998. Informal negotiations proceeded within the government as Westman and his colleagues persuaded their colleagues that the new perspective on nature conservation was consistent with the party's commitment to cooperative efforts to improve the human condition. Negotiations between the government and implement-ing agencies presented another challenge. Westman reported that the SEPA resisted the Ministry's efforts at first, explaining that "we at the Ministry tried to get it into the [annual appropriations directive from the government to agencies[2]].... The Environmental Protection Agency more or less refused two times. Then, the third time, we succeeded to get it in" (22.06.11).

Simultaneous to working within the government to legitimize the devel-opment of a dialogue programme in the annual appropriations directive, Westman also initiated discussions with Björn Risinger, who was the director of the department of natural resources at the SEPA, and with other SEPA personnel. Risinger (28.09.12) reported that the agency already was involved in several discussions about how to improve public involvement in NRM throughout Sweden. Although he had been focused on how to shift from centralized to regional management of Sweden's national parks, he realized that the proposal from the Ministry was consistent with the agency's efforts. Just as Westman faced resistance to his efforts to institutionalize such a program, so Risinger faced opposition as he endeavoured to decentralize Swedish NRM. Risinger had already encountered significant internal resist-ance to his attempts to increase local participation in both the planning and the implementation of environmental policy. He noted that he

> had to struggle a lot to convince both the Ministry and the people in the SEPA that it's better to push the management at least one step down to the regional level because they are closer to the local environment.
>
> (28.09.12)

The government's appropriations directives during the following years support Westman's assertion of resistance to institutionalizing a dialogue pro-gramme (*Regleringsbrev för budgetåret* [2003–2007]). The Social Democrats again won the election in 2002, which enabled the Ministry to continue pushing forward its vision for the DNC as a fundamental part of a new nature conserva-tion policy. The directive for 2003 merely told the SEPA to "work for more collaboration between nature conservation, cultural values and outdoor recreation". The directive for 2004 told the SEPA to "develop a procedure of nature conservation to strengthen the dialogue with citizens and meet the objective of good participation". This policy was reemphasized and further motivated in the government's statement on Swedish environmental objectives presented to the Swedish parliament in 2005 (Svenska miljömål – ett gemensamt uppdrag 2004/2005: 150), and in the directive for 2005 the government repeated the instruction to "strengthen the dialogue with citizens and meet the objective of good participation". The Ministry finally achieved their objective of including the DNC in the appropriation directive for 2006. This directive provided both funding and instructions for the SEPA to launch a programme to develop "competence in dialogue, local participation and local governance and conflict resolution mechanisms addressing practitioners working with nature conservation and natural resource management" (*Regleringsbrev för budgetåret 2006*, Mål 4) by 1 July 2007. Risinger explained that the rationale behind this programmatic shift was "to make the whole work of nature conservation more legitimate" (28.09.12).

Prime Minister Persson lost the 2006 election and the government switched to Conservative leadership, under Fredrik Reinfeldt as prime minister and Andreas Carlgren as minister of the environment. Despite the shift of government, however, the appropriation directive for budget year 2007 maintained the momentum for launching the DNC in 2007 (*Regleringsbrev för budgetåret 2007*, Mål 3). The only change was that the launch deadline was postponed from 1 July to 30 September.

Planning and developing the program

Faced with a hard deadline in 2007, the SEPA began "to very actively prepare [a program]" (Risinger, 28.09.12). As Risinger noted, the DNC programme was the direct result of "a proposal from the Ministry" (28.09.12). The Ministry intended that the directive should mandate the development of a programme to remedy a perceived gap in the education received by natural scientists working in conservation. As Westman explained,

> If you are employed in the government system you have no experience, you have not read a single word of ... how to deal with people, how to interact, how to mitigate conflicts. This is something totally new for these guys who are brilliant in lichens and fungi and so on.
>
> (22.06.11)

Risinger shared Westman's opinion regarding the relative ignorance among personnel working in the SEPA regarding how to interact productively with the citizenry. He assigned the task of developing a programme focused on, "dialogue, local participation and local governance and conflict resolution mechanisms" (*Regleringsbrev för budgetåret 2006*, Mål 4) to a handpicked team of SEPA personnel.

Risinger selected a leadership team that included professional backgrounds in anthropology, biology and communication. Team members were selected because of their past experience, their current responsibilities and their personal interest in being part of what they hoped would bring about positive change in Swedish NRM. As one member explained,

> It was supposed to be local management so Björn [Risinger] figured: "Well ok, this task must be with the people involved in management of protected areas"..., and they figured we had the right background and so on, that we could probably handle this task.
>
> (Team, 23.06.11)

Although their professional backgrounds differed, all team members were enthusiastic about the task. One member noted, "I thought that with my background I should be in on this.... I thought that I know what this is all about, and I got in to it of course" (Team, 11.07.11). Another member reported that she was "really interested in this with communication and so on, so I guess it was very natural for me to be in this project" (Team, 23.6.11). A third person, who noted that this was her first task "working with communication", explained further that, "it was a nice task to work with. I felt very engaged to it" (21.06.11).

As indicated above, the team identified the DNC as a communication program. With this definition in mind, they immediately began to attend relevant conferences and short-courses. They studied existing communication training programmes and interviewed a wide variety of social scientists, especially those working with NRM. When interviewed, all team members explicitly differentiated the purposes of the DNC from those of management. From their perspectives, management referred to the processes used to ensure that the agency fulfilled its primary mission and that agency tasks were completed efficiently. For example, one of the team members who claimed to have no experience working in communication also self-described her career as primarily focused on management. The entire team agreed with Westman and Risinger's assessment that few personnel working with environmental conservation in Sweden were good communicators. They did not know "how to talk to people, how to listen and how to involve people" (Team, 21.06.11). From their perspectives, this weakness posed an unnecessary threat to the legitimacy of nature conservation, and the DNC was intended to remedy the weakness.

The resulting DNC programme grew out of their attempts to interpret the "intentions of the government". Although they were pleased to have the resources to respond to a problem they already recognized, they also were nervous about the responsibility of designing both the form and content of a completely new program, based on "one short line written in this *regleringsbrev* [directive]". As one team member explained, "a program can mean so many things. It can be a learning program or it can just be a program on how we are supposed to work; more like regulations or guidelines or something". When they requested further clarification, "Björn [Risinger] ... had some dialogue with the Ministry to try to figure out what they meant". Apparently this dialogue did not clarify the government's intentions; in fact, "he didn't really get very clear instructions" (23.06.11). Left with considerable freedom to interpret the directive, they relied on their cumulative experience at SEPA, combined with their research into existing programmes, and "decided it should be some sort of competence development program, since the level of knowledge about communication and dialogue was so low" (23.06.11).

In developing the DNC programme, the SEPA team was responding to four points highlighted in the government directive: The programme should promote competence in (1) dialogue, (2) local participation, (3) local governance and (4) conflict resolution (*Regleringsbrev för budgetåret 2006*, Mål 4). They determined that enhancing the communication knowledge and skills of SEPA personnel could provide the basis for promoting all four competencies listed in the directive. Despite this potential, however, team members developed a programme that emphasized dialogue, participation and conflict resolution over governance. This may have occurred because they associated governance most closely with management, and "a lot of people at the EPA were also afraid of the words local management" (Team, 23.06.11). Team members expressed both nervousness about losing control of resources for which they were responsible, and anxiety about misinterpreting the directive's intent regarding governance. One team member noted that, "we were anxious not to – to give away enough control, but still feel – that we were in control, so to speak". Another explained, "there was a lot of anxiety ... if we would go too far, so to say, that we would actually – not follow the laws and regulations that we're supposed to follow" (Team, 23.06.11). When explaining the challenges associated with enabling local governance of conservation initiatives undertaken at the behest of national and international governments, a third team member noted that, "the people working with these questions ... have a task that is not possible to fulfil in many ways" (21.06.11). The team also explained that Risinger faced stiff resistance from the SEPA leadership, especially to efforts to increase local control of nature reserves.

Although he did not talk with us about internal resistance, Risinger expressed concern with the legal aspects of local governance, noting that,

> the legal problem is actually, as heads of state agencies we are responsible to the government and to the parliament that we are in control of what we are doing and that we are in control of the properties we own. And if we first buy property to have nature conservation, and then let other actors decide what's happening in them, we are not in control.
>
> (28.09.12)

He preferred that local governance should be enhanced through a separate (although related) effort, suggesting that, if we want more of the nature conservation overall to be; to work as local initiatives we should actually allocate more of the money to fund local projects than to fund the state system. For instance, we should give money to the municipalities to create nature reserves instead of letting the state agencies buy land for state reserves because you have a problem if you have state management where the state has no responsibility.

Risinger suggested that programmes providing conservation funds directly to local governments (such as municipalities), exemplified a politically and legally appropriate response to the desire for increased local control of NRM. Given both the anxiety about failing to fulfil agency responsibilities and concerns about potential legal challenges, the leadership team decided that the DNC programme would only include governance indirectly, and would emphasize dialogue, participation, and conflict management.

The decision to focus on communication meant that the term itself was subjected to meticulous consideration. Although communication may be viewed as purely instrumental, it may also be viewed as constitutive. When team members explained the importance of communication to us, they demonstrated awareness of both its immediate instrumentality and its constitutive potential. From their perspective, communication extends far beyond information transfer. When attempting to explain why they chose to focus the programme on communication training, one said that communication "should permeate – communication isn't just a task or something separate. It should be everywhere" (21.06.11). They also rejected a definition of communication that limited it to influence and manipulation, noting that some "say this is just cosmetic; that we do these courses so that we sound nicer". She rejected that assessment, explaining that, "we want it to be real. We want people who work with these questions; that they are actually listening and they are actually taking in the knowledge from other people" (21.06.11). Another team member said they had attempted to develop a programme that would give those working with NRM the "tools that they need to be ... secure or feel comfortable when they go out and meet people" (23.06.11). Team members recognized that, although information transfer is "one part" of communication, the DNC programme could not be limited to that aspect. Rather, "if we're going to be serious about it, [we have to include education] about the processes and how you act in those situations" (Team, 11.07.11).

Team members were passionate about the necessity of taking an expansive approach to communication, while at the same time they recognized how difficult it would be to incorporate the principals taught by the DNC programme into everyday work situations. As one noted, "Yes, we have to protect these areas. Yes, we have to work with democratic processes. And you should do both. You will manage.... You have to work with both these questions" (21.06.11). They also recognized that the programme would be most effective if they were able to institutionalize the dialogic aspects of communication, or "deliver some sort of idea [describing] how do we change our way of working so that we have time to work with dialogue?" Regretfully, however, "[they] didn't get that in to it" (11.07.11). From our perspective, these team members understood that their organization was stuck within instrumental rationality, and that the transformation Westman had imagined would not be realized without moving beyond that form of rationality. Further, they indicated awareness that they would need to come up with ways to meaningfully incorporate both community and dialogic communication to move in order to facilitate that transformation.

The role of individual subjects in transforming nature conservation

In this chapter we have explored to what extent and in what ways the DNC programme reflected the political awareness of a legitimacy gap between environmental policy makers and the citizenry, and the socio-political processes leading to its implementation. All of our informants were civil servants during the time the DNC programme was envisioned and during its development. As civil servants, they functioned as system representatives, and the systems where they worked functioned as tools to accomplish the goals that society has established (in this case, conservation of nature). But in some cases, it seems the tools, or organizations, have exceeded their boundaries. The participants have forgotten that individual subjects built the system, and that it can be remodelled if it is not fulfilling the goals that society has set for it. The civil servants themselves are humans who are driven by complex and conflicting rationalities that include, but are not limited to, the instrumental rationality most frequently used in public settings. Yet, as they strive to follow institutional rules and procedures that may need remodelling, they sometimes are complicit in the erasure of their personal sensibilities about appropriate relations between citizens, and between human society and its environment.

Westman was part of a government that sought to expand its mandate to include specific attention to environmental concerns. For that to work, nature conservation had to be reimagined in a way that was consistent with human freedom, equality and solidarity, ideals claimed by the Swedish Social Democratic Party. Westman's experience and perspectives made him an ideal individual to act as a change agent in this situation. His experiences with nature conservation in Africa and Asia had persuaded him that the legitimacy of nature conservation was dependent on dialogue with people who lived and worked with the nature being conserved, and he saw no reason why that principal would not apply to Swedish nature. While he was thoroughly enmeshed within the semi-permanent political structure of the Social Democratic Party, he did create meaningful change. Communicative ethics at the level of personal interaction are equally important, with questions of procedural fairness and accountability, and measurements of formal representation at the organizational level. He sought to transform the role of NRM professionals from instruments of legal process and institutional structures to individual subjects by emphasizing a dialogic approach to public participation. This does not necessarily preclude strategic approaches to public administration, but it does necessitate the inclusion of genuinely communicative approaches.

An analysis of the interviews with key actors, supported by the analysis of official documents enabled us to trace how the goals of transforming nature conservation policy into a more dialogically based and participative policy process shifted and were reinterpreted at various governmental levels. The new paradigm envisioned by Westman and his colleagues brought a fundamentally different logic to environmental conservation in Sweden, but it tended to be reduced to instrumental reasoning, with concomitant weakening of attentiveness to the needs of individual subjects, who would need to act as change agents, thus putting their sense of community with other civil servants at risk. Although the discourse includes more than language, linguistic choices themselves are powerful. For example, the linguistic shift from "competence" to "skill" illustrates narrowing the discursive frame to the point that the constitutive dimensions of communication were largely hidden by instrumental dimensions.

Lessons learned

Examining the genesis of the DNC programme enabled us to identify both opportunities and challenges that are likely to be encountered when public institutions attempt to incorporate non-instrumental, and explicitly value-based rationalities into the policy arena. Rather than presuming that, within liberal democracies, institutions (whether governmental or nongovernmental) serve as the primary receptacles of social values, this approach would emphasize the importance of the individual subjects to whom social values adhere, and who have varying degrees of freedom.

These subjects jointly construct social values through their interaction with other subjects. Institutions of course remain significant players, but no longer are the only important players. From this perspective, those who seek to build an inclusive conservation paradigm should focus on enhancing horizontal communicative processes between citizens of society, and the legitimacy problem becomes more than just a matter of vertical democracy (e.g. legal rights and regulations).

Questions of communicative ethics at the level of personal interaction become equally important to questions of procedural fairness and accountability. While formal representation at the organizational level remains important, it cannot be the *sine qua non* for democratic legitimacy. Development of the DNC demonstrates that a strategic focus on public participation as an opportunity for community engagement offers a model of public administration that has the potential to transform the role of environmental professionals from instruments of legal process within institutional structures to self-conscious subjects who interact with other citizens as individual subjects. To the degree that the DNC enables environmental professionals to experiment with new ways of interacting with citizens of communities where environmental conservation efforts are envisioned, it may strengthen democratic legitimacy as envisioned by Westman. At the same time, the gradual turn to legalistic concerns that occurred may limit the DNC's ability to generate a process that builds meaningful citizen participation into environmental policy development and implementation.

Notes

1 Swedish *Naturvårdsverket*.
2 Swedish *Regleringsbrev*.

References

Beierle, T. C. (2002) *Democracy on-line: an evaluation of the national dialogue on public involvement in EPA decisions*. Resources for the future: Washington, DC. Online, available at: www.rff.org/rff/Documents/RFF-RPT-demonline.pdf (accessed 30 March 2013).

Bomberg, E. (1998) *Green parties and politics in the European Union*. London: Routledge.

Boonstra, W. J. and Frouws, J. (2005). Conflicts about water: a case study about conflict and contest in Dutch rural policy. *Journal of Rural Studies* 21: 297–312.

Bsumek, P. K., Schneider, J., Schwarze, S. and Peeples, J. (2014) Corporate ventriloquism: corporate advocacy, the coal industry, and the appropriation of voice. In: Peeples, J. and Depoe, S. (eds) *Voice and environmental communication*. Basingstoke, Hampshire: Palgrave Macmillan, pp. 21–43.

Burke, K. (1950) *A rhetoric of motives*. London, UK: Prentice-Hall.

Conquergood, D. (2002). Lethal theatre: performance, punishment, and the death penalty. *Theatre Journal* 54: 339–367.

Dialogue for Nature Conservation. (2009) EECN Newsflash, 74, August 2009. Online, available at: http://ec.europa.eu/environment/networks/doc/newsflash/newsflash74.pdf (accessed 13 May 2014).

Elling, B. (2008) *Rationality and the environment*. London, UK: Earthscan.

Eurobarometer. (2008) *Attitudes of European citizens towards the environment*. Online, available at: http://ec.europa.eu/public_opinion/archives/ebs/ebs_295_en.pdf.

Global Greens: The partnership of the world's Green parties and political movements. Online, available at: www.globalgreens.org/.

Habermas, J. (1981) *Theorie des kommunikativenhandelns*. Frankfurt am Main: Suhrkamp. Two volumes. Translated by McCarthy, T. as *The theory of communicative action: reason and the rationalization of society* (1984) and *Lifeworld and system: a critique of functionalist reason* (1987). Boston, MA: Beacon Press.

Habermas, J. (1989) *The structural transformation of the public sphere: inquiry into a category of bourgeois society*. Boston, MA: MIT Press.

Habermas, J. (1997) *Between facts and norms*. Cambridge, MA: Polity Press.

Hajer, M. A. (1995) *The politics of environmental discourse: ecological modernization and the policy process*. Oxford, UK: Oxford University Press.

Hansen, H. P. (2008) *Demokrati&Naturforvaltning – enkritisksociologisk-historisk analyse afnationalparkudviklingeniDanmark* [Democracy and nature conservation – a critical sociologic-historical analysis of the development of national parks in Denmark]. Roskilde: Roskilde University.

Huspek M. and Kendall L. (1991) On withholding political voice: An analysis of the political vocabulary of a "non-political" speech community. *Quarterly Journal of Speech* 77: 1–19.

Innes, J. E. (2004) Consensus building: clarifications for the critics. *Planning Theory* 3: 5–20.

Jameson, C. M. (2012) *Silent Spring Revisited*. London, UK: A & C Black.

Jensen, C. and Hansen, H. P. (2008) "ArvenfraVadehavet" In: *Økologiskmoderniseringpå Dansk – Brudogbevægelserimiljøindsatsen* [Ecologic modernization in Denmark – shifts and changes in environmental policy]. Denmark: Frydenlund.

Jordan, A. J. and Adelle, C. (eds) (2012) *Environmental policy in the European Union: contexts, actors and policy dynamics*. London: Earthscan.

Jordan, A. J. and Liefferink, D. (2004) *Environment policy in Europe: the Europeanization of national environmental policy*. New York: Routledge.

Klassen, J. A. and Feldpausch-Parker, A. M. (2011) Oiling the gears of public participation: the value of organisations in establishing trinity of voice for communities impacted by the oil and gas industry. *Local Environment* 16: 903–915.

Laessoe, J. (2007) Participation and sustainable development: the post-ecologist transformation of citizen involvement in Denmark. *Environmental Politics* 16: 231–250.

Lear, L. (2009) *Rachel Carson: witness for nature*. New York: Henry Holt and Company.

Naturvårdsverket. (2003) *Lokalförankringavnaturvård, genomdeltagandeoch dialog, Rapport* 5264–0.

Naturvårdsverket&Skogsstyrelsen. (2005) *NationellaStrategierförformellsskyddavskog* (National strategies for formal forest protection). Swedish Environmental Protection Agency and Swedish Forest Agency, Stockholm. Online, available at: www.naturvardsverket.se/ Documents/publikationer/620-1243-6.pdf.

Nielsen, K. A. and Nielsen, B. S. (2006) *Enmenneskelignatur* (A human nature). Frydenlund, Denmark: Forlaget.

Nielsen, K. A. and Nielsen, B. S. (2007) *Demokratiognaturbeskyttelse*. Frydenlund, Denmark: Forlaget.

Packham, R. G. and Sriskandarajah, N. (2004) Systemic action research for postgraduate education in agriculture and rural development. *Systems Research and Behavioral Science* 22: 119–130.

Petersen, L. K., Læssøe, J., Holm, J., Remmen, A. and Hansen, C. J. (2008) *Økologiskmoderniseringpå Dansk – Brudogbevægelserimiljøindsatsen* ("Ecologic modernization in Denmark – shifts and changes in environmental policy"). Frydenlund, Denmark: Forlaget.

Peterson, T. R. (ed.) (2004) *Green talk in the White House: the rhetorical presidency encounters ecology*. College Station, TX: A&M University Press.

Peterson, T. R., Witte, K., Enkerlin-Hoeflich, E., Espericueta, L., Flora, J. T., Florey, N., Loughran, T. K. and Stuart, R. (1994) Using informant directed interviews to discover risk orientation: how formative evaluations based in interpretive analysis can improve persuasive safety campaigns. *Journal of Applied Communication Research* 22: 199–215.

Regleringsbrevförbudgetåret 2003 avseendeNaturvårdsverket, 2002.

Regleringsbrevförbudgetåret 2004 avseendeNaturvårdsverket, 2003.

Regleringsbrevförbudgetåret 2005 avseendeNaturvårdsverket, 2004.

Regleringsbrevförbudgetåret 2006 avseendeNaturvårdsverket. 2005. 1.1.2.2; Mål 4.

Regleringsbrevförbudgetåret 2007 avseendeNaturvårdsverket. 2006. 1.1.2.2; Mål 3.

Reus-Smit, C. (2007) International crises of legitimacy. *International Politics* 44: 157–174.

Rowell, A. (1996) *Green backlash: global subversion of the environmental movement.* London: Routledge.

Sanjek, R. (1990) *Fieldnotes: the making of anthropology.* Ithaca, NY: Cornell University Press.

SLIM. (2004) *Social learning for the integrated management and sustainable use of water at catchment scale.* Final report to the EU. Online, available at: http://slim.open.ac.uk/ (accessed 14 July 2006).

Svenskamiljömål – ettgemensamtuppdrag 004/05:150. Online, available at: www.riksdagen.se/sv/Dokument-Lagar/Utskottens-dokument/Betankanden/Arenden/200506/MJU3/.

Swanson, E. (2013) Poll finds Americans less concerned about the environment now than when Earth Day began. *Huffington Post.* Online, available at: www.huffingtonpost.com/2013/04/22/environment-poll-earth-day_n_3117003.html.

Swedish Government. (2001) Ensamladnaturvårdspolitik Skr. 2001/02:173.

Swedish Social Democratic Party: an introduction. Online, available at: www.socialdemokraterna.se/upload/Internationellt/Other%20Languages/TheSwedishSocialDemocraticParty.pdf (accessed 1 April 2013).

Tipton, F. and Aldrich, R. (1987) *An economic and social history of Europe from 1939 to the present.* Baltimore, MA: Johns Hopkins University Press.

UNEP (United Nations environment program). (1972) *Stockholm declaration of the United Nations conference on the human environment.* Online, available at: www.unep.org/Documents.multilingual/Default.asp?DocumentID=97&ArticleID=150.

van Dijk, T. A. (2001) Critical discourse analysis. In: Schiffrin, D., Tannen, D. and Hamilton, H. E. (eds) *The handbook of discourse analysis.* Oxford, UK: Blackwell Publishers, Inc, pp. 352–371.

von Essen, E., Hansen, H. P., Källström, H. N., Peterson, M. N. and Peterson, T. R. (2014) The radicalization of rural resistance: how hunting counterpublics in the Nordic countries contribute to illegal hunting. *Journal of Rural Studies*, in press. Online, available at: http://dx.doi.org/10.1016/j.jrurstud.2014.11.001.

Waddell, C. (ed.) (1998) *And no birds sing: rhetorical analyses of Rachel Carson's Silent spring.* Carbondale, IL: Southern Illinois University Press.

Westberg, L. Hallgren, L. and Setterwall, A. (2010) Communicative skills development of administrators: a necessary step for implementing participatory policies in natural resource management. *Environmental Communication* 4: 225–236.

Whiteside, K. H., Boy, D. and Bourg, D. (2010) France's "Grenelle de l'environnement": openings and closures in ecological democracy. *Environmental Politics* 19: 339–367.

Agonistic politics – instantiating community through dissent and nontraditional practice

9 Deconstructing public space to construct community

Guerrilla gardening as place-based democracy

Anne Marie Todd

In Los Angeles, sunflowers line the median of Imperial Drive. In London, street corner planter boxes bloom. In Berlin, a rose garden blossoms behind apartment buildings. These gardens, seemingly random against the broader urban milieu, are political acts (Ralston, 2012). Guerrilla gardening is the planting of public, often abandoned, land. The first known use of the term was by Liz Christy, who in 1973 started a Green Guerrilla group to transform an abandoned lot in New York City into a lush flower garden. That garden is now an official city park (McKay, 2011; Pasquali, 2006; Wilson and Weinberg, 1999).

Despite the decades-old history of this practice, recent surges of guerrilla gardening in cities around America have gained media attention. A story in the *Washington Post* (published in the Style section, underscoring the widespread view of gardening as a leisurely pastime) noted the rise of guerrilla gardening activity in cities like Pittsburgh, Detroit, Portland and Washington, DC, and reported its presence in over 30 countries (Wax, 2012a). An article published in the *Boston Globe* and *Seattle Times* to correspond with Earth Day 2012 declared "young urbanites are redefining the seemingly fusty pastime as a tool for social change" (Wax, 2012b, 2012c). The *Village Voice* shared the media fascination with guerrilla gardening, ascribing a resurgence of guerrilla gardening activism to the Occupy movement (Schwendener, 2012).

This chapter explores guerrilla gardening as environmental communication. The goal of this activism is to create "green community spaces in cities" (Reynolds, 2008: 43). Ultimately, guerrilla gardening is "gardening public space with or without permission" (Tracey, 2007: np). Guerrilla gardening communicates through symbolic action: "the illicit cultivation of someone else's land" (Reynolds, 2008: 16). A garden's natural beauty signifies growth and environmental health. Guerrilla gardening is a form of environmental communication, defined as a "symbolic medium" used in "constructing environmental problems and in negotiating society's different responses to them" (Cox, 2013: 19). A garden invites audiences to "view the garden, like the land, as a fully functioning ecosystem – and to incorporate the awareness that its impacts extend far beyond its footprint" (Reichard, 2011: 2–3). As James Cantrill and Christine Oravec (1996: 2) note, the "environment we experience and affect is largely a product of how we come to talk about the world". Guerrilla gardening is public discourse that aims to shape our understanding of urban environments.

Guerrilla gardening constructs community through communication: responding to the ills of urban development and negotiating a local response to them. Daniel Deudney (1996: 130) argues that, "communities are constituted by a 'here-feeling' derived from the shared habitation of a place, as well as by a 'we-feeling' of group solidarity and attributes shared in common". As environmental communication, guerrilla gardening redefines urban environments as public space to establish a here-feeling of place and constructs community through a shared sense of aesthetic responsibility.

In the next section of this chapter I lay out the context for this argument, discussing gardening as a discursive and aesthetic practice and as place-based communication. I then outline the method of rhetorical analysis and introduce the artefact. I present the findings of my analysis along two themes: deconstructing public space and constructing community. In the discussion, I consider the ethical implications of guerrilla gardening as place-based democracy. I conclude with a review of the theoretical frame of this chapter and offer a recommendation that follows from this analysis.

Context: gardening as environmental communication

Environmental communication is "the pragmatic and constitutive vehicle for our understanding of the environment as well as our relationships to the natural world" (Cox, 2013: 19). Environmental communication is pragmatic because it increases awareness of environmental issues and has the potential to mobilize community action. Guerrilla gardening is pragmatic because it alerts passers-by to a redefined place and it draws people in, mobilizing support for community gardens. Environmental communication is constitutive because it shapes our perceptions of the world around us and ourselves. Guerrilla gardening is constitutive because it reshapes our perceptions of the urban world around us, and thus renovates our understanding of ourselves as urban inhabitants. In this section I explain gardening as a discursive and aesthetic practice and discuss its function as place-based communication.

Discursive and aesthetic practice

Guerrilla gardening is a discursive practice. Richard Reynolds, a London-based activist whose website many guerrilla gardeners cite for its inspiration and instruction, notes in his handbook *On Guerrilla Gardening* that guerrilla gardening is a "powerful form of communication" (Reynolds, 2008: 28). He continues: "Gardening is a vivid form of expression. Doing it in public, on land that is not yours, sends an even stronger message" (52). Guerrilla gardening aims to change our perception of our environments and the way we experience them daily.

The environments we experience every day and our perceptions of ourselves within these settings influence the way we engage the world and how we understand environmental messages (Cantrill, 2004). Gardening is a symbolic act, while gardens themselves communicate, shaping public space and thus our perceptions of our environments. The transformation of an empty lot into a wildflower garden makes a declaration. David Tracey, author of *Guerrilla Gardening: A Manualfesto*, advocates using gardening as a communication tool: "if you have something to say in a guerrilla display, don't be afraid to shout" (Tracey, 2007: 72).

Guerrilla gardening is also an aesthetic practice, "tending a defined space for the cultivation or appreciation of natural things" (Tracey, 2007: 4). Our aesthetics emerge in our appreciation of natural settings, our grand and everyday environs. An awareness of natural beauty support for ongoing environmental preservation (Chapple and Tucker, 1994). Environmental aesthetics considers the role of place in how we interpret experience and rests on the assumption that the world's environments offer much to appreciate (Carlson, 1992, 2001, 2002, 2009). Aesthetic appreciation reveals the history of a place through its "configuration of features, its ways of holding those who live there, its resources for living, its affordances and limitations" (Carbaugh and Cerulli, 2013: 5). Guerrilla gardens cultivate a sense of place through "the perception of what is most salient in a specific location", which influences personal and social values and public appraisal of a place's significance to the public interest (Cantrill and Senecah, 2001: 187). Guerrilla gardening defines urban spaces in such a way that fosters an understanding and appreciation of the transformation of public places.

Place-based communication

Guerrilla gardening is an example of what Spurlock (2009: 5) calls "place-based, embodied experiences". Gardening is "meaning-making, enhancing attachments to place and engaging with [the] natural environment to create identity" (Kiesling and Manning, 2010: 317). Guerrilla gardening transforms urban spaces into meaningful places – inviting human interaction through discursive and aesthetic practices.

James G. Cantrill and Susan Senecah (2010: 188) explain that our "sense of place is socially constructed upon an edifice of the environmental self that, in itself, is a product of discourse and experience". We define our community environment by talking about and moving through a place. Human interaction and communication transform our terrestrial environment into places of significant meaning in public imagination (Thompson and Cantrill, 2013). Guerrilla gardening activists engage public spaces in unexpected ways by transforming typical urban scenes into gardens.

Guerrilla gardening establishes community through activism. A healthy public sphere relies on democratic engagement in communicative processes (Peterson and Horton, 1995). In this way, environmental discourse becomes a set of social practices that create a more engaged community (Peterson *et al.*, 2007). Guerrilla gardens thus promote a democratic aesthetic, fostering a sense of cultural connection among residents with diverse cultural customs and values (Hariman, 2000; Hariman and Lucaites, 2002). Community gardens are sites of democratic engagement. They are places where residents engage in activities to transform their environments. Tending a garden is a social activity: as residents come together to sow seeds for flowers and vegetables, they establish roots in the community: making connections to each other and investing in their environs.

Analytical method: rhetorical criticism

This chapter uses rhetorical criticism to explore guerrilla gardening as a rhetorical practice. I consider rhetoric as the "epistemic grounds upon which people base their everyday choices" (Gallagher and Zagacki, 2005: 192–193). Environmental rhetoric concerns communication that appeals to ecological implications of our actions. "Although nature is more than a rhetorical text, human actions and political institutions associated with it function rhetorically" (Peterson *et al.*, 2010: 418). Guerrilla gardening is an example of environmental rhetoric in that it attempts to persuade audiences to adopt a certain perspective about the environment.

To analyse the environmental rhetoric of guerrilla gardening, I engage in a process of rhetorical criticism, which "investigates the situated uses and effects of language (or symbolic action) by particular human agents, in particular times and places for particular purposes" (Spoel and Hoed, 2014: 272). Rhetoric connects knowledge with action, mobilizing "the democratic potential in society" (Myerson and Rydin, 1996: 32). This "is an interpretive method of research not aimed at producing broad generalizations about human communication, but instead concerned with developing context-specific interpretations of the situated complexities of human symbolic action" (Spoel and Hoed, 2014: 272). In conducting this criticism, I interpret guerrilla gardening as rhetorical activism within the specific context of place.

I inquire how guerrilla gardening rhetoric promotes environmental community. Rhetoric animates social action, engaging public audiences by creating meaning around shared experiences that build identification with community. "The abstract forms of civic life have to be filled in with vernacular signs of social membership" (Hariman and Lucaites, 2003: 25). In this way guerrilla gardening is rhetorical – it seeks to develop attachments with place and to inspire community engagement.

This chapter analyses the rhetorical strategies of guerrilla gardening manuals to demonstrate how guerrilla gardening discourse constructs and deconstructs community. To exemplify an activist discourse of guerrilla gardening, I examine the two most prominent published guerrilla gardening manuals: from England, Richard Reynolds's *On Guerrilla Gardening: A Handbook for Gardening without Boundaries*, and from Canada, David

Tracey's *Guerrilla Gardening: A Manualfesto*. I chose these two manuals because they are the only published guerrilla gardening books readily available in the United States, and because they are the two most frequently cited in popular press articles about guerrilla gardening. As such they influence the actions of guerrilla gardeners and shape public perception about the movement. I read these handbooks as examples of place-based communication practice, artefacts that exemplify what Carbaugh and Ceruli (2013: 5) call "the various discursive devices available to communicate our nature and our environments in linguistically and culturally particular ways". Reynolds and Tracey's manuals are the rhetoric of the guerrilla gardening movement. I identify significant patterns in their rhetorical strategies and weave their words throughout the analysis as examples of guerrilla gardening discourse. In the next section I discuss the findings that emerge from my analysis along two themes: deconstructing public space and constructing community.

Findings

This analysis of guerrilla gardening discourse reveals that guerrilla gardening deconstructs preconceived notions about public space in order to reconstruct a sense of community rooted in place. Such activism constructs community through civic engagement aimed at social change. This section first explains the two ways in which guerrilla gardeners deconstruct public space: through a critique of the urban spaces and the transgression and transformation of these spaces into community places. Following that is an analysis of how guerrilla gardens construct community through aesthetic appeal and civic engagement.

Deconstructing public space

Reclaiming public space means reshaping the places where community members live, work and play. Spurlock (2009: 5) notes that embodied place-based discourse has "significant potential for challenging unsustainable discourses of consumerism".

Critique

Guerrilla gardeners critique city spaces that encourage "isolation, alienation, disembodiment and waywardness" (Tracey, 2007: 37). Guerrilla gardening focuses on "the smaller details of public spaces that give a place personality [and] are being erased by globalized commerce and globalized landscape architecture, planning rules and codes of conduct. Public space is increasingly anodyne" (Reynolds, 2008: 52). Gleaming office towers house global financial networks. Industrial warehouses are designed for the efficient production and distribution of goods. Chain store facades caricature revered architectural styles. These all erase the diversity and personality of urban centres. Guerrilla gardeners create a visual critique by constructing salient spaces that are meaningful for local identity. "By breaking rules, guerrilla gardeners are challenging the conventions of society. Doing so in public space is a direct rejection of our political environment" (Reynolds, 2008: 246). This is what Ross Singer (2011: 345) calls "a visual, affective, embodied, and place-based refutation of a dominant cultural logic that dissociates bodies and particularities from spaces they inhabit". Guerrilla gardeners change the urban environment and thus change the way that city residents experience urban landscapes. By transforming the environment that urban dwellers move through, guerrilla gardening influences their perspective on the world and their place in it.

Guerrilla gardeners critique a central precept of capitalism – private property. Guerrilla gardeners "argue that vacant land should serve the community, and that owning the land does not release anyone from this responsibility. Such a practice challenges the concept of private property, particularly in an area of high-population density" (Green, 2008: 1). Land ownership is not a meaningful way to organize public space. Reynolds explains, "there is neglected orphaned land all over the place. Pockets of resistance have broken out in some areas as guerrilla gardeners fight back to reclaim this precious resource and cultivate it" (Guerrilla Gardening, 2013). Reynolds' comments reflect the view of many guerrilla gardeners that private owners neglect their responsibility to the community. Guerrilla gardens are a visual statement declaring community responsibility for the neglected land.

> An empty city lot makes a classic guerrilla gardening site, and a good place for a dramatic entry into the campaign. If we agree that a city is a shared experience, something we all create together, what kind of anti-social message is made by someone who buys a prominent space in a crowded district and leaves it to collect litter?
>
> (Tracey, 2007: 50)

This critiques a lack of accountability by property owners and city officials and a broader attitude of complacence toward urban blight.

Guerrilla gardening critiques the development mind-set that pervades city planning. Reynolds likens the continual process of maintaining a garden to the ongoing activist movement.

> Cultivating a garden is always a fight. We cut back one plant to allow another one to flourish; we scatter seeds, but we rip up weeds and snatch away flowers and fruit before their seed has dispersed. Our gardens are scenes of savage destruction. Animals uproot, frosts cripple, winds topple, rains flood. The guerrilla gardener shares this constant battle with nature with other gardeners. But we have other enemies and ambitions.
>
> (Reynolds, 2008: 9)

This description might as well portray classic tales of bureaucratic struggle in which administrative red tape thwarts institutional change and environmental reform meets obstacles and setbacks at every turn. Guerrilla gardening is an ongoing critical act. It attempts to redress a lack of a sense of place by deconstructing the boundary between public and private space.

Transgression and transformation

Guerrilla gardening challenges public norms, transgressing rules and traversing borders to claim public space. In doing so, guerrilla gardening deconstructs the notion of public and private spaces. The manuals define public space as "places we share environmentally", which "can include private land even if the only access is visual" (Tracey, 2007: 5). Guerrilla gardening arises from a belief that a cultural emphasis on private property has undervalued community spaces. This premise refutes the concept of private space and expands public space to include all visual features of the urban landscape.

Tracey explains, guerrilla gardening is a "reclaiming of public spaces by the public for the public" and thus "a way to begin taking back control" (Tracey, 2007: 47). By showing how abandoned private land affects public life, guerrilla gardening responds to erroneous city planning and the compartmentalization of public and private space. Planting areas without permission "breaches a sacrosanct boundary, the line between public and private space. To intervene, however benignly, on property that is not one's own, is one of the ultimate transgressive acts in a social system based on private ownership" (Johnson, 2006). Guerrilla gardeners physically cross the line between public and private land and in doing so cross legal lines that prohibit this act. The deconstruction of existing public spaces opens the possibility that these spaces could be more usable and more liveable. By cultivating vegetation, guerrilla gardeners cultivate a sense of community.

Thompson and Cantrill (2013) identify the transformation of place through human interaction. Through community activities around tending a shared space, guerrilla gardening transforms previously uncared for places. The goal of guerrilla gardening is to "take a public place of wasted opportunity and turn it into a garden" (Reynolds, 2008: 219). Guerrilla gardening is

> a surreptitious act that leaves hard-to decipher traces on the landscape. Who really knows if those sunflowers along the laneway are the result of intention or serendipity? But perhaps that's the main point – unexpected growth with a hint of purpose opens up questions, invites consideration.
>
> (Johnson, 2006: 11)

Guerrilla gardens influence people's perceptions of their environment and themselves. Unexpected flowers in unanticipated places invite passers-by to reconsider the beauty of their urban environment and revaluate their relationship to it. "Even a transformed roadside verge signals the potential for change.

We know we should take greater responsibility for the health of the planet by changing our patterns of consumption and production" (Reynolds, 2008: 247). Guerrilla gardeners encourage citizens to be more aware of their complicity in the degradation of urban environments and take responsibility. Reynolds describes such activism as "a battle for resources, a battle against scarcity of land, environmental abuse and wasted opportunities. It is also a fight for freedom of expression and for community cohesion. It is a battle in which bullets are replaced with flowers" (Reynolds, 2008: 16). Guerrilla gardeners chip away at the dominant urban landscape by creating pockets of beauty. By changing the configuration of urban features, guerrilla gardeners declare gardens to be part of the urban landscape, and thus resources for urban living. Ultimately, guerrilla gardening transforms public spaces and creates the possibility for change.

Reynolds and Tracey's manuals are explicitly activist: they include detailed how-to guides for successful guerrilla gardening, with tips about what to plant and how to not get caught. Reynolds describes an

> organic movement.... Like a virulent plant, it has sprung up whenever the environmental conditions of society have been conducive to it. Like seeds blowing from one patch to flower in another nearby, guerrilla gardens grow and adapt to local conditions, and in time take on new characteristics, almost like new species of a genus.
>
> (Reynolds, 2008: 22–23)

Here Reynolds compares the gardening movement to the changing environment, describing the urban landscape as an ecosystem. Guerrilla gardens create a sense of connection within an urban environment, engaging humans in the world around them.

Constructing community

Guerrilla gardeners deconstruct public space through a critique of the broader social systems that create urban landscapes. They transgress private property lines between public and private space to transform urban spaces into meaningful places. Carbaugh and Cerulli (2013: 6) note that "by losing sight – or touch, or feel, or smell – of our places, we risk being unsettled in our thoughts, floating above and beyond our immediate circumstances, where we indeed live". Guerrilla gardening responds to the problem of being unrooted in urban spaces. Activists reshape the city to create public places that are more reflective and supportive of the community. Guerrilla gardeners construct community in two ways: through aesthetic appeal and through civic engagement.

Aesthetic appeal

Guerrilla gardening constructs community by "growing beauty out of urban blight" (Tracey, 2007: 1). The visual beauty of a flower garden in an abandoned lot highlights and transforms urban blight. In guerrilla gardening discourse, "the message is about the potential for creating beauty and productivity in the landscape" (Reynolds, 2008: 14). For example, the Southern California group, Los Angeles Guerrilla Gardening, publicizes its mission as "to get our hands dirty by starting gardens all over Los Angeles. To be a resource for other potential Guerrilla Gardeners and a home base for people interested in brightening their own communities" (Los Angeles Guerrilla Gardening, 2013: np). Guerrilla gardening improves community beauty and in doing so aims to strengthen community health.

In this way, guerrilla gardening communicates an aesthetic of sustainability. A catchphrase of one guerrilla gardening handbook – "say it with sunflowers!" – resonates with the idea of gardening as a discursive practice. Sunflowers are "an antidote to the problems within cities" expressing "beauty, productivity, community and a great deal of optimism" (Reynolds, 2008: 57). Guerrilla gardening changes the appearance of the landscape and in doing so shifts the mindset of urban community members. The aesthetics of a place shapes the identity of those who live there. Guerrilla gardening increases the salience of the urban environment, fostering attachments and a shared sense of community.

Gardens are created through human activity – cultivated through the symbolic transformation of place. The choice of when and where to plant flowers and vegetation can be a powerful "expression of the gardener's vision and sometimes a specific message. The guerrilla gardener in public space reaches out to others and uses plants to draw people in" (Reynolds, 2008: 28). Planter boxes around utility poles and blubs planted in medians configure the features of urban landscape to hold those who live, work and play there. Tracey explains,

> people might enter a newly gardened space for a closer look, decide to linger and even mingle. It could have seating with footrests for seniors and a place for new mothers to park strollers. It could be a garden to stimulate not the eye but the nose: imagine sidewalk blooms designed to remind a commuter crowd that life can still be sweet even when the job isn't, or a grassy, earthy aroma meant to evoke the idyll of the meadow on a summer day.
>
> (Tracey, 2007: 101)

Green spaces enhance the sensual experiences of the urban landscape, promoting an environmental aesthetic that fosters attachment to place.

Aesthetic improvements do more than invoke appreciation. As people walk past and observe a garden's growth over time, their awareness of the natural world, often obscured by urban development, increases. Aesthetically appealing gardens amidst urban blight signal a change in approach and promote a sense of shared responsibility. "Just the display of volunteer activity – a sign that somebody cares – can be enough to stop others from littering.

It may go beyond that to uplift a neglected or shunned place into an attraction" (Tracey, 2007: 101). In transforming public spaces, guerrilla gardens transform public attitudes toward the environment.

Guerrilla gardening offers a way for individuals to "reclaim public space for the public good" (Tracey, 2007: 1). Responding to the alienation of many urban environments, guerrilla gardens can create pleasant places for community gathering outside of the consumer economy.

> There are very few places in this city or country where people can come together without paying money, do not have to buy a drink to sit there, can come and go as they please, garden, build art, or just socialize, have a barbecue and be in a positive space, not a concrete box, learn stuff, get job skills, just getting their hands in the dirt.
>
> (Reynolds, 2008: 44)

Guerrilla gardens create places where people socialize as community members, not as consumers. This is an alternative to cities designed for industry and commerce, not community.

These manuals demonstrate how guerrilla gardening discourse emphasizes the role of a healthy, vibrant environment in sustaining a healthy community. This is a vision for social change, based on "happier, more sociable and sustainable" communities (Reynolds, 2008: 247). Guerrilla gardens "can create social legacies that last generations. They can turn lives around and reshape derelict city spaces into urban wonders" (Tracey, 2007: 139). Guerrilla gardening communicates a vision for sustainable communities, creating public spaces that emphasize our relationship to place. This vision of community imbues all citizens with responsibility for the health of their surroundings. Moreover, such gardening discourse establishes the role of a healthy, vibrant environment in sustaining a thriving urban community.

Civic engagement

Guerrilla gardening manuals define public space as "places we share environmentally" (Tracey, 2007: 5). This invokes the "we-feeling" that Deudney describes as essential to community. In turn, this promotes civic engagement. "Choosing to cultivate someone else's neglected land is taking responsibility where others have not" (Reynolds, 2008: 247). This vision of community imbues all citizens with responsibility for the health of their surroundings. Frauke 242, a guerrilla gardener in Berlin notes that, "everything happens through the community. That means exchange, learning from one another, self-organization, ecological aspects, waste reduction" (Reynolds, 2008: 46-47). Guerrilla gardening creates spaces of discourse through social interaction and grassroots activity.

The guerrilla gardening community promotes civic engagement by inviting individuals to participate in the transformation of previously unused public spaces into usable places. Community members participate in the creation of the garden and community engagement continues through the use of the transformed space. Guerrilla gardeners see themselves as doing a "public service that the city cannot afford to pay for" (Reynolds, 2008: 47). Guerrilla gardening offers individuals a chance to reinvent their role in the community:

> You may redefine your role as a citizen as you discover new ground on which to make a stand. Start by shedding that urban exoskeleton of cynicism and dread. Continue by merging into a larger movement of all things living. No longer a passive consumer, you become what has never been needed more: an active citizen engaged in your environment.
>
> (Tracey, 2007: 1)

These handbooks seek to instil a sense of responsibility that each guerrilla gardener is

> an active participant in the living environment. You're no longer content to merely react to what happens to the spaces around you. You're a player, which means *you* help determine how those spaces get used. And when you're in tune like this, every plant counts.
>
> (Tracey, 2007: 32)

Guerrilla gardens change our perception of the city as environment, establishing the possibility of crowd-sourcing city planning. Gardens allowed to thrive suggest the permissibility of this type of activism and (un)pave the way for more gardens. Ultimately community gardens construct "spaces of discourse … through social interaction and grassroots activity" (Ralston, 2012: 12). Guerrilla gardeners are "part of an ecosystem" and thus "share a responsibility for the web of life that supports you and everything else". In this way, guerrilla gardeners, promote an "eco-based code of ethics" (Tracey, 2007: 31).

Hariman might call this a democratic aesthetic: creating cultural continuity across diverse norms and practices. Tracey notes "guerrilla gardening thrives on differences. Different gardeners, different styles, different attitudes, different tactics – all leading to the same results: a healthier environment and a better city" (Tracey, 2007: 31). Gardeners of different backgrounds and perspectives – one person preferring succulents, another choosing narcissus bulbs – can promote a community vision based on a sense of connectedness to place. Guerrilla gardening handbooks ask individuals to reclaim public space to create more vibrant, healthy communities.

Discussion

In his book, *A Philosophy of Gardens*, David Cooper (2006) suggests that an ethic of gardening derives from a moral sense of a good life. Cultivating a plot of earth, no matter where or how large, contributes to a sense of place, and as such gardening is "our principal means of being connected to the earth" (Endicott, 1996: 10). The handbooks I analyse promote this perspective. They offer an approach to gardening that starts with safe, sustainable seeds that provide "the material and intellectual conditions for an entire community to flourish" (Ralston, 2012: 12). The sustainability ethic promoted by these manuals raises the possibility of gardening as an ethical practice based on a sense of place. Guerrilla gardening advocates particular visions of community through sensory appeals of environmental sustainability.

Civic environmentalism draws upon individuals' connection to place to persuade them to actively participate in their local communities (Baber and Bartlett, 2005: 195). Guerrilla gardening engages citizens by linking environmental problems to the experience of daily life and providing opportunities for individuals to identify with the environment. (Killingsworth and Palmer, 1992). This can have implications for global action. As Cantrill and Oravec (1996) note, individuals' broad understanding of the "world at large" directly influences their local actions. Guerrilla gardens represent a microcosm of broader human development. "The challenge of fighting scarcity and neglect on a global scale seems distant and insurmountable as you dig away trying to transform a tatty tree pit" (Reynolds, 2008: 219). The guerrilla gardener focuses on addressing the ills of global industrialization that are evident in her own city. "Community gardens are more than gardens. They're community-building resources that use the ripple effect of good ideas to spread beyond the immediate area and time" (Tracey, 2007: 139). Guerrilla gardening cultivates a sense of place through a radical form of community engagement. Guerrilla gardeners build community by claiming public places for the public good. Such activism takes back the (urban) commons to develop community sustainability. In taking responsibility for previously unkempt lands, activists reclaim a sense of community that has been lost in the urban milieu. The guerrilla gardening manuals discussed here reflect a belief that the neglected public spaces signify the deterioration of the cultural worth of public spaces, either publically or privately owned. By cultivating gardens to claims such spaces, guerrilla gardeners attempt to reclaim a lost sense of community. Highlighting the connection between guerrilla gardening practices and cultivating community, this study furthers our understanding of gardening as an environmental practice and its implications for the relationship between community and place. This research demonstrates the possibilities of social change in sustainable gardening discourse and explicates the importance of gardening discourse's aesthetic in constructing ethical principles of sustainable community.

Conclusion

Guerrilla gardening is at once a commentary on urban aesthetics, a critique of private property ownership, and a call for civic engagement. This chapter establishes a theoretical frame for place-based democracy. Embodied place-based practices that challenge the status quo construct community and promote civic engagement. Guerrilla gardeners deconstruct public space through the embodied critique of the urban environment, and through the transgression of public norms and boundaries and the transformation of geographic and social space. Guerrilla gardens construct community through aesthetic appeal and civic engagement.

This analysis suggests that guerrilla gardening can enhance a sense of place in urban communities and promote civic engagement. The power of places is in "their ability to communicate with or to us as we are there in them". Such discourse is central to our knowledge of our places and our ability to understand their influence on us (Carbaugh and Cerulli, 2013: 20). Guerrilla gardens can enhance urban experiences for residents by beautifying the land and drawing them in. Guerrilla gardens offer an alternative for cities looking for ways to incorporate more green spaces and to keep residents engaged. Guerrilla gardens cannot be regulated, cannot be sanctioned, or they lose the critique that animates them, but cities would do well to look the other way and recognize the virtue of these citizen-planted gardens as symbols of a thriving city environment, made better by individuals who care about their community.

References

Baber, W. F. and Bartlett, R. V. (2005) *Deliberative environmental politics: democracy and ecological rationality*. Cambridge, UK: MIT Press.

Cantrill, J. and Oravec, C. (1996) *The symbolic earth: discourse and our creation of the environment*. Lexington, KY: University Press of Kentucky.

Cantrill, J. G. (2004) A sense of self-in-place for adaptive management, capacity building, and public participation. In: Senecah, S. L. (ed.) *Environmental communication yearbook*. Mahwah, NJ: Lawrence Erlbaum Associates, pp. 165–185.

Cantrill, J. G. and Senecah, S. L. (2001) Using the "sense of self-in-place" construct in the context of environmental policy-making and landscape planning. *Environmental Science and Policy* 4: 185–203.

Carbaugh, D. and Cerulli, T. (2013) Cultural discourses of dwelling: investigating environmental communication as a place-based practice. *Environmental Communication: a Journal of Nature and Culture* 7(1): 4–23.

Carlson, A. (1992) Environmental aesthetics. In: Cooper, D. (ed.) *A companion to aesthetics*. Oxford: Blackwell, pp. 142–144.

Carlson, A. (2001) Environmental aesthetics. In: Gaut, B. and Lopes, D. M. (eds) *Routledge companion to aesthetics*. London: Routledge, pp. 423–436.

Carlson, A. (2002) *Aesthetics and the environment: the appreciation of nature, art and architecture*. London: Routledge.

Carlson, A. (2009) *Nature and landscape: an introduction to environmental aesthetics*. New York: Columbia University Press.

Chapple, C. K. and Tucker, M. E. (1994) Introduction. In: Chapple, C. K. (ed.) *Ecological prospects: scientific, religious, and aesthetic perspectives*. Albany, NY: State University of New York Press, pp. xi–xxi.

Cooper, D. (2006) *A philosophy of gardens*. New York: Oxford University Press.

Cox, R. (2013) *Environmental communication and the public sphere*. Thousand Oaks, CA: Sage Publications.

Deudney, D. (1996) Ground identity: nature, place and space in nationalism. In: Lapid, Y. and Kratochwil, F. (eds) *The return of culture and identity in IR theory*. London: Lynne Rienner, pp. 129–146.

Endicott, K. G. (1996) *Northern California gardening: a month-by-month guide*. San Francisco, CA: Chronicle Books.

Gallagher, V. and Zagacki, K. S. (2005) Visibility and rhetoric: the power of visual images in Norman Rockwell's depictions of civil rights. *Quarterly Journal of Speech* 91(2): 175–200.

Green, M. (2008) Guerrilla gardeners: when push comes to shovel. *San Francisco Chronicle*, 29 March.

Guerrilla gardening. (2013) *Guerrilla gardening*. Online, available at: www.guerrilla gardening.org/ (accessed 20 March 2013).

Hariman, R. (2000) Aversion to and a version of the democratic aesthetic. In: Hollihan, T. A. (ed.) *Argument at century's end: reflecting on the past and envisioning the future*. Conference Proceedings at the National Communication Association, Annandale, PA, pp. 286–293.

Hariman, R. and Lucaites, J. L. (2002) Performing civic identity: the iconic photograph of the flag raising on Iwo Jima. *Quarterly Journal of Speech* 88: 363–392.

Hariman, R. and Lucaites, J. L. (2003) Public identity and collective memory in US iconic photography: the image of "accidental Napalm". *Quarterly Journal of Speech* 20(1): 35–66.

Johnson, L. (2006) Guerrilla gardening. *Alternatives* 32(4/5): 10–12.

Kiesling, F. M. and Manning, C. M. (2010) How green is your thumb? Environmental gardening identity and ecological gardening practices. *Journal of Environmental Psychology* 30: 315–327.

Killingsworth, M. J. and Palmer, J. S. (1992) *Ecospeak: rhetoric and environmental politics in America*. Carbondale, IL: Southern Illinois University Press

Los Angeles Guerrilla Gardening. (2013) *Los Angeles guerrilla gardening*. Online, available at: www.laguerrillagardening.org/ (accessed 20 March 2013).

McKay, G. (2011) *Radical gardening: politics, idealism and rebellion in the garden*. London, UK: Frances Lincoln Limited.

Myerson, G. and Rydin, Y. (1996) *The language of environment: a new rhetoric*. London: University College London Press.

Pasquali, M. (2006) *Loisaida. NYC Community Gardens. Ediz. italiana e inglese*. Milan, Italy: A + M Bookstore.

Peterson, M. N., Peterson, M. J. and Peterson, T. R. (2007) Environmental communication: why this crisis discipline should facilitate environmental democracy. *Environmental Communication: a Journal of Nature and Culture* 1(1): 74–86.

Peterson, M. N., Peterson, T. R., Lopez, A. and Liu, J. (2010) Views of private-land stewardship among Latinos on the Texas–Tamaulipas border. *Environmental Communication: a Journal of Nature and Culture* 4(4): 406–421.

Peterson, T. R. and Horton, C. C. (1995) Rooted in the soil: how understanding the perspectives of landowners can enhance the management of environmental disputes. *Quarterly Journal of Speech* 81: 139–166.

Ralston, S. J. (2012) Educating future generations of community gardeners: a Deweyan challenge. *Critical Education* 3(3).

Reichard, S. H. (2011) *The conscientious gardener: cultivating a garden ethic*. Berkeley, CA: University of California Press.

Reynolds, R. (2008) *On guerrilla gardening: a handbook for gardening without boundaries*. London: Bloomsbury Publishing.

Schwendener, M. (2012) Gardening art grows into activism in the age of occupy. *Village Voice.* Online, available at: www.villagevoice.com/arts/gardening-art-grows-into-activism-in-the-age-of-occupy-717208.1 (accessed 2 February 2016).

Singer, R. (2011) Visualizing agrarian myth and place-based resistance in south central Los Angeles. *Environmental Communication: a Journal of Nature and Culture* 5(3): 344–349.

Spoel, P. and Hoed, R. C. D. (2014) Places and people: rhetorical constructions of "community" in a Canadian environmental risk assessment. *Environmental Communication: a Journal of Nature and Culture* 8(3): 267–285.

Spurlock, C. M. (2009) Performing and sustaining (agri)culture and place: the cultivation of environmental subjectivity on the Piedmont Farm tour. *Text and Performance Quarterly* 29(1): 5–21.

Thompson, J. L. and Cantrill, J. G. (2013) The symbolic transformation of space. *Environmental Communication: a Journal of Nature and Culture* 7(1): 1.

Tracey, D. (2007) *Guerrilla gardening: a manualfesto.* British Columbia: New Society.

Wax, E. (2012a) "Guerrilla gardeners" spread seeds of social change. *Washington Post,* 14 April.

Wax, E. (2012b) Guerrilla gardeners plant seeds of activism. *Seattle Times,* 15 April.

Wax, E. (2012c) Social activists find cause as urban "guerrilla gardeners". *Boston Globe,* 22 April.

Wilson, P. L. and Weinberg, B. (1999) *Avant gardening: ecological struggle in the City and the World.* New York, NY: Autonomedia.

10 Communicating emotions in conflicts over natural resource management in the Netherlands and Sweden

Legitimation and delegitimation of communities

Elin Ångman, Arjen E. Buijs, Irma Arts,
Hanna Ljunggren Bergeå, and Gerard Verschoor

Introduction

During the last decades natural resource management (NRM) has been increasingly embedded in the paradigm of participation. Participatory governance has been the word of honour ever since Agenda 21 and the Rio conference on sustainable development in 1992. This increase in discourse about participatory governance stems from a critique claiming that contemporary liberal democratic institutions are employing decision-making techniques that misrepresent the nature of environmental values as well as the emotions involved in environmental issues (Mattijssen *et al.*, 2014; Rauschmayer *et al.*, 2009). While the role of values and value-conflict is widely acknowledged, the role and legitimacy of *emotions* in NRM conflicts has received less attention thus far (Buijs and Lawrence, 2013).

One way of understanding participatory governance is through the concept of deliberative democracy. Deliberative democracy suggests a form of decision-making based on inclusive and unconstrained dialogue and allows for better-informed decisions and the participation of active and empowered citizens (Smith, 2003). In Chapter 8, Hansen and Peterson explore the potential value of deliberative democracy for improving the legitimacy of NRM. Meanwhile, deliberative democracy theory has been criticized for its focus on consensus and for neglecting the conflictual dimension of the political process (Mouffe, 2009). In Chapter 2, Hallgren offers additional suggestions for applying Mouffe's concept of agonism to NRM conflict. The indiscriminate use of consensus processes in environmental disputes can create apathy by setting unrealistic expectations of harmony for participants who may have very different goals (Peterson *et al.*, 2005). Furthermore, actors may not always be empowered as power relations are reproduced (Smith, 2009). Such power relations may be expressed openly but, more often, power is hidden in the discourses used to construct the legitimacy of actors and arguments. In this chapter we move beyond the debate between deliberative and agonistic approaches to NRM conflict to investigate the mostly hidden process of the de-legitimation of emotions in communication and decision-making.

Our starting point is that communication always involves power. We define communication therefore as "symbolic process whereby reality is produced, maintained, repaired and transformed" (Carey, 2007). Through communication people express opinions, values, views and emotions regarding their surroundings. Communication is crucial in the development of relevant discourses as well as in the struggle for hegemony between different discourses (Hajer, 1995). Power is expressed through the legitimation of certain discourses and affects whether people feel marginalized or empowered to participate in community change processes, and whether they feel they have the right to participate (Manzo and Perkins, 2006).

It is through our communication with each other that "everyday experiences of self-in-place form and mutate" (Dixon and Durrheim, 2000: 32). Consequently, people's attachment to a specific place can be seen as a dynamic process in which people are active in shaping their lives in their interaction with other people. This interaction can lead to a socially constructed sense of community. This sense of community has a strong emotional basis, entailing feelings of mutual trust, membership, shared concerns, and community values along with place attachments (Manzo and Perkins, 2006; Perkins and Long, 2002). Still, a community does not need to be geographically fixed, but to have reference to a group of people sharing a common resource, such as a place, and who are connected through communication (Sprain, 2014). People's relation to this place, including the practices, ethical considerations and emotions will influence how they act towards the space. When emotions create a shared sense of place and connectedness, cohesion between the people who might constitute the community will increase. Such cohesion may be constructive for planning processes, including communication between stakeholders as individual views and opinions may become translated and reformulated into common concerns and outlooks. On the other hand, emotions can also be destructive for such a process if emotions create a polarization between different parties (stakeholders/people) connected to a common resource. However, whether emotions become a constructive or destructive element depends on the process of legitimization and management of expression of emotion. This chapter explores how expressions of emotions were managed in two cases and discusses the consequences of this for the construction of community as well as for the opportunities for deliberation and participation. The conflicts we describe in this chapter are generally characterized by strong emotions around a natural resource. We focus on how these emotions are highlighted or downplayed in the interaction between those who hold these emotions and the other parties.

Emotions and legitimacy

Research on environmental decision-making displays how difficult it is for decision-making-bodies to listen to and incorporate the values and emotions relative to nature that stakeholders express (for example connectedness to nature, ethics and aesthetics). These arguments are overlooked or delegitimized and often have to give way for rational-technical argumentation (see for example Carolan and Bell, 2003; Ljunggren Bergeå, 2007; Clausen *et al.*, 2010; Buijs and Lawrence, 2013). Expert discourses (Ljunggren Bergeå, 2007) and scientifically based argumentation (Clausen *et al.*, 2010) can make actors feel that their emotionally charged arguments are less legitimate and may also prevent authorities from incorporating non-scientific ideas and visions into their plans (Turnhout *et al.*, 2012). By opposing affective concerns with rational or technical ones, the legitimacy of the actor with affective concerns is effectively undermined (Devine-Wright, 2005).

Such a focus on the rationality and scientification of nature has been inherent in the Western world from the rise of modernity (Adams, 1997). Modernity comprises all the rapid changes in social, economic and cultural spheres, starting already with the Enlightenment in the 1700s when science displaced theology (Elling, 2003), describing us now in a bureaucratized society governed by naturalized scientific ideals. However, ever since the eighteenth century romanticism (a counter-movement to the Enlightenment) and its different heirs (e.g. post-structuralism) have called into question many philosophical, ethical and aesthetic views that had been dominant in the Enlightenment era. This criticism particularly focused on the utilitarian, mechanistic, and rather detached view of nature. Because of this unease about the results of the Enlightenment, Romantic writers and painters called for the re-enchantment of nature (Honour, 1979). This tension between the rational, utilitarian and scientifically based discourse on the natural environment and the deeply felt emotional connectedness to nature has been infusing conflicts ever since the rise of modern conservation in the late nineteenth century.

Ever since the Enlightenment it has been argued that emotions are biasing evaluations and disrupting rational thought (Eisenberg, 2000). However, a parallel understanding with roots back to romanticism is that emotions help people to motivate their moral stances and reveal their values and concerns to others (Eisenberg, 2000). When people explain emotions or show how they feel this contributes to social interaction. Emotions signal that something is of importance; hence emotions should be taken seriously. As such, emotions are indicative of some valuable bond beyond mere personal feelings, and help people make the step from personal passion to a kind of generalized argument where emotion is valued as a common good. The judged authenticity of emotions plays an important role, as social actors use this information about others to be able to navigate in the social context, to understand what is important for others, and to negotiate status and power (Warner and Shields, 2009). Thévenot *et al.* (2000: 252) argue that whether emotionally inspired gestures and claims can be publicly displayed, commonly evaluated, and criticized, closely relates to the type of community in which they are expressed and how such communities construct the value and valuation of natural resources.

Emotions, place and community

An important base for the discussion of emotions in NRM is the relationship between people and their natural environment. This relationship gives rise to usually positive emotions regarding non-human animals (Jacobs, 2012), a specific geographical area (Relph, 1976) or the greater topic of nature (Mayer and McPherson Frantz, 2004). These bonds between person and location can typically be made explicit by a threat to a place we hold dear (Brown and Perkins, 1992), These emotions are often, but not always, related to feelings of care and responsibility. Manzo (2003) for example describes place attachment as a positive emotional connection with familiar locations. In turn, emotional connection (both in terms of bonds among people *and* attachment to place) has been described by Manzo and Perkins (2006) as the core sense of community: emotional connection motivates communities to an ethic of care (Nussbaum, 2001) and also encourages residents to participate in planning efforts and improve their surroundings. Such emotions, related to the content of NRM are usually seen as positive emotions. To increase public support, environmental managers want people to care about issues and places, to be engaged and active in their community and in politics (Nassauer, 1997). An important concern in many countries is however the decreasing number of people voting or getting engaged in other ways and the negative consequences this may have for political support for NRM (Buijs *et al.*, 2014).

Moral emotions as an indicator for common concerns

In understanding the role of emotions in NRM, it may be helpful to differentiate between *moral* and *non-moral* emotions. When talking about emotions, most people refer to the non-moral emotions, also called "basic emotions", like anger, fearfulness, happiness and sadness. In NRM, a second type of emotions is probably at least as important: moral emotions (Buijs and Lawrence, 2013). Moral emotions relate emotions to ethics (Keltner and Haidt, 2003; Nussbaum, 2001; Tangney *et al.*, 2007) and usually stem from or inform important ethical considerations. Moral emotions are those "that are linked to the interests or welfare of either a society as a whole or at least of persons other than the agent" (Haidt, 2003). Examples include feelings of guilt, shame and sympathy (Eisenberg, 2000). In this understanding emotions help people to distinguish moral features and motivate moral behaviour, and as such they reveal an individual's values and concerns to others. For example, if a person fails to help someone or something in need, such as an animal, that person's behaviour is not in line with an ethic of care they may adhere to.

Consequently, they may experience feelings of guilt or shame. As such emotions relate to morality and ethics of the self, they differ fundamentally from emotions such as anger that relates to the interpretation of the behaviour of *others* being unjust or morally wrong. Since emotions are usually understood as motivating an individual concern, considering emotions as an indicator of the ethical importance of certain issues in NRM management may be helpful in understanding and preventing environmental conflicts. Hence we see emotions and expression of emotions as vital for building community in the sense that a person's moral emotions signal what is important for the group when seen from that person's point of view.

Non-moral emotions in NRM

Although moral emotions are essential emotions in nature conservation, people usually think of non-moral emotions when the word "emotion" is used. Non-moral emotions relate to most experiences in life. People may get disappointed in or angry at people or processes, they may have fear for the consequences of political decisions or be sad about the particular outcome of a participation process. Such emotions relate to all kinds of decision-making and for the last decade also social movement research has focused on the role of emotions in societal change and conflict (Jasper, 2011).

Feelings of anger, fear and loss are important for understanding people's reactions to NRM. The fear that one can no longer hunt or pick berries in an area or anger over the lack of community participation in decision-making may evoke strong emotional reactions from the local community (Fried, 2000). Feelings of anger can be strong motivators to act, especially when events are personally relevant, inconsistent with personal goals, and seemingly caused by a responsible other (Eisenberg, 2000). These emotions are not only linked to the environment or a specific place, but also incorporate evaluations of the behaviour of the actors involved and the process as such (Glasl, 1999; Carpenter and Kennedy, 2001).

The construction of legitimacy

It is interesting how sometimes emotions are perceived as socially appropriate (people should care, they should be engaged) and some as socially inappropriate (the fact that people love a place is not considered a relevant NRM argument). Based on our constructivist interpretation of communication and conflicts in NRM, we claim that whether emotions are seen as constructive or destructive is something that is socially constructed in communication between stakeholders. We turn to theory about the construction of legitimacy to understand the role of emotions in conflict and participatory processes. We follow Bernstein (2011) who conceives of legitimacy as the process of the (discursive) justification of a shared rule by a community. A useful way to define the concept of *justification* is provided by Boltanski and Thévenot

(2006) who see these as the argumentations actors use in public disputes to assess what counts as legitimate argument – especially in relation to realizing "the common good". Justifications can involve positive arguments, claims, or position statements, but might also be critical denunciations of opposing views. Boltanski and Thévenot consider six different "orders of worth" or "evaluative frameworks" that serve as a philosophical basis for different types of legitimate discourses or legitimate types of arguments: "rational efficiency and planning", "environmentalism", "tradition and locality", "the free market", "civic equality", and "inspiration". For example within the "rational efficiency and planning" discourse, scientific expertise and expert-based arguments are seen to be legitimate, i.e. the value and expected loss of biodiversity in a specific area (Thévenot *et al.*, 2000: 255).

Following from this, we propose that the construction of legitimacy does not hinge on the question of *who is a legitimate spokesperson* (an essentialist stance that obscures the means by which an actor becomes a legitimate spokesperson) but, rather, on the question of what type of arguments are seen to be legitimate by the different stakeholders involved in a controversy (Arts *et al.*, under review). One type of argument of which the legitimacy tends to be controversial is argument based on emotional accounts (Buijs and Lawrence, 2013).

Description of cases and methods

We draw from the experiences of two different cases; one from the Netherlands and one from Sweden. In this section we describe the overall events and actions in these cases, while the emotional aspects will be unfolded in the subsequent section.

The Dutch case explores how dog-owners and Natuurmonumenten (the National Heritage Foundation, NHF) came into conflict over the management and use of Saint Peter's Hill in the city of Maastricht. A part of the hill was assigned as a dog walking area, but was at the same time appointed as a Natura2000 area, a class of protected areas under the EU regulations, to protect nardus grassland. As nardus grassland is sensitive to distortion, the NHF wanted to close the dog area in order to optimally manage this grassland. As compensation, they proposed that dog-owners would be allowed to use a different piece of the slope in return. Conflict arose when these plans were made public.

Dog-owners organized into a foundation called the *Gebete Hoond*. They turned to the municipality in an attempt to protect their previously arranged access Saint Peter's Hill. A two-year process of consultation, initiated by the municipality, brought the parties closer together and a revised plan was drawn up. But this plan was rejected by some of the members of the *Gebete Hoond*. This splinter group claimed that *Gebete Hoond* had too easily given in to the NHF and the municipality. To accommodate this new voice a final meeting was organized. Here an agreement was reached for a management plan, although dissatisfaction remained among residents and dog-owners.

The Swedish case explores a conflict over the clear-cutting of a forested area. A forest owner decided to log part of his forest and informed the forestry board of his intention to harvest. The plans met no formal hindrance. When other villagers understood that the forest, which they commonly used for recreation, was to be felled, they initiated an action group to stop the felling. The forest owner was unaware of this opposition until faced with a petition formulated by the action group. The action group and forest owner both contacted the relevant authorities and the local media. In response to these activities, the environmental coordinator at the municipal authority initiated a meeting in the forest between the different stakeholders. Eventually, and despite efforts from the local action group, the forest was logged.

The two cases have in common that they comprise situations connected to emotions around a recreational area. Together they enable us to investigate in what way emotions are used and responded to in the argumentation around NRM, be it in a city environment with 3,000 people engaged as in the Dutch case, or as in the Swedish case in a smaller and more privately owned area. The two cases together offer the possibility to study how different organizations react to emotional arguments and how this relates to the construction of the legitimacy of emotionally based arguments within the realm of environmental policy.

The empirical data from the Swedish case consisted of semi-structured interviews with the people involved in the conflict; the interviews were conducted one year after the felling took place. All interviews were recorded and transcribed. In addition to the interviews, articles in local newspapers as well as publicly available correspondence between the parties provided additional information. In the Dutch case semi-structured interviews also were held among the parties involved in the conflict. All interviews were recorded and transcribed. In addition to the interviews, informal talks (and walks) with several dog-owners provided additional information, as well as articles in local newspapers, on blogs and the Facebook page of the dog-owners' group. Because of the nature of our data our analysis is built on the basis of interviewees' own stories about their and other participants' emotions.

Results: legitimacy of emotions in natural resource conflicts

Dogs or nature on Saint Peter's Hill

In this section we take a closer look at the emotions involved in the discussion between dog-owners, residents, the municipality and the NHF. These are both *moral emotions* of beauty linked to the area and its history, but also non-moral emotions such as anger and disappointment linked to the way the design and management of the area was handled.

Saint Peter's Hill has a rich history. Residents of the adjacent neighbourhood feel closely bonded to this area, as do a lot of other residents of

Maastricht. As a local resident in the local paper describes it: "Everyone who knows the history intuitively knows it is our hill. And our love for [the hill] is huge. That huge that we call the plateau on top of the hill the living room of Maastricht".

However a large part of the hill also contains marlstone, which was excavated for cement for several decades. Residents of Maastricht have slowly seen the hill shrink, leaving an empty hole. The use of the remaining part of the hill therefore became very important for the residents, and any new plan for, or proposed changes to, the use of the hill are delicate topics.

Moreover dog-owners feel that they often have been required to comply with the interests of others. While they do not wish to come into conflict with non-dog-owners, they consider it important to let their dogs run free and be able to meet other dogs. When the new plans to reduce the area for dog walking were drawn, the dog-owners quickly organized into a foundation with close to 3,000 members. They had seen each other passing on the hill when walking their dogs, but it was not until their dissatisfaction on the changes to come, that they were given an impulse to unite. They shared a purpose, a love for dogs and a feeling of responsibility to their dogs to let them run free. These moral emotions allowed for the construction of a community in which the dog-owners became very committed to this case. Social media and local press helped them in reaching a large group of supporters among the residents of the neighbourhood surrounding Saint Peter's Hill. A shared history of connectedness to the place between residents and dog walkers, and anger about the changes that had come to the hill brought a wide set of actors to rally around the issue of the "space for dogs":

> What they [the NHF] forgot, and this is why they think we're rigid and do not want to compromise, is that we already compromised as dog-owners when the hill was transferred [to the NHF] and we were no longer allowed to walk on the entire hill, but had to confine ourselves to the dog-area.
>
> (Respondent citizen initiative)

This statement was recognized by the municipality of Maastricht:

> looking back, as government we forgot that the Sint Pietersberg is a very sensitive issue. It is sensitive because it is a place which people feel is theirs. It is a public park that belongs to no-one, and which should not exclusively belong to anyone.
>
> (Respondent municipality)

All parties involved, including the NHF, acknowledged that the way the planning had been done in the past had not taken account of the sensitivities involved; hence, a certain anger or resentment on the part of the residents was seen as legitimate by all stakeholders. The municipality looked at itself and admitted a certain responsibility for these emotions, and the need to organize a (deliberative) consultation process.

While the moral emotions were predominantly constructive in building community and allowing deliberation, non-moral emotions influenced the consultation process in a destructive manner. Emotions such as anger and resentment caused, for example, strife among the membership of the *Gebete Hoond*, which led to the dissolution of the group. These emotions stimulated a few of the dog-owners to take a firm and explicitly emotional stance against the plans. This group of dog-owners was described as obstructive to the process, including members of the *Gebete Hoond*, who were seen as more constructive members of the citizen initiative. The municipality and NHF mainly attributed this to the emotional behaviour exhibited by the small group who dissented from the final decision. According to the more constructive group of dog-owners, NHF employees and municipal officers gave too much attention to a few people who shouted the loudest. This resulted in the feeling, shared by some of the dog-owners, that they were not being listened to, which in turn made them more rigid in terms of their opposition towards the NHF's handling of the situation, as illustrated by the following example:

> Not to mention the enormous clearing of trees Natuurmonumenten carried out on our beautiful Saint Pietersberg! There is barely a tree left, while everyone knows how very important trees are for the environment and air quality. And the citizens of Maastricht? They will have to buy a ticket to walk on the tight, fenced path over the arid design-grassland!
>
> (Resident's opinion in a local paper)

For some of the residents and dog-owners the consultation and the eventual decision turned into a disappointment, and a confirmation that citizens were not listened to by NHF and municipality:

> Even when we established the foundation people predicted that nothing would be achieved anyway. The general feeling was that nothing would be done with our point of view. I still wanted to do something, but eventually it became clear that the others had been right. We weren't really heard.
>
> (Dog-owner)

Although during the process emotions of disappointment, anger and pain from the past were evoked for all parties engaged in the controversy, the site itself was recognized as a place of beauty. However, what constituted the beauty of the site was defined differently by different groups, and in fact became one of the core contested issues in the discussion about the dog area. Furthermore, place attachment played an important role, as residents and dog-owners clearly felt attached to the area, with some calling it their "living room". Yet, this emotional attachment to place was not seen as a legitimate argument to question the plans. It was not denied that people may feel strong emotions related to the hill, but when discussing its management these emotions were not accepted as a valid argument to be used when negotiating for a different approach. Rather, it was the ecological background these plans built upon ("Nature on the hill is unique and rare, and this is why it is important to preserve it") that was seen as the legitimate argument on the basis of which to make management changes. As a respondent from the NHF put it:

> Resistance [to for example the felling of trees] is based more on emotion than on the knowledge needed to understand the background for the felling of trees. Forest is nature, but heathland is also nature. Heathland, just as grassland, is home to different plants and animals. Often they are even richer in natural value than a forest. But it is the emotional value that plays a role. Take for example an acacia. An acacia is in itself very beautiful. But when it grows in a rare piece of land you do not want it there. While for a lot of people a beautiful fragrant acacia has a lot of emotional value. But it is not the right experience … in terms of natural value we would say, we choose the lime-tree. This seems a small thing for a visitor [of the area] but to us it is crucial.
>
> (Respondent Natuurmonumenten)

One spokesperson for the NHF did state that ecological concepts are often a bit vague:

> Nature is what leads us; we are a nature organisation and nature is what we stand for … that is our core business. Recreation is allowed, but only when there is no damage done to nature … but of course recreation, or what is damage, are very flexible terms. And "nature" is of course not tangible, and neither is vulnerability. This is also the difficulty we are faced with. We are always put in a certain corner, because we have to prove that something is rare or special, just to have an argument.
>
> (Respondent Natuurmonumenten)

To gain a foot in the discussion, some of the dog-owners accepted the premise of the NHF, thereby agreeing to limit the issue to an issue of nature management, and to exclude recreation. As one respondent from *Gebete Hoond* explained, "To be honest I do have my doubt sometimes [about the management], but I am not an ecologist, so I will not argue with it". Others, on the contrary, actively searched for a scientific foundation of their point of view:

> We are not unreasonable; we understand that you cannot do everything and that nature is important. But this grassland will never grow here and

could be developed elsewhere. We looked for articles.... Moreover a lot of species of this grassland are already here [in the dog walking area].

(Dog-owner)

However, the scientific arguments brought to the fore by these dog-owners were not taken seriously by the municipality and the NHF, as the dog-owners were not attributed with the scientific credentials needed to read, understand and interpret these texts correctly. The citizens tried to shift their discursive field towards that of the NHF and municipality, to be able to "talk the talk" of the management plan. However, they were unsuccessful as the NHF had a much more powerful voice in this field as they already had reached the status of experts in this evaluative framework. In the end, the decision about what type of nature was most valuable remained in the hands of the ecologists of the municipality and NHF. So even though the dog-owners tried to align their arguments to the arguments that were seen as legitimate by the responsible authorities, they did not feel they had been successful. Although they were compensated for the loss of a large part of their present dog-area, they did not feel their doubts and arguments were heard.

Logging or recreation in a privately owned Swedish forest

In accordance with Swedish forestry law, the decision-making mandate around the forest is in the hands of the forest-owner and does not involve a mandatory participation process with local people. However, citizens have user rights to forest through the Right of Public Access, allowing recreational use of privately owned forests.

The villagers in the Swedish case were using the forest for recreation. The resident who discovered the planned logging started an action group called "Save our Forest" with the mission to save the forest from being logged; four persons ran the group and represented it to the larger public. A handful of other supporters discussed with and supported the core group. The group contacted other forest networks and organizations like Greenpeace to get ideas and inspiration. The two leading members of the action group had lived in the village for ten years, close to the forest and made use of it every day. They highlighted their connection to the forest, the sound of birds and the beauty of the forest, as well as, in a more user-oriented sense, the possibility to use it as a playground, for hiking and for riding. Thereby the emotional connectedness was tangible for them:

Because all of us here have children, and the children had a hut in here, in the forest and we don't have a playground here. So, we who live right next to [the forest], we send the children to the forest. And they had a swing, a hut, and everything up there. All natural, not like we had built anything or so, but you know like falling trees ... and the like.... We have no school transport, nothing, but at least we have our forest. And that is why we live here! To be close to nature!

(Respondent Save our Forest)

When describing the forest, villagers used wordings like "our old, beautiful walking paths", the "magical forest", and particulars like the "coolest foxhole". It was not only the leaders of the action group whose connectedness to the area inspired them to stand up against the logging, but also the positive feedback the action group founders received from people in the local community who encouraged them to form the "Save our Forest" action group. Place attachment often emerges from a combination of love for the specific place, connected to more general societal concerns; a moral emotion which is linked to the interests or welfare of society: "I am doing this for my children, for the future, you have to say STOP at some point, we cannot keep destroying the earth like this, ruining all forests" (Respondent Save our Forest).

The two interviewees from the action group explained how, in the beginning, they sensed they did not know enough about forest management; therefore, in a first step to find out how to reverse the decision on the logging they decided to contact the forestry board, the municipal authority, the SEPA and the County Administrative Board (CAB) to find out who owned the land and the rules concerning logging: "They gave us a lot of information and that was when they told us to, well, if you find a key habitat you can stop the felling".

Key habitats are smaller areas with plants and animals worthy of protection that should be preserved through habitat protection (Swedish Forestry Act 1979:429/SFS 2014:890). From that moment on the action group focused their work on finding biodiversity values. There is no evidence, either in the interviews or in our correspondence with them, that the action group used their "place attachment" arguments in the process. During the interviews the action group explained their commitment through emotional reasoning, but during the decision process they used exclusively rational argumentation, which they were told would give them a strategic advantage. A key habitat is something measurable (it exists or not) that authorities claim to be important and that has to be saved. This can be interpreted as legitimate to mention during the process to stop the logging; "key habitats" are accepted as appropriate to discuss within this discursive field. However, the key habitat that the action group claimed to have found was not an approved key habitat according to the definition of the CAB. The action group, with no education in natural sciences, had to argue with the ecologists at the CAB about biodiversity and species. Relating to the six evaluative frameworks/discourses (Thévenot *et al.* 2000) the action group shifted to a different evaluative framework when trying to use the scientific-rational arguments. They were not successful because within this discourse the CAB was stronger, had more knowledge, and had the interpretative authority.

This case is interesting from a process perspective: there existed no opportunity during the process of interaction between citizens and authorities to raise the issue of *why* emotional attachment (and its underlying values) was important for the forest users. For the activists, their reason for feeling attached to the area could not be raised to discussion with anyone outside their own group, they did not get a chance to discuss it, defend it or justify it. The actual motivation for becoming engaged soon was lost when the action group tried to learn the new language of the scientific-rational framework. From a democracy point of view a valuable input from a different perspective was lost and from the "moral emotion" perspective the chance to dig deeper into what this place attachment represents in terms of community and commons was disregarded.

Positive emotional connections to their surroundings often motivate community members to be active (Manzo and Perkins, 2006), and the action group's next step was to create a petition, which they placed at the local gas station and the local store that read: "Sign here to stop the felling of [name of the specific forest]". The petition to stop the logging was signed by 300 persons, which according to the group showed that they had strong support in the area. When a friend showed the forest owner the petition it was the first time he had heard of an organized opposition against the logging. The forest owner expressed how he had been very emotional during this entire process. Also during the interview the forest owner expressed his emotions. "And they think they can say this! I have managed this forest all my life! And they say I am after some fast money! I mean ... that is just rude!" He felt uncomfortable with the situation that developed with his neighbours: "It is such a madly unpleasant situation, with the neighbours, and the attacks on me" and "it is sad to have such neighbours, such hating people that have nothing else to do".

The forest owner depicted his neighbours as "rude" people who seemed to do this to him out of spite; he did not recognize the neighbours' ties to the area, considering the members of the action group as persons who have "come here during the last ten years and consequently has no tradition here". He perceived that they were doing this *against him*, rather than *for the place*. The forest owner responded by writing to all conceivable relevant authorities. He expressed how hurt and sad he felt, he did not (in the interview) connect his feeling for the forest to place attachment, but rather his feeling for his neighbours. The sense of community that now was threatened by the behaviour of his neighbours seemed to be a significant loss for him.

The situation above is not uncommon in NRM conflicts (see for example Carpenter and Kennedy, 2001) when actors' focus turns away from the topic (forest management) to relationships instead. The forest owner's expressed emotions were not moral in the sense that he was referring to, for example, the importance of private ownership for society, instead he directed his feelings outwards, towards the action group. At the same time he might very well have felt shame (a moral emotion) because he explained during the interview how he saw himself as a good, righteous person, but had been treated as a mean crook, and his integrity and reputation may have been damaged (see also Ångman *et al.*, 2011). As Turner (2002) explains, moral emotions that are not lifted and examined can easily turn into anger.

In all probability both the forest owner and the action group had common cares; they wanted the area to develop in a sustainable manner, they wanted nature for their children, etc. However, there were no opportunities to explore and develop these common values. Similarly to the Dutch case, the process and quality of the communication in this conflict thus had consequences for what could be expressed and what was valued as legitimate argumentation. We will use a meeting that took place as part of this conflict to highlight the connection between process and emotions.

The forest owner and members of the action group produced a series of letters, emails and newspaper articles connected to the topic of the forest management. In response to these communications, the environmental coordinator at the municipal authority initiated a meeting between the different stakeholders so that they "could listen to each other and understand each other's point of view". The power of decision-making remained in the hands of the forest owner but the meeting could be used to exchange information and provide – according to the municipal authority – a possibility for a sharing of perspectives. The meeting took place in the forest. Besides the forest owner, representatives from the landowner association, the action group, the logging company, a national environmental NGO, the municipality and the Swedish forestry board were present. One member of the action group pleaded for the group's cause while another member kept silent and took notes during the meeting. The representative of the logging company explained how he experienced the situation:

> They [the "Save our Forest" action group] had a bit of a nasty attitude because one of them was the one talking and then there was another one who just wrote it down, everything what we said. Yes, it was sort of "everything you say can be used against you"; if we ... happen to say the wrong thing.
>
> (Respondent Logging Company)

The rules, mandates and obligations applied for the meeting in the forest were unclear to the participants. All present had some knowledge of the previous story of petition, letters and email circulation. The feeling of being frightened of exposure is not conducive to listening to others' knowledge and experience – which would have been an important part of a successful meeting. Despite their small numbers, the behaviour of the action group members seemed to be controlling the space of others during the meeting, since the others perceived them as threatening. Also the fact that the meeting took place at all suggests that the claims of the action group were legitimate in the eyes of the authorities (the municipality who arranged the meeting). Although the municipality has no formal role in forestry planning on private land, the decision to hold a meeting may have given some participants, such as the forest owner and the logging company, a feeling that the action group had been able to influence the municipality, which may have adversely affected the legitimacy of the process.

However, the power of decision-making remained in the hands of the forest owner, and he and other people in the meeting did not see the action group as a legitimate entity with legitimate views. During the meeting the parties agreed that specific stands of trees should be saved. Apart from them, the forest was to be logged in the conventional way.

The forester from the forestry board present at the meeting in the forest disparaged the action group when he explained how he viewed their argumentation: "It is all about emotions really. That you have a feeling for old forest". Having a "feeling" for a forest was not seen as a legitimate topic to introduce into discussion.

One of the members of the action group happened to meet the forest managers and the representative of the municipality in the forest after the felling, and they told her that they were satisfied and that the logged area looked "quite good" from their perspective. The action group member described the situation: "and there were such deep tracks [from forest machinery], and I was so angry, the tears were just pouring and I was screaming, I mean I was pissed off, because they were so unaffected". Here the professional's view, that the logging was satisfactorily managed by their standards seemed offensive to the woman because they were *not* showing any emotions. From her point of view her sense of anger was completely legitimate, and she became more emotional because the civil servants seemed "unaffected". As pointed out in the introduction, the emotional driving forces of engagement and involvement are complex. As one of the action group told us, "I was driven by such aggressiveness from the beginning. That was my fuel ... and that came from how we were treated. It was so unprofessional. Really not professional". Here anger at another's behaviour seems to be spurring engagement, the engagement that authorities are always claiming they want from citizens. This anger led the actors to search for new knowledge and to organize themselves.

On the other hand, the local community as such seems not to have gained from the conflict. When asked to reflect on his community after the logging, the forest owner said he had no contact with the members of the action group: "They stay away. I don't know. I rarely see them. I guess I nod but I mean, if I see someone and they greet me I will greet back, but else, I have nothing to say" (Forest owner). A member of the action group reflected over the struggle:

> So now we are ... we really messed things up, there are a lot of people that you meet in the forest that used to say hello and be nice, they take big detours when they see me, like that.
>
> (Member of the action group)

In this case, centrally motivating emotions were not discussed and the process became destructive. The community ended up with a logged forest and damaged relationships. We will now explore how a focus on moral emotions could help produce more constructive processes.

Discussion and lessons for research and practice

As we have argued earlier, emotional expressions and arguments based on emotions are usually overlooked or delegitimized and have to give way for rational-technical argumentation. This is consistent with the institutional paradigm and the domination of technical rationality discussed in Chapters 2, 8 and 12, and the domination of technical rationality discussed in Chapter 8. Yet, according to the paradigm of participation and the deliberative ideal, it is desirable that many voices are heard and that everyone is respected. In our two cases, citizens have been mobilized to influence the decision-making process both in terms of procedural questions (communication and access to participation) and outcome. When people feel they have not had a say, that their arguments have not been accepted as legitimate arguments, anger and other negative non-moral emotions towards process and others involved in the conflict increase. If it were acceptable for people to admit that their constructive emotions of connectedness to land and nature serve as motivating forces in their efforts to influence NRM, an awareness and acceptance of these emotions may result in more constructive processes. Meanwhile, we also need to acknowledge the ongoing motivational force of all types of emotions, including anger and the like.

By displacing affective arguments with more scientific, economic or other less affective arguments, the legitimacy of people's connections to place is undermined, which effectively makes them feel inferior; hence authorities miss the opportunity of incorporating citizens into the construction of ideas and visions for their communities. It is not the persons but the arguments of the lay persons that are considered illegitimate, according to the civil servants we interviewed.

Although it would be too simplistic to claim that community is kept together around emotions, both of our cases show how communities are constructed through protest and collaboration. In both cases, at least two opposing communities were created. In the Swedish case a former "good neighbour" community was divided into an "activist" community and a "forest owner" community. In the Dutch case, the dog-owners seemed to have strengthened their sense of community by organizing themselves around the conflict. Although this is a very weak community, the 3,000 signatures of dog-owners, along with the organization of *Gebete Hoond* could be seen as a first step towards the construction of community among this group of stakeholders.

The tension between rationalism versus romanticism can be seen in both our cases; it was clear that, while emotions drove much of the action, they were excluded from public discussion. In this sense rationalism is built into NRM's structural arrangements; there is simply no space to discuss emotions in the public sphere. The real tension between rational-technical decision-making and the emotional foundations for argumentation lies in the construction of legitimacy for emotion. Legitimizing moral emotions such as sense of place and connectedness to animals, nature or nature based activities is an important step. Most environmental managers have difficulty imagining what could happen if there was an arena where it was possible and legitimate to discuss emotional attachment to land. Providing stakeholders with opportunities to discuss emotions could open up space to consider what type of emotions (moral, non-moral) are legitimate in what kind of situations. Talking explicitly about emotions could be understood as a way of constructing legitimacy, because as we communicate about connections between emotion and nature, we are actively forming an arena where it is legitimate to say that one has emotions and that they are important in this context, hence legitimizing certain practices and relations independently from personal characteristics.

Our ambition in this chapter has been to increase awareness about how important emotions are as drivers of NRM, and to suggest that organizations tasked with managing natural resources should explore ways to allow emotion into planning and decision-making activities. In both cases we described, emotions were primary motivators and remained important throughout the conflicts, although they were not openly discussed. Since demonstrating openness to others' perspectives may encourage recognition of others as well as recognition of the common good (Smith, 2003), these processes limited participation and may have hindered a hypothetically constructive dialogue of shared understanding. Instead of focusing on the common good, participants concentrated on not saying anything that could be perceived as inappropriate.

A raised awareness among practitioners and researchers about the importance of valuing emotions could improve the quality of communication and decision-making in NRM. When environmental communicators and managers encounter emotional accounts they should appreciate that as a sign of strong engagement. This engagement can be positively harnessed in the process, ideally to learn more about different perspectives and to obtain a richer picture of the situation. The emotions and the engagement they presuppose can be used as an opening for the process.

Theorists of democratic deliberation claim that actors can widen their perspectives by being exposed to others' knowledge and experience, which will in turn encourage recognition of others as well as recognition of the common good (Smith, 2003). This moralizing effect is suggested as a means to minimize egoistic preferences (Miller, 1992: 61). However, deliberative democracy theory has been criticized for its focus on the forming of consensus and for neglecting the conflictual dimension of the political process (Mouffe, 2009; Peterson et al., 2005). If emotions are understood as a way of helping people to distinguish moral features and motivate moral behaviour (Eisenberg, 2000), emotional argumentation and emotional expression have the possibly to act as a key in communicating values and concerns to others in conflictive NRM processes. Emotions signal what is important and should be taken seriously because multiple voices are important in deliberative democracy. Emotions are something that human beings have *in common* and can understand as a "common" – thus they may facilitate shifting from an exchange of individual interests to finding common ground, without forcing consensus on a process.

References

Adams, W. M. (1997) Rationalization and conservation: ecology and the management of nature in the United Kingdom. *Transactions of the Institute of British Geographers* NS 22: 277–291.

Arts, I., Buijs, A. E. and Verschoor, G. (Submitted) Actors or arguments? The construction of legitimate participatory spaces in Dutch nature conservation practices. *Land Use Policy*.

Bernstein, S. (2011) Legitimacy in intergovernmental and non-state global governance. *Review of International Political Economy* 18: 17–51.

Buijs, A., Mattijssen, T. and Arts, B. (2014) The man, the administration and the counter-discourse: an analysis of the sudden turn in Dutch nature conservation policy. *Land Use Policy* 38: 676–684.

Buijs, A. and Lawrence, A. (2013) Emotional conflicts in rational forestry: towards a research agenda for understanding emotions in environmental conflicts. *Forest Policy and Economics* 33: 104–111.

Boltanski, L. and Thévenot, L. (2006) *On justification: economies of worth*. Princeton, NJ: Princeton University Press.

Brown, B. and Perkins, D. (1992) Disruptions in place attachment. In: Altman, I. and Low, S. (eds) *Place Attachment*. New York: Plenum Press, pp. 279–304.

Carey, J. W. (2007) A cultural approach to communication. In: Craig, R. T. and Muller, H. L. (eds) *Theorizing communication: readings across traditions*. Thousand Oaks, CA: Sage Publications, pp. 37–49.

Carpenter, S. L. and Kennedy, W. J. D. (2001) *Managing public disputes: a practical guide for government, business, and citizens' groups*. San Francisco, CA: Jossey-Bass Publishers.

Clausen, L. T., Hansen, H. P. and Tind, E. (2010) Democracy and sustainability: a lesson learned from modern nature conservation. In: Nielsen, A. K., Elling, B., Figueroa, M. and Jelsøe, E. (eds) *A new agenda for sustainability*. Ashgate: Ashgate studies in environmental policy and practice, pp. 229–247.

Devine-Wright, P. (2005) Beyond NIMBYism: towards an integrated framework for understanding public perceptions of wind energy. *Wind Energy* 8: 125–139.

Dixon, J. and Durrheim, K. (2000) Displacing place-identity: a discursive approach to locating self and other. *British Journal of Social Psychology* 39: 27–44.

Eisenberg, N. (2000) Emotion, regulation, and moral development. *Annual Review of Psychology* 51: 665–697.

Elling, B. (2003) *Modernitetens miljøpolitik*. Köpenhamn: Frydenlund Grafisk.

Glasl, F. (1999) *Confronting conflict: a first-aid kit for handling conflict*. Gloucestershire: Hawthorn Press.

Haidt, J. (2003) The moral emotions. In: Davidson, R. J., Scherer, K. R. and Goldsmith, H. H. (eds) *Handbook of affective sciences*. Oxford: Oxford University Press, pp. 852–870.

Hajer, M. A. (1995) *The politics of environmental discourse: ecological modernization and the policy process*. Oxford: Clarendon Press.

Honour, H. (1979) *Romanticism*. New York; Hagerstown, MD; San Francisco, CA; London: Harper & Row.

Jacobs, M. H. (2012) Human emotions toward wildlife. *Human Dimensions of Wildlife* 17: 1–3.

Jasper, J. M. (2011) Emotions and social movements: twenty years of theory and research *Annual Review of Sociology* 37: 285–303.

Keltner, D. and Haidt, J. (2003) Approaching awe, a moral, spiritual, and aesthetic emotion. *Cognition and Emotion* 17: 297–314.

Ljunggren Bergeå, H. L. (2007) *Negotiating fences: interaction in advisory encounters for nature conservation*. Acta Universitatis Agriculturae Sueciae, Uppsala: Doctoral Thesis No. 2007:130.

Manzo, L. C. and Perkins, D. D. (2006) Finding common ground: the importance of place attachment to community participation and planning. *Journal of Planning Literature* 20: 335–350.

Mattijssen, T. J. M., Behagel, J. H. and Buijs, A. E. (2014) How democratic innovations realise democratic goods: two case studies of area committees in the Netherlands. *Journal of Environmental Planning and Management* 58(6): 997–1014.

Mayer, F. S. and McPherson, F. C. (2004) The connectedness to nature scale: a measure of individuals' feeling in community with nature. *Journal of Environmental Psychology* 24: 503–515.

Miller, D. (1992) Deliberative democracy and social choice. *Political Studies* 40: 54–67.

Mouffe, C. (2009) Democracy in a multipolar world. *Millennium: Journal of International Studies* 37: 549.

Nassauer, J. I. (1997) Cultural sustainability: aligning aesthetics and ecology. In: Nassauer, J. I. (ed.) *Placing nature: culture and landscape ecology*. Washington, DC: Island Press.

Nussbaum, M. C. (2001) *Upheavals of thought: the intelligence of emotions*. Cambridge, UK: Cambridge University Press.

Perkins, D. D. and Long, D. A. (2002) Neighborhood sense of community and social capital: a multi-level analysis. In: Fisher, A., Sonn, C. and Bishop, B. (eds) *Psychological sense of community: research, applications, and implications*. New York: Plenum, pp. 291–316.

Peterson, M. N., Peterson, M. J. and Peterson, T. R. (2005) Conservation and the myth of consensus. *Conservation Biology* 19: 762–767.

Rauschmayer, F., van den Hove, S. and Koetz, T. (2009) Participation in EU biodiversity governance: how far beyond rhetoric? *Environment and Planning C: Government and Policy* 27(1): 42–58.

Relph, E. (1976) *Place and placelessness*. London: Pion.

Smith, G. (2003) *Deliberative democracy and the environment*. New York: Routledge.

Smith, G. (2009) *Democratic innovations: designing institutions for citizen participation*. Cambridge: Cambridge University Press.

Sprain, L. (2014) Voices of organic consumption: understanding organic consumption as political action. In: Peeples, J. and Depoe, S. (eds) *Voice and environmental communication*. New York: Palgrave Macmillan, pp. 127–147.

Tangney, J. P., Stuewig, J. and Mashek, D. J. (2007) Moral emotions and moral behavior. *Annual Review of Psychology* 58: 345–372.

Thévenot, L., Moody, M. and Lafaye, C. (2000) Forms of valuing nature: arguments and modes of justification in French and American environmental disputes. In:

Lamont, M. and Thévenot, L. (eds) *Rethinking comparative cultural sociology: repertoires of evaluation in France and the United States.* Cambridge, UK: Cambridge University Press, pp. 229–272.

Turner, J. H. (2002) *Face-to-face: towards a sociological theory of interpersonal behavior.* Stanford, CA: Stanford University Press.

Turnhout, E., Bloomfield, B., Hulme, M., Vogel, J. and Wynne, B. (2012) Conservation policy: listen to the voices of experience. *Nature* 488(7412): 454–455.

Warner, L. R. and Shields, S. A. (2009) Gender, status, and the politics of emotional authenticity. In: Salmela, M. and Mayer, V. (eds) *Emotions, ethics, and authenticity.* New York: John Benjamin.

Ångman, E., Hallgren, L. and Nordström, E. M. (2011) Managing impressions and forests: the importance of social interaction in the co-creation of a natural resource conflict. *Society and Natural Resources* 24(12): 1335–1344.

11 Community construction through culturally rooted celebration

Turtles all the way down

Michael J. Liles, Eduardo Altamirano, Velkiss Gadea,
Sofia Chavarría, Ingrid Yañez, David Melero,
José Urteaga and Alexander R. Gaos

After a lecture on cosmology and the structure of the solar system, James was accosted by a little old lady.

"Your theory that the sun is the center of the solar system, and that the earth is a ball which rotates around it, has a very convincing ring to it, Mr. James, but it's wrong. I've got a better theory", said the little old lady.

"And what is that, madam?" inquired James politely.

"That we live on a crust of earth which is on the back of a giant turtle".

"If your theory is correct, madam", he asked, "what does this turtle stand on?"

"You're a very clever man, Mr. James, and that's a very good question", replied the little old lady, "but I have an answer to it. And it is this: the first turtle stands on the back of a second, far larger, turtle, who stands directly under him".

"But what does this second turtle stand on?" persisted James patiently.

To this the little old lady crowed triumphantly, "It's no use, Mr. James – it's turtles all the way down".

> J. R. Ross, *Constraints on Variables in Syntax*, 1967

Introduction

One of Earth's most profound sustainability and social justice challenges is including the full spectrum of society in decision-making and actions regarding the use of natural resources. Because most of the world's threatened species are found in biodiversity hotspots in low-income regions, these areas are top priorities for conservation action (Myers *et al.*, 2000). Sound policy-making by governments and civil society based on current ecological knowledge is considered an essential element of multifaceted approaches to protect remaining biodiversity in hotspot areas (Brooks *et al.*, 2002). However, biodiversity loss continues unabated in many of these countries, suggesting that existing conservation policy and practice may be ineffective (Butchart *et al.*, 2010). Risk of failure increases when conservation actions underestimate or disregard the diverse relationships between conservation needs and human wellbeing (Adams *et al.*, 2004), particularly in low-income regions where the direct use of natural resources remains an important livelihood strategy for many people (Hutton and Leader-Williams, 2003). As Banerjee notes in Chapter 6, conservation policy and practice that fail to account for dynamic social contexts, distributions of power, and interests of local stakeholders are less likely to succeed (Ekoko, 2000).

Communication plays a fundamental role in negotiation among diverse groups and communities with distinct values and goals, particularly in areas of acute poverty where the self-governance of commonly shared resources occurs. When we refer to community, we follow Cnaan *et al.*'s (2008) and Hunter's (2008) description of community as a three-dimensional concept, where any group of people can vary from weakly to strongly communal in its degree of "communityness": 1) shared ecology in space and time, 2) social organization, and 3) shared cultural and symbolic meanings. By motivating and facilitating the organization of individuals, communicative practices can potentially forge the construction of community. For example, a common symbol system can create and maintain a sense of community, where members assign value or meaning to a symbol to which they adhere and around which they establish boundaries (McMillian and Chavis, 1986).

In this chapter, we explore the symbolic relevance of a flagship species – the hawksbill turtle (*Eretmochelys imbricata*) – in constructing community through a culturally based competition that strives to protect the species and improve the wellbeing of local residents in El Salvador and Nicaragua. To provide a context for understanding hawksbills as a locally relevant symbol and its ability to form community, we first draw from the historical record to briefly outline the evolving role of local people in natural resource conservation and then describe the local importance of hawksbills in these two Central American countries. Second, we explain the methodology of our project, including the creation of the Hawksbill Cup, a culturally based sporting competition, and interviews with local residents who participated in the competition in El Salvador and Nicaragua. Third, we provide a detailed analysis of the interviews to help explain how local residents who participated in the Hawksbill Cup viewed hawksbills and their conservation, as well as their experiences with fellow participants in both countries. Finally, we discuss what our results tell us about hawksbills, and how their conservation through sport may constitute a community that includes both humans and extrahumans (see Callister's Chapter 3 in this volume) centred on the mutual wellbeing of hawksbill and human populations.

The role of local people in conservation: from exclusion toward inclusion

For more than a century after Yellowstone National Park (US) was created in 1872, the North American, or Western, model of national parks and protected areas was considered by ecologists and conservationists to be the most effective method for biodiversity preservation (Adams, 2004). This approach traditionally relied on top-down management by centralized government agencies to maintain "pristine" wilderness and to prohibit permanent human residence within demarcated park borders, engendering a nature–culture binary (McNeely, 1994). Park numbers grew consistently in the United States during the twentieth century, ceasing only momentarily during the Second World War (Harrison *et al.*, 1982). By the late 1960s, the Western model of protected areas had been exported to low-income regions worldwide and was becoming commonplace as an international strategy for biodiversity conservation (Adams, 2004).

During the 1970s–1980s, the process of identifying and establishing protected areas expanded considerably in Central America (Herlihy, 1992), due largely to a growing concern with deforestation and associated environmental impacts (Hecht and Cockburn, 1989). The application of this Western model of protected areas in low-income regions has, however, been criticized for its inability to protect biodiversity outside of the cultural context in which it emerged (Goldman, 2003; Lu *et al.*, 2005; Nepal and Weber, 1995). Additionally, the establishment of exclusionary reserves has fostered opposition by resource-dependent populations and threatens the success of conservation goals (Brandon and Wells, 1992). Over the past three decades, pragmatic and justice concerns have spurred a shift from top-down exclusionary approaches imposed by central governments, toward bottom-up decentralized alternatives that encourage the inclusion and empowerment of local communities (Adams and Hutton, 2007). The core element of these alternative practices is the recognition of local residents as key stakeholders in biodiversity conservation, whose participation is essential for the achievement of sustained conservation outcomes (Oldekop *et al.*, 2015; Pimbert and Pretty, 1995). Considering the limited capacity of many Central American governments to enforce environmental laws, in conjunction with the increasing shift toward social inclusion and transfer of ownership of natural resources to private individuals and corporations, co-management models of joint administration by civil society and the government have taken on greater importance for conservation endeavours in the region (Andrade and Rhodes, 2012; Brown *et al.*, 2013). Despite these perceived shifts from exclusion toward inclusion, however, historic marginalization of local people and continued social inequalities have engendered scepticism toward government intentions and actions that persists today in many low-income regions, including El Salvador and Nicaragua (Gammage *et al.*, 2002; Larson and Soto, 2008; Liles *et al.*, 2014).

Raising a common flag: hawksbills as a locally relevant flagship species

Sea turtles are globally distributed reptiles that spend the vast majority of their lives at sea, coming ashore only to deposit their eggs in sandy beaches. Seven species of sea turtles exist worldwide – olive ridley (*Lepidochelys olivacea*), green (*Chelonia mydas*), loggerhead (*Caretta caretta*), flatback (*Natator depressus*), leatherback (*Dermochelys coriacea*), Kemp's ridley (*Lepidochelys kempii*), and hawksbill

(*Eretmochelys imbricata*) – all of which are long-lived, late-maturing, and highly migratory species that frequently cross jurisdictional boundaries while traveling between foraging areas and nesting beaches (Luschi *et al.*, 2003; Nichols *et al.*, 2000). The complex life cycles of sea turtles and their pressing conservation status – all species, except the flatback, are listed on the IUCN *Red List of Threatened Species* as critically endangered, endangered, or vulnerable on a global scale – draw interest from the international conservation community (Marine Turtle Specialist Group, 1995). At the same time, sea turtles often are considered a subsistence resource in low-income regions (Thorbjarnarson *et al.*, 2000), which can be rooted in cultural heritages (Morgan, 2007; Nietschmann, 1973). Despite differences between international and local priorities, opportunities exist to integrate local realities with international conservation priorities to simultaneously support long-term sea turtle recovery efforts and human well-being in low-income regions (Liles *et al.*, 2014).

Hawksbills are critically endangered globally (Mortimer and Donnelly, 2008) and the population of hawksbills in the eastern Pacific Ocean is among the most threatened (Wallace *et al.*, 2011) and least resilient (Fuentes *et al.*, 2013) sea turtle populations in the world. Myriad historical and contemporary threats, including their intentional capture for egg consumption and the tortoiseshell trade, as well as incidental capture in fisheries, and have reduced population numbers to fewer than 500 hawksbills nesting along 15,000 km of coastline from Mexico to Peru, where more than 75 per cent of known nesting activity is concentrated at two sites, Bahía de Jiquilisco-Xiriualtique Biosphere Reserve (Bahía de Jiquilisco) in El Salvador and Estero Padre Ramos Nature Reserve (Estero Padre Ramos) in Nicaragua (Gaos *et al.*, 2010; Liles *et al.*, 2015). Despite moratoriums that prohibit sea turtle consumption in both countries (República de El Salvador, 2009; República de Nicaragua, 2005), the exclusion of local egg collectors in their development and limited enforcement by authorities has contributed to the inability to halt egg extraction, which reaches nearly 100 per cent at most beaches. For example, many *tortugueros* (i.e. local sea turtle egg collectors) in El Salvador feel that the moratorium stripped them of a traditionally important source of income without providing alternatives and that they are being excluded from decision-making regarding sea turtle conservation, which they contend is biased toward powerful, elite interests (Liles *et al.*, 2014). Conservation programmes in El Salvador and Nicaragua now collaborate with *tortugueros* by purchasing hawksbill eggs directly from local residents for protection, which provides an alternate economic incentive to sale for consumption. This approach has gained acceptance among members of coastal communities and stimulated strong local support for hawksbill conservation (Altamirano *et al.*, 2011; Liles *et al.*, 2011). Given that the local priorities of coastal residents tend to focus on the socio-economic development and needs of humans communities, hawksbill eggs have historically been collected by *tortugueros* working independently, and the primary value placed on hawksbills by *tortugueros* often has been the economic value attached to egg sales (Liles *et al.*,

2014). Decades-long implementations of neo-liberal monetary incentive schemes – both market and conservation based – have fostered this individualist perspective of egg collection by rewarding *tortugueros* for the number of eggs collected on an individual basis that offers little incentive for collaboration among *tortugueros*, and may hamper the achievement of sustained conservation outcomes.

As we thought about ways to expand opportunities for local residents to participate in biodiversity conservation beyond neo-liberal monetary incentives, two ideas came to mind: Flagship species and football. Veríssimo *et al.* (2011, 2) define a flagship species as one "used as the focus of a broader conservation marketing campaign based on its possession of one or more traits that appeal to the target audience". Whether a flagship species succeeds in raising conservation awareness can depend on the cultural context, socio-economic conditions and perceived value of the species at the local level (Bowen-Jones and Entwistle, 2002). Sea turtles capture significant public attention (Campbell, 2003) and are perceived to have high intrinsic value (Witherington and Frazer, 2003). Given that they appeal to a wide range of audiences, sea turtles can be effective symbols that garner far-reaching and deep support for conservation (Eckert and Hemphill, 2005; Veríssimo *et al.*, 2011). Football is followed with a fevered and passionate intensity around the world (Mason, 1995), and is inextricably embedded in the social, political and cultural fabric of most Latin American countries (Taylor, 1998). The Fédération Internationale de Football Association (FIFA) World Cup is an unrivalled cultural phenomenon in Latin America. Football's firmly established cultural roots in Latin America seemed to offer a prototype for the development of a locally relevant celebration to spark community passion for hawksbill conservation outcomes in El Salvador and Nicaragua. We developed the Hawksbill Cup in an attempt to harness Central Americans' passion for football and competition, to enhance hawksbill conservation and to stimulate positive interactions among *tortugueros* at Bahía de Jiquilisco and Estero Padre Ramos.

Materials and methods

Study areas

Our study was conducted at Bahía de Jiquilisco (13°13′N, 88°32′W) in El Salvador and Estero Padre Ramos (12°48′N, 87°28′W) in Nicaragua, which are located on the western and eastern borders of Gulf of Fonseca on the Pacific coast of Central America, respectively (Figure 11.1).

High levels of poverty are common to both areas, with most households earning $162 per month, discontinuing education at middle school level and lacking waste collection services and potable water (ICAPO, 2012). Impoverished residents of Bahía de Jiquilisco and Estero Padre Ramos rely upon the exploitation of wild natural resources, such as fishing, mollusc extraction, and sea turtle egg collection, a highly variable but important source of income.

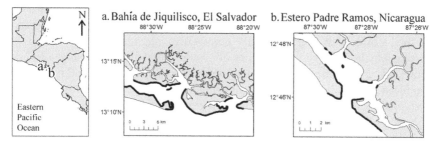

Figure 11.1 Location of hawksbill nesting beaches, with patrolled shoreline marked with black lines, at a) Bahía de Jiquilisco, El Salvador and b) Estero Padre Ramos, Nicaragua, 2012–2014.

Because poverty is rampant and employment options are limited at both sites, additional constraints to effective resource management and conservation by local residents often include low self-esteem, a general distrust of others, particularly in El Salvador where crime is prevalent, and minimal communication among human settlements (Liles *et al.*, 2014).

Beach monitoring and nest protection

Bahía de Jiquilisco and Estero Padre Ramos host 35 and 40 per cent respectively, of known hawksbill nesting activity in the eastern Pacific Ocean (Altamirano *et al.*, 2011; Gaos *et al.*, 2010; Liles *et al.*, 2015). Hawksbill nesting occurs primarily between May and September, with a peak in June and July, along sandy beaches (54.9 km) in mangrove estuaries at these two sites (Figure 11.1).

We facilitated beach patrols at both sites from 1 May to 15 October 2012–2014, where project personnel and a network of more than 200 *tortugueros* monitored the nesting habitat from 18:00 to 06:00 daily by foot and boat in search of female hawksbills and nests. Encountered clutches of eggs either were relocated to a hatchery or protected in situ (i.e. original site of deposition), depending on their location. We excavated nest contents following hatchling emergence and counted hatched eggs, unhatched eggs and hatchlings.

Participatory development of the Hawksbill Cup

The Hawksbill Cup emulates the World Cup such that the hawksbill nesting season (i.e. April–October) represented the final match between the two most important nesting sites in the region to determine which team (i.e. Team Bahía de Jiquilisco or Team Estero Padre Ramos) scored more hawksbill conservation "goals" at their respective sites. Working together with *tortugueros*, we designed the scoring system that encompassed conservation and research objectives, while simultaneously ensuring that each team had a chance of winning. Seven categories were established whereby teams could score goals: 1) total number of nesting female emergences recorded, 2) percentage of nesting females observed, 3) number of nests protected, 4) percentage of nests protected, 5) number of hatchlings produced, 6) percentage of hatchlings produced, and 7) number of *tortugueros* that participated in the protection of nests. Each category was worth one goal per month for a total of seven possible goals per month for seven months in 2012–2013 and for eight months in 2014, totalling a maximum of 49 and 56 possible goals, respectively, during the season. The team that had the highest number or percentage in a given category for a given month received one goal and the team with a lower number or percentage for that same category received zero goals. Both teams reported their results at the end of each month, goals were awarded, and publicly-displayed scoreboards were updated at both sites and shared via media outlets. The team that scored the most hawksbill conservation goals at the end of the final match had their name engraved on the Hawksbill Cup trophy that travelled between sites and resided at the site of the winning team each year.

Ethnographic approach

Since the discovery and systematic documentation of hawksbill nesting at Bahía de Jiquilisco in 2008 (Liles *et al.*, 2011) and Estero Padre Ramos in 2010 (Altamirano *et al.*, 2011), we have partnered with *tortugueros* to conduct participatory research and conservation activities at both sites, including multi-sited ethnographic research (Coleman and von Hellerman, 2011). Recognizing that the way humans communicate *about* the environment influences relationships *with* the environment, we used an ethnographic approach to collect data that enabled us to perceive how personal experiences and their social contexts shaped informants' perceptions of reality and how language was used to construct that reality (Lincoln and Guba, 1985). At least one member of our team was immersed in local contexts with *tortugueros* during the past eight years (2007–2014) at Bahía de Jiquilisco, and five years (2010–2014) at Estero Padre Ramos.

In preparation for conducting this analysis, members of our team spent over 7,000 hours (2012–2014) at both sites, during which time we conducted hundreds of informal interviews with local residents, and participated in over 200 night patrols with *tortugueros* searching for nesting hawksbills. These encounters allowed us to observe interactions with hawksbills and with fellow *tortugueros*, which facilitated trust building and increased the likelihood of obtaining authentic information in interviews and other conversations.

During the process of conducting formal interviews, we adhered to Hammersley and Atkinson's (2007) instruction on selecting ethnographic informants, where individuals are purposively selected as informants based on their knowledge, roles, insights and willingness to discuss their experiences. The purpose of these interviews was to better understand Hawksbill Cup participants' experientially based relationships with hawksbills, their conservation, and fellow human participants, particularly as it related to the symbolic construction of community through participation in the Hawksbill Cup.

Collection and analysis of interview data

In 2012–2014, we conducted 172 interviews with Hawksbill Cup participants (i.e. *tortugueros*, family store owners, local field staff and other local residents) from Bahía de Jiquilisco and Estero Padre Ramos, using open-ended questions in Spanish. We included questions regarding perspectives toward and value of hawksbills, factors that motivate participation in hawksbill conservation, and the role of the Hawksbill Cup in relationship building. To identify potential informants, we contacted residents that participated in the Hawksbill Cup and arranged interviews with interested individuals. Interviews lasted between 10 and 30 minutes. We used a variety of techniques to manage issues of accuracy with the data, including triangulation, informant validation and clarification questions (Lincoln and Guba, 1985).

We conducted a thematic analysis of the interview text (Peterson, 1994) and supplemented interview data with information from meetings, published literature, and unpublished reports. Whenever possible, we used the informants' own words to describe their perspectives and experiences.

Results

Beach monitoring and nest protection

In 2012–2014, the Hawksbill Cup contributed to the achievement of record-breaking results at Bahía de Jiquilisco and Estero Padre Ramos, including 226 individual hawksbills observed, 1,135 nests protected (more than 95 per cent protection rate), 111,971 hatchlings produced, and more than 150 *tortugueros* that participated directly in research and nest protection. These results are particularly important for the species given that prior to 2008 so few adult hawksbills were sighted in the eastern Pacific Ocean that scientists considered them extirpated and few, if any, hawksbill eggs escaped human consumption.

Of the 1,135 hawksbill nests protected, 46 and 54 per cent were protected by Team Bahía de Jiquilisco and Team Estero Padre Ramos, respectively. The cumulative scoring of the seven categories during the three years of this analysis yielded the following annual winners of the Hawksbill Cup: 2012, Team Estero Padre Ramos (28:14); 2013, Team Estero Padre Ramos (25:21); and 2014, Team Bahía de Jiquilisco (31:20).

Figure 11.2 Local participants from Team Estero Padre Ramos proudly displaying the Hawksbill Cup trophy after their victory over Team Bahía de Jiquilisco in 2013.

Emergent themes from interviews

Four primary themes emerged from interviews with Hawksbill Cup informants, which we describe below:

1   Most informants viewed hawksbill conservation as a process of reciprocal wellbeing for their communities – local human residents provide protection for hawksbill residents because hawksbills provide economic assistance to local humans.
2   Many informants identified the conservation status and ecological role of hawksbills as reasons for protection.
3   Many informants indicated that hawksbills cultivate feelings of patriotism and pride in their unique natural heritage.
4   Most informants stated that participating in hawksbill conservation improves human-to-human connections and relationships within and between sites.

Reciprocal wellbeing in conservation

Most interviewees regarded hawksbill conservation as a reciprocal relationship they share with hawksbills – local human residents provide protection for hawksbill residents and their nests because hawksbills provide economic assistance to local people through providing eggs to sell for conservation.

Because employment opportunities often are scarce in coastal areas with acute poverty, the livelihoods of impoverished residents invariably depend on natural resources from their local environment, including hawksbill eggs. Many informants acknowledged this reality, including a beach patroller from Estero Padre Ramos who stated: "[Hawksbills] are extremely valuable because they help us survive, they provide money for the community". Not surprisingly, the high economic value of hawksbill eggs resulted in the historic extraction and sale for human consumption of nearly 100 per cent of eggs at Bahía de Jiquilisco and Estero Padre Ramos prior to the initiation of conservation programmes in 2008 and 2010, respectively. Until recently, many local residents did not consider the exploitation of hawksbill eggs a factor that contributed to the perceived decline in current hawksbill nesting from historic levels, where fewer nesting hawksbills translated into fewer economic benefits from egg sales. A *tortuguero* from Estero Padre Ramos summarized this point: "Before, we only extracted [hawksbill eggs for human consumption] and did not protect [them]. Today, we understand that [protection] is important and we are concerned because we survive off of them". Most informants echoed this statement and preferred to sell hawksbill eggs for conservation rather than for human consumption because they viewed their own wellbeing as intertwined with that of hawksbills. One *tortuguero* described this reciprocal relationship as "human–nature feedback".

Although all informants valued hawksbills for their ability to relieve the immediate economic hardship of local residents, some also expressed the belief that the fundamental link between people and turtles transcended short-term self-interest and extended to future descendants. When asked about his primary motivation for protecting hawksbill nests, one *tortuguero* from Bahía de Jiquilisco responded: "For the conservation of the turtles so that they do not go extinct ... it benefits present and future generations because they also will be able to see the turtles". Informants did not isolate short-term economic benefits from longer-term sustainability. They explained that their commitment to the protection of hawksbill nests over the long-term should lead to an increase in the number of nesting turtles, which would provide greater economic benefits from egg sales, which would in turn provide greater stability in a region where economic conditions are constantly in flux: "We know that [by protecting hawksbill eggs] we are taking care of ourselves for the future ... there will be more turtles and that will generate more income". Although biologists often have depicted local residents who are primary resource users, and *tortugueros* specifically, as having simplistic and superficial relationships with sea turtles, usually guided by a self-interest that lacks concern for the wellbeing of the turtle (Campbell, 2000, 2002; Shaw, 1991), our informants described relationships with hawksbills that were based on respect and appreciation, and rooted firmly in a process of reciprocal wellbeing that fundamentally linked human and hawksbill residents for present and future generations.

Conservation status and ecological role of hawksbills

Many informants identified the conservation status of hawksbills and their eco-logical role in marine ecosystems as reasons for protection. Hawksbills are highly endangered in the eastern Pacific Ocean. With the exception of leatherbacks (Wallace *et al.*, 2013), their population numbers are dwarfed by those of the other species found along the Pacific coast of Central America (Abreu-Grobois and Plotkin, 2008; Gaos *et al.*, 2010; Hart *et al.*, 2015). Reflecting on the status of eastern Pacific sea turtle species, one *tortuguero* from Bahía de Jiquilisco commented: "[Hawksbills] hold greater value than the other sea turtles, the hawks-bill is the most coveted for its [critically endangered] status". Many informants reiterated this point and highlighted that the importance of hawksbills hinges, in part, on their rarity and the imminent threat of extinction. One hatchery manager from Estero Padre Ramos referred to the hawksbill's status as a factor that motives his participation in conservation activities: "It motivates me because I am helping to protect a species that is on the edge of extinction".

Many informants projected toward the future when speaking about the threat of extinction and emphasized the need to protect hawksbills today so they will exist tomorrow. By connecting present actions to future con-sequences, local residents recognized their agency in influencing conservation outcomes for hawksbills. While commenting on the importance of hawks-bills, one fisher from Estero Padre Ramos stated: "[Hawksbills] are important to us because if we harm them [today], in the future they may go extinct. That is why it is necessary that we protect them by protecting their eggs".

Although reasons for offering hawksbills protection varied, most of our informants identified future descendants as those that would ultimately benefit from the persistence of hawksbills. For example, one *tortuguero* from Bahía de Jiquilisco responded: "For me, [hawksbills] are special because they are species that are critically endangered and it is important [to protect them] because my grandchildren need to know them". This *tortuguero* was not unique in high-lighting the importance of *knowing* the turtles, rather than simply seeing them or gaining economic value from them. Informants at both sites echoed the desire for future residents to see and interact with hawksbills. Despite clear agreement among local residents that hawksbill abundance during their grandparents' time was much greater than that found today, some interview-ees expressed cautious optimism, viewing the slightly increasing number of turtles in the estuaries as a sign that conservation actions are slowly paying off. As one beach patroller from Estero Padre Ramos put it: "[Recently] there were almost no hawksbills, but now with the [conservation] project you see a few more hawksbills". Many local residents in the Bahía de Jiquilisco, par-ticularly fishers that spend hours on the water, shared the perception that hawksbill numbers are increasing in the estuary and stated that juvenile turtle sightings are on the rise at inshore feeding areas, which they attribute to the release of thousands of hatchlings each year, a practice that relies almost exclusively on eggs sold for conservation.

Because local residents rely on the extraction of wild natural resources for essential goods and services, their experiences while immersed in the natural environment give them unique insight into species interactions, abundance and ecosystem change over time. When asked about the value of hawksbills, one local resident in Estero Padre Ramos commented: "[Hawksbills] are an important emblematic species in the ecosystem. They are valuable because they are indicators of ecosystem health". Some residents in Bahía de Jiquilisco used an example in informal interviews that mirrored this sentiment, suggesting that once-abundant hawksbills effectively suppressed jellyfish populations in the estuary in the past. Now, however, they claim that depleted hawksbill abundance contributes to the upsurge of previously rare occurrences of jellyfish irruptions, which can wreak havoc in local fisheries. Although they may not be familiar with the technical term, they recognize that trophic cascades – the top-down regulation of ecosystems by predators – are key components of ecosystem function and wellbeing (Terborgh and Estes, 2010), and understand the role of hawksbills in shaping coral reef ecosystem structure and dynamics (Leon and Bjorndal, 2002; Meylan, 1988). Regardless of their specific role, informants at both sites reiterated that hawksbills "maintain the ecosystem in equilibrium" and "give balance to the ecosystem", and for those reasons they deserve protection.

Patriotism and pride in natural heritage

Our findings echo the importance of emotion Ångman *et al.* described in Chapter 10. Many informants indicated that hawksbills cultivate feelings of emotional attachment to their homeland and pride in the natural heritage it comprises. Despite the lament that local residents expressed regarding the near disappearance of hawksbills and concern for their wellbeing, many interviewees simultaneously celebrated the surviving members of the population and the habitat they share with the turtles. When asked about the value of hawksbills, one *tortuguero* from Estero Padre Ramos stated: "[Hawksbills] are valuable because they have raised the name of my Nicaragua high – it is not everywhere that hawksbills nest". Another *tortuguero* from Estero Padre Ramos echoed this comment while replying about factors that motivate a person to sell a nest for protection: "The conservation of hawksbills [motivates me] so that we can say, HERE WE HAVE HAWKSBILLS!"

Many informants asserted that the sense of pride that arises from sharing a community with critically endangered hawksbills also carries a sense of stewardship that brings a unique responsibility to care for this irreplaceable species. While reflecting on his motivations for participating in conservation, one *tortuguero* from Bahía de Jiquilisco explained: "It motivates me to live where this species is – we are the only ones that can take care of our turtles".

We designed the Hawksbill Cup to empower and strengthen local residents' feelings of pride and a sense of responsibility for *their* hawksbills at both sites, while at the same time encouraging friendly competition between sites to motivate residents to maximize collaborative hawksbill conservation in both countries. When asked how the Hawksbill Cup contributed to hawks-bill conservation, one long-time *tortuguero* from replied: "[Because of the Hawksbill Cup] we take greater care of hawksbills in El Salvador so everyone sees that here we care for our turtles". Interviewees often viewed their natural heritage – and conservation ethic – as a legacy that must be protected and nurtured not only out of self-interest and in search of public recognition today, but also as a revered obligation to future generations. In many ways, hawksbill conservation preserves a way of life and offers a promise that future descendants could follow the same path as their predecessors. Many inform-ants considered conservation as a vehicle that enabled them to pass the know-ledge and experience amassed from years living with hawksbills to their children and grandchildren so they could continue to protect the turtles. While discussing his motivation for participating in conservation activities, one *tortuguero* from Bahía de Jiquilisco commented: "[My motivation is] to conserve the species and to teach my children to do the same. [This way,] our children can continue [what we have started]".

Overall, informants at both sites expressed high levels of pride in sharing their homes with hawksbills and noted that living with an endangered species also bears an inherent responsibility to care for its wellbeing. With few excep-tions, interviewees considered themselves caregivers for hawksbills and viewed their protection as an integral component of a conservation ethic and legacy to be passed on to future generations so they may continue what their predecessors started.

Human-to-human connections

Moving beyond the individual space-based communities in Bahía de Jiquilisco and Estero Padre Ramos, the Hawksbill Cup also appears to have contributed to the construction of a larger community encompassing both places. Most informants stated that their participation in efforts to protect hawksbills – primarily through the Hawksbill Cup – improves human connections and relationships within and between sites. Whereas traditional economic incen-tive schemes for sea turtle conservation (e.g. price per dozen eggs) reward individualist effort and can reduce the role of local residents in the conserva-tion milieu to little more than an ephemeral business transaction, the Hawks-bill Cup formally expands the scope of hawksbill conservation beyond both biodiversity and economic concerns, rewarding collective action by local resi-dents toward the achievement of long-term conservation goals through friendly competition. Competitiveness often has strong motivational qualities (Abra, 1993) and can fuel cooperation in reaching shared goals – in this case, protecting hawksbills more effectively than the opposing team. Rivalry between competitors that are socially similar and that repeatedly compete in evenly matched contests can further increase motivation and performance (Kilduff, 2014). When asked how the Hawksbill Cup influenced conserva-tion, one *tortuguero* from Estero Padre Ramos stated:

[The Hawksbill Cup] is a competition between El Salvador and Nicaragua. I personally work hard to collect eggs in order to beat El Salvador. We push ourselves harder so that they do not beat us – all of us are in this [together].

Interviewees from Bahía de Jiquilisco shared this competition-oriented attitude based on collective performance: "[The Hawksbill Cup creates] enthusiasm and motivation to lose not even one turtle [nest to consumption]. We strive to beat Nicaragua, which generates interest in conservation".

The transition from viewing participation in conservation as an individualist endeavour to a team effort can facilitate increased collaboration among local residents, which ultimately can increase motivation for interpersonal communication and enhance community relations. When asked how the Hawksbill Cup influenced relationships among participants, one *tortuguero* from Bahía de Jiquilisco replied: "The competition unites the community, [which helps us] take better care of the turtles. There is a change in our way of thinking". One beach patroller from Estero Padre Ramos emphasized this point stating:

In order to conserve [hawksbills] we need to have energy and [the Hawksbill Cup] energizes us ... we are fighting together because we want to improve and we are united. [Because of that,] we have better relationships and there has been better communication.

Many interviewees expanded on the perceived benefits of solidarity, such as improved organization, increased information sharing, and a greater sense of responsibility to each other: "Now we support each other and we share opinions. If there is a [participating] *tortuguero* from any town we will offer him transportation and so far no [hawksbill] nests have been [sold for consumption]". Informants from both sites asserted that relationship building through the Hawksbill Cup occurred not only with compatriots, but also extended to their competitors in the neighbouring country. Participants from both countries exhibited mutual respect in shared interests and striving to reach a common goal: "We are sister countries and we are together in [hawksbill] conservation. We are both fighting to protect the turtles". This symbolic brotherhood between the teams of both countries was transformed into material reality during exchanges between sites. One *tortuguero* explained his perspective toward exchanges of Hawksbill Cup participants: "[The experience] is positive. People come from [Estero Padre Ramos] and when it is time to announce the winning team, people from [Bahía de Jiquilisco] travel to Nicaragua – friendships are made". Exchanges also aided knowledge sharing and information flow between sites, which were limited prior to the Hawksbill Cup.

Hawksbills and their conservation through the Hawksbill Cup mobilized local residents to unite around a common goal infused with passion. Local residents that participated in collective efforts to protect hawksbills often improved interpersonal connections with compatriots as well as formed relationships with members of the competing team that transcended geographical boundaries. The shared passion exhibited by both teams is exemplified in the videos they created to boost the spirit of competition (see the videos, online, available at: www.hawksbill.org).

Discussion

The Hawksbill Cup slogan of "We are one team!" rings throughout the videos of both teams and highlights their conviction that no matter which team wins the contest in a given year, the Hawksbill Cup participants at both sites form one team in the fight to protect hawksbills in the eastern Pacific Ocean. Our informants viewed participation in hawksbill conservation as a process of reciprocal wellbeing, where human residents provided protection for hawksbill residents because hawksbills provide economic relief to local residents through egg sales for conservation. Informants underscored hawksbills' conservation status and their ecological role in marine ecosystem maintenance as additional reasons for protection, and emphasized their desire for future humans to experience and interact with hawksbills. Interviewees expressed pride and honour in sharing their homes with the last remaining hawksbills and considered their protection part of a conservation ethic to be entrusted to future descendants. Finally, our informants viewed hawksbill conservation through the Hawksbill Cup as an exciting enterprise that increased local motivation for conservation and strengthened relationships among participants within and between sites.

Symbolic construction of community – turtles all the way down

In low-income regions where NRM and environmental law enforcement are lax, primary resource users often self-govern resource use in their local environment (Dietz *et al.*, 2003), such as the collection of hawksbill eggs in Bahía de Jiquilisco in El Salvador and Estero Padre Ramos in Nicaragua. This local reality highlights the power and control *tortugueros* wield in determining the success or failure of hawksbill conservation initiatives (Liles *et al.*, 2014) and underscores the importance of understanding the factors that motivate or discourage their participation in conservation, particularly as it relates to the formation of a conservation community that strives to collectively reach shared goals.

We follow Cnaan *et al.* (2008) in envisioning community as constructed by shared ecology, social organization, and shared cultural and symbolic meaning. From this perspective, a community is considered less robust if one or more dimensions are weak or non-existent and a community is considered more robust if all three dimensions are strong (Cnaan *et al.*, 2008; Hunter, 2008). We use this multidimensional concept of community as a lens to examine the four themes that emerged from our interviews and, in turn, the symbolic power of hawksbills in constructing community through the Hawksbill Cup.

The dimension of shared ecology encompasses the aspects of spatial location and time wherein a community exists. Bahía de Jiquilisco and Estero Padre Ramos are strikingly similar in terms of geographic location (~110 km distant) on the Pacific Ocean and natural resource composition (mangrove ecosystems). Human residents at both sites are inextricably tied to the extraction of wild natural resources for their livelihoods. Additionally, Bahía de Jiquilisco and Estero Padre Ramos host the largest remaining rookeries for hawksbills in the eastern Pacific Ocean, and represent the last hope for the survival of the species in the region. Our informants were cognizant of this fact and expressed high levels of pride in their natural heritage, particularly because they were able to share their homes with, and protect, this highly endangered species. The Hawksbill Cup – rooted firmly in the competitiveness of local culture – draws from the pride that local people feel for being part of a community that includes hawksbills and from the competitive spirit that motivates them to protect the species more comprehensively than their competitors. Interviewees reiterated their fundamental connection to time as a motivating factor for conservation, namely the devotion of local residents to collectively protect hawksbills during their lifetime so that future generations can have the opportunity to experience and interact with the turtles as well. Some researchers argue that improved technology has rendered the dimension of shared ecology less salient in contemporary community formation (Wellman, 2001). We found, however, that the depressed socioeconomic and relatively remote conditions at both our sites limited access to technological innovations and further fomented a shared place-based identity.

The dimension of social organization centres on interpersonal networks, or networks of social interaction that emerge from and are strengthened by common values and interests, shared characteristics and norms, and common community-level goals. Our informants explicitly stated that participants in the Hawksbill Cup at both sites are primarily interested in improving hawksbill and human wellbeing, in the present and future, and in the thrill of competition and the human connection that accompanies it. To enhance its appeal to local residents and through the participatory process of its design, the interests expressed by local residents were the pillars upon which the Hawksbill Cup was crafted and from which shared conservationist norms and communal goals emerged. For example, Hawksbill Cup participants thwart exploitive behaviour by upholding an instantiated informal norm that prohibits the sale of hawksbill eggs for human consumption. During a meeting in Bahía de Jiquilisco, one participant conveyed concern about *tortugueros* from a nearby town that did not adhere to this norm and its implications for reaching conservation goals established in the Hawksbill Cup:

> Two *tortugueros* from Madresal have found five [hawksbill] nests so far this year, and they sold them all to the market [for consumption]. The loss of those nests can affect our chances of winning the [*Hawksbill*] *Cup*. We need to go and speak with them so they collaborate with us [for conservation].

Subsequent conversations with the two non-participating *tortugueros* resulted in their active participation in the Hawksbill Cup and adherence to its conservationist norms. This example, together with other informant interviews, highlights how communicative processes among local residents underpin and can strengthen interpersonal relationships in collective efforts to reach communal goals, such as increased hawksbill protection in a self-governed system. As illustrated in a parade celebrating the Hawksbill Cup, this event has helped *tortugueros* from both Bahía de Jiquilisco and Estero Padre Ramos expand the community of humans involved in turtle conservation to include other residents who may not have previously considered themselves so closely connected to turtles.

The dimension of shared cultural and symbolic meanings constitutes the meanings and convictions members share that lead them to identify with and value their community. Our informants described how local residents at both sites regard hawksbills as a symbol of shared identity that holds experiential meaning and value in their everyday lives. Hawksbills can be viewed as a

Figure 11.3 Hawksbill Cup participants leading a local parade comprised of coastal residents, NGOs and national authorities to celebrate hawksbill conservation during the annual Hawksbill Festival at Estero Padre Ramos, Nicaragua in 2013.

locally relevant flagship species whose message and what it represents extends well beyond the species itself to the natural and cultural environments it shares with local people. As our interviewees explained, hawksbills represent a diverse set of symbolic and material realities for local residents, including a locally important livelihood resource and a source of pride that emanates from the species' scarcity and a perceived responsibility to care for it. The Hawksbill Cup mobilizes hawksbills as a symbol and transfers the meanings and values it holds into a sporting competition rooted in local culture. This shift transforms the role of local participants from the "invisible worker" in conservation into the protagonist in the saga of hawksbill conservation in the eastern Pacific (Peterson *et al.*, 2010). Such a reconfiguration in character affords them an elevated collective voice and additional agency in determining the intertwined fate of human and hawksbill wellbeing.

Before concluding our discussion, we offer two caveats in the interpretation of our results. First, we recognize that "the politics of the local" and a multiplicity of interests aside from hawksbills likely influence decision-making and actions regarding conservation in a community, and we understand that actors within a community seek their own interests in conservation programmes (Agrawal and Gibson, 1999). We contend, however, that the democratic and participatory processes employed during the development of the Hawksbill Cup encouraged local human residents to express their interests and preferences in an effort to minimize inherent power inequalities, facilitate negotiated outcomes, and foster joint-ownership of the competition. Our immersion in the study sites over long periods of time, during which we constantly interacted with local residents, facilitated our ability to identify power distributions and to better understand the local political context. Second, the purchase of hawksbill eggs from *tortugueros* by conservation programmes for protection at both sites is unquestionably a primary motivating factor for most local residents that participate in conservation (Liles *et al.*, 2014). Most informants stated that the discontinuation of payments for hawksbill egg protection would force the great majority of *tortugueros* to alleviate economic need by selling collected eggs in local markets for human consumption. This reality underscores the need to employ integrated conservation approaches that include short-term economic incentives, as well as strategies that transcend neoliberal economics and increase the non-economic values of hawksbills. The Hawksbill Cup is just one example of an innovative programme that provides income while also generating passion, instilling pride, and motivating a sense of responsibility in sustaining long-term conservation outcomes. This is one reason why the Hawksbill Cup's ability to transform local participants from invisible workers to protagonists is so important.

Conclusion

Our study demonstrates how endangered hawksbills as a shared symbol of identity and the Hawksbill Cup as a mobilizing force function together as a constructive instrument in the formation of a conservation community. Given Cnaan *et al.*'s (2008) three-dimensional concept of community, the analysis demonstrated that these recently crafted conservation communities are relatively robust, but remain vulnerable to destruction if direct payments for hawksbill egg protection cease. While our case demonstrates that the symbolic construction of community can gradually dismantle the array of context-specific constraints to resource management provoked by the historic marginalization and systematic disfranchisement of impoverished residents, this does not remove economic and other material constraints. To effectively protect the Earth's biodiversity and improve human well-being in low-income regions where most biological diversity occurs, further delineation of the efficacy of communicative processes in constructing conservation communities using additional case studies should be a fundamental and normative task.

Acknowledgements

We thank the Hawksbill Cup participants who shared the experiences and insights they gained over many years living with sea turtles in El Salvador and Nicaragua. We greatly appreciate the numerous people and organizations that supported this work, including A. Henriquez, P. Torres, N. Sanchez, L. Manzanares, O. Rivera, D. Melero, T. R. Peterson, M. J. Peterson, G. Serrano Liles, C. Cea, C. Rivas, M. Pico, E. Possardt, the Hawksbill Committees of Bahia de Jiquilisco and Estero Padre Ramos, and the Ocean Foundation. We thank the National Fish and Wildlife Foundation and the US Fish and Wildlife Service for financial support.

References

Abra, J. (1993) Competition: creativity's vilified motive. *Genetic, Social, and General Psychology Monographs* 119: 289–342.

Abreu-Grobois, A. and Plotkin, P. (2008) *Lepidochelys Olivacea: the IUCN red list of threatened species*. Version 2015.2. Online, available at: www.iucnredlist.org (accessed 28 August 2015).

Adams, W. M. (2004) *Against extinction: the story of conservation*. London: Earthscan.

Adams, W. M. and Hutton, J. (2007) People, parks and poverty: political ecology and biodiversity conservation. *Conservation and Society* 5: 147–183.

Adams, W. M., Aveling, R., Brockington, D., Dickson, B., Elliot, J., Hutton, J., Roe, D., Vira, B. and Wolmer, W. (2004) Biodiversity conservation and the eradication of poverty. *Science* 306: 1146–1149.

Agrawal, A. and Gibson, C. C. (1999) Enchantment and disenchantment: the role of community in natural resource conservation. *World Development* 27(4): 629–649.

Altamirano, E., Torres, P., Manzanares, L., Maradiaga, E., Seminoff, J. A., Urteaga, J., Yañez, I. L. and Gaos, A. R. (2011) Surpassing the wildest of expectations: a newly discovered hawksbill (*Eretmochelysimbricata*) nesting rookery in the Estero Padre Ramos Natural Reserve, Nicaragua, provides new hope for recovery of the species in the eastern Pacific. In: Jones, T. T. and Wallace, B. P. (eds) *Proceedings of the thirty-first annual symposium on sea turtle biology and conservation*. NOAA Technical Memorandum NOAA NMFS-SEFSC-631.

Andrade, G. S. M. and Rhodes, J. R. (2012) Protected areas and local communities: an inevitable partnership toward successful conservation strategies? *Ecology and Society* 14(4). Online, available at: http://dx.doi.org/10.5751/ES-05216-170414.

Bowen-Jones, E. and Entwistle, A. (2002) Identifying appropriate flagship species: the importance of culture and local contexts. *Oryx* 36(2): 189–195.

Brandon, K. E. and Wells, M. (1992) Planning for people and parks: design dilemmas. *World Development* 20: 557–570.

Brooks, T. M., Mittermeier, R. A., Mittermeier, C. G., da Fonseca, G. A. B., Rylands, A. B., Konstant, W. R., Flick, P., Pilgrim, J., Oldfield, S., Magin, G. and Hilton-Taylor, C. (2002) Habitat loss and extinction in the hotspots of biodiversity. *Conservation Biology* 16: 909–923.

Brown, N. K., Gray, T. S. and Stead, S. M. (2013) Co-management and adaptive co-management: two modes of governance in a Honduran marine protected area. *Marine Policy* 39: 128–134.

Butchart, S. H. M., Wapole, M., Collen, B., Van Strien, A., Scharlemann, J. P. W., Almond, R. E. A., Baillie, J. E. M., Bomhard, B., Brown, C., Bruno, J., Carpenter, K. E., Carr, G. M., Chanson, J., Chenery, A. M., Csirke, J., Davidson, N. C., Dentener, F., Foster, M., Galli, A., Galloway, J. N., Genovesi, P., Gregory, R. D., Hockings, M., Kapos, V., Lamarque, J., Leverington, F., Loh, J., McGeoch, M. A., McRae, L., Minasyan, A., Hernández Morcillo, M., Oldfield, T. E. E., Pauly, D., Quader, S., Revenga, C., Sauer, J. R., Skolnik, B., Spear, D., Stanwell-Smith, D., Stuart, S. N., Symes, A., Tierney, M., Tyrrell, T. D., Vie, J. and Watson, R. (2010) Global biodiversity: indicators of recent declines. *Science* 328: 1164–1168.

Campbell, L. M. (2000) Human need in rural developing areas: perceptions of wildlife conservation experts. *Canadian Geographer* 44(2): 167–181.

Campbell, L. M. (2002) Science and sustainable use: views of marine turtle conservation experts. *Ecological Applications* 12(4): 1229–1256.

Campbell, L. M. (2003) Contemporary culture, use, and conservation of sea turtles. In: Lutz, P. L., Musick, J. A. and Wyneken, J. (eds) *The biology of sea turtles, volume 2*. Boca Raton, FL: CRC Press.

Cnaan, R., Milofsky, C. and Hunter, A. (2008) Creating a frame for understanding local organizations. In: Cnaan, R. A. and Milofsky, C. (eds) *Handbook of community movements and local organizations*. New York: Springer.

Coleman, S. and von Hellerman, P. (2011) *Multi-sited ethnography: problems and possibilities in the translocation of research methods*. New York: Routledge.

Dietz, T., Ostrom, E. and Stern, P. C. (2003) The struggle to govern the commons. *Science* 302: 1907–1912.

Eckert, K. L. and Hemphill, A. H. (2005) Sea turtles as flagships for protection of the wider Caribbean region. *MAST* 3(2): 119–143.

Ekoko, F. (2000) Balancing politics, economics and conservation: the case of the Cameroon forestry law reform. *Development and Change* 31: 131–154.

Fuentes, M. P. B., Pike, D. A., DiMatteo, A. and Wallace, B. P. (2013) Resilience of marine turtle regional management units to climate change. *Global Change Biology* 19: 1399–1406.

Gammage, S., Benitez, M. and Machado, M. (2002) An entitlement approach to the challenge of mangrove management in El Salvador. *Ambio* 31(4): 285–294.

Gaos, A. R., Abreu-Grobois, F. A., Alfaro-Shigueto, J., Amorocho, D., Arauz, R., Baquero, A., Briseño, R., Chacón, D., Dueñas, C., Hasbún, C., Liles, M., Mariona, G., Muccio, C., Muñoz, J. P., Nichols, W. J., Peña, M., Seminoff, J. A., Vásquez, M., Urteaga, J., Wallace, B., Yañez, I. L. and Zárate, P. (2010) Signs of hope in the eastern Pacific: international collaboration reveals encouraging status for a severely depleted population of hawksbill turtles *Eretmochelysimbricata*. *Oryx* 44(4): 595–601.

Goldman, M. (2003) Partitioned nature, privileged knowledge: community-based conservation in Tanzania. *Development and Change* 34: 833–862.

Hammersley, M. and Atkinson, P. (2007) *Ethnography: principles in practice*. New York: Routledge.

Harrison, J., Miller, K. and McNeely, J. (1982) The world coverage of protected areas: development goals and environmental needs. *Ambio* 11: 238–245.

Hart, C. E., Blanco, G. S., Coyne, M. S., Delgado-Trejo, C., Godley, B. J., Jones, T. T., Resendiz, A., Seminoff, J. A., Witt, M. J. and Nichols, W. J. (2015) Multi-national tagging efforts illustrate regional range scale of distribution and threats for east Pacific green turtles (Cheloniamydasagassizii). *PLOS ONE* 10(2): e0116225. Online, available at: http://journals.plos.org/plosone/article?id=10.1371/journal.pone.0116225.

Hecht, S. and Cockburn, A. (1989) *Fate of the forest*. London: Verso.

Herlihy, P. (1992) "Wildlands" conservation in Central America during the 1980s: a geographical perspective. *Yearbook. Conference of Latin Americanist Geographers* 17/18: 31–43.

Hunter, A. (2008) Contemporary conceptions of community. In: Cnaan, R. A. and Milofsky, C. (eds) *Handbook of community movements and local organizations*. New York: Springer.

Hutton, J. M. and Leader-Williams, N. (2003) Sustainable use and incentive-driven conservation: realigning human and conservation interests. *Oryx* 37(2): 215–226.

ICAPO (Eastern Pacific Hawksbill Initiative). (2012) *Socio-economic baseline of hawksbill egg collectors in Bahía de Jiquilisco, El Salvador and Estero Padre Ramos, Nicaragua, San Salvador, El Salvador*. San Salvador, El Salvador: ICAPO–USAID.

Kilduff, G. J. (2014) Driven to win: rivalry, motivation, and performance. *Social Psychological and Personality Science* 5(8): 944–952.

Larson, A. M. and Soto, F. (2008) Decentralization of natural resource governance regimes. *Annual Review of Environment and Resources* 33: 213–239.

Leon, Y. M. and Bjorndal, K. A. (2002) Selective feeding in the hawksbill turtle, an important predator in coral reef ecosystems. *Marine Ecology Progress Series* 245: 249–258.

Liles, M. J., Jandres, M. V., Lopez, W. A., Mariona, G. I., Hasbún, C. R. and Seminoff, J. A. (2011) Hawksbill turtles *Eretmochelysimbricata* in El Salvador: nesting distribution and mortality at the largest remaining nesting aggregation in the eastern Pacific Ocean. *Endangered Species Research* 14: 23–30.

Liles, M. J., Peterson, M. J., Lincoln, Y. S., Seminoff, J. A., Gaos, A. R. and Peterson, T. R. (2014) Connecting international priorities with human wellbeing in low-income regions: lessons from hawksbill turtle conservation in El Salvador. *Local Environment*. Online, available at: http://dx.doi.org/10.1080/13549839.2014.905516.

Liles, M. J., Peterson, M. J., Seminoff, J. A., Altamirano, E., Henríquez, A. V., Gaos, A. R., Gadea, V., Urteaga, J., Torres, P., Wallace, B. P. and Peterson, T. R. (2015) One size does not fit all: importance of adjusting conservation practices for endangered hawksbill turtles to address local nesting habitat needs in the eastern Pacific Ocean. *Biological Conservation* 184: 405–413.

Lincoln, Y. S. and Guba, E. G. (1985) *Naturalistic inquiry*. Newbury Park, CA: Sage.

Lu, D. J., Chou, Y. F. and Yuan, H. W. (2005) Paradigm shift in the institutional arrangement of protected areas management in Taiwan – a case study of Wu-Wei-Kang Waterfowl Wildlife Refuge in Ilan, Taiwan. *Environmental Science and Policy* 8: 418–430.

Luschi, P., Hays, G. C. and Papi, F. (2003) A review of long-distance movements by marine turtles. *Oikos* 103(2): 293–302.

McMillian, D. W. and Chavis, D. M. (1986) Sense of community: a definition and theory. *Journal of Community Psychology* 14: 6–23.

McNeely, J. A. (1994) Protected areas for the 21st century: working to provide benefits to society. *Biodiversity and Conservation* 3: 390–405.

Marine Turtle Specialist Group. (1995) *A global strategy for the conservation of marine turtles*. Gland, Switzerland: International Union for Conservation of Nature.

Mason, T. (1995) *Passion of the people? Football in South America*. London: Verso.

Meylan, A. (1988) Spongivory in hawksbill turtles: a diet of glass. *Science* 239: 393–395.

Morgan, R. C. (2007) Property of spirits: hereditary and global value of sea turtles in Fiji. *Human Organization* 66(1): 60–68.

Mortimer, J. A. and Donnelly, M. (2008) *Eretmochelysimbricata: the IUCN Red List of Threatened Species*. Version 2014.3. Online, available at: www.iucnredlist.org.

Myers, N., Mittermeier, R. A., Michener, C. D., Da Fonseca, G. A. and Kent, J. (2000) Biodiversity hotspots for conservation priorities. *Nature* 403: 853–858.

Nepal, S. K. and Weber, K. E. (1995) The quandary of local people – park relations in Nepal's Royal Chitwan National Park. *Environmental Management* 19: 853–866.

Nichols, W. J., Resendiz, A., Seminoff, J. A. and Resendiz, B. (2000) Transpacific migration of a loggerhead turtle monitored by satellite telemetry. *Bulletin of Marine Science* 67(3): 937–947.

Nietschmann, B. (1973) *Between land and water: the subsistence ecology of the Miskito Indians, Eastern Nicaragua*. New York: Seminar Press.

Oldekop, J. A., Holmes, G., Harris, W. E. and Evans K. L. (2015) A global assessment of the social and conservation outcomes of protected areas. *Conservation Biology*. Online, available at: http://dx.doi.org/10.1111/cobi.12568.

Peterson, T. R. (1994) Using informant directed interviews to discover risk orientation: how formative evaluations based in interpretive analysis can improve persuasive safety campaigns. *Journal of Applied Communications Research* 22(3): 199.

Pimbert, M. P. and Pretty, J. N. (1995) *Parks, people, and professionals: putting "participation" into protected area management*. Geneva: United Nations Research Institute for Social Development.

República de El Salvador. (2009) Veda total y permanente al aprovechamiento de huevos, carne, grasa, aceite, sangre, huesos, especimenes disecados, caparazones, fragmentos y productos elaborados de caparazones de todas las especies de tortugas marinas. *Diario Oficial No. 23. Tomo No. 382*. San Salvador, El Salvador.

República de Nicaragua. (2005) Veda indefinida para todas las especies de tortugas marinas en Nicaragua. *Resolucion Ministerial No. 043–2005*.

Shaw, J. H. (1991) The outlook for sustainable harvest of wildlife in Latin America. In: Robinson, J. G. and Redford, K. H. (eds) *Neotropical wildlife use and conservation*. Chicago, IL: Chicago Press.

Taylor, C. (1998) *The beautiful game: a journey through Latin American football*. London: Victor Gollancz Ltd.

226 M. J. Liles et al.

Terborgh, J. and Estes, J. A. (eds) (2010) *Trophic cascades: predators, prey, and the changing dynamics of nature*. Washington, DC: Island Press.

Thorbjarnarson, J., Lagueux, C. J., Bolze, D., Klemens, M. W. and Meylan, A. B. (2000) Human use of turtles: a worldwide perspective. In: Klemens, M. W. (ed.) *Turtle conservation*. Washington, DC: Smithsonian Institution Press.

Veríssimo, D., MacMillan, D. C. and Smith, R. J. (2011) Toward a systematic approach for identifying conservation flagships. *Conservation Letters* 4: 1–8.

Wallace, B. P., DiMatteo, A. D., Bolten, A. B., Chaloupka, M. Y., Hutchinson, B. J., Abreu-Grobois, F. A., Mortimer, J. A., Seminoff, J. A., Amorocho, D., Bjorndal, K. A., Bourjea, J., Bowen, B. W., Briseno Dueñas, R., Casale, P., Choudhury, B. C., Costa, A., Dutton, P. H., Fallabrino, A., Finkbeiner, E. M., Girard, A., Girondot, M., Hamann, M., Hurley, B. J., López-Mendilaharsu, M., Marcovaldi, M. A., Musick, J. A., Nel, R., Pilcher, N. J., Troeng, S., Witherington, B. and Mast, R. B. (2011) Global conservation priorities for marine turtles. *PLOS ONE* 6(9): e24510. Online, available at: http://journals.plos.org/plosone/search?q=Global+conservation+priorities+for+marine+turtles&filterJournals=PLoSONE.

Wallace, B. P., Tiwari, M. and Girondot, M. (2013) *Dermochelyscoriacea: the IUCN Red List of Threatened Species*. Version 2015.2. Online, available at: www.iucnredlist.org (accessed 28 August 2015).

Wellman, B. (2001) Physical place and cyberplace: the rise of personalized networking. *International Journal of Urban and Regional Research* 25(2): 227–252.

Witherington, B. E. and Frazer, N. B. (2003) Social and economic aspects of sea turtle conservation. In: Lutz, P. L., Musick, J. A. and Wyneken, J. (eds) *The Biology of Sea Turtles, volume 2*. Boca Raton, FL: CRC Press.

Cases that integrate the above perspectives

12 Seized and missed opportunities in responding to conflicts

Constructivity and destructivity in forest conflict management in Finland and British Columbia, Canada

Kaisa Raitio

Introduction

The conflict literature identifies conflicts as neither positive nor negative but as having the potential to be either depending on how they are addressed (Carpenter and Kennedy, 1988; Daniels and Walker, 2001; Deutsch, 2011; Glasl, 1999). Despite this, there is a strong focus in natural resources management research and practice on conflicts as an obstacle or a problem to solve, or simply to get out of the way. Without downplaying the potentially significant harmful effects of protracted and escalated conflict (Hellström, 2001; Ramsbotham *et al.*, 2005), I argue in this chapter that an excessive focus on conflict resolution may be problematic for at least two reasons. It increases the likelihood that parties will achieve superficial agreement that ignores underlying issues, and it risks delegitimizing contestation and protest as part of the democratic process.

First, it risks rushing to a superficial agreement or consensus-seeking without taking the time to fully explore the problematic situation and the full diversity of causes underlying the most obvious contradictory interests (Rothman, 1997). The settlement of immediate differences (Yasmi, 2007), rather than attending to the underlying, often more difficult and enduring, causes becomes more attractive. This reduces the constructive, transformative potential that conflicts at best entail, because the potential of discovering more in-depth or innovative solutions beyond the ones already envisaged unilaterally by the parties is lost. For example, this mind-set would preclude the approach Sprain *et al.* suggest in Chapter 13 because it is simply too time consuming. Second, if conflicts are predominantly perceived as obstacles, there is a risk of delegitimizing contestation and protest as democratic rights and forms of political action leading to social change. The result may be the "sterilization" of politics (Mouffe, 1999; Poncelet, 2001; Hillier, 2003) to the extent that conflict in itself is perceived as a problem. Critics of collaborative, consensus-seeking approaches worry that they may lead actors away from addressing inherently contentious, yet important issues because both researchers and practitioners have a tendency to conceptualize collaboration or partnerships as contradictory to conflictual relations: disagreement or protest is considered the opposite and a threat to collaboration, even though successful collaboration may require that disagreements are first expressed and dealt with (Poncelet, 2001; see also Tjosvold, 1991).

The purpose of this chapter is to attend to both of these issues – underlying causes of conflicts and the role of conflict in social change – through two case studies on enduring old-growth forest conflicts. The analysis focuses on the constructivity of conflict as a communicative process to the extent it contributes to the inclusion of different actors and perspectives in the community and to the willingness and trust of the actors to contribute to collective problem solving. The conflicts in Inari in northern Finland and in Great Bear Rainforest in British Columbia, Canada both functioned as drivers of social change. At the same time, the differences in the communication and planning approaches adopted by the Finnish and British Columbia public forest management agencies show how the outcomes of the conflicts were not dependent of the characteristics of the conflicts themselves, but on the ways in which their underlying causes were, or were not, addressed during the conflict management processes. In the Great Bear Rainforest case, the constructive potential of the conflict was captured through a long process of trust building and learning that resulted in institutional innovation. In the Inari case, these opportunities were missed as the state agency managing the forests opted for the settlement of the most immediate concerns without attending to the lack of trust, knowledge disagreements or structural causes of the conflicts.

The chapter draws on three different types of literatures and theoretical discussions that together contribute to a multi-causal analytical framework: policy regime framework, collaborative planning theory and conflict theory. The purpose is to bring together the more critical, macro level analysis on power relations and the role of conflict as drivers of change in any given policy regime with the planning theory discussion on the design of collaborative processes and conflict management research focused on in-depth conflict analysis. Analysing the ways in which a conflict affects and changes the actors, institutions and discourses within a policy regime (Cashore et al., 2001) is helpful for understanding the nature of conflicts as drivers of social change, and as motivators for collaborative communication between adversaries to emerge (Saarikoski et al., 2013). It is well established in research on collaborative planning that an inclusive process design is often decisive for successful conflict management (Innes, 2004; Beierle and Cayford, 2000), but the process design characteristics are rarely explicitly connected to the analysis of the causes of a conflict, which is the focus in conflict theory and literature on conflict management (Carpenter and Kennedy, 1987; Daniels and Walker, 2001). In this chapter I bring these theoretical discussions together to explicate the connection between different process design features and the ways in which they focus on the different causes of a conflict. I argue that this approach helps us to understand the difference between different approaches to working with a conflict.

To summarize, the purpose of the chapter is to analyse:

1   the role of conflict as driver of change both on the macro level of society and on the level of collaborative process design,
2   the role of the process design components of collaborative planning in addressing the immediate and underlying causes of a conflict, and
3   the way these choices affect the constructivity or destructivity of the communicative process and its outcomes.

Conflicts in this chapter are understood as communicative processes in which the dynamic interaction between actors is central. Communication is defined as an inter-subjective process of "constructing the world in dialogue" (Waldenström, 2001). In this chapter "community" is not limited to a locality, such as a village or a city, but can encompass regions or even virtual communities. The key to our understanding of community is the sense of "gemeinschaft" or sense of belonging to a group of people who are dependent on one another for collective problem solving.

In the next section I will develop the theoretical approach in more detail, after which I will introduce the two case studies and describe the data and methods used in the study. The results section is divided into two parts, with the first focusing on the role of conflict and contestation as a driver of changes in the policy regime, and the second on the differences in the responses of the management agencies to the pressure of the conflict in the both cases, while the resulting differences are presented in the outcomes section. In the discussion section I focus on the potential explanations for the identified differences in conflict management strategies before ending with general remarks on the role of conflict in the construction and destruction of sense of community.

Theory

Collaborative approaches that gather the relevant actors to joint problem-solving are commonly seen as an appropriate strategy for making progress and – optimally – to resolve conflicts (e.g. Crowfoot and Wondolleck, 1990; Susskind *et al.*, 1999; Daniels and Walker, 2001).

Collaborative approaches aim at anticipating conflicts by promoting a deeper involvement of the different actors throughout the planning process. In contrast to "conventional" public participation methods, such as public hearings and the collection of written statements, these consensual problem-solving efforts use a higher level of collaboration between stakeholders who work together in face-to-face meetings to reach a consensus agreement – ideally in advance of disputes (Gunton and Day, 2003; Wondolleck and Yaffee, 2000). Selin and Chavez (1995: 190) define "collaboration" as "a joint decision-making approach to problem resolution where power is shared and the stakeholders take collective responsibility for their actions and the subsequent outcomes from those actions".

Indeed the inclusion of all affected parties has been found to be central in addressing conflicts in ways that satisfy the diversity of interests and actors typically involved in environmental issues (Beierle and Cayford, 2000). At the same time, the collaborative planning literature has been criticized for focusing too much on finding agreement at the expense of identifying and addressing the underlying causes of the conflict. These causes often relate to the broader context within which inter-personal interactions and collaborative planning take place (Fischler, 2000). The broader societal structures, within which the planning processes are embedded, including legal and other regulatory constraints, asymmetrical distribution of negotiation skills, resources and power of the parties, restrict the options of both the management agencies and the leverage of the different stakeholders in a conflict (Hillier, 2003; Mouffe, 1999). In fact, some actors may be so dominant that they simply do not see any need to join collaborative processes with the disempowered groups. Collaborative planning theory offers no advice in such a situation. In line with the critique of collaborative planning, conflict is not understood in this chapter as opposite to collaboration, but as a potentially necessary precondition and a legitimate communicative strategy for moving towards more democratic and collaborative processes. The chapter speaks to the literature on the role of protests and conflict in social and institutional change (Ganesh and Zoller, 2013; Mouffe, 1999; Young, 2001).

In analysing the mechanisms through which conflicts contribute to changes in wider power relations and hence policy and institutions, we need to look beyond the local level to society at large. In doing this, the chapter builds on the analytical approach developed by Saarikoski *et al.* (2013), who have combined collaborative planning theory with Cashore *et al.*'s (2001) *policy regime framework* in their analysis of the Great Bear Rainforest conflict. The policy regime framework looks at the ideas, institutions and actors (relations) in policy systems and policy-making. Combining policy network analysis, institutionalism, discourse analysis, and the advocacy coalition framework, the framework provides a multi-causal approach that "illustrates the role of actors and their networks, the institutions which constrain and enable actors, and discourses that provide actors with the narratives to make sense of policy problems" (Saarikoski *et al.*, 2013). The policy regime is embedded in a broader political-economic context that consists of public opinion, elections, market forces, the macro-political system and other policy sectors. Cashore *et al.* perceive these background conditions to be deeply influential for the dynamics of the policy regime.

Saarikoski *et al.* (2013) used this multi-causal approach to understand "the ways in which institutional rules and social discourses open up opportunities for agreement, while closing off others" and hence affected the success of the collaborative conflict management process in the Great Bear Rainforest. This chapter uses the analytical approach for the purposes of discussing the constructive role of conflicts in societal change more broadly (beyond the success in resolving conflicts), and adds to it a third theoretical component – that of the analysis of the causes of conflicts (below). The comparison between the Great Bear Rainforest conflict and the one in Inari brings forth the consequences of the different conflict management approaches for the constructivity and destructivity of the conflict processes despite the seemingly similar outcomes of both conflicts as solved.

Although one explicit aim of collaborative planning is to anticipate, manage and resolve conflicts, the literature on collaborative planning does not typically make an explicit connection between the process design factors of collaborative planning and how these contribute to addressing the different causes of conflicts. To address this gap, I complement the collaborative planning literature with insights from conflict research in terms of analysing the causes of conflicts. According to Daniels and Walker (2001: 36), progress needs to take place on three fundamental dimensions of a conflict: procedural, substantial, and relationship. These inter-linked factors are called the "progress triangle" or "satisfaction triangle" (Figure 12.1). The different causes of conflict, as they are typically conceptualized in the literature (Daniels and Walker 2001; Moore 1996) can be organized under these three main categories (see Table 12.1).

Causes related to the substance include knowledge disagreements, goal or interest interference (including uneven distribution of benefits and costs), and incompatible ways of framing the character of the conflict (Gray, 2003). Procedural aspects are closely related to the design of the collaborative planning process itself, but also to other societal decision-making processes related to the issue at hand (such as permitting or impact assessment). Key questions here concern how decisions are made, who has the right to participate, and how to set the agenda (Dahl, 1999).

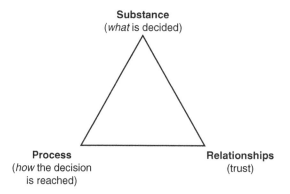

Figure 12.1 Situation improvement triangle (adapted from Walker and Daniels, 1997).

Note: In order to improve a conflict situation, progress needs to be made on three dimensions: substance of the conflict (what is decided), the process of addressing the conflict (how the decision is reached) and the relationships (trust) between the parties in the conflict.

Table 12.1 Causes of a conflict

	Causes of a conflict
Substance	Disagreement over facts Conflicting interests Uneven distribution of costs and benefits Framing of the issue: what is the conflict about?
Process	How are decisions made? Who has the right to participate? Whose agenda?
Trust/relationships	Inter-personal Between organizations Process

Finally, relationships – or trust – often depend on the history of the situation on the inter-personal level, or between organizations. Trust has been found to be one of the most important factors enabling collaborative behaviour, which can in turn produce innovative outcomes needed in conflict management (Schön and Rein, 1994; Gillroy, 2000). Indeed, it has been said that trust is the "glue" or "lubricant" of cooperation in modern societies (Misztal, 1996: 77–87). The problem is that many disputes related to NRM escalate over time to the point where individual actors no longer trust each other in the sense that they would be assured of the cooperative behaviour of others (Kyllönen *et al.*, 2006). The escalation of a dispute can be caused by several factors, including lack of direct communication or failed attempts to resolve the issue. The stage of mutual distrust can be described as an assurance problem. Under such circumstances people are more likely to change the strategies into non-cooperative ones, even at the expense of their own goals (Gillroy, 2000: 200–227; Glasl, 1999).

While structural causes are sometimes classified as a separate category in the conflict literature, this chapter departs from a perception that all the above causes of conflict – substance, process, trust – can become institutionalized in the social structures to different degrees. Regulations and policies that are a part of the policy regime typically privilege some interests over others. They define the appropriate processes for decision-making, and these institutionalized processes may be one of the topics of contestation in themselves. Certain forms of knowledge and ways of framing an issue become privileged depending on the type of professionals that are given the task of managing a natural resource. For example, in both the forest conflict analysed by Banerjee (Chapter 6) and that analysed by Ångman *et al.* (Chapter 10), professional foresters were responsible for management decisions. As such, policies and institutions are "imprints of power" (North, 1990), both part of the causes of the conflict as well as determining the opportunities and limitations for how those same conflicts can be managed within a given policy regime.

Cases and methods: Inari and the Great Bear Rainforest

Two similar cases of old-growth forests with different outcomes

The above combination of theoretical ideas has emerged out of and is tested through the analysis of two forest conflicts in Inari in northern Finland and in the Great Bear Rainforest in British Columbia. Both cases concern conflicts over publicly owned old-growth forests that have initially been designated for timber harvesting.

Inari is a large municipality of 17,000 km², situated some 300 km north of the Arctic Circle in the timberline between the northern boreal forest zone and the hemi-arctic zone. It has a population of 7,000 inhabitants, of which one-third belong to the indigenous Sámi people. Most livelihoods in Inari depend directly on the surrounding environment. The most important livelihoods are forestry, reindeer husbandry and, to an increasing extent, tourism. Some 60 per cent of the total land area of the municipality and 40 per cent of the forests are protected.

Reindeer husbandry, together with hunting and fishing both for subsistence and for commercial sale, are traditional livelihoods of the Sámi people and as such protected by the Finnish Constitution. The state currently owns 90 per cent of the land area in Inari, which is managed by the Forest and Park Service, a state enterprise with the dual role of producing timber and managing the lands for the benefit of multiple land uses. The forest conflict concerns reindeer husbandry and forestry and stems from the fact that old forests are attractive for timber harvest and also important winter pastures for the semi-domesticated reindeer. Reindeer depend on tree-hanging lichens, abundant in old-growth forests, during the crucial winter months when another central winter food, ground lichen, is covered by thick snow and ice. Underlying the conflict are the unsettled land rights of the Sámi people, who contest the Finnish state's claims of land ownership. (For details on the conflict, see Raitio, 2008, 2012; Saarikoski and Raitio, 2013.)

Great Bear Rainforest is the name that environmental NGOs gave to the central and north coast in British Columbia in the 1990s when the conflicts over the area emerged between them, the forest industry, the provincial government and the First Nations (indigenous people). Covering an area of 32,000 km², the region is known as the largest remaining unprotected temperate rainforest in the world, with high biodiversity and habitat variety, with the iconic white Spirit Bear as its symbol. The area is also the home of 27 First Nations, whose traditional uses of the area include subsistence fishing, picking plants and berries, and using the massive cedar tree logs to build boats and totem poles. Many of the small remote communities are only accessible through air and water, and suffer from high unemployment and related social problems. For the First Nations, the central issues concern their need to develop the communities and improve their wellbeing, and to gain recognition for their land rights. Unlike other parts of Canada, the First Nations in British Columbia have not signed treaties with the Crown. For some of the communities, protecting remaining old-growth forests is a crucial part of their wellbeing and rights. Others live in areas that have been logged previously and are therefore less concerned directly with logging that is carried out by a number of international forest companies. Their tenure gives them the right and duty to harvest timber and manage the forests that are owned by the Crown, and under the jurisdiction of the provincial government of British Columbia.

Data and methods

The data for both cases consisted of policy and planning documents, as well as key informant interviews with actors that had in-depth knowledge of policy processes and who played important roles in their resolution.

The data on the Inari case consisted of 13 in-depth interviews with the Forest Service representatives, conducted in 2003 and 2004, as well as an additional five interviews conducted with the representatives of both the Forest Service (two individuals) and the reindeer husbandry communities (three individuals) after the settlement of the conflict in 2012. Participatory observation was also carried out on field visits with the reindeer herding communities and the Forest Service. The documents analysed included formal regulations on state owned forests, finalized forest management plans, and unpublished written statements by the Forest and Park Service, Ministry of Agriculture and Forestry, reindeer herding communities and other actors involved in the dispute.

Primary data for the Great Bear Rainforest conflict came from 14 thematic in-depth interviews conducted in 2009. The interviewees represented the British Columbia government (4), First Nations (3), environmental groups (4) and forest industry (3). The interviews were supplemented by a document analysis that included the Central Coast Land and Resource Management Plan completion table report (CCLRMP 2004) and related background documents, as well as press releases, policy documents, presentations and websites produced by the actors from 1996 to 2009.

Results

Causes and escalation of the conflicts

Both the Great Bear Rainforest conflict and the one in Inari concern *conflicting interests* over publicly owned forests that have initially been designated for timber harvesting. Timber harvesting is of economic interest to the international forestry corporations procuring wood from the areas, and thereby to the national and provincial governments, municipalities and local community members concerned with employment opportunities, tax revenues, and local and regional development. Those arguing for increased forest conservation include local, national and international environmental nongovernmental organizations (ENGOs) that are concerned with high biodiversity and wilderness values, but also significant parts of the indigenous community, whose traditional uses of the forests (hunting and gathering, and in Inari, centrally, reindeer husbandry) are dependent of intact forest landscapes.

Besides these immediate interests regarding the use of the forests, for the indigenous groups the conflicts concern their rights to self-determination over their traditional territories, their traditional livelihoods, and their social well-being. Both Northern Finland and British Columbia lack treaties between the indigenous populations and the state, and land ownership remains disputed (Barry, 2012). The local and national/provincial governments as well as forestry corporations have tended to *frame* the conflicts as balancing between diverse interests. However, the indigenous groups (and some of the ENGOs that allied with them as the conflicts escalated) have contested this view as ignorant of their perspective that the conflict is a question of rights. From the rights perspective, the primary focus is not on balancing between local interests, but on the responsibilities of the legislators to respect the land rights of the indigenous peoples and to seek agreement with the indigenous representatives.

The differences between these ways of framing the conflict have in both cases been reflected in the ways in which the first attempts at collaborative planning were designed in the late 1990s and early 2000s. Both in the Natural Resource Planning (NRP) carried out by the Finnish Forest and Park Service and in the Land and Resource Management Planning (LRMP) organized by the provincial government agencies in British Columbia, the first rounds (1999–2000 and 1996–2001, respectively) treated indigenous groups as stakeholders among other citizen stakeholders, as opposed to indigenous governments with sovereignty. This led, most explicitly in the Inari case, to the arguments of the indigenous representatives being countered with the opposition from the majority. In both cases, those questions of most concern for the indigenous groups did not gain attention at the negotiation table. For both of these reasons, the concerned Sámi reindeer herding communities and some of the First Nations in British Columbia chose to leave the planning processes. Environmental groups were equally frustrated with both of the planning processes, as logging of the disputed old-growth forests was carried out while the planning proceeded. A majority of them opted for leaving the "talk and log" processes in protest.

Thus, the *process* for deciding on management strategies for the forests – including the management authority of the governments – was in itself contested, and this affected the *relationships* and the *trust* between the actors negatively. Difficulties in addressing the conflict have also included *knowledge disagreements* over the actual impacts of forestry on biodiversity and on reindeer husbandry, over the impacts of increased forest conservation on timber production and employment, as well as general lack of knowledge about the indigenous land uses and needs related to them (Saarikoski and Raitio, 2013; Saarikoski *et al.*, 2013).

Following the decisions to leave the planning processes that had failed to address the major concerns of many of the indigenous communities and ENGOs, these groups developed alternative strategies to push for their agenda. The indigenous groups became organized in coalitions of several First Nations and several reindeer herding communities with a joint message and strategy. They started collaborating with environmental groups to gain resources and competence on protesting, and to gain access to market campaigns the ENGOs were running (Raitio, 2012; Saarikoski et al., 2013). The Saami Council – a Sámi NGO supporting the reindeer herding communities – also contacted ethical indexes and investors, advising them to remove paper giant Stora Enso from their listings as long as the company was buying wood from the disputed areas (Lawrence, 2007).

Another alternative strategy that contributed to the escalation of the conflict was court cases initiated by the indigenous groups against governments either directly in relation to the conflicts analysed here (Inari) or in other areas, but with relevance for the NRP concerning the conflict (British Columbia) (Barry, 2012; Saarikoski et al., 2013). In Inari, three herders chose to file a civil law suit against the state, with the argument that the forestry operations were threatening their right to practice their culture in accordance with the UN Covenant on Civil and Political Rights (Raitio, 2008; Lawrence, 2007).

Ultimately, the market campaigns targeting the forestry industry's paper customers in the United States, Central Europe and, most of all, in Germany were the central game changer in both cases. German publishing houses and other buyers of the wood or the forest products demanded a moratorium on logging in the disputed forests until an agreement was established (Saarikoski et al., 2013; Lawrence, 2007).

These ways of contesting the governments' conflict management strategies caused vocal critique and counter-protests both in the national level debates as well as locally, leading to boycotts of reindeer meat from Sámi who collaborated with Greenpeace, as well as threats and attacks against environmentalists present in the local communities in both cases. In short, they were perceived as destructive by some of the other actors, which in turn led to increased escalation of the conflicts with decreasing levels of trust (Carpenter and Kennedy, 1987; Glasl, 1989). Nonetheless, the more confrontational communication strategies were successful in changing the power relations underlying these conflicts on the level of the policy regime (Saarikoski et al., 2013). The *networks* built within the indigenous community and between the indigenous and the ENGO community led to changes in the *actors'* resources and capacities, affecting their ability to influence their counterparts. By changing the locus of the conflict from government agency controlled planning processes to the international marketplace and the courts, the alliances were able to change the rules of the game (the *institutions*). In the international media and markets, the ways of framing the conflict as the last wildernesses of the world and as indigenous peoples under threat resonated with the international *discourses* on biodiversity conservation and indigenous rights (ibid.).

Taken together, these shifts in the policy regime changed the power relations between the previously dominant governments and industry on one side, and the environmental and indigenous groups on the other. The shifts compelled all the parties and, crucially, the responsible government agencies to turn to new ways of addressing the conflict. This is where the trajectories of the cases differ. In the following two sections, I use the collaborative planning literature and conflict analysis literature to pinpoint the differences in the approaches adopted by the forest management agencies in Finland and British Columbia, respectively.

Settling the immediate interest conflict in Inari

Finnish Forest and Park Service (FPS) had on several occasions during the conflict invited the reindeer herding communities to bilateral negotiations. However, since the agenda of these negotiations remained unchanged from the multi-stakeholder NRP and did not include the key concern of the Sámi communities in terms of excluding some forests from logging, the negotiations ended without progress. It was not until after the court case initiated by the three herders from Nellim village that the state offered a new negotiating position. Interestingly, the first court had ruled in the favour of the state party, but the decision had been appealed by the herders. The United Nations Human Rights Committee was following the case and had demanded that the state refrain from logging in the contested forests as an interim measure. This international attention and intervention may have increased the incentive for the state to get the issue off the table.

The first round of negotiations only concerned the three herders and their winter group in Nellim. The process was simple bargaining without attempts to actually agree on issues beyond "who gets what, where and how". After some months, the parties were able to reach an agreement on these issues, and a few months later similar negotiations were initiated between the FPS and the remaining five reindeer herding communities. In September 2010, after five years of court proceedings, a final agreement was reached. In total, 77 per cent of the disputed areas (and 90 per cent of old-growth forests within them) are protected either permanently or for the next 20 years. Both parties expressed satisfaction with the outcome and with bringing the conflict to an end.

The adopted approach with focus on settling the interest conflict through bargaining had clear implications for the constructivity/destructivity of the conflict (Table 12.2). The interviewees pointed out explicitly that the parties never agreed on the extent to which forestry actually is detrimental to reindeer pastures and hence, to what extent the demands of the reindeer herding co-operatives were legitimate. Thus, all knowledge disagreements (see Saarikoski and Raitio 2013 for details) remained unaddressed, and frame reflection was not even attempted. The fact that the parties were able to reach an agreement did improve the trust between them somewhat, even though the implementation of the agreement has proven demanding. Furthermore,

Table 12.2 Addressing the causes of the Inari conflict

Causes of the conflict		Responses
Substance	Knowledge	Disagreement over impacts not addressed—persist
	Interests	Conflicting interests settled through bargaining
	Framing	Frame conflicts not addressed—persist
Process	Access to decision-making	Not all parties included/connected to negotiations
Relationships	Trust	Improved between reindeer herding communities and Forest Service, but other actors not included

the bargaining approach did not lead to new, innovative solutions in terms of how to best accommodate the interests of both parties. Neither did it lead to learning in terms of how to develop the NRP tool – or the broader institutional context (Raitio, 2012) – so that reindeer herding rights could be better accommodated and conflicts anticipated and mitigated in the future. Other local people, and other parties in general, were also left out of the process, the results of which were simply communicated to the stakeholders working on revisions to the NRP.

All in all, while being successful in getting the conflict of interests off the table and thus improving the situation for both parties, the process did not attend to any of the other underlying causes of the conflict on the local, national or structural level. The Great Bear Rainforest, on the other hand, provides an illustrative example of understanding what difference addressing the full spectrum of causes can make for the constructivity and destructivity of the conflict.

Addressing the underlying causes of the Great Bear Rainforest conflict

In the Great Bear Rainforest conflict, the involvement of the German publishing houses in the conflict between the British Columbian forest industry and various other stakeholders that resulted from the ENGO-led market campaign led to a number of changes in the conflict dynamics, both in the communication processes between industry and ENGOs, as well as in the formal planning process design. Although a number of activities and resources provided by the forest industry and ENGOs were important in making the process successful (on these governance relations, see Raitio and Saarikoski, 2013; Saarikoski *et al.*, 2013), here the focus is on the possible impacts that these activities and resources may have had on the government planning process, and the ways in which the government adapted its strategies to better accommodate the different interests and views.

The process design for the second round of LRMP was essentially different from the first round, and fundamental for making progress with the conflict.

By accepting a logging moratorium for the 100 ecologically most valuable valleys for the duration of the process, a meaningful decision space was created for the ENGOs. The provincial government came to recognize the First Nations as a government entity, and established separate government-to-government negotiations (between the provincial and First Nations governments) in addition to the collaborative stakeholder LRMP, while at the same ensuring close communication between the two. The number of parties around the table was reduced by clearer representation, and the province clarified and separated its own roles in the planning process (facilitation, general public interests and forestry interests). In short, key procedural aspects of the conflict were effectively addressed by these changes. The province also established and funded a separate Coast Information Team to specifically focus on the knowledge disagreements and to acknowledge traditional knowledge alongside scientific knowledge. The changed power relations meant that the parties had an incentive to listen to one another. To succeed in building trust and in perspective taking (or frame reflection (Schön and Rein, 1994) necessary for identifying workable solutions, the process benefitted from the use of professional facilitators and mediators, and from long meetings organized in isolated locations. The government also allocated funds to alleviate the adverse impacts of conservation on forestry workers. All of this contributed to increased levels of trust, and also opened up for solutions that would not have been available otherwise.

After five years of intensive work, the multiple processes resulted in the Land Use Decision in 2006, known by the media as the Great Bear Rainforest Agreement. It meant that 2.1 million hectares (36 per cent) of the forests were protected, and a new ecosystem-based management approach was introduced to the rest of the area, with varying levels of old-growth forests maintenance across the landscape. Some 120 million Canadian dollars were allocated to First Nations community wellbeing and for the development of new, sustainable jobs. These funds consisted of 25 per cent provincial and 25 per cent federal government money, as well as another 50 per cent from the forest industry and money raised by the ENGOs (Raitio and Saarikoski, 2013). On the level of innovations, the process led to the establishment of a new category of protected areas in the British Columbia legislations, called *Conservancies*, that recognized the user rights of First Nations. Further, the process became "a key site in a larger re-imagining of the possibilities for government-to-government (G2G) relations between indigenous peoples (First Nations) and the state" (Barry, 2012) far beyond the coast of the province.

The outcomes of the Great Bear Rainforest process differed from those in Inari in two important respects. First, the comprehensive conflict resolution process addressed multiple diverse causes underlying the conflict, ranging from knowledge disagreements to major institutional issues related to indigenous peoples' rights (Table 12.3). In other words, the parties took the time, and the government agency crafted a process that allowed for the in-depth exploration

Table 12.3 Addressing the causes of the Great Bear Rainforest conflict

Causes of the conflict		Response
Substance	Knowledge	Joint fact finding
		Government resources
	Interests	Increased protection
		New category of protected areas
		Ecosystem based management
	Framing	Meetings in isolated locations
		Listening
Process	Access to decision-making	First Nations as rights holders (G2G)
		Connection between stakeholder process and G2G
Relationships	Trust	Use of mediator
		Funding
		Exploring the underlying causes

of the differences. Second, the progress that was made due to this approach was not limited to the area or to the case itself; the process also contributed to bottom-up changes in the policy regime regarding institutions, relations between actors, and ideas (Barry, 2012; Saarikoski *et al.*, 2013). Constructive conflict management thus worked as a driver for bottom-up policy change, highlighting the broader ramifications of how individual conflicts are addressed.

Discussion

In this chapter, I have demonstrated differences between the approaches to two forest conflicts, both of which on the surface, led to an agreement. I have also argued for recognizing differences in the consequences of these two approaches in terms of building trust and capacity, for learning, and for broader policy change and development. Paying attention to, and dealing with the underlying causes of the conflicts – beyond the settlement of immediate interests – helped capture the constructive potential of the conflict in British Columbia, and led to social change both locally and province-wide. An appropriate collaborative process design was instrumental in achieving this. In Inari, the conflict was an important tool for affected Sámi reindeer herding communities and the ENGOs to change power relations, and to achieve desirable changes in forest management. At the same time, many opportunities were missed as the focus of the Forest and Park Service throughout the conflict was on bargaining and settling of interests. The underlying causes of the conflict were neither considered legitimate nor explicitly and systematically addressed. The opportunities for improved recognition of Sámi rights, exploring of different types of knowledges, or building trust and understanding within the local community between the different parties were missed.

The contrast between the two cases and policy regimes presented here encourages us to ask what led to the different approaches. Why did the government agency in British Columbia choose to address the underlying causes of the conflict and the one in Finland chose not to? I have argued above that in both cases shifts took place in the policy regime that changed the power relations between actors in essential ways, yet clearly the policy regime changes in Finnish forest policy were not as significant as in the case of British Columbia. Despite the attempts of the reindeer herding communities and the ENGOs to tap into the international discourse on indigenous peoples' rights, this framing did not gain larger support.

In comparison to Canada, the overall status of Sámi as an indigenous people and the recognition of indigenous issues as a policy field on its own right are much more weakly established in Finland. Tuulentie (2003: 288) notes that the principle of "equal citizenship" has dominated the discussions in the Finnish parliament regarding the rights of the Sámi as indigenous people. She notes that one interpretation of the liberal concept of equality between citizens in fact denies all kinds of group-based collective rights or benefits. They are seen as morally arbitrary and inherently discriminatory (for the same debate concerning Sweden, see Lawrence, 2007; Mörkenstam, 1999). The Sámi parliament – a self-governing body of the Sámi in Finland – has noted that the rights of the minority will always lose in a democracy if they are simply weighed against the majority. Indeed, the municipalities in Finnish Sapmi and the members of the parliament elected from Northern Finland have been opposed to any special rights for the Sámi. Likewise, there has been a "resistance movement" of the ethnic Finns living in Sapmi (Tuulentie, 2003). As Tuulentie (2003: 290) summarizes the situation:

> The value of Sámi culture is not directly denied in any statement or parliamentary speech. However, after the positive attitude comes "but" which is often presented to separate principle from practice or to refer to the locus of quantity to overcome that of quality.

This politics of "but" summarizes also the position of the state forest administration, in particular as far as the Forest Service and its superior Ministry of Agriculture and Forestry are concerned. The rights of the Sámi as an indigenous people are considered important, yet they are only taken into account within the frame of balancing equally important local land uses and perspectives. While it is important to look at the needs and rights of the local community as a whole, it would be equally important to show that in doing so, the state recognizes the position of the Sámi not as a regular stakeholder, but as a sovereign nation. Only once this has been accepted and recognized through some type of government-to-government institutional arrangement can the discussion proceed in how these rights and the rights of the local population as a whole can be reconciled. Such discussions have taken place in the different governmental committees addressing Sámi rights, but this approach still remains largely excluded from the frames of the state forest administration.

While the forest sector is significant in both Finland and British Columbia, there are still relative differences in this respect. The role this one single economic sector has played for the independence and economic growth of Finland provides a unique position for it in the society. According to Koskinen (1985), it is impossible to understand the Finnish economy, politics, culture and national coherence in general without understanding the role the forest sector – forestry and forest industry – has had as a central economic resource and hence as a central power player in the Finnish economic policy and society as a whole (see also Oinis, 2005 and Tainio and Lilja, 2003). A whole mythology has been developed to tell the story of a small and poor country that through hard work and by skilful utilization of a single resource – wood – has, since the beginning of forest industry development in the 1870s, been able to gain independence from Russia in 1917 and become one of the wealthiest economies and welfare states with some of the largest forest corporations in the world (Donner-Amnell, 1991: 265–267). The forests in Inari and the small amount of cubic meters they provide annually are not of importance for the industry – this has in fact been explicitly stated by the paper company Stora Enso. However, the symbolic meaning of surrendering in the face of a small and marginalized non-timber forest use cannot be underestimated, and it could have ramifications beyond the local context. Indeed, Tuulentie (2003) has shown that the forestry industry has been actively lobbying against legislation that would recognize the Sámi land rights.

In her analysis of the state and market relations in the Inari conflict, Lawrence (2007) has also highlighted the particular dynamics caused by the fact that the Finnish Forest Service is a state-owned enterprise and its biggest buyer of wood, paper giant Stora Enso, a corporation with considerable state ownership. In her analysis of Stora Enso's corporate social responsibility, Lawrence shows how markets are neither universal nor abstract but instead "entangled in local, national and global relations" (2007: 174). In contrast to its operations in other parts of the world, Stora Enso has in Inari maintained that as a "mere customer" of Metsähallitus it is responsible for contributing neither to the resolution of the conflict nor to the recognition of Sámi indigenous rights. Thus paradoxically, the strong presence of the state within the market actors has worked to weaken the market mechanisms and pressures, and enabled the forest company to take on a passive role instead of a proactive one as in the Great Bear Rainforest, where the forest corporations invested large amounts of time and financial resources to drafting lasting solutions.

Finally, it is worth noticing that the role of ENGOs differed between the cases, not least in terms of providing resources. In the Great Bear Rainforest the ENGOs covered parts of the costs of the professional mediator in negotiations between the industry and ENGOs, and fundraised 25 per cent of the money put into the Coast Opportunity Funds. This was made possible by active ENGOs and other foundations across North America, whereas similar funding for the Finnish conflict did not emerge from European ENGOs. In the Scandinavian context, this is strongly embedded in the traditional perception of the good strong state providing for central services, such as the planning of public forest management.

Conclusions

This chapter has compared two high profile forest conflicts to show the important and constructive role conflicts can play as drivers of social change by improving the access of previously disadvantaged groups to decision-making processes. By comparing the conflict management responses adopted by the government forest agencies in Finland and British Columbia, the analysis has shown how the extent to which conflicts contribute constructively to change depends not only on the intention of those who challenge the system, but centrally on the response of those in power. By attending to the underlying, long-enduring causes of the conflicts and seeking structural changes to them, the actors in British Columbia have, I argue, learnt more from their experiences and built both concrete institutional innovations as well as capacity and sense of community (respect and relationships) that will help them address challenges in the future.

For both policy-making and planning practice, the lesson from the cases is to think of protests as a message of something that needs attention and constructive engagement. Protests should be understood not as opposite to dialogue, but as an invitation to dialogue on more equal terms (Ganesh and Zoller, 2013). I argue that approaching conflicts with such an understanding would help policy makers and planners to start listening earlier to the concerns that protesters are trying to convey. It is possible to avoid conflicts by only attending to the immediate concerns, but for the long term benefit, policy makers and planners should see and attend to the full potential that conflicts have as drivers of constructive social change. This is likely to have positive effects beyond the particular conflict in the form of increased legitimacy of the natural resource governance at large.

Acknowledgements

I want to thank all the informants for their collaboration, without them this study would not have been possible. I thank Janice Barry and Heli Saarikoski for previous collaborations, Theo Verwijst and Rebecca Lawrence for asking me questions that drove the analysis forward, and Lars Hallgren for on-going discussions on constructivity and destructivity in conflicts. I acknowledge the financial support of Formas (project 211–2014–545).

References

Barry, J. (2012) Indigenous–state planning as inter-institutional capacity development: the evolution of "government-to-government" relations in Coastal British Columbia, Canada. *Planning Theory and Practice* 13(2): 213–231.

Beierle, T. and Cayford, J. (2000) *Democracy in Practice: Public Participation in Environmental Decisions*. Washington, DC: Resources for the Future.

Carpenter, S. L. and Kennedy, W. K. D. (1988) *Managing Public Disputes: a Practical Guide to Handling Conflicts and Reaching Agreements*. San Francisco: Jossey-Bass.

Cashore, B., Hoberg, G., Howlett, M., Rayner, J. and Wilson, J. (2001) *In Search of Sustainability: British Columbia Forest Policy in the 1990s*. Vancouver: University of British Columbia Press.

CCLRMP. (2004) Central Coast LRMP completion table, British Columbia. Report of consensus recommendations to the provincial government and First Nations. Victoria, British Columbia. Online, available at: www.for.gov.bc.ca/tasb/slrp/lrmp/nanaimo/cencoast/plan/consolidated%20central%20coast%20lrmp%20completion%20table%20recommendations%20may%202004.pdf.

Crowfoot, J. E. and Wondolleck. J. M. (1990) *Environmental Disputes: Community Involvement in Conflict Resolution*. Washington, DC: Island Press.

Dahl, R. A. (1999) *Democracy and its Critics*. New Haven, CT: Yale University Press.

Daniels, S. and Walker, G. B. (2001) *Working through Environmental Conflict: the Collaborative Learning Approach*. Westport: Praeger.

Deutsch, M. (2011) Cooperation and competition. In: Coleman, P. T. (ed.) *Conflict, Interdependence and Justice – the Intellectual Legacy of Morton Deutsch*. New York: Springer.

Donner-Amnell., J. (1991) Metsäteollisuus yhteiskunnallisena kysymyksenä Suomessa. [Original in Finnish, The forest industry as a societal phenomenon in Finland] In: Massa, I. and Sairinen, R. (eds) *Ympäristökysymys: ympäristöuhkien haaste yhteiskunnalle* [The environmental question – Environmental threats as a challenge in society]. Helsinki: Gaudeamus. 265–306.

Ehrmann, J. and Stinson, B. (1999) Joint fact-finding and the use of technical experts. In: Susskind, L., McKearnan, S. and Thomas-Larmer, J. (eds) *The Consensus-building Handbook: a Comprehensive Guide to Reaching Agreement*. Thousand Oaks, CA: Sage, 375–400.

Fischler, R. (2000) Communicative planning theory: a Foucauldian assessment. *Journal of Planning Education and Research* 19: 358–368.

Ganesh, S. and Zoller, H. M. (2013) Dialogue, activism and democratic social change. *Communication Theory* 22(1): 66–91.

Gillroy, J. M. (2000) *Justice and Nature: Kantian Philosophy, Environmental Policy, and the Law*. Washington, DC: Georgetown University.

Glasl, F. (1999) *Confronting Conflict. A First Aid Kit for Handling Conflict*. Stroud, Gloucestershire, UK: Hawthorn Press.

Gray, B. (2003) Framing of environmental disputes. In: Lewicki, R. J., Gray, B. and Elliot, M. (eds) *Making Sense of Intractable Environmental Conflicts: Concepts and Cases*. Washington, DC: Island Press, 11–34.

Gunton, T. I. and Day, J. C. (2003) Theory and practice of collaborative planning in resource management. *Environments* 32(2): 31–46.

Hellström, E. (2001) *Conflict Cultures – Qualitative Comparative Analysis of Environmental Conflicts in Forestry*. Silva Fennica Monographs 2. Helsinki: Finnish Forest Research Institute.

Hillier, J. (2003): Agonizing over consensus: why Habermasian ideals cannot be "real". *Planning Theory* 2(1): 37–59.

Innes, J. (2004) Consensus building: clarification for the critics. *Planning Theory* 3(1): 5–20.

Koskinen, T. (1985) Finland – a forest sector society? Sociological approaches, conclusions and challenges. In: Kari, Lilja K., Rasanen, K. and Tainio, R. (eds) *Problems in the Redescription of Business Enterprises*. Proceedings of the first summer seminar of the Research Group on the Theory of the Firm 3. Helsinki School of Economics Studies B-73.

Kyllönen, S., Colpaert, A.., Heikkinen, H., Jokinen, M., Kumpula, J., Marttunen, M., Muje, K. and Raitio, K. (2006) Conflict management as a means to the sustainable use of natural resources. *Silva Fennica* 44(4): 687–728.

Lawrence, R. (2007) Corporate social responsibility, supply-chains and Saami claims: tracing the political in the Finnish forestry industry. *Geographical Research* 45(2): 167–176.

Misztal, B. A. (1996) *Trust in Modern Societies: the Search for the Bases of Social Order*. Cambridge: Polity Press.

Mörkenstam, U. (1999) Om 'Lapparnas Privilegier' [Original in Swedish About the 'Lapps' Privileges']. Unpublished PhD thesis, Department of Political Science, Stockholm University, Sweden.

Moore, C. (1996): *The Mediation Process: Practical Strategies for Resolving Conflict*. San Francisco: Jossey-Bass.

Mouffe, C. (1999) Deliberative democracy or agonistic pluralism? *Social Research* 66(3): 745–758.

North, D. C. (1990) *Institutions, Institutional Change and Economic Performance*. Cambridge, UK: Cambridge University Press.

Oinis, P. (2005) Finland: a success story? *European Planning Studies* 13: 1227–1224.

Poncelet, E. C. (2001) A kiss here and a kiss there: conflict and collaboration in environmental partnerships. *Environmental Management* 27(1): 13–25.

Ramsbotham, O., Woodhouse, T. and Miall, H. (2005) *Contemporary Conflict Resolution: the Prevention, Management and Transformation of Deadly Conflicts*. Cambridge, UK: Polity Press.

Raitio, K. (2008) *You Can't Please Everyone: Conflict Management Practices, Frames and Institutions in Finnish State Forests*. Joensuu: University of Joensuu Publications in Social Sciences 86.

Raitio, K. (2013) Discursive institutionalist approach to conflict management analysis: the case of old-growth forest conflicts on Finnish state-owned land. *Forest Policy and Economics* 33: 97–103.

Raitio, K. (2012) New institutional approach to collaborative forest planning: methods for analysis and lessons for policy. *Land Use Policy* 29(2): 309–316.

Raitio, K. and Saarikoski, H. (2012) Governing old-growth forests: the interdependence of actors in Great Bear Rainforest in British Columbia. *Society and Natural Resources* 25(9): 900–914.

Rothman, J. (1997) *Resolving Identity-Based Conflict in Nations, Organizations, and Communities*. Jossey-Bass. San Francisco.

Saarikoski, H. and Raitio, K. (2013) Science and politics in old-growth forest conflict in Upper Lapland. *Nature and Culture* 8(1): 53–73.

Saarikoski, H., Raitio, K. and Barry, J. (2013) Explaining "success" in conflict resolution – policy regime changes and new interactive arenas in the Great Bear Rainforest. *Land Use Policy*, 32: 271–280.

Schön, D. A. and Rein, M. (1994) *Frame Reflection: Towards the Resolution of Intractable Policy Controversies*. New York: Basic Books.

Selin, S. and Chavez, D. (1995) Developing a collaborative model for environmental planning and management. *Environmental Management* 19: 189–195.

Susskind, L., McKearnan, S. and Thomas-Larmer, J. (1999) *The Consensus-building Handbook: a Comprehensive Guide to Reaching Agreement*. Thousand Oaks: Sage.

Tainio, R. and Lilja, K. (2003) The Finnish business system in transition: outcomes, actors and their influence. In: Czarniawksa, B. and Sevón, G. (eds) *The Northern Lights– Organization Theory in Scandinavia*. Oslo: Liber AB. 69–90.

Tjosvold, D. (1991) *The Conflict-positive Organization: Stimulate Diversity and Create Unity*. Madison, WI: Addison-Wesley.

Tuulentie, S. (2003) For and against the rights of the Sami people: the argumentation of the Finnish majority in the debate on the Sami rights. In: S. Jentoft, H. Minde and R. Nilsen (eds) *Indigenous Peoples: Resource Management and Global Rights*. Delft: Eburon. 275–295.

Waldenström, C. (2001) *Constructing the World in Dialogue. A Study of Advisory Situations in Swedish Agriculture*. Stockholm University.

Walker, G. B. and Daniels, S. E. (1997) Foundations of natural resource conflict. In: Solberg, B. and Miina, S. (eds) *Conflict Management and Public Participation in Land Management*. European Forest Institute Proceedings 14. Joensuu. 13–36.

Wondolleck, J. M. and Yaffee, S. L. (2000) *Making Collaboration Work: Lessons from Innovation in Natural Resource Management*. Washington, DC: Island Press.

Yasmi, Y. (2007) *Institutionalization of Conflict Capability in the Management of Natural Resources: Theoretical Perspectives and Empirical Experience in Indonesia*. Wageningen University, Wageningen, the Netherlands. PhD Thesis.

Young, I. M. (2001) Activist challenges to deliberative democracy. *Political Theory* 29(5): 670–690.

13 Divergent meanings of community

Ethnographies of communication in water governance

Leah Sprain, Brion van Over and Eric L. Morgan

Introduction

A major challenge facing democratic communities is how to make decisions together in the face of diversity and disagreement. If, as Dahl (2000) argues, inclusion, effective participation, and enlightened understanding are the criteria for measuring democracy, political theorists have long debated how to address the challenges of meeting these goals in plural societies (Dahl 2005). Recognizing the importance of inclusion and effective participation, in particular, environmental decision-making processes increasingly seek stakeholder and citizen involvement. Indeed, the dominant presumption is that environmental governance requires a wide range of stakeholder involvement (Paavola and Adger 2006; Few, Brown and Tompkins 2007). As Bulkeley and Mol (2003) note, "increasingly, non-participatory forms of policy-making are defined as illegitimate, ineffective and undemocratic, both by politicians and by stakeholders themselves" (144).

Participation is a democratic right that reduces marginalization, increases public trust, increases empowerment, and contributes to civic capacity (Reed 2008; Stringer *et al.* 2006). Pragmatically, participation can help ensure that solutions are better adapted to the local context, transform adversarial relationships, lead to ownership of decisions, reduce implementation costs, introduce better information, and include diverse perspectives and ways of knowing (Reed 2008), thereby enhancing the quality of assessments or decisions (Ferkany and Whyte 2011). Nonetheless, public participation is not beyond criticism. Most of the instrumental claims that collaborative approaches are more effective have not been systematically supported by empirical research (Newig and Fritsch 2009). Furthermore, accomplishing procedural democracy does not necessarily result in environmental protection (Davies 2001). Done poorly, participation can result in undemocratic outcomes by reinforcing existing power inequalities, marginalizing minority perspectives, creating dysfunctional consensus, or fostering cynicism if decisions are overruled by other levels of governance (Reed 2008). For example, Martin (2007) analysed the public participation in India's Allain Dunhangan environmental impact assessment process to show how the process was compromised by inadequate access to information, predetermined outcomes controlling the definition of issues, and relying on consultative forms of communication that promote one-way flows of information. Martin concluded that communications within the public processes were acts of power that privileged the ways of speaking and meaning-making of decision-makers.

One move to create more effective participatory processes is to begin by trying to understand stakeholders' concerns, information needs and desire for involvement (Jardine *et al.* 2007). Several of the chapters in this volume have suggested ways to develop an understanding of stakeholders' desires and needs. In this chapter we advocate for a different approach: focus on the cultural dynamics of communication within public participation. A cultural perspective on communication examines the speech events (Hymes 1972) wherein publics are invited to participate, including the divergent expectations and meanings that citizens and event designers hold for communication, public participation and political life. These differences reveal ways communication is used to invoke, construct, destruct and imagine community during two public processes on water issues in the American West. In this sense, community is not so much geographically fixed as it is fundamentally connected to communication (Sprain 2014).

To analyse our case studies, we draw on the ethnography of communication (Hymes 1972; Philipsen and Coutu 2005) as a theoretical and methodological framework. The ethnography of communication focuses on the relationship between language and social life, seeking to understand local systems of meaning, values, norms and beliefs related to communication. Public meetings, and participation processes more broadly, are conceptualized in terms of a speech event, an event with shared rules and norms for communication (Hymes 1972). We then focus on the cultural discourses (Carbaugh 2007) and related discourse practices in play during the meetings. However, this analysis does not purport to isolate a singular cultural discourse employed by a single bounded community, but rather seeks to understand participation processes such as these as a cultural chorus where a myriad of cultural meanings are voiced in concert, though not always in congress, in an ongoing co-production. The focus of this work is not on evaluating the process from normative criteria (e.g. what is an effective democratic process?), but instead on analysing the local discourses used among community members and decision-makers before, during and after the public process.

In the next section, we briefly introduce our two case studies: the Marine Life Protection Act (MLPA) and the *Poudre Runs Through It* (PRTI) series. These case studies provide two distinct scenes for understanding participation within water governance. The MLPA case analysis investigates the practices and premises that organizers of the process and its participants employ in making sense of what constitutes desirable and effective participation from the vantage of multiple distinctive communities. The PRTI case focuses on a single meeting and how organizers and participants drew on different interactional frames that connect to divergent cultural discourses about communication and community. Together these cases demonstrate how participation processes are one way that communities are bounded, sustained and transformed through their participation. In the conclusion we draw on both cases to propose a set of considerations that these cases make salient for future attempts at locally driven decision-making.

Case studies

The MLPA was passed by California legislators in 1999, mandating the development of a network of marine protected areas (MPAs) along the California coast that extant research suggested would be more effective at sustaining and conserving marine life than the ad-hoc arrangement that existed prior to the act. Two attempts were made to implement the law in 2000–2001 and 2002–2003. Both attempts failed to create a new MPA network for a variety of reasons including lack of staff, funding and technical tools, general lack of stakeholder involvement, unclear goals and objectives for the MPAs, misunderstandings about the mandate and limited time for public input (Gleason *et al.* 2010).

In 2004, the mandate was revived through a public–private partnership between the state and the Resources Legacy Fund Foundation (RLFF). A Blue Ribbon Task Force (BRTF) of "distinguished citizens" was created to "guide the design process", a science advisory team (SAT) to "develop guidelines and evaluate alternative MPA packages", and stakeholder groups for each region that would make recommendations to the BRTF. Our analysis focuses on the deliberative processes of the regional stakeholder group (RSG), as well as non-RSG members of the community, which produced this proposal for the MPA package, working with information and guidelines provided by the SAT and under the supervision of the BRTF.

Our second case comes from the semi-arid desert of Northern Colorado, where water has long been the key resource that determines the development of cities, industry and agriculture. Early settlers in the area developed a system of reservoirs and ditches to ensure a year-round supply of water. Growing populations and their demands for water have led to recent proposals to build new reservoirs. These proposals faced tremendous opposition as local activists expressed concerns that these projects would adversely impact stream flows, fisheries, recreation and more. Simultaneously, a public–private partnership called UniverCity Connections convened a group of local businesses, government and university partners to discuss issues of shared concern in Fort Collins, Colorado. Initial processes identified key issues held by stakeholders, including a prominent interest in the river that resulted in the creation of a task force to explore issues related to it.

This group faced a dilemma. Members recognized the significant public interest in the river and the need to have discussions about its future, yet they did not want to get mired in controversies over specific reservoir proposals, especially since they had no decision-making power nor influence over these projects while environmental impact assessments were being conducted. The group decided to develop a three-part series titled *The Poudre Runs Through It* (PRTI) that would both educate the public on issues related to the health and management of the river and begin a conversation about how to meet future water needs that would build democratic capacity for making future decisions.

These two cases provide a fruitful space for exploring the theoretical problems of how community is constructed and destroyed through local practices employed in public participation on environmental controversies. What follows is a brief overview of the ethnography of communication and its implications for work in environmental communication for scholars and practitioners. To begin, we present an anecdote that illustrates how an ethnographer of communication may approach environmental communication.

Conceptual framework and methodology

In 2014, US president Barack Obama issued an executive order designating a large swathe of land in Southern New Mexico as the Organ Mountains and Desert Peaks National Monument. This designation removes that land from the possibility of being commercially, residentially, or agriculturally developed. During the deliberative process leading up to this decision there were numerous arguments in favour of designation and against it. One of the more interesting claims was that this designation was being perpetuated by "people who aren't even from the area". Not only in public meetings about the designation, but also in everyday conversation, there were numerous characterizations of these "outsiders". The outsiders were characterized as being different than locals and not supporting local interests. Most interesting, for one to engage the local/outsider dimension, one did not have to necessarily be in residence or even from the area. Indeed many people from the area were in support of the national monument designation.

In this talk there is a locally produced sense of community being used by participants. Presumed in this exchange is a shared sense of who counts as a community member and who does not. For the ethnographer of communication, a few questions would become immediately relevant. What sense of community is operative here? Who can be a member of the community? What are the various criteria for community membership? How is being a member of the community performed? What are culturally meaningful ways to engage public discussions about environment? This anecdote is presented as a way to gain entry into the world of the ethnographer of communication – a world in which cultural discourse is paramount.

The ethnography of communication is a research tradition that provides a well-developed apparatus for understanding the diversity of cultural communication practices and their meanings as people employ them in a variety of contexts. We do not define culture as synonymous with community, but rather as a system of meaning that can be characterized as deeply felt among cultural members, widely accessible to potential participants and, at least to some degree, commonly intelligible among interactants (Carbaugh 1989).

When we use the term culture, we denote some shared set of symbols that, to follow Carbaugh,

> say something about our common senses of acting (what we are doing together and how we do it), of being (who we are), of relating (how we are linked together), of feeling (about people, actions, and things), and of dwelling together (how we relate to the world around us.)
>
> (2005: 1)

Ethnographers of communication seek to identify and understand local ways of speaking according to those who practise them (Philipsen and Coutu 2005). At the forefront of this analysis is a commitment to understanding meaning from the perspective of the participant.

In the field of communication, Philipsen (1989) restated the ethnography of communication in one essential axiom, the axiom of particularity. This axiom consists of four subsequent assumptions about communication, culture and action. The first assumption is that of communicative meaning, which states that as people communicate, meanings about their social worlds emerge. The second assumption concerns coordinated action, and takes people to be agents who coordinate their actions in what seems like, at least from a native point of view, a coherent manner. Language, then, plays an essentially communal function establishing a set of shared symbolic resources for accomplishing various social ends. Third is the assumption of particularity in meaning and action. This assumption reiterates Hymes' (1972) point that meaning and action are particular to specific communities. Finally, ethnographers of communication hold to an assumption of cultural particularity, which states that people, as they exist in cultural groups, make sense of their world in distinct and systematic ways. In later work, Philipsen (1992) summarized these assumptions by stating simply that communication is structured, distinct and social.

Communication is also cultural in that it is how people create, transform, and maintain beliefs and values about who people are, what society is, and, in part, what nature is (Carbaugh 1996; Carbaugh and Cerulli 2012). Communication is, therefore, partially constitutive of social life. As people interact they re-animate society. Much as Mead (1962) and other symbolic interactionists of the Chicago School (Blumer 1969; Manis and Meltzer 1972) argued, with each interaction, society, complete with consequences for future interactions, is accomplished. Thus, social worlds are continually being reacted to, acted upon and, ultimately, recreated. Subsequent work has extended this tradition to consider how communication creates and sustains cultural orientations to the natural environment (see Carbaugh 1996, 2014; Scollo Sawyer 2004; Carbaugh and Ceruli 2012).

Many chapters in this volume presume that communication represents the central political challenge as communities contend with a number of environmental concerns. The ethnography of communication prioritizes differently; beginning with local practices and commitment to understanding them in their own terms (an emic perspective) before moving to consider theories of community, democracy, or political life (see Townsend 2009; Sprain and Gastil 2013). Thus we orient to questions of the de/construction of community as a problem of communication from the standpoint of communication. So, understanding communication as a political challenge would likely be a characterization that would arise only after ethnographic investigation had identified this symbolic conceptualization deployed in a given community.

Following the data collection tenets of the ethnography of communication, Sprain and van Over collected participant observation data separately for each of the two cases. Each of these case studies are part of broader projects (for other work see Webler and van Over 2011; Sprain, Carcasson and Merolla 2014; Carcasson and Sprain 2015). Van Over collected data for the MLPA case, and Sprain collected data on the PRTI. Van Over's involvement in the North Coast MLPA process began as part of a research team from the Social and Environmental Research Institute, led by Thomas Webler. Seeking to understand the local communicative resources that residents of the North Coast employed in participating in the process and how the resources functioned, the team reviewed relevant literature, process outreach materials, online public comment databases and archived video recordings of RSG meeting. They worked to identify interested organizations or communities and read any opinions they, or members of their organization, had expressed about the process.

Van Over and Webler further took two trips, totalling just over three weeks, to the North Coast to personally meet with local interest groups, some of whom were officially represented in the RSG. They interviewed local political, social and economic leaders and attended local community meetings to hear what people were saying about the process, as well as a variety of stakeholders, both formally and informally, and had numerous conversations with staff who worked for the Marine Life Protection Act Initiative (MLPAI). Finally, they attended one meeting of the RSG in person to meet other interested parties in the audience and hear what inevitably does not make it onto televised or streaming broadcasts.

Sprain was invited to participate in early planning meetings of the PRTI series based on her affiliation with the Colorado State University Center for Public Deliberation (CPD). The CPD had previously designed and facilitated meetings for UniverCity Connections, and the organizing group sought their contributions. Ultimately, Sprain participated in organizing meetings, helped design the processes and supported meeting activities (e.g. taking public notes projected on a screen). She was deeply familiar with the community since she lived and worked there and had grown up in a nearby town. She took field notes of planning meetings and public meetings. Her research team also collected data from these processes, including audio recordings of deliberative groups. Video recordings of the public forum and educational sessions were aired on public television and remain publicly accessible. Transcripts of the public forum are the primary source of data for this analysis.

Across both cases, we draw on the ethnography of communication as a framework for data analysis. That our cases use different data sources and the authors have different roles in the cases demonstrates the utility and strength of our analytical approach to explore a variety of local contexts. In our analysis section, we entertain a central question – What communicative actions constitute a desirable and satisfactory form of participation in a given community? – within the context of each case, before turning to general insights about public participation and community in the conclusion section.

MLPA analysis

Generally, in order to understand the cultural foundations of what counts as a desirable and satisfactory form of participation, we must understand at least two distinct dimensions. First, what kinds of communicative activities constitute *participation* in the community? It may be, as in the MLPA case here, that many channels presumed to be communicative by some were available in the process, such as two-minute public comments at RSG meetings, a written public comments section on the state process website, discussion with local groups and local leaders, etc. (Sayce *et al.* 2013). But if these are not imagined by community members as the kinds of activities that constitute *participation* then they likely will not be effective at generating the kind of participation-based buy-in that these processes are hoped to generate.

Second, we need not only to understand what kinds of activities constitute participation in any given community, but in what ways these are unequally *valued*. For instance, in a comment submitted to the MLPA website, one tribal member writes: "private funding – private dining – private parties = private decisions". "Private dining" refers to a practice where during meal breaks at RSG meetings members of the public who had come to watch, and possibly speak at the meeting, were excluded from entering the dining area where "off-camera" discussions and deals were made between RSG members trying to come into agreement about items on the table. From these community members' perspective the participatory form they were offered, the two-minute slot for public comment, was not constitutive of a desirable and satisfactory form of participation.

Another tribal member references this practice saying "where everything really happens" is "behind the closed doors" of group meals at RSG meetings, and further claims that everything that happens when they come out of that room is for the public spectacle of the televised meeting. This claim was also forwarded by a member of the Yurok Tribe, who reported to us that since RSG meetings were broadcast, people would be unwilling to speak honestly about these issues in such a highly documented fashion, and would likely prefer to speak their "true" thoughts in a more private setting, making the private dining practice an attractive and effective space for participation. For this tribal member then, being denied access to spaces off-camera at RSG meetings, which RSG members were privy to, meant that even though he was allowed to speak in the public meeting, he could not truly do so, and from his view, neither could anyone else barred from those private spaces.

From this vantage, because no one is presumed able to speak freely in an event structured in this way, interlocutors cannot sincerely communicate with other speakers. This connects to a claim forwarded by another Yurok tribal member, "in these places, no one really listens". "Listening", as it is formulated here, does not refer to the bio-mechanics of the ear, nor information transmission, but rather to a communicative act that presumes an established connection between two interlocutors who deeply consider, and ultimately act, on the basis of what they have heard. Related forms of listening as a communicative practice have been identified by Carbaugh among the Blackfeet (Carbaugh 1999), and Basso among Western Apache (Basso 1970, 1996). In the communication event of the recorded public meeting, then, a double-bind is produced where simultaneously one is presumed unable to speak, nor listen, because the content of that speech is deemed always and already insincere, or at least produced with the understanding that this speech is now public and may be used in a variety of ways that can no longer be controlled by the speaker.

This sentiment was repeatedly expressed enough to be included in the *Summary of Input from North Coast Tribes and Tribal Communities* document generated by the MLPAI (2010). The concern is cast here from the perspective of the MLPAI author, who summarizes: "Tribes also chose not to share information because they were concerned with maintaining the confidentiality of their sacred sites and gathering methods, and they felt uncertain in how the data would be used in the future" (2010: Appendix E, 2). This uncertainty "in how the data would be used in the future", while possibly motivated by a lack of trust between tribal members and the MLPAI, speaks to the problem produced for native participants who are invited to speak and listen, but from whose vantage this cannot be done.

Taken together, the instances above suggest a cultural premise that one is able to more freely speak and act, to express one's "true" thoughts and feelings when in a more private setting, when the cameras are off, with those one trusts. This cultural premise that *one cannot speak and act freely in a documented public space with unknown others*, means efforts to publicize the meetings for the sake of transparency may actually be in conflict with a particular community's sense that there are places where they can in fact speak and listen, and forms through which this can be accomplished – the two-minute recorded public comment being neither. Similar preferences for not disclosing information about native culture or beliefs to outsiders among some native communities have been documented by Wieder and Pratt (1990) as well as Carbaugh and Wolf (1999).

Other communicative forms and channels were available for community members to express concern, some of which included "teas" and "potlucks", and may have afforded those members the ability to speak in a more private setting, but we would suggest not in a way that produced the satisfaction of influence over decisions that many sought. This suggests another potential premise that might be identified as *speech only yields influence at the right times and places and through the right actions*. The question then becomes, for a given community, what forms of participation are presumed important and influential, are these available, and can one participate in those ways without violating other deeply held premises? What we are working at here, then, is the elaboration of a set of cultural premises that together constitute a local cultural discourse for the influence of decisions through meaningful participation.

While a number of other concerns over participation were raised in our conversations with members of the North Coast community, including the participation of "outsiders" perceived to be "legislating our livelihood" (much as in the National Monument designation anecdote above), or issues of inclusiveness surrounding membership on the SAT (no tribal scientists were included in the SAT), or suspicions about the motives of those participating (some stakeholders were paid for their time/involvement, and scientists on the SAT were perceived to be there solely to increase their publications and thereby advance their careers), we focus here in the remainder of this case on the cultural constitution of money *as* participation.

For some community members, spanning tribal and non-tribal membership, an additional channel, presumed more influential than speech, was formulated as powerfully participatory – money. Because the state simply could not pay for the process on its own a public–private partnership with the Resource Legacy Fund Foundation (RLFF) was formed. For some, this was simply an organization that broadly supported conservation by funding a process where the state could not.

Others formulated this financial contribution as deeply and powerfully communicative, akin to the popular idiom "Money talks". For them, this was not simply money to fund an independent process, but influence bought for outcomes desired and communicated through backchannels or other nefarious methods. Here, money is shaped as a channel for participation through which one can attain one's desired ends. This is frustrating for those who constitute money *as* participation, because this kind of participation is inherently unequal and violates broadly held premises that all participants in the process should yield equal influence on the outcome.

The constitution of money as participation carries a moral dimension as well, communicated in written public comments like "not good to have private $$ funding public resource management". The extent to which private funding is perceived as an always and automatic wrong is further evidenced in another participant's comment, "private funding influenced the process". However, rarely did such comments point to particular practices wherein the influence of money could be traced, but rather seem to implicate a deeply felt sense that the combination of private money and public process is inherently untoward.

Other comments such as, "private orgs should not make public policy!!" are suggestive of the perceived link between the money used to fund a process and the influence that such funding will surely buy. Another participant elaborates this connection in the following comment:

> it is unconstitutional for one group with unlimited money and power to fund a process that tells the government to deny access to a natural resource based on the personal beliefs of a group of wealthy environmentalists and not accurate science.

In the above comment the perceived link between "unlimited money and power" and its ability to "deny access" is clear. The ultimate concern appears to be that those who would contribute money to a cause are vested parties with their own agenda, and that with money comes the power to influence the outcome of a process toward their own ends. This logic then connects to powerful beliefs about equity, and fair play, positing an untrustworthy other who seeks only to forward their own ends above the public good. In this comment, the "denial of access" to a "natural resource" by another individual or group is of paramount import and invokes a political and social discourse of personal freedom, where the presumed role of government is simply to prevent the "wealthy" from infringing on the freedom of the individual to exercise their rights to "natural resources".

If money is constituted *as* participation, wherein no particular communicative practices or observable actions need occur for money to *become* action, then money itself is constructed in these messages *as* action. A cultural premise at work in this discourse can then be identified: *money is action* and by extension, *participation*. Additionally, one can formulate the moral dimension of this premise in a normative claim that *in public participation processes, if participation and influence on outcomes is to be equal, private money cannot be used for funding*. This is suggestive of the difficulty process designers face when the careful checks and balances to assure equal opportunity for participation at the level of communicative action (equal available turns at talk, access to locations, etc.) are overrun by the constitution of money as an always-engaged actor on the scene.

PRTI analysis

Within the PRTI, questions about participation can be explored by looking at the cultural basis for participation within a single public forum, which reveals that the participants and organizers of the public forum did not share the same understanding for how to communicate during the meeting. As noted in the introduction of this chapter, a cultural perspective begins by considering these venues as speech events (Hymes 1972) wherein there are shared, structured ways of communicating. This analytical lens reveals an important disconnect between the participants and organizers of the public forum: they do not share the same understanding for structured ways of communicating during the meeting. Indeed, this is a case where the explicit event framing by organizers was insufficient for creating a shared interactional frame (Goffman 1974) for participants.

The first speaker opened the meeting by introducing several elected officials and describing the general format for the entire series. Then she attempted to create an interactional frame for the public forum:

> So welcome to our community dialogue on water issues basically focusing on the Poudre River. This is our opportunity to develop some common knowledge, some shared knowledge of the Poudre, and some common understandings. We can as a group raise the quality of the discussion around water, and we can do it in a positive and a collaborative way. And that's our intent tonight. We know that water can be a divisive issue. No doubt about it. But this is our chance to listen to each other in a respectful way sharing our insights with each other and working creatively together to forge our future. The Poudre River is our greatest natural asset in Fort Collins.... So this is going to be an informal dialogue we hope about our very own Poudre River. This dialogue that will be both educational and productive. So once again thank you, we are looking forward to input from all of you.

She frames the event as a "community dialogue" oriented to "developing common understandings". This communication event is for the community to come together through communication by "sharing our insights" and "listening" in a respectful way. Dialogue is typically constructed as a verbal co-production (Carbaugh *et al.* 2006), and the speaker draws on this sense even though the communication practices for participants to contribute to this co-production are less clear. Most of this framing is being done in comparison to something else that goes unlabelled. This forum will "raise the quality of the discussion" and be "positive", "collaborative", "educational", and "productive" in ways that the unnamed discourse on proposed reservoirs has not been.

Four community leaders are then invited to share short speeches about what they value about the river. Each has been selected to describe a relevant stake: history, ecology, economics and the spirit of the river. These speeches all draw, in their own way, on a *rhetoric of community* that ties this community (Fort Collins, the people in this room, the social-ecological system) with a particular way of dealing with public problems that is collaborative, thoughtful, and balances multiple needs and perspectives. There are important issues related to the river, and "we have to grapple with them as a community". And, this community has successfully done this before. As the historian urges,

> look for those turning points in the past when people tried to turn away from conflict and when they realized that the answer was not in complete self-interest in individualism, but somehow there was a collective, a community good, that was embedded in the resolution of problems. And they worked together to try to solve those.

There is a need to "work together to balance all of our community's needs". Yet this is possible because, "we are not an ordinary community. And nor is this an ordinary place". Matching a legacy of prior visioning is possible. "For those willing to see, listen, and feel our land, nature is sending us warning signs to read and act upon. If we so choose, we can come together".

After about an hour of these presentations, it is time for "your deliberation and discussion". A communication professor who is helping facilitate the event highlights the role for the public in engaging in discussions about what is important to the community because "experts can't make the decisions about values for us, the public have to and that's why we need to engage this issue broadly". Much of his talk develops a sense of how people should talk about controversial issues. He too draws on a rhetoric of community:

> you know Fort Collins is really such a great community. Can we become an example to the nation especially to the west on how a community can really take on a tough issue and really understand the competing values and work together to make good decisions and keep this community great?

Here he reinforces a desire to voice diverging interests while working together as a community. He outlines some of the values discussed in the presentation, sets up ways that participants can share their perspective by speaking and filling out forms that will inform the design of subsequent sessions, and discusses ground rules for the discussion (be honest and respectful, listen to understand, assume good intentions, it's ok to disagree but do so with curiosity not hostility). He asks people to speak for around 30 seconds, following one of the prompts on a handout (a prompt in this case is a short statement designed to elicit talk e.g. what I value about the river...; one thing I need to know to decide...).

The first five citizen-speakers all rely on expertise discourse (Sprain 2015), including technical language and credentialing themselves using their professional expertise ("a retired hydrologist", "a retired professor"). None of them use the prompts. They all speak for over a minute; two are interrupted by facilitators. These speaking turns resist the interactional frame that was offered by organizers. Instead of focusing on values, they raise issues about water use efficiencies and attempt to correct "erroneous" understandings of return flow. The facilitators handle this by attempting to paraphrase comments in terms of values, interrupting speakers when speaking goes on over a minute, and invoking their desired interactional frame. The facilitator notes,

> And certainly figuring out some of those technical aspects and thinking about possible ways for efficiency is going to be an important part moving forward. And we want as many ideas as possible because dealing with these tensions is about creativity. But we also want to hear not just from the experts tonight but we want to hear from the public to talk about you know what's important to you and those type of things as well.

In terms of ideal participants, the facilitator is working from two distinct categories: experts and publics. For the facilitator, this forum is for publics, and publics talk about values and the tensions between different values. Yet these initial members of the public choose to speak as experts. They also frame the issue under discussion as a technical issue, calling for "a position paper" on "ag[ricultural] to urban transfer" – a hot button topic within water policy.

Several citizen-speakers, through their discourse, orient to expertise even though they do not seem to consider themselves experts. One speaker introduces himself and states, "I'm not a big professional. I'm a carpenter; work on my own. But I want to talk about the values". Other participants credential themselves in terms of how long they have lived in the area, recreational interests, or their professions unrelated to the issue (e.g. dentist). Several introduce themselves as, "just citizens". Although they inhabit the interactional frame sought by organizers, these discourse practices suggest that speakers view themselves as violating a desired norm of speaking as an expert on a technical issue – despite the facilitator's explicit framing for the public to speak on values.

These discourse practices end up contributing to predictable groupings among public participants – between experts and citizens. These groups do not necessarily exist a priori but are enacted through communication practices (Witteborn and Sprain 2009). These groups draw on different ways of speaking, different public personae, and different ways of framing their contribution to the discussion (values versus expert knowledge). The grouping works against the rhetoric of community that leaders used in an attempt to develop a singular community poised to tackle this controversial issue.

Conclusion

The analysis of the cases presented here is suggestive of the necessity of public participation processes to treat seriously the ongoing constitution of social reality through symbolic means and the deeply cultural nature of that constitution. Well-intentioned public participation processes can fall well short of their democratic and instrumental goals when participants and organizers do not share cultural premises about ideal forms of participation, communication and communal life, in general and within specific meetings. We do not presume that organizers are naive to these possibilities. Indeed, the attention to issues of inclusion within the academic and practitioner literatures on public participation (see Ryfe and Stalsberg 2012 for review) suggests a sincere and abiding interest in how to design public participation to be not only efficient but also democratic. Rather than focus on utilizing more channels and more methods of public engagement, we argue that attending to the cultural dynamics in play can reveal important gaps in cultural premises that process designers can then address. This attention can both increase the cultural competence of process designers and inform locally appropriate deliberative designs (Sprain and Boromisza-Habashi 2013).

While we are not insensitive to the various constraints on public participation processes, including time, money, human resources, etc. we assert there is much process designers can do with the existing data that many are already gathering. Having come to realize the absolute necessity of localizing process design, many processes like the MLPA and PRTI collect data through a variety of means in an attempt to better develop local strategies for outreach and participation. The question, then, is what to do with those data. We advocate an analysis that attends to the ways that community members presume and enact 1) the identities of those involved in the process (personhood), 2) the social relations among those identities (relations), 3) proper ways of feeling and acting (emotion), 4) proper ways of being in place (dwelling), and 5) available means and meanings of symbolic action (communication) (Carbaugh 2007).

We advocate this kind of analysis not simply for the cultural dynamics it can reveal, but because we believe it provides opportunities for rethinking the design of processes in ways that will help meet the goals of participants and designers alike. In the MLPA case analysis, certain practices were revealed to have distinctly different meanings for some members of the North Coast than were likely intended. Among those are the practice of two-minute televised public comment, private dining at RSG meetings, and the public–private partnership with the RLFF that helped fund the process. All of these practices, from one vantage, can be understood as helpful ways to assure that the public has some influence over outcomes of policy. However, from another vantage these same practices are impotent, lacking any influential capacity because what it means to participate, and the kind of practices that engender the feeling one has done so, are distinctly different. Armed with this knowledge, the process might have been designed to create avenues for participation that were discovered in the local emic discourse and about what it is to be included, involved and effectual from the perspective of distinctive speech communities.

Overall, our analysis demonstrates how communication practices within public participation can be used to both construct a unified community that can take on public problems (as was desired in PRTI) and divide participants into different groups (e.g. experts and citizens; insiders and outsiders) who have different standing to participate in shared governance. The ethnography of communication reminds us that community is not an entity that always, already exists. Instead, it is accomplished through a locally determined set of communication practices that, when enacted, lay claims to membership in particular communities rather than others. Indeed, it is through those very practices of communication in participation processes that members of a community become recognizable, or not, to each other. Public participation processes are one way that communities are bounded, sustained and transformed – often in ways that work against the organizers' intentions. In turn, a cultural perspective might offer some insight into local, cultural ways to help organizers design processes that do not, unintentionally, undermine communal life.

Acknowledgements

Data used in the analysis for the MLPA case was gathered as part of a project funded by the National Science Foundation under Grant Number: SES-1024585. Dr Thomas Webler from the Social Environmental Research Institute was the primary investigator for the grant and without him the MLPAI analysis presented here would not be possible.

References

Basso, K. H. (1970) To give up on words: silence in Western Apache culture. *Southwestern Journal of Anthropology*. 26(3): 213–230.

Basso, K. H. (1996) *Wisdom sits in places: landscape and language among the Western Apache*. Albuquerque, NM: University of New Mexico Press.

Blumer, H. (1969) *Symbolic interactionism: perspective and method*. Englewood Cliffs, NJ: Prentice-Hall.

Bulkeley, H. and Mol, A. P. J. (2003) Participation and environmental governance: consensus, ambivalence and debate. *Environmental Values* 2(2): 43–154.

California Marine Life Protection Act. (2010) Summary of input from north coast tribes and tribal communities regarding the MLPA North Coast Project. Online, available at: https://nrm.dfg.ca.gov/FileHandler.ashx?DocumentVersionID=73866 (accessed 12 October 2011).

Carbaugh, D. (1989) Fifty terms for talk: a cross-cultural study. *International and Intercultural Communication Annual* 13(93): 120.

Carbaugh, D. (1991) Communication and cultural interpretation. *Quarterly Journal of Speech* 77(3): 336–342.

Carbaugh, D. (1996) Naturalizing communication and culture. In: Cantrill, J. and Oravec, C. (eds) *The symbolic earth: discourse and our creation of the environment*. Lexington, KY: University Press of Kentucky, pp. 38–57.

Carbaugh, D. (1999) "Just Listen": "listening" and landscape among the Blackfeet. *Western Journal of Communication* 63(3): 250–270.

Carbaugh, D. (2005) *Cultures in conversation*. Mahwah, NJ: Lawrence Erlbaum Associates.

Carbaugh, D. (2007) Cultural discourse analysis: communication practices and intercultural encounters. *Journal of Intercultural Communication Research* 36(3): 167–182.

Carbaugh, D. (2014) Response essay: environmental voices including dialogue with nature, within and beyond language. In: Peeples, J. and Depoe, S. (eds) *Voice and environmental communication*. New York: Palgrave Macmillan, p. 241.

Carbaugh, D. and Cerulli, T. (2013) Cultural discourses of dwelling: investigating environmental communication as a place-based practice. *Environmental Communication: a Journal of Nature and Culture* 7(1): 4–23.

Carbaugh, D. and Wolf, K. (1999). Situating rhetoric in cultural discourses. *International and Intercultural Communication Annual* 22: 19–30.

Carbaugh, D., Boromisza-Habashi, D. and Xinmei, G. (2006) Dialogue in cross-cultural perspective: deciphering communication codes. In: Aalto, N. and Reuter, E. (eds) *Aspects of intercultural dialogue*. Köln: SAXA Verlag, pp. 27–47.

Carcasson, M. and Sprain, L. (2015) Beyond problem solving: Re-conceptualizing the work of public deliberation as deliberative inquiry. *Communication Theory* 26: 41–53.

Carey, J. W. (1989) *Communication as culture: essays on media and society*. London: Unwin Hyman.

Dahl, R. A. (2000) *On democracy*. New Haven: Yale University Press.

Dahl, R. A. (2005) What political institutions does large-scale democracy require? *Political Science Quarterly* 120(2): 187–197.

Davies, A. (2001) What silence knows – planning, public participation and environmental values. *Environmental Values* 10(1): 77–102.

Ferkany, M. and Whyte K. P. (2011) The importance of participatory virtues in the future of environmental education. *Journal of Environmental Ethics* 25(3): 419–434.

Few, R., Brown, K. and Tompkins, E. L. (2007) Public participation and climate change adaptation: avoiding the illusion of inclusion. *Climate Policy* 7(1): 46–59.

Fiske, J. (1991) Writing ethnographies: contribution to a dialogue. *Quarterly Journal of Speech* 77(3): 330–335.

Gleason, M. G., McCreary, S. T., Miller-Henson, M. A., Ugoretz, J. K., Fox, E., Merrifield, M. S., McClintock, W. J., Serpa, P. and Hoffman, K. (2010) Science-based and stakeholder-driven marine protected area network planning: a successful case study from north central California. *Ocean and Coastal Management* 53(2): 52–68.

Goffman, E. (1974) *Frame analysis: an essay on the organization of experience*. Cambridge, MA: Harvard University Press.

Hymes, D. (1972) Models of the interaction of language and social life. In: Gumperz, H. H. and Hymes, D. (eds) *Directions in sociolinguistics: the ethnography of communication*. New York: Holt, Rinehart & Winston, pp. 35–71.

Jardine, C. G., Predy, G. and Mackenzie, A. (2007) Stakeholder participation in investigating the health impacts from coal-fired power generating stations in Alberta, Canada. *Journal of Risk Research* 10(5): 693–714.

Manis, J. G. and Meltzer, B. N. (1972) *Symbolic interaction: a reader in social psychology*. Boston, MA: Allyn and Bacon.

Martin, T. (2007) Muting the voice of the local in the age of the global: how communication practices compromised public participation in India's Allain Dunhangan environmental impact assessment. *Environmental Communication* 1(2): 171–193.

Mead, G. H. (1962) *Mind, self, and society: from the standpoint of a social behaviorist*. Chicago: University of Chicago Press.

Newig, J. and Fritsch, O. Environmental governance: participatory, multi-level – and effective? *Environmental Policy and Governance* 19(3): 197–214.

Paavola, J. and Adger, W. N. (2006) Fair adaptation to climate change. *Ecological Economics* 56(4): 594–609.

Philipsen, G. (1989) Speech and the communal function in four cultures. *International and Intercultural Communication Annual* 13: 79–92.

Philipsen, G. (1991) Two issues in the evaluation of ethnographic studies of communicative practice. *Quarterly Journal of Speech* 77(3): 327–329.

Philipsen, G. (1992) *Speaking culturally: explorations in social communication*. New York: SUNY Press.

Philipsen, G. and Coutu, L. (2005) The ethnography of speaking. In: Fitch, K. L. and Sanders, R. E. (eds) *Handbook of language and social interaction*. Mahwah, NJ: Lawrence Erlbaum Associates, pp. 355–380.

Reed, M. S. (2008) Stakeholder participation for environmental management: a literature review. *Biological Conservation* 141: 2417–2431.

Ryfe, D. M. and Stalsburg, B. (2012) The participation and recruitment challenge. In: Nabatchi, T., Gastil, J., Weiksner, G. M. and Leighninger, M. (eds) *Democracy in motion*. Oxford University Press, pp. 43–58.

Sayce, K., Shuman, C., Connor, D., Reisewitz, A., Pope, E., Miller-Henson, M., Poncelet, E., Monie, D. and Owens, B. (2013) Beyond traditional stakeholder engagement: public participation roles in California's statewide marine protected area planning process. *Ocean and Coastal Management* 74: 57–66.

Scollo Sawyer, M. (2004) Nonverbal ways of communicating with nature: a cross-case study. *Environmental Communication Yearbook* 1: 227–249.

Sprain, L. (2014) Voices of organic consumption: understanding organic consumption as political action. In: Peeples, J. and Depoe, S. (eds) *Voice and environmental communication*. New York: Palgrave Macmillan, pp. 127–147.

Sprain, L. (2015) Expertise discourse. In: Tracy, K., Illie, C. and Sandel, T. (eds) *International encyclopedia of language and social interaction*. Boston: John Wiley & Sons.

Sprain, L. and Boromisza-Habashi, D. (2013) The ethnographer of communication at the table: building cultural competence, designing strategic action. *Journal of Applied Communication Research* 41: 181–187.

Sprain, L. and Gastil, J. (2013) What does it mean to deliberate? An interpretive account of jurors' expressed deliberative rules and premises. *Communication Quarterly* 61: 151–171.

Sprain, L., Carcasson, M. and Merolla, A. (2014) Experts in public deliberation: lessons from a deliberative design on water needs. *Journal of Applied Communication Research* 42: 150–167.

Stringer, L. C., Dougill, A. J., Fraser, E., Hubacek, K., Prell, C. and Reed, M. S. (2006) Unpacking "participation" in the adaptive management of social–ecological systems: a critical review. *Ecology and Society* 11(2): 39.

Townsend, R. M. (2009) Town meeting as a communication event: democracy's act sequence. *Research on Language and Social Interaction*. 42(1): 68–89.

Webler, T. and van Over, B. (2011) *Assessing the north coast MLPA process*. Project Report. Greenfield MA: Social and Environmental Research Institute.

Wieder, L. and Pratt, S. (1990) On being a recognizable Indian among Indians. In: Carbaugh, D. (ed.) *Cultural Communication and Intercultural Contact*. Hillsdale, NJ: Lawrence Erlbaum Associates, pp. 45–64.

Witteborn, S. and Sprain, L. (2010) Grouping processes in a public meeting from an ethnography of communication and cultural discourse analysis perspective. *International Journal of Public Participation* 3: 4–35.

Part III

Conclusion and summary

14 Social transformation and sustainability

Communication and community construction/destruction

Tarla Rai Peterson, Hanna Ljunggren Bergeå, Andrea M. Feldpausch-Parker and Kaisa Raitio

This book was inspired by the theme of *Participation Revisited: Openings and Closures for Deliberations on the Commons*. Our hope is that revisiting participation may enable engagement that helps humans to transform their communities in ways that at least prefigure more sustainable habitation of Earth as a home shared with other humans, as well as with extrahuman residents of Earth. The preceding chapters critically examined environmental communication in a variety of community venues, searching for signs that public participation may be re-crafted to open meaningful opportunities for citizen engagement. They have identified and explored varying forms of critique and contestation that challenge the status quo; threatening the destruction of existing community patterns while opening possibilities for constructing new ones. Each chapter demonstrates in multiple ways that communication not only provides channels for exchanging information and meaning but also constitutes possibilities for environmental politics. Here, we briefly summarize the main points made in the cases explored in Chapters 3 through 13, and then suggest potential opportunities for connections between environmental communication and the constructivity and destructivity that is entailed in social transformation.

Summary

Citizen communication about environmental issues generally occurs within the limits of existing institutional structures, and the changes it enables come about through symbolic processes. Chapters 3, 4 and 5 examined ways that language and other images may persuade people to think, feel and act in certain ways rather than others. In Chapter 3, Callister suggested an approach to conflict communication designed expressly to encourage collaboration, while maintaining space for dissent. She focused attention on how language can function as a "discursive lubricant" for community members who have previously seen each other as enemies, while also noting the importance of creating appropriate structures wherein this symbolic interaction can operate. Although she recognizes the importance of developing institutional arrangements that will allow participants to carry their incipient collaborative attitudes beyond the relatively safe space of facilitated conversation, Callister's analysis focuses on getting the symbolic interaction right as a prelude for striding into the rough and tumble world of politics.

In Chapter 4, Endres and her co-authors examined a professional community of scientists and engineers engaged in developing and deploying a suite of technologies aimed at mitigating climate change by reducing CO_2 emissions from fossil fuel combustion. The authors focus on the rhetorical significance of changing the name of the technology, which also entails changing the name of the community. Their analysis details the wide range of responses by community members, ranging from some who claim that the name makes no difference at all, to others who explain that the name change compels them to leave the community. As their analysis demonstrates, something as apparently simple as a name change may have significant political repercussions for a community; in this case, language had decidedly material consequences.

In Chapter 5, the focus shifted from a single name to an entire story line. Bernacchi and Peterson explained how tenacious devotion to a community narrative narrowed the possibilities for engagement, discouraging political action regarding biodiversity conservation among a group of citizens who were dedicated conservationists. Their analysis easily could be extended to suggest the value of deconstructing a community narrative that seemed to encourage citizens to obsess over aspects of the situation they could not influence (the number of blue crab in the area) to the exclusion of equally important aspects they could have influenced (the hectares of habitat available to the endangered whooping cranes).

Chapters 6, 7 and 8 shift the focus from language and other images to the institutional arrangements that communication may call into being, and that subsequently provide boundaries for further communication. The authors of these chapters examine organizational arrangements for forest conservation in India, wildlife conservation in North America, and nature conservation in Sweden. As Banerjee notes in Chapter 6, India's Joint Forest Management (JFM) programme was intended to change the practice of forest conservation from simply another post-colonial endeavour to alienate residents from their places and from each other by obliterating their informal, but longstanding and deep place relationships. She found that, at least in east Sikkim, JFM operates very similarly to previous, more overtly exclusionary forest management schemes. Her analysis includes an attempt to discover underlying causes for the program's relative failure to provide meaningful participation opportunities for local residents and suggestions for how to revise it, using ideas consistent with "process literacy", as envisioned by Callister in Chapter 3.

Chapter 7 takes readers to the North American Continent to examine the North American Model of Wildlife Conservation (NAMWC), an approach to managing wildlife that supporters credit as the reason for successful wildlife conservation in the United States and Canada, as well as for successful wildlife conservation efforts on other continents. Although Feldpausch-Parker and her co-authors note that claims of the NAMWC's global pre-eminence may be overstated, their focus is on how it is framed by communities of practice within North America. The central problem they identify is similar to that identified in Chapter 4; a risk of community rupture. Based on their analysis of rhetoric discussing the NAMWC, they note that, as currently framed, the NAMWC excludes a majority of those who may be eager to participate in wildlife conservation.

Hansen and Peterson turned to a programme celebrated throughout the European Union (EU), the Swedish Dialogue for Nature Conservation (DNC), for an institutional approach to the construction of more inclusive community relations. They trace the DNC from its emergence as an idea offered by a Swedish minister of the environment through its eventual development and deployment as an education programme for personnel working for *Naturvårds-verket*, the Swedish agency responsible for environmental management. They use a traditional Habermasian perspective on deliberative democracy to guide an analysis of the challenges faced when formal organizations attempt to institutionalize public participation. Their analysis demonstrates that, despite the best intentions of everyone involved, the communicative rationality originally envisioned by the environmental minister became increasingly technologized as the agency developed, and then deployed the DNC. This chapter raises the question of whether it is possible to institutionalize public participation opportunities without simultaneously technologizing them.

The fundamental transformations needed to invigorate public participation in environmental policy-making can come about only through the third mode of engagement suggested in the introductory chapter, agonistic politics. This offers ways to counter the depoliticization of prevailing techno managerial solutions and open up new possibilities for citizens of sustainable communities to participate fully in decisions about environmental policy. Chapters 9, 10 and 11 explored communities that took nontraditional routes to public participation. Todd's reading of guerrilla gardening as political resistance to the radical privatization of urban space suggests ways that ordinary citizens, some of whom have been complicit in removing themselves from meaningful participation in decisions about the future of their communities, may exercise political power without engaging in direct confrontation with the scions of private ownership. The lack of direct confrontation does not, however, mean that guerrilla gardeners are passive observers. Todd's quotation from Reynolds' handbook proclaims that, "cultivating a garden is always a fight.... Our gardens are scenes of savage destruction. Animals uproot, frosts cripple, winds topple, rains flood. The guerrilla gardener shares this constant battle with nature with other gardeners. But we have other enemies". Those other enemies include planners who arrange cities with no regard for neighbourhoods and decision-makers who seem unaware of the importance of maintaining common spaces to nurture care for other humans, as well as for the environments where they live.

Ångman and her co-authors explored a different route to radical resistance, proposing that emotion should become a legitimate dimension in public participation (bring emotion into traditional practices). Both of their cases demonstrate opportunities lost by excluding, or at least delegitimizing emotion from the public process. These authors note that, since moral emotions are fundamental to the process of connecting with particular places, their exclusion from the formal process of deciding how to manage those places is irrational. They suggest that natural resource managers can enhance both the quality of the decision-making process and the sustainability of its outcomes by making space for emotion within public participation venues such as public hearings.

Liles and his co-authors offer a fiesta. Like Todd's guerrilla gardeners, the humans who share their communities with hawksbill turtles have been complicit in their own political erasure. They are more likely to have engaged in legally forbidden activities than to have spoken in a public hearing. The thought of participating in formally organized processes sponsored by the central government is completely alien. At the same time, they feel the same closeness with *their* turtles as did community members with *their* cranes (Chapter 5). Working collaboratively with community residents, Liles and his co-authors hit upon the idea of using another cultural icon, the game of football, and developed the Hawksbill Cup, which has transformed turtle conservation from a peripheral activity led by outsiders to a celebration of village life led by local heroes.

The analyses presented in Chapters 12 and 13 draw liberally from all three theoretical traditions described thus far. Raitio contrasted the management of conflicts in the Great Bear Rain Forest (GBRF) in Canada and Inari Forest in Finland, claiming that the ways these conflicts were handled was constructive for the community in the first case, and destructive in the second. She notes, for example, that in the GBRF conflict, leaders took care to honour important symbols and to recognize the broader cultural context within which the conflict had emerged, whereas in the Inari Forest conflict leaders seemed to ignore the cultural context in the interest of efficiency. Further, she explains how the GBRF conflict resolution process led to institutional innovation, while the Inari process did not. Finally, she notes that those involved in the GBRF conflict struggled with the democratic paradox between liberality and democracy, using the struggle to negotiate the pre-existing power relationships among conflict participants, where the people managing the Inari conflict chose to ignore, and even bury the paradox.

We concluded the case studies with Chapter 13, where Sprain and her co-authors explicitly returned the focus to communication as the basic building block of community and society. They argue for an analysis of local communicative practices, "before moving to consider theories of community, democracy, or political life". From their perspective, this sort of analysis is crucial, even when the primary goal is to discover modes of social transformation that enable greater sustainability, because neither community nor polity exist until they are enacted through communication. Like Raitio, Sprain and her co-authors compared and contrasted two environmental conflicts, but unlike Raitio, their analysis focused explicitly on communication as a process whereby individual members of the communities in conflict constituted and enacted their identities, relations among those identities, and acceptable ways of feeling and being in those communities.

Environmental communication for social transformation

Circling back to communication as the keystone is important, because we want this book to provide ideas about how environmental communication may enable social transformation toward greater sustainability, recognizing that such transformation always entails both constructivity and deconstructivity. Analysing symbolic interaction is valuable in itself, but also as a guide for thinking about how institutional arrangements, ranging from specific public participation processes to broader law and policy frameworks, can facilitate broader public participation in democratic politics.

If we define the political realm as a space where citizens voluntarily engage with processes of debate and decision-making on collective issues where highly diverse values, ideals and desires are played out and opposed, we must recognize and plan for situations where people's political subjectivities determine their orientations to democratic participation. Because much of contemporary political communication predominantly constitutes citizens into passive consumers of decisions determined by technical rationality, a transformative process of emancipation is needed to enable the political dimensions of public life to emerge. This transformation demands the creation of spaces for marginalized voices in face-to-face encounters, in mainstream and alternative media, as well as in other communication spaces, where dissent is as fully normalized as consensus. Such recognition could contribute to further civic mobilization, to engagement with social movements, and to incorporation of diverse views in political parties, among other political developments.

Political identities are not fixed but are relational and fluid. Rather than looking at citizenship as a legal status, we have followed Asen (2004) in viewing it as a process and hence open ended and variable in its expressions. Noting that what matters is how people *enact* citizenship, he described a vital public sphere as one that welcomes "fluid, multimodal, and quotidian enactments of citizenship" (191). Mouffe's (1993/2005) rejection of essentialism in relation to political identities is consistent with Asen's process-oriented perspective and maintains that political identities emerge from the "contingent and pragmatic form of their articulation" (7). The analyses in this book offer diverse contributions to rethinking community and the role of communication practices in promoting or hindering different forms of political engagement.

Researchers who study phenomena that have demonstrable policy implications do not have the luxury of pursuing their research in neutral isolation.

Industry, environmental NGOs, consumer advocates and others will dissect research publications on environmental policy in the hope of finding a sentence or two that can be used to justify predetermined goals. Those goals may or may not be consistent with constructing and deconstructing communities to enable more sustainable futures. Communication itself is not a science, and neither is the environment. The systematic study of both communication and the environment, however, *is* a science. If one assumes that continued human life on Earth is a good thing and that justice for all human beings is worth seeking, then the moves between environmental science and environmental policy matter. Environmental communication mediates that move, for better or worse, and understanding how it operates increases the likelihood of crafting a more sustainable and democratic existence. This existence requires various types of online platforms and other new media, traditional media, the street, community centres, art galleries, workplaces, and other face-to-face and mediated spaces.

Rather than discussing *the* public sphere, it may therefore make more sense to speak of *multiple* public spheres (Breese 2011; Carvalho and Peterson 2012) formed by different types of communities. The appropriate scale for these communities is not self-evident, but as suggested by Sprain and her co-authors in Chapter 13, is called into being through communication. As demonstrated by the analyses in this book, communities may be highly local, transnational and varying scales in between. Whatever the scale, Mouffe's claim that real democracy "must make room for competing conceptions of our identities as citizens" (1993/2005: 7) reminds us that citizens are as diverse as are their communities. Though not simple, the ways to transform society toward greater sustainability need to involve increased pluralism in addressing natural environments at all junctures of political life. But rather than seeking consensual deliberation, perhaps we should celebrate opportunities to work within agonistic politics.

The analyses in this book support Mouffe's claim that antagonism is a condition of, rather than an obstacle to, democracy. There is never going to be a unanimous solution or a final closure to the heterogeneous worldviews of political subjects. Designing spaces and mechanisms of expression of a wide range of views on environmental problems, including those in disagreement with hegemonic discourses, may need to be prioritized. Out of respect for both liberty and equality, such arrangements would need to recognize and respect the "different social relations and subject positions in which they are relevant" (Mouffe 1993/2005: 71). These arrangements must enable the confrontation of conflicting perspectives about how much one should risk and allow to be destroyed, about the worth of economic growth, about consumption and about other social and political issues. Accommodating such a diversity of environmental views opens space for those who view official policy as insufficient and inadequate, who strive for more substantial and ambitious goals, as well as for those who view any environmental policy as wrong-headed. Obviously, this would pose new challenges. Still, defining institutional mechanisms to accommodate agonistic politics is an important part of producing better – if only temporary – responses to the enormous environmental challenges faced by contemporary society (Peterson *et al.* 2006).

As shown by the analyses in this book, communication can draw attention to resources, spaces and structures that offer key opportunities for inventing alternatives that enable citizens to breathe new life into their communities and that sanction policies that engage the multiple implications of environmental policy. The paths leading to such transformation are, to a large extent, still to be drawn. We offer this book as one piece of the ongoing experimentation with alternative forms of communication that are redefining the meanings of political action, public participation and sustainable communities.

References

Asen, R. (2004) A discourse theory of citizenship. *Quarterly Journal of Speech* 90: 189–211.

Breese, E. B. (2011) Mapping the variety of public spheres. *Communication Theory* 21: 130–149.

Carvalho, A. and Peterson, T. R. (eds) (2012) *Climate Change Politics: Communication and Public Engagement*. Amherst, NY: Cambria Press.

Mouffe, C. (1993/2005) *The Return of the Political*. London: Verso.

Peterson, T. R., Peterson, M. N., Peterson, M. J., Allison, S. A., Gore, D. C. (2006) To play the fool: can environmental conservation and democracy survive social capital? *Communication and Critical/Cultural Studies* 3: 116–140.

Reynolds, R. (2008) *On Guerrilla Gardening: a Handbook for Gardening without Boundaries*, London: Bloomsbury Publishing.

Index

Page numbers in **bold** denote figures and those in *italics* denote tables

For Product Safety Concerns and Information please contact our EU representative GPSR@taylorandfrancis.com Taylor & Francis Verlag GmbH, Kaufingerstraße 24, 80331 München, Germany

Printed and bound by CPI Group (UK) Ltd, Croydon, CR0 4YY

08/05/2025

01864310-0002